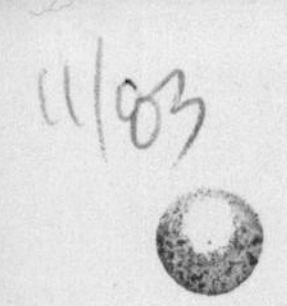
11/83

BK 770. F299F
FEININGER ON PHOTOGRAPHY
/FEININGER,
R 1953 6.95 M
3000 615613 40019
St. Louis Community College

D0913183

WITHDRAWN

St. Louis Community
College

FEININGER ON PHOTOGRAPHY

REVISED EDITION

by
ANDREAS FEININGER

CROWN PUBLISHERS, INC
New York

Library of Congress Catalog Card Number: 52-11816

Unless otherwise credited, all photographs by Andreas Feininger

PRINTED IN THE UNITED STATES OF AMERICA

To Wilson Hicks—

—without whose active interest
this book would never have been finished.

CONTENTS

INTRODUCTION

THIS BOOK contains the conclusions resulting from twenty years of experimenting in photography. Into it I have put all the things I found important, and left out the ones that, today, I think are no longer necessary for the making of good photographs. This makes it a very personal book, and other photographers may not always agree with me.

I believe that photography at its best is an Art, and photo-technique is but a means to an end: the creation of the picture. Today, even a fool can learn to operate any of our modern foolproof cameras, and produce technically perfect pictures—but is this knowledge really all he needs for taking purposeful and pictorially exciting photographs? Naturally, as in any other art, there are artists and here are dabblers. If photography really were nothing but the simple and purely mechanical reproduction process the majority of people still think it is, why are there so many dull and meaningless photographs around?

Obviously, there still must be some indefinable "something" a photographer has to have besides technical knowledge in order to make pictures with a meaning, and to express this meaning graphically in moving and exciting form.

The vast majority of books on photographic topics is concerned with purely technical problems. They are textbooks written to teach people how to improve their technique, with the result that today the technical standard of the average photographer is at an all-time high. But there are few, if any, books, and only a few occasional articles scattered through photo magazines, which attempt to show photographers how to use their technical knowledge and skill to best advantage for the creation of purposeful and graphically exciting pictures. If photographers were told how to use their brains and imagination as well as they use their cameras, if they would learn, for instance, to consider composition as important as finegrain development, many of them might produce photographs of a quality and an impact comparable to the best they see in national picture magazines.

In this book, photo-technique is treated strictly as a means to an end: the final photograph. Throughout the following pages emphasis is put not only on how to do things, but even more so on why to do them, and when. Everything that is of no direct importance for the making of good pictures has been eliminated in order to avoid ballast and to provide additional space for more essential matters, with the result that certain things found traditionally in other photographic books will not be found in this one—for instance, intricate sensomitrikal lectures, explanations of the technical reactions occurring in emulsions under the influence of light and developer, historical and lens-evolutionary discussions, etc. These may be fascinating to research-technicians or students of photo-history, but are completely valueless as far as the actual making of good photographs is concerned. On the other hand, a vast amount of unusual information will be presented on the following pages—for instance, how the photographer should select his equipment; how to use filters for transformation of colors into any desired shade of gray; how to control perspective in every possible (and sometimes apparently impossible) respect; how to make light look radiant in a picture instead of merely white; how to create impressions of movement and action in still photographs; and many other equally interesting and exciting facts necessary to make good pictures.

I want this book to be useful to both amateurs and professionals. If you are so far advanced that you cannot find helpful information in Part I, please turn to Part II, and I think you will find surprises. On the other hand, if you only recently got interested in photography, don't be afraid that you may not "understand" this rather voluminous book. In spite of its ambitious goals, it starts with fundamental photographic principles. Actually, you may find it even easier to digest than other much simpler-looking books—and less insulting to your intelligence.

I trust it will help you to see and think in terms of photography and to work like any other creative artist.

BROOKFIELD CENTER, CONN.
January, 1953

Andreas Feininger

PART ONE

The Technique of Making a Photograph

CHAPTER 1

THE MAKINGS OF A PHOTOGRAPHER

TAKING photographs is getting simpler and easier all the time. Most of the basic technical problems have been solved during the last ten or twenty years, and the various steps in producing the picture have been streamlined to a degree where success is achieved almost automatically. Gadgets, accessories, newly invented instruments of all kinds not only successfully substitute for the skill and experience without which no photograph could have been taken yesterday, but even lead to results which yesterday would have been considered impossible. Electronic exposure meters, lens-coupled rangefinders, synchronized flashguns, miniature cameras built to the rigid specifications of precision watches, speedlight enabling exposures down to one ten-thousandth of a second, infrared and microfilms, black-out flashbulbs and invisible light, etc., are only a few of the better known of these recently perfected marvels which today's photographers have at their disposition without giving much thought to the immense amount of research, ingenuity, money, sweat, and disappointment that had to be spent before these things were ready for us to enjoy. . . .

Technically, the use or operation of the majority of these inventions is so simple that any person of average intelligence can learn how to master them within a few days. All he has to do is read a few instructions and not let himself get confused by the sometimes very complicated principles that make them work. There is no need to study intricate electric or chemical laws in order to operate a photoelectric exposure meter, or to take a picture on infrared film.

Boiled down to plain English, this means: Technical perfection is no longer a major problem in modern photography, and to judge a photograph by its technical perfection or imperfection alone would be the same as to judge a book by the correctness of its grammar or spelling. Technique in modern photography should be considered no more than a matter of course. Surely, we have to learn it, once and for all, and to teach it in an easily understandable form I have written Part I of this book. But as soon as we have mastered the technique of photography, let's not talk about it any more, let alone boast about it—just as no writer would boast about his ability to spell words correctly.

The mark of the really good photographer is the way in which he makes use of the rich potentialities of modern photo-technique. And this is a theme that has been rather neglected by most writers on photographic topics. I have tried to make up for this negligence in the second and main part of this book.

If you have an eye for the photogenic, if you instinctively discriminate between a good, a purposeful, a stirring subject, and one that is better left alone because it would never look interesting in a photograph—in other words, if you can see and think "graphically" in terms of black and white, then you don't have to worry about your present lack of "technique"; sooner or later you are bound to become a good photographer.

Otherwise—no. Not even with the help of the most brilliant "technique."

THE RISE OF A PHOTOGRAPHER

Many of our very best photographers have been something else before they made photography their profession. They started by taking pictures as a hobby; they were amateurs, and today—in spite of impressive salaries and nationwide reputations—they are still amateurs at heart, which is one of the reasons why they are so good.

"Amateur" means "lover," and amateurs are people who do something because they love to do it; they are interested in the thing for itself and not just as a means of making money. Amateurs are idealists. And amateurs are people who don't take "no" for an answer when it comes to their hobby. They slave and they save for their hobby's sake, to earn a few free hours and a few extra dollars to make possible those moments which for them make life worth living. Amateurs make good photographers. . . .

And by the same token, amateurs make the best professionals if they have sufficient courage to drop an earlier profession, to shelve everything they worked so hard for, and to start anew as photographers because they love making pictures more than doing anything else, then one can be pretty certain that they will have interest and energy enough to be successful. The facts confirm this belief: Among *Life's* regular photographers are Alfred Eisenstaedt, who was a button manufacturer; Fritz Goro, a sculptor and magazine editor; George Karger, a banker; Gjon Mili, an engineer; Dmitri Kessel, a fur merchant; Wallace Kirkland, a social worker; and Eric Schaal, who sold ladies' undergarments.

I had been an architect myself for many years before I found the courage to chuck everything connected with architecture and to switch over to photography. I never regretted this step. I was already an amateur photographer during my last years in school, and even today, having been a professional for close to fifteen years, I still consider myself an amateur at heart, a lover of the art of picturemaking. I have encountered many amateurs—in France, in Sweden, and in Germany as well as in the United States. I have listened to them and talked to them; I know their problems, the dangers and pitfalls that threaten their development, and the obstacles they must overcome. As a result of those years of experience, I believe today that photography as a profession should always start with photography as a hobby. You cannot "learn" photography as you can, for instance, study law, or learn how to make shoes, or how to repair a car, or how to sell vacuum cleaners. You should become a photographer only if you can't imagine enjoying anything but photography, if photography has fascinated you right from the beginning, and if you don't mind taking photographs for years and years just for the fun of it and not because somebody told you people make a lot of money out of pictures. And, remember, the *only* thing anyone can "learn" about photography is photo-technique; but, as we will see later, even the slickest photo-technique by no means guarantees that a photograph will be great as a "picture," too. For everything else that makes a photograph successful you need a feeling and an understanding which you either have or have not, but which you cannot "learn"—the urge to create with your mind and your hands, for the sake of creation and your personal satisfaction and not for any money value the work you created may represent. Unless you feel this compulsion, you may one day become a fair photo-illustrator, but never a creative photographer. . . .

Photography as a hobby costs money. I know that, because I had to earn every cent I wanted to spend on photography. And I made very little money during the time I was a struggling amateur. Today, I know that this was only good for me, and that having too little money is better for a beginner than having all he needs. For one thing, if a photographer has to slave and save before he can finally buy a new piece of equipment, you may be sure that he will select this piece more carefully, that he will value it more highly, use it more wisely, take better care of it, and get more fun out of it, than a man to whom money makes no difference and who at any time can buy anything he wants. But, paradoxically enough, of even greater value to a beginner can be the things he cannot get because of the limitations of his budget. They can do him—indirectly—the greatest favor a photographer could ask: they force him to develop his ingenuity and imagination. They teach him to rely on his own resources, to invent, to take good pictures with simple means—and if he is the type of amateur who doesn't take "no" for an answer, he still will—somehow—find a way to get the results he wanted *without* the means he couldn't afford . . . and all throughout his later career as a photographer he will profit from the lessons he forcibly took when he was still an unknown amateur.

I know what I am talking about, because I speak from personal experience. Almost thirty years ago I built my first enlarger out of wood, without instructions or drawings, inventing as I went ahead. It was of the horizontal type, operated with two 100-watt bulbs and indirect light, and got so hot that I never could use it for more than ten minutes at a time because my negatives curled and the darkroom (a corner in a basement) filled up with smoke. Two months later I built the second machine, an improved model with an effective ventilation system. Its dimensions were awe-inspiring, filling three-quarters of the darkroom. . . . It worked with six 100-watt bulbs and didn't overheat any more, and I learned a lot about enlarging and enlargers, and especially about their deficiencies. I became ambitious, and, profiting from my mistakes, constructed a third enlarger half a year later. This time I used thin, hard plywood and built the enlarger so it could be knocked down flat within a few minutes and stowed away when not in use. Besides, each one of the six lamps could be turned on or off individually, which helped a lot in dodging, and the negative carrier could be tilted for easy correction of undesirable perspective. It worked so well that I used it for many years, even after my budget had improved enough to permit the purchase of a "real" enlarger. At that time none of the commercial models had the tilting negative carrier which I badly needed because much of my photographic work was architectural and correction of converging verticals was important. So one day I wrote to the makers of a well-known enlarger and suggested an improved tilting device for redistortion of distorted negatives. They liked my ideas so well that they adopted them and incorporated them into a new enlarger model, and later they sent me one of these improved machines. I have had it now for over twenty years and still use it exclusively.

Quite early in my amateur days I got interested in telephotography. I had seen some telephotographs which fascinated me because of their beautiful and distortion-free perspective—and because everything looked so monumental. . . . I longed to make some myself, but the price of a telephoto lens was way beyond my budget.

So I shopped around for weeks looking for an old rectilinear lens with an extra-long focal length. I finally found it on the "flea market" (I was studying architecture at that time in Paris), and bought it for the equivalent of one dollar since it was so old-fashioned and slow that nobody else wanted it. But its definition was perfect, and its front element, used by itself, had a focal length long enough to give me what I wanted. I built a very primitive box camera out of wood to accommodate it and learned more about telephotography than I would have learned if I hadn't had to struggle with inadequate means to get a decent picture. . . . Many years later, in 1944, experience gained with that old telephoto outfit proved invaluable when I constructed another telecamera with a 40-inch lens for taking pictures of the New York skyline (see photographs on opposite page).

I mention these examples because I think they will convince you that a limited budget is no real excuse for failure. Only too often beginners complain to me: "If only I had a camera as good as the great Mr. X, a darkroom fitted like that of Mr. Y, or the means for buying tele-equipment like you must have, I, too, could make outstanding pictures!" This is a defeatist attitude which occasionally grips all of us, but has to be fought the moment it becomes apparent; otherwise, it will eventually take all the fun out of photography and prevent a person from ever becoming a good photographer himself. If things look really dark and everything seems to go wrong at once, just remember: Even the great Mr. X has once been nothing but a beginner, fumbling with two left hands and ten thumbs to persuade an obstreperous film into the grooves of a developing reel while trying desperately not to get his fingerprints all over the emulsion.

One of the highlights in the career of a beginner is the moment when he buys his first "real" camera. He may have knocked around with a box Brownie or simple folding camera, but now he wants to take photography seriously. He has saved his dollars and is going to invest them in the real McCoy—a camera "exactly like the one the great Mr. X himself uses." This really is an important moment, a moment as decisive for the future development of a photographer's career as is marriage for the future development of his life. For if the two don't fit together—man and wife, photographer and camera—unhappiness and failure are bound to result, in marriage as well as in photography.

Again, I speak from personal experience. My marriage is a very happy one, but my first "real" camera was a regrettable mistake. Previously, I had only worked with a cheap, big, and clumsy, but highly adaptable 4x5 camera with an old-fashioned, slow, but exceedingly sharp lens. I always have been (and still am) a rather slow worker. I want to take my time and do things carefully and thoroughly. I love technical perfection, sharp definition, and large-size negatives. And I, of all

New York City skyline, from seven miles away. This photograph was taken with the homemade telephoto camera illustrated below, from the location shown in the center picture below. It was taken with a standard lens, showing the skyline as it appears to the eye, all but invisible because of haze and distance.

Specifications of the telecamera: Lens—an old-fashioned Ross lens of 21-inch focal length; its front element with a focal length of 40 inches was used by itself. Purchased in 1944 for $25. Filter—Wratten A, gelatine, mounted between two pieces of cardboard. Camera—two plywood boxes, one telescoping inside the other; bellows of old view camera in rear for focusing. Tripod—five legs joined together with wooden "backbone"; the crossbeam is a "wind brace" to prevent vibrations when taking pictures on a windy day. Cost of the complete outfit: $60, to do practically the same job as a thousand-dollar "Big Bertha."

Closeup of camera.

Location shot for comparison.

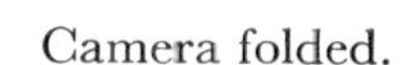

Camera folded.

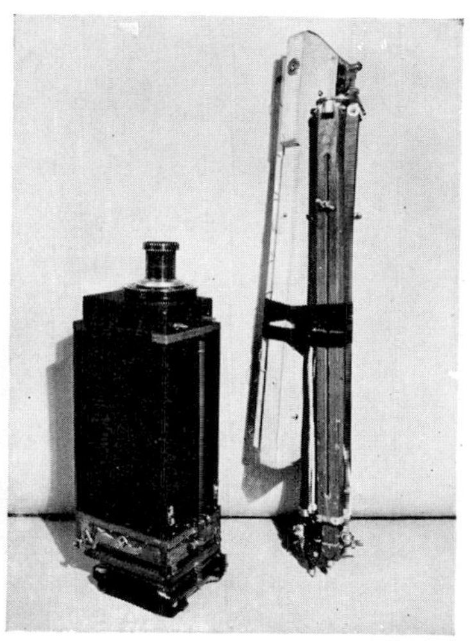

people, had to fall for the seductive beauty of a Leica, because, at that time, my hero, my great Mr. X, was Dr. Paul Wolff, the German Leica specialist whose books I then admired greatly. Naturally, the inevitable happened almost from the start: my Leica and I were incompatible. I loved to handle it; I loved its technical beauty; I loved to listen to the smooth click of its shutter. But I never got a single picture out of it that I really liked. I struggled with my Leica for almost a year; I tried desperately to make a go of it, for after all, didn't I have the same camera and thus the same opportunities as the great Dr. Wolff? What did he have that I didn't have? The struggle was always in vain; Dr. Wolff and I had different temperaments; our ways of working were not the same; my Leica and I were desperately unhappy with each other. . . . And finally, I sold it at a big loss. . . .

I bought a Rolleiflex instead. It was a success right from the start, thanks mainly to its larger negative size which resulted in pictures of almost the same quality as I was used to getting from my old 4x5 . . . and we lived happily ever after . . . do you really think so? Not I. . . . Believe it or not, but a year or so later I got the itch once more; I didn't like the square of the Rollei any more; I didn't like to be limited to a single lens—especially a lens which had a relatively short focal length. I thought I had learned enough in the meantime; in short, as you may already have guessed, I traded my good Rolleiflex for another Leica.

Once more the same thing happened—no go. . . . Again, it didn't work! In spite of all its beauty and perfection, in spite of all the wonderful pictures others took with it, in spite of the fact that the Leica was *the camera* that could do everything—certified by authorities who proved by their work that they knew what they were talking about—I still couldn't get a single decent photograph out of it! I used up negatives by the yard, hoping against hope that, according to the law of averages, one in a hundred would be good, at least. But with me the average must have been one in a million, for I never got that single picture that would have kept the flame alive, and once more I had a Leica for sale.

I went back to a 4x5, a sadder but wiser man. And lo and behold, right away I started making PICTURES!

Years later, after I got a position with *Life* magazine, I watched other photographers work, professionals with a nationwide reputation. I marveled at the lot of equipment they had. Some actually never took less than four different cameras to cover a simple assignment that I, in my innocence, would have tackled with only a single camera! Apparently I still had a lot to learn. . . . They had 4x5 Deardorffs; they had 3¼x4¼ Linhofs; they had Rolleiflexes (most of them had at least two, some had three and four); they had Contaxes; and they had Leicas. They had Leicas. . . . And they got beautiful pictures with these Leicas! I went with Eisenstaedt on a job, and didn't he swing a wicked Leica! The pictures he got . . . every single one a hit! So there I was again, unable to resist the temptation, and for the third time I went and bought myself a Leica—with all the trimmings. Some people only learn the hard way.

Naturally, it didn't work out this time either. But this time I found the reason: the Leica is too beautiful for me! To me, a Leica is a work of Art, is mechanical perfection personified, is not a means to an end, but the end itself. I could put a Leica on my desk and keep it there as an ornament, I can play around with it and enjoy it like a piece of "technical jewelry"—but I can never treat it casually, as casually as a camera should be treated. I sold this third Leica outfit of mine four months after I had bought it. I wonder when I shall buy my next one. . . . I tell this story of trouble in such detail because I believe that others may profit by it. I am not proud of myself; but on the other hand, I know that I am no exception when it comes to stubbornness. Many beginners have exactly the same kind of trouble I had. They buy a camera because some other guy did beautiful work with it. But it doesn't fit their temperament, and they trade it for another camera which usually doesn't satisfy them either for some reason or other. Then they trade again. . . . Thus, the vicious circle goes on and on for years. Each change is connected with a more or less serious financial loss; interest remains concentrated on the equipment and is never free to be applied where it belongs: to the making of photographs. Maybe, if he wouldn't give up so easily, such a photographer would eventually get acquainted with his camera and get good pictures out of it, but usually—in his eternal search for the "ideal" camera which exists as little as the "ideal" woman—if something doesn't work out right away, he gets discouraged, runs to the dealer, and "trades."

One of the most valuable lessons learned during my work for *Life* is to keep my equipment simple. Especially during the war years, traveling would have been positively killing if I hadn't cut my equipment down to essentials. And during this process of elimination I made the wonderful discovery that I could get along with only a fraction of the things I thought a *Life* photographer would need. This simplicity, however, doesn't merely make life more comfortable by reducing the necessary equipment, even for a big assignment, to two small suitcases. Its real value doesn't manifest itself until I get started on my job, which is to take pictures: no more worry which camera to take, what lens to use, no more chance of taking the wrong-size filters on location and leaving the right set at home, of mixed-up lens shades, of cable releases that don't fit the shutter, etc.—nothing to work with, to think of and to worry about, but one camera and *two* lenses, fitted with adapter rings to take *one* size of filters, *one* adjustable lens shade, and a single cable release.

All my energy and interest remain free from worry about technicalities and can be concentrated one hundred per cent on the job of taking pictures.

Another source of confusion is the habit of many photo magazines and annuals of mentioning technical data beneath each picture. Unless there are really unusual circumstances that warrant special attention, such data have absolutely no practical value—unless it is publicity value for the manufacturers of the materials. Or, can anyone tell me what difference it makes, so far as the impact of a photograph is concerned (and especially in print!) whether it was taken, for instance, on Ansco instead of Kodak film, with a Wollensack instead of a Zeiss lens, printed on Eastman instead of Defender paper, enlarged with an Omega instead of a Beebee enlarger?

Besides, I'm still waiting to see such data that are really complete. For infinitely more important than, for instance, camera, paper, enlarger, and even exposure time used, are facts referring to light conditions (indicated in meter readings), time of development, temperature of the developer, and gradation of the printing paper. Unless these, too, are mentioned, all other facts are completely senseless and can never be used for successful duplication of the technical conditions responsible for the making of that particular photograph.

If such data were simply valueless, but otherwise harmless, I wouldn't mention them here. Actually, however, they give many a beginner the idea that if only he, too, would take his pictures with a "prize-winning" Speed Graphic, or would use a Wollensack lens for enlarging, or Defender paper for printing, etc., his troubles would be over and his pictures would be terrific. And straightaway he trades camera and enlarger, switches to paper he doesn't know, etc., and generally invites an entirely new set of troubles on top of those he had already—which probably didn't result from inferiority of materials anyway, but from inadequate knowledge of their proper use. Today, all products made by nationally known manufacturers are practically alike with regard to quality and uniformity.

From twenty years of experience, the best advice I have for a beginner is this: never mind "the other guy," even if his name is Eisenstaedt or Mydans or McGinnicuddle. Don't imitate, be yourself, and be proud of it! Be honest with yourself, decide what you want to do, and don't buy more equipment than you need for doing it. The less you have to worry about, the better off you are and the greater chance you have to get to know your tools intimately and to get the most out of them. Always listen to experience. Profit from the mistakes of others, but don't be gullible. Accept advice only if you are convinced it really will be good *for you!* Be critical, test equipment and materials wherever you can, use your common sense. Never forget that even the most expensive camera won't do your thinking for you.

CHAPTER 2

THE EQUIPMENT OF A PHOTOGRAPHER

WITH THE purchase of his tools—his equipment—the beginning photographer to a certain degree decides the trend of his future activities. So, if he is to make this decision himself, and not leave it to chance and the clerk in the photo shop, he must know what he wants to do as a photographer and what he needs for doing it *before* he goes out buying things. Only in this way can he hope to avoid situations like the following one—typical of many I have involuntarily witnessed while waiting in a camera store: on one side of the counter a prosperous-looking customer intent on buying a camera; on the other side a glib-tongued clerk intent on playing the sucker for all he is worth; between them an array of half a dozen or so cameras from Contax and Leica up to 4x5 Speed Graphic. The customer takes up one camera after another, fondles it, cocks and trips the shutter, peeps through the viewfinder, sights through the door at the building across the street, puts the camera down, takes up another one, and repeats the performance while the clerk pours out a running comment on the merits of each model, guessing the shifting thoughts of his victim with uncanny accuracy, praising whatever the customer would like to hear praised, but never for a moment forgetting to emphasize the special advantages of the most expensive of all the cameras on the counter, a Contax with an *f* 1.5 lens. The salesman climaxes his arguments by whipping out one of the complete Contax catalogues describing the several hundred different accessories "adapting this camera for every conceivable purpose," and finally closes the deal by selling the, by now, completely bewildered customer the Contax.

When our man entered the camera shop all he apparently knew was that he wanted to buy "a camera." What he apparently did *not* consider sufficiently was the fact that there are about as many different types of cameras as there are breeds of dogs, and just as different in looks, size, and purpose. The camera customer behaved exactly like "a dog lover" who went to buy a dog without having made up his mind

The equipment of a photographer: What he needs; what else he should have

Drugstore stage—this is all you need for making snapshots:

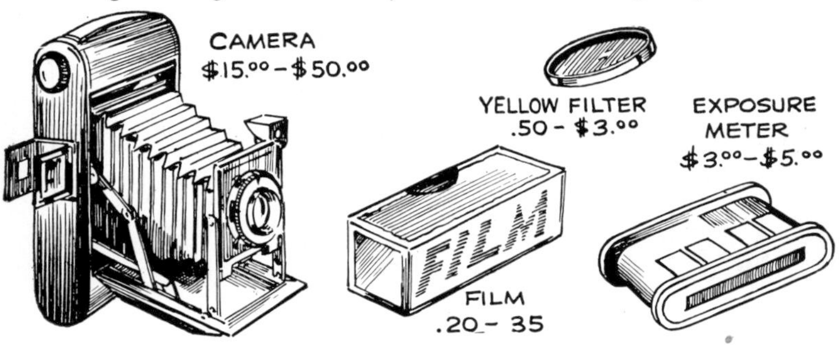

Amateur stage—this is what you need for serious work:

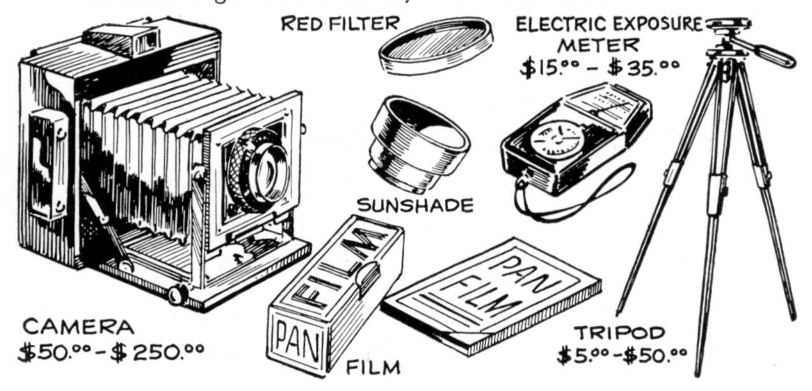

Advanced amateur and first professional stage—requires a darkroom:

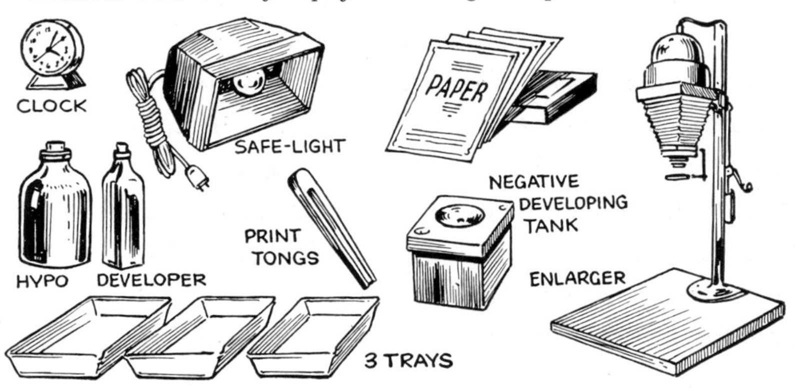

Lighting equipment for amateurs and professionals:

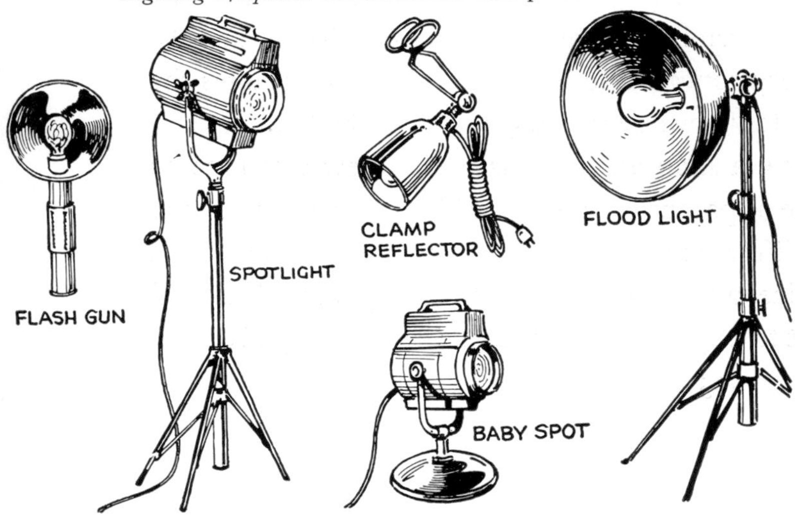

The only things you positively need for taking photographs are *camera* and *film*. But unless you are satisfied with the simplest type of snapshot, you should acquire two more things simultaneously with the camera: *a medium-yellow color filter* which will make your pictures richer in tone and bring out the clouds (see pages 48-49, 227), and an *exposure meter* which will pay for itself in a short time by saving you the cost of film that otherwise would be lost because of faulty exposure (page 50).

The scope of your work will grow considerably if you treat yourself to *a better camera with groundglass-focusing, double extension, and interchangeable lenses.* To make fullest use of these more advanced features you need *a tripod* (page 51) for firm support of the camera, and a *lens-shade* for the lens. *A red color filter* gives more dramatic black-and-white effects than a yellow one, but can be used only in connection with *panchromatic* film (page 68). *A photoelectric exposure meter* (page 50) is infinitely more accurate and reliable than any other type of meter, and more than worth its higher price to anybody who can afford it.

Real creative work—and the real fun in photography—begins the moment you start to develop and print your own negatives. For this you need a darkroom (which can be improvised, page 88) equipped with: *negative developing tank; enlarger; three trays* for developer, hypo, and water; *safelight; clock; thermometer; print tongs; towel; sensitized paper; and chemicals.* Convenient, but not absolutely necessary, are: *print washer* (otherwise: bathtub), *print dryer, trimming board,* and electrically heated *mounting press.*

If you want to be independent of sunlight and practice photography indoors as well as at dusk and night and dawn, you have to have your own sources of light. For fast work, and for photographing action and motion, you have to use *flashbulbs* on speedlights (pages 61-63) synchronized to the shutter of your camera by means of a *synchronizer* (pages 57-59). For carefully posed work in the studio or at home you need *floodlights* and *spotlights* (pages 52-56) which come in all sizes from tiny portable lights to heavy units for use in the studio only.

whether he wanted a Pekinese or a Chow or a Great Dane, long hair or short hair, a pet for his wife or a watchdog for his factory. . . . And the odds are more than ten to one that our camera buyer did *not* get "the" camera that was best adapted for his needs, for his temperament, for his way of taking pictures, for taking the subjects he most wanted to take—but got just "a" camera. This despite the fact that he bought one of the finest and most expensive cameras on the market. And that small difference between "a" camera and "the" camera may for him take all the fun out of photography. . . . Before you buy any kind of equipment you should decide just what you want to do with it. Naturally, in the case of a camera, you want it for taking pictures; but what type of pictures? Good ones, of course. . . . Yes, but good portraits? Or good landscapes? Or good pictures of children? Or good architectural photographs? Or good closeups of insects and flowers? Or good candid shots of people? You see, the use you want to put the camera to is so terribly important. There are so many, many types of cameras, and in spite of uniformity of price or workmanship some of them are *better* adapted to do certain things in photography than others. Specialization goes so far that actually the more expensive camera may be the one less well adapted to solve *your* special problem! The section "How to Select Your Camera" (pages 28-32) advises you how to choose the camera that is best adapted to *your* special needs!

Another type of eternally frustrated photographer is the gadgeteer and collector. The gadgeteer must always have the complete line of accessories for his camera, even if he will never need them. He is the man who buys photo novelties as fast as they appear on the market, and his type is so common and he buys so much that serious photographers actually should be grateful for his existence because his buying sprees make quantity output of photographic supplies possible and thus keep prices low. . . . Most beginners pass at one time or another through this stage of collecting. And little harm is done—if they can only get it out of their systems early in the game. But many a photographer with a future never gets past this stage of gadgeteering, never tears his interest away from the *means* in photography and concentrates on the *purpose*—making pictures! I used to know such a man who had the makings of a first-class photographer but who never arrived simply because he couldn't help falling in love with beautiful equipment. And his wasn't the only case. I know of another photographer making pictures whose quality was inverse in proportion to the amount of money and equipment spent in producing them. These people are living examples proving convincingly that it is *not* the quantity of expensive means used in making a photograph that accounts for its greatness as a picture, but the qualifications of the man who knew how to put these means to intelligent use.

Demonstration of the "pinhole principle." Rays of light from brilliantly illuminated object (Lincoln head) are focused by a pinhole cut in sheet of cardboard (*center*) on groundglass (*left*). As in all cameras, image is reversed.

THE CAMERA

Fundamentally, a camera—any camera—is nothing but a light-tight box with a lens at one end and a piece of light-sensitized film inside at the other end. Actually, not even a lens is absolutely necessary; instead, a very fine hole in the front end of the box will do, too, and will throw a reasonably clear if extremely faint image of any object in front of it on the film in the rear.

The best way to understand once and for all the workings of a camera and the functions of its different parts is to build one oneself. This can be done within half an hour from material available everywhere: take any strong cardboard box—preferably between five and seven inches long and a little less wide and high—and cut a hole about a quarter of an inch in diameter in the center of one of its short sides. Take a piece of thin metal foil about one inch square, stick it over the hole with Scotch tape, and pierce the center of this tin foil with a very fine sewing needle (watch out that this tiny hole—your future "lens"—is exactly in the center of the quarter-inch hole you cut into the cardboard box). Then cut a piece of black paper (a tab from a filmpack) about two inches square and "hinge" it with Scotch tape on the front end of the box (outside) so it covers the "pinhole" and prevents light from entering the box until you are ready to take a picture. Secure the hinged "shutter" lightly with another piece of Scotch tape so that the black paper cannot flap open accidentally. Finally, go into a perfectly dark room and fasten a piece of sheet film with Scotch tape inside the box on the wall opposite the one with the hole in it. To take a photograph, set your box camera on a rigid support—a windowsill, or a table near the window, with some books on the top of the box to keep it absolutely still while you make the exposure. Aim your "camera" at the scenery outside the window. Carefully unfasten one side of the black paper shutter and then lift it to admit light through the pinhole for about ten seconds (in bright sunlight). Close and fasten it again, take the box back into the darkroom, and develop the film. If you timed your exposure right (exposure time depends on brightness of the illumination, sensitivity of the film, diameter of the pinhole, and distance from pinhole to film; if necessary, correct your exposure time after the first trial), you will get a picture which naturally is not needle sharp, but which nevertheless is amazingly good, considering: it was taken with a cardboard box that was converted into a camera without a lens within half an hour, from valueless waste material, without the help of tools. . . . The principle of such a "pinhole-camera" is illustrated on the opposite page; a "pinhole-picture" is reproduced on the following page.

A pinhole camera has two inherent weaknesses: 1. Its "lens" is exceedingly slow (which means that pictures can never be "snapped." Only perfectly still objects can be photographed at all, and a tripod or similar camera support has always to be used.) 2. Pinhole pictures are not sharp enough for critical work. Making the pinhole larger would shorten the time of exposure, but would simultaneously increase the fuzziness of the picture tremendously and thus is out of the question. The only way to surmount these shortcomings is to replace the pinhole with some kind of a "lens," and if we want to improve our experimental camera this is the way to do it:

We get hold of a medium-sized reading-glass lens with a diameter of two inches; we cut a circular hole one and a half inches in diameter in the front of our cardboard box (where the pinhole was), cover it with the reading-glass lens, and fasten

Picture taken with a pinhole camera. Compared with a photograph taken with a regular lens, the pinhole picture looks softer all over without actually being "blurred." Its outstanding quality is perfect uniformity of softness which renders near and distant objects equally unsharp, eliminating the need for "focusing" when working with a pinhole camera. Changes in distance from pinhole to film affect the angle of view, the scale of the image, and the time of exposure, but *not* the sharpness of the rendering, which solely depends on the size of the pinhole: the smaller the hole, the sharper will be the picture—but never so sharp as a photograph taken with a regular lens.

the lens with Scotch tape; we cut a large square hole in the opposite end of the box (as large as possible without weakening the box too much) and cover it with a piece of groundglass that we Scotch tape on. Then we aim our box at some object or out of the window, watch the groundglass, and—we will probably see nothing, or only a hazy blur. The reason: the distance between lens and groundglass is not yet adjusted to the distance between lens and object. No more is everything sharp regardless of distance (as in the case of the "pinhole lens"), but objects must now be brought "into focus" by adjusting the distance between lens and groundglass (or film) to the distance between lens and object. This operation is called "focusing."

Picture taken with a simple reading-glass lens (double-convex). Notice the "distortion" of the straight lines of the window which here appear curved, and the high degree of unsharpness, increasing toward the edges of the picture. To get rid of these "faults," a lens must be "corrected," which accounts for the complexity and the high price of modern lenses.

We do it now by cutting out the entire rear wall of our "camera" and moving it back and forth inside the box until we get an image on the groundglass. Such an image is shown in the picture at the top of this page: it will be increasingly unsharp toward the edges, and straight lines will appear increasingly curved the closer they are to the edges of the picture. However, we have gained one valuable point over the pinhole lens: the image has tremendously increased in brightness. To get rid of that annoying unsharpness we have only to "stop down" the lens, i.e. use only its center for producing the image: we take a piece of black cardboard, cut a one-eighth inch circular hole in it, and put it over the lens, covering all but its exact center. This way, of course, we again lose part of the image's brightness (although it is much brighter than the image made by a mere pinhole), but as a result we get a picture

Picture taken under identical conditions as that on preceding page, but with the reading-glass lens "stopped down." A piece of cardboard with a circular, three-millimeter hole in it was placed over the lens, covering all except its center, which alone was used to produce the image. The resulting picture is fairly sharp all over, but the curvilinear distortion remains. It can be avoided only by using a "corrected" photographic lens.

that is sufficiently sharp all over. To get rid of the curvilinear distortion, however, we would have to use a "corrected" camera lens, an "aplanat." In order to get an undistorted, sharp picture even with the lens "wide open" (i.e. not "stopped down") so we can use the maximum light transmission of the lens (its full "speed"), make "instantaneous" exposures and "stop motion" even of fast-moving objects, we would have to employ an even more perfectly corrected type of camera lens, an "anastigmat."

We will hear more about lenses, their faults and the way they are corrected, in the discussion of lenses beginning on page 33.

Every camera, from the simple folding camera to the most elaborate and expensive professional type, consists of the same few fundamental parts as our experimental cardboard-box camera. Naturally, construction and execution of these parts is infinitely more complex and elaborate, but this is no reason for getting confused, for viewing, for instance, a Leica or a Speed Graphic with reverence, and for believing that a beginner in photography has to begin with the simplest type of camera because he "cannot understand" the more complex types unless he starts at the very bottom. In my opinion, the unsurpassed best camera for any beginner is one of the "twin-lens reflex type," a class to which belong among others the Rolleiflex and the Ikoflex, two of our most expensive cameras.

However, no matter which camera is chosen, it will have:

A light-tight compartment (the "cardboard box"), the backbone of any camera, consists either of an accordion-like "bellows" (Vestpocket Kodak, Speed Graphic), or a rigid metal casting (Contax, Rolleiflex). In the first case, focusing is done either by lengthening or shortening the bellows by means of "rack and pinion," or by screwing the front element of the lens inwards or outwards; in the second case, forward and backward movement of the lens is built right into the lens mount, usually in the form of a screw ("helical mount," Leica). *For complete information on "focusing" see the section beginning on page 102.*

A lens (the "pinhole" or the "reading glass") is not only the most expensive part of any camera, but the most important one, too: on its quality—its degree of "correction"—depend sharpness, crispness, and definition, and on its "focal length" depends the scale of our picture. It is attached to the front of the light-tight compartment, and may be either permanently attached or removable so that it can be easily interchanged with other lenses, a feature which is invaluable for any type of creative work. *For exhaustive information on lenses see pages 33-47.*

A diaphragm (the cardboard with the small hole in front of our reading-glass lens) is built right between the elements of the lens (with the exception of some of the very cheapest box cameras). Its function is to regulate the amount of light that is permitted to pass through the lens onto the film, and to control the extension of sharpness in depth in our pictures. *For information on the use of the diaphragm (the "stop") turn to page 107.*

A shutter (the hinged black paper in front of our pinhole) automatically times the length of an exposure—the time during which the lens is "open" permitting light to pass through it to the film. It can be preset for a great number of different exposure times from "Time," for time exposures of any desired length, down to smallest fractions of a second (Contax: 1/1250 second, Rolleiflex: 1/500 second). The shutter is either built right into the lens ("between-the-lens shutter," for instance, the "Compur" shutter of the Rolleiflex), or operates in the form of a curtain directly in front of the film ("focal-plane shutter"—Nikon, Contax, Leica, Graflex). Cheaper shutters have fewer different "speeds" than more expensive ones; focal-plane shutters permit shorter exposure times and are more efficient than between-the-lens shutters—but the latter are easier to "synchronize" with flash-bulbs (see page 61).

A filmholder (we used Scotch tape in our pinhole camera) is connected to the end of the light-tight compartment opposite the lens. Its form depends on the type of film a camera uses: "sheet film" ("cut film") has to be loaded piece for piece into individual filmholders, and filmpack into a filmpack adapter which accommodates in one holder a magazine containing twelve sheets of film; both filmholder and filmpack adapter slide into grooves at the rear of the camera (for instance: Speed Graphic, Graflex, view cameras). "Roll film" is wound on spools. One roll contains material enough for from eight to thirty-six individual pictures ("frames") and can be loaded into the camera in daylight, the same as filmpack. Sheet film has to be loaded into filmholders in the darkroom. However, always load roll film or filmpack in the shade, *never* in full sunlight which would almost certainly penetrate to the film along the edges of the pack or roll.

A viewfinder (the groundglass of our cardboard camera with the reading-glass lens) is indispensable for accurate "aiming" of the camera at the object we want to photograph. Without its help we would never know exactly what would be included in a picture, and what would be cut off. The best type of viewfinder is a groundglass that shows both degree of sharpness and extension of the future picture in a size as large as the negative itself, before, during and after an exposure (all twin-lens reflex-type cameras). Single-lens reflex-type cameras have the same type of viewfinder, but the image disappears the moment we release the shutter. View cameras have the kind of groundglass viewfinder we used in our experimental box camera, giving, like the reflex-type cameras, a negative-size image showing not only extension of the future picture, but its degree of sharpness, too; this image, however, disappears when we insert the filmholder into the camera. Optical direct-vision viewfinders, and brilliant finders, show a very much reduced image of the future picture only, and say nothing at all about its sharpness. Wire-frame viewfinders are good only for very fast work, since they are not too reliable in their indication of the future picture's extension and say nothing about its degree of sharpness.

Principal types of cameras and their characteristics

Box and fixed-focus cameras: cheapest and simplest of all cameras. Cannot produce really sharp negatives at all, and well-exposed ones only in bright sunlight. Lenses extremely slow (*f* 12.5 to *f* 16), are either adjusted once and for all for taking pictures from a certain distance (fixed focus), or have two focusing positions for near and distant objects only. Shutters very simple with one or two different slow speeds. This type of camera is ideal for children and beginners since it is simple, foolproof, and practically indestructible.

Folding rollfilm cameras: we have to differentiate between two types: one has no direct control for focusing (uses focusing scale instead of groundglass or rangefinder); cameras belonging to this group are often referred to as "blind cameras," and from the viewpoint of the serious photographer, are hardly superior to boxes and fixed-focus cameras.

Cameras belonging to the second group have lens-coupled rangefinders for accurate focusing (the same as the Ektra has), and include, especially among the smaller sizes, several outstanding models designed to become constant and valuable companions of even very critical photographers, filling the functions of "photographic sketchbooks." Lenses usually have fair to excellent correction, and apertures from *f* 6.3 to *f* 2.8; shutter speeds of the better types in this camera group range from "time" down to 1/250 and 1/500 second. Prices from $15 to over $200.

Sheet-film and filmpack cameras are the ideal all-around heavy-duty cameras for the creative and versatile photographer who strives for pictures of highest technical quality. The Speed Graphic, the typical "press camera," is the prototype of this group which includes some of the most universally adaptable of all cameras, combining in their most highly developed representatives features such as the following: negative-size groundglass for accurate focusing and composing of the picture; lens-coupled rangefinder for quick and accurate shooting; interchangeability of lenses for wide-angle and telephotographs; double or triple extension to accommodate lenses of unusually long focus and for super closeups showing objects several times their natural size; "swings" of both camera back and front, and horizontal and vertical shift of the lens, for correction of perspective distortion; alternative use of focal-plane or between-the-lens shutters for stopping fastest action or flashbulb synchronization; revolving camera back for quick change from horizontal to vertical picture and vice versa; rugged construction, completely enclosing the whole camera mechanism when shut, enabling these

cameras to withstand years of rough professional treatment and making them easy to transport.

Almost any lens can be used in this type of camera, from wide-angle to telephoto lenses, high-speed lenses, portrait lenses, etc. Shutter speeds down to 1/1,000 second. Negative sizes from 2¼x3¼ to 5x7 inches. Prices depend on type of lens, and presence or absence of rangefinder, focal-plane shutter, etc. Ask your dealer for literature and details.

Single-lens reflex cameras: the only weakness of the sheet-film and filmpack cameras—disappearance of the groundglass image the moment we slide the filmholder into place—has been overcome in the reflex cameras. Here the lens-produced image is reflected from a hinged 45-degree mirror inside the camera onto a horizontal groundglass the size of the negative, permitting the photographer to check focus and extension of the picture with extreme accuracy up to the moment of the exposure, when pressure on the shutter-release lever or button makes the mirror snap upwards, out of the way of the light, while simultaneously the shutter is being released and the exposure of the negative is made. A camera of this type is ideal whenever it is important to observe the object up to the very moment of the exposure, especially in action shots where last-minute corrections of focus have to be made; in portraiture, where success of the picture depends on catching the right expression on a face; and when making extreme closeups where even the slightest movement of object or camera would throw the image out of focus.

Single-lens reflex amecra

Single-lens reflex cameras come in all sizes from 35 mm up to 5x7 inches for either roll film or sheet film and filmpack, and combine in their most highly developed forms features like interchangeability of lenses (actual wide-angle lenses, however, can not be used because minimum distance between lens and film is limited by the size of the hinged mirror); double extension; rising and tilting front; revolving back; automatic diaphragm which permits focusing with the lens wide open but will stop down the lens to a predetermined aperture the moment the shutter is released; built-in flash synchronization, etc. Features common to all single-lens reflex cameras are their perfect freedom from "parallax" (in contrast to twin-lens reflex cameras), which means that extension of the picture will rigorously correspond with the extension of the groundglass image; the disadvantage that stopping down the diaphragm automatically makes the groundglass image so much darker, (this is where the automatic diaphragm proves itself invaluable!); and the fact that between-the-lens shutters cannot be used since they would prevent the light from forming an image on the groundglass via the mirror.

With the exception of wide-angle lenses, any kind of lens can be used alternately in most of the better single-lens reflex cameras, shutter speeds of which usually go down to 1/1,000 second. Prices range from $50 to $400 and $500, depending on camera model and lens.

Twin-lens reflex cameras differ from single-lens reflex cameras in so far as two lenses of identical focal length are employed for producing the visible groundglass image and recording the picture on the negative, respectively. As a consequence, the negative-size groundglass image is visible at all times before, during, and after an exposure; adjustments with regard to sharpness and composition can be made up to the last moment; and brightness of the image is not affected by stopping down the lens that takes the picture. On the other hand, sharpness in depth (depth of field of the negative) cannot be checked on the groundglass and has to be determined with the help of a depth-of-field guide, and parallax compensation becomes necessary (the more expensive cameras of this group have automatic parallax compensation). An advantage over the single-lens reflex camera is the fact that now between-the-lens shutters which are more easily synchronized can be employed (with speeds down to 1/500 second); but it is a sometimes decisive disadvantage of this camera type that interchangeability of lenses is not practical for technical reasons (however, focus-shortening slip-on lenses may be used within certain limits).

Twin-lens reflex camera

Most twin-lens reflex cameras make square pictures 2¼x2¼ inches large on No. 120 or No. 620 roll film. Their quality usually is so high that enlargements up to 11x14 inches and more are possible which are so sharp and so free from grain that they compare favorably with enlargements made from much larger negatives.

Lenses range from *f* 4.5 to *f* 2.8, prices from about $50 to over $300. Twin-lens reflex cameras are the ideal all-round cameras for the photographer who wants to be prepared for all kinds of subjects without particularly specializing in any one of them, as well as for amateurs and beginners. Their popularity is still increasing steadily.

Thirty-five millimeter miniature cameras: their outstanding features are compactness and light weight (easy to carry and easy to conceal when taking candid shots); economy (35 mm film is relatively cheap); relatively short focal length of standard-lens (greater depth of field than long-focus lenses of same aperture); wide choice of highly specialized interchangeable lenses (including high-speed lenses with relative apertures of *f* 2 and *f* 1.5 which would be prohibitively heavy and expensive for larger-size cameras); adaptability to practically any field in photography, such as microphotography, copying, portraiture, wide-angle,

35mm miniature camera

tele- and infrared photography, etc., thanks to highly specialized attachments and accessories of every imaginable kind.

On the other side, just that special advantage of small size creates a number of rather serious disadvantages, such as: 1. Extreme delicacy of the mechanism which necessitates precision work of the highest degree in order to function properly, which again results in extremely high prices for miniature cameras and their accessories. 2. The need for using special slow-speed finegrain film, and finegrain developers with resulting further loss of film speed if grainless enlargements have to be made, practically offsetting the advantages of special high-speed lenses. 3. The need for extra-careful processing of negatives and prints since blemishes and faults would be enlarged in the same proportions as the negative with the result that otherwise negligible defects can completely ruin a picture. 4. Sectional enlargements of a negative are not practical if grainlessness and sharpness are important, since magnification would have to be higher than graininess of the film would permit, a fact which forces the miniature-camera photographer to compose his pictures even more carefully than a man working with a larger-size camera, since he always has to make the motif proper fill the whole of his negative.

Most minicameras are equipped with focal-plane shutters, their speeds ranging usually from one full second down to 1/500 or 1/1,000 second, with a few models going down to 1/1,250 second.

Prices depend on the type of lens a specific camera is equipped with and range from $25 to $500. The average for a first-class minicamera with a 3.5 lens is around $250.

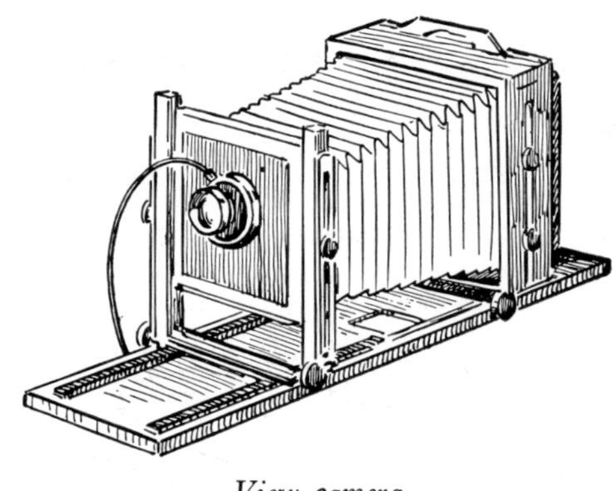
View camera

Standard view cameras are in many respects the most flexible of all types of cameras, characterized by features like negative-size groundglass, double or triple bellows extension, extensive back and front swings, reversible back, and rising, falling, and lateral-sliding front. Compared to all but the cheapest types of cameras, view cameras are relatively inexpensive, easy to operate, and because of their basic simplicity more universally useful than many other more specialized types of cameras. They use filmpack in sizes up to 5x7 inches and sheet film in all sizes to 11x14 inches. Reduction backs are available for most of the larger-size view cameras so smaller-size film can be used in them. View cameras can be fitted with any kind of lens, from wide-angle to telephoto, from super-sharp apochromat to soft-focus portrait lens. The unique advantage of view cameras—their super-flexibility—has to be paid for with one disadvantage: they have to be used on a tripod, and hand-held pictures cannot be taken. The reason: because of the many swings, sharpness and extension of the image have to be checked on the groundglass, and once adjusted to satisfaction the camera cannot be moved without the danger of creating serious disturbances with regard to distribution of sharpness in depth and composition of the picture; no viewfinder but the groundglass has been invented so far that can account for and make visible all the subtle changes introduced through use of swings and lens shifts. Prices for view cameras range from $40 to $250 for negative sizes from 4x5 to 8x10 inches, always without the lens.

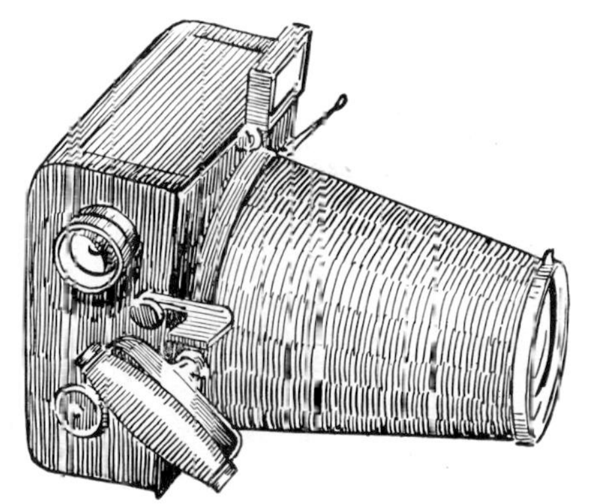

Aerial camera

Most of the 200-odd cameras available today fall into one or another of the classifications above. A few extreme types, however, deserve to be mentioned by themselves:

Aerial cameras usually have fixed-focus (fixed on infinity), large negative-size, bellows-less construction (slipstream in a plane would immediately collapse a bellows!), and often motor-driven, shutter-coupled film transport. They are not suitable for anything but aerial photography.

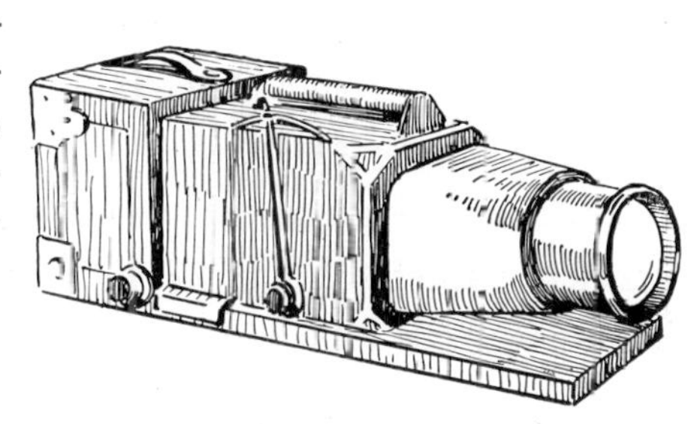

Big Bertha

Big Berthas usually are 5x7-inch Graflex cameras fitted with extreme telephoto lenses of 24- to-40-inch focal length, used mostly for taking closeups of sport scenes and speakers at conventions, etc. See page 9 for instructions on how to build a similar telecamera yourself.

Super wide-angle lenses as for instance the Goerz Hypergon have to be used in special boxes of very shallow depth, since the bellows of ordinary cameras usually cannot be compressed tightly enough for these lenses with extremely short focal lengths.

Super wide-angle lens in shallow box

How to select your camera

The selection of a camera should be governed by nothing but the three factors of *personality* of the photographer, the *purpose* to which the camera will be put, and the *purse* of the buyer, which decides how much he can spend on equipment. All else is immaterial; there are no "prize-winning cameras," there are only prize-winning photographers. . . .

The personality of the photographer (it determines the negative size of the camera). Today there are two decidedly different trends in photography. One is characterized by a demand for highest photographic quality and is personified by photographers like Edward Weston, Ansel Adams, and Paul Strand. The other school puts dynamic action and human interest above everything else and has its prototypes in photographers like Alfred Eisenstaedt, Eugene W. Smith, Leonard McCombe, Carl Mydans, and others. In between these two extremes, of course, we find all kinds of intermediate stages with perhaps the majority of photographers trying to combine the best features of both "schools." Parallel with the development of these two groups—which we could call the "conservatives" and the "radicals"—two types of cameras have been developed and perfected to such a degree that today the best cameras in *both* groups are capable of covering practically every field in photography equally well (judged by editors who care nothing about cameras and look only at results). These two camera types, each with its peculiar advantages, are the 4x5 sheet-film and filmpack camera (greatest technical perfection), and the 35 mm miniature camera (extreme mobility). Both types have in common such features as interchangeable lenses, including highly specialized lenses for every conceivable purpose, shutters with speeds down to 1/1000 second, lens-coupled rangefinders for quick action shots, double and triple extensions (minicameras: extension tubes) for super closeups, and flash synchronization. For both types a long line of different and sometimes highly specialized negative emulsions (high-speed, finegrain, infrared-sensitized, etc.) is available. And the advantage derived from "swings" of the 4x5 camera is practically compensated for by the fact that perspective distortion can be corrected during the process of enlarging (*see* page 163) almost as well as during the taking of the picture. So far, so good.

However, the very fact that *two* so highly developed and still so different types of camera can exist side by side, without one crowding the other out of the competition, proves that each of these types must have at least *one definite advantage* over the other: *its size.* Its larger size, which admittedly makes it heavy and bulky and comparatively slow to operate, gives the 4x5 camera over the minicamera the advantages of greater sharpness and better definition, makes for easier and faster processing (rapid developer!) because negatives don't have to be enlarged as many times as those of the 35 mm size, thus minimizing the effects of grain, dust particles, and minute blemishes. On the other side, its smaller size gives the miniature camera the advantage over the 4x5 of compactness and lightness, inconspicuousness for candid work, lightning-fast maneuverability, greater independence from artificial lighting (lenses with higher speed available!), rapid-fire action backed up by a magazine containing material for 36 consecutive exposures, which with several camera models can even be shot mechanically by means of a "motor" (Leica, Robot, and Foton cameras). These features, however, must be paid for with a lower grade of sharpness and definition, loss of film speed if grainless pictures are desired, and painstakingly careful processing if clean photographs with good tone modulations are to result.

The decision between these opposed types of camera depends upon the temperament and interests of the photographer. If he is more interested in movement and action than in texture and definition, if he wants to travel light with a maximum of equipment taking a minimum of space, if he is impulsive and likes (or needs!) to shoot fast on the spur of the moment in order to get a certain picture at any cost, even if definition and composition may not be perfect, and if he is willing to pay the price for these advantages in the form of a somewhat lower print quality than the man with the 4x5 can get—no matter how much care he has taken in processing his negatives—then he may safely buy a minicamera and the chances are that he will not regret it. But if he wants to get the utmost in photographic quality, if he doesn't mind lugging heavy equipment and enjoys working patiently and painstakingly on lighting and composition if only he gets exactly what he wants, if he demands perfection in every respect—from himself as well as from his camera—and if he would rather miss a slightly imperfect picture than accept a lowering of his standards—then only the 4x5 or an even larger camera will ever satisfy him. In the long run, such a man can never be really happy with a minicamera, and if ever he should be persuaded to buy one, will sooner or later regret this step and eventually go back to his old reliable 4x5.

The majority of photographers, whose temperaments and interests generally are not as one-sided as the examples mentioned above, and who are willing to make slight sacrifices toward both ends in order to get a maximum of the combined advantages of both camera types, will doubtless find what they need among the intermediate sizes using No. 120 roll film or 2¼x3¼ and 3¼x4¼ sheet film and film pack, respectively.

The purpose to which the camera will be put (it determines the type of camera). Having decided on the negative size of the future camera, the next step would be to select one of the several basically different camera designs which offer constructionally different features, as for instance "swings" for correction of perspective distortion, or extreme extension for extreme closeups, or a reflex viewfinder for fast and accurate work, etc. Most of these features can be found in small cameras as well as in large ones.

Let's illustrate this with a few examples. One photographer may want to specialize in portraits. For this purpose he would need a camera that takes a lens with relatively long focal length in order to insure a natural and distortion-free perspective (see page 36). He may also want interchangeability of lenses so he can use special soft-focus portrait lenses whenever the occasion demands. Furthermore, he would need a type of viewfinder which permits constant observation of the subject so he wouldn't miss an interesting expression and wouldn't have to ask his model to "hold it" while he switches from groundglass to film holder. These demands would be met perfectly by the larger Graflex reflex cameras for 3¼x4¼ to 5x7 film, by the Hasselblad 2¼x2¼ as a representative of a medium-sized camera, and by the Nikon, Leica, Contax, and Kine-Exacta 35mm reflex in the miniature-camera class.

Another photographer may be interested predominantly in architectural subjects. Since he would be concerned primarily with perspective he would need a camera with plenty of "swings" to correct unwanted distortion, and since his objects are stationary he would prefer sharpness and definition of the photograph to speed and maneuverability of the camera. Many times, especially when working on interior shots, he would be badly crowded for space, and would have to use more or less extreme wide-angle lenses in order to get his picture, which makes interchangeability of lenses and provision for the use of wide-angle lenses essential. Cameras which fulfill these demands are: all sizes of view cameras from 4x5 up to 11x14, and certain sheet film and filmpack cameras 3¼x4¼ and 4x5 with "swings" and "drop-bed," as, for instance, the Deardorff-Triamapro and the Linhof-Technica cameras. In this case, there are no smaller models which would give one hundred per cent satisfactory results in all conceivable cases, even if perspective distortion can frequently be corrected afterward while enlarging.

I believe these two examples will suffice to give a rough idea of how, in other cases, requirements essential for producing good results should be analyzed along similar lines. Thus the 200-odd different cameras may be reduced to a few possibilities, among which a final selection can be made comparatively easy on the basis of negative size and price. For photographs of children or candid shots of people, lightness and maneuverability, short focal length for greater sharpness in depth, and large viewfinder would be the most desirable features, pointing straight to the group of twin-lens reflex cameras 2¼x2¼ inches. If, for the same purpose, greater versatility is needed, one of the better-class 35mm minicameras with interchangeable lenses would probably be the solution, despite the fact that the combination of rangefinder and optical viewfinder is a bit slower and more difficult to use than a focusing groundglass. And so on. As long as a photographer knows what he wants to do with his camera, uses his head when selecting it, and doesn't let himself get confused by questionable "advice" there is no earthly reason why he shouldn't get exactly the camera he needs—"the" camera that alone can make photography a *pleasure.*

The purse of the buyer (it determines the quality of the camera). Advice here is as easy to give as it is often hard to follow: always buy the best you can afford! In photography, as anywhere else, quality speaks and pays for itself, and consequently, an expensive camera can be expected to last longer and to give more satisfaction (and to need fewer repairs) than a less expensive one, thus actually being cheaper in the long run than a cheaper camera that has to be discarded or traded much sooner—usually with more or less heavy financial loss. However, don't make the common mistake of buying a more expensive camera merely because you think it is a better investment. Unless it actually fits your needs better than a cheaper model, it is merely another way of getting inferior pictures, and not a very original one at that.

A good way to get an expensive camera comparatively cheap is to acquire it secondhand. However, never buy it outright, but insist on a trial period during which you can test it and find out if it meets your specifications (every reputable dealer will agree to that). Examine the lens especially (see page 47). Check the camera for light-tightness by loading it with high-speed film (if sheet film or filmpack, insert the holder and remove the slide), rack the front all the way out and leave the camera for several minutes in the bright sun (with the shutter closed, naturally!), rotate it so that it gets light from all sides, then develop the film in absolute darkness. It should come perfectly clear out of the hypo. Black smudges or all-over fog indicate a light leak. Click the shutter repeatedly using all its speeds; even if it hesitates or sticks only once out of 50 times it needs an overhaul. Extend the tracks as far as they go, or pull out the lens and lock it. Wiggle them sideways as well as up and down (carefully!) and notice if there is any play. Only the very slightest "give" is permissible; actual movement would later cause unsharp pictures. Similarly, test the front of the camera and find out whether it is steady or not. Finally, take several test shots of clearly defined, contrastful objects from different distances, focusing as carefully as you can on the groundglass or with the help of the rangefinder. If the camera is equipped with both, make parallel exposures using once the groundglass only and the other time the rangefinder. Don't hold the camera in your hand when making these tests, *put it on a solid tripod* in order to eliminate the possibility of unsharpness because of movement during the exposure. Make blowups of the negatives and check them for sharpness. Have the rangefinder adjusted if necessary before you definitely buy the camera.

Conclusions: There is no "ideal" camera, equally well suited for every purpose and demand; often, however, two or three different models make an ideal team. . . .

The larger the negative size of a camera, the higher will be the photographic quality of the print, the greater its sharpness, the richer its tone, and the smaller the danger of graininess; and vice versa. On the other side, the bulkier and heavier the camera, the slower it will be to operate, and the narrower will be the zone of sharpness in depth with any given stop in the picture; and vice versa.

Large negative sizes are preferable for rendering of texture, for long-distance shots (telephotographs), for big enlargements (exhibition prints, murals), wherever speed doesn't matter and a tripod can be used, wherever highest technical quality is important.

Small cameras are preferable for fast work, for action shots, for picture sequences that have to be taken in rapid succession, for unobserved candid shots; they are better for closeups than for long shots which usually don't come out sharp enough.

Small cameras are easier to operate than large ones, but small negatives are more difficult to process and to print than larger ones.

The best camera for you is the one with which you are most familiar!

How a lens forms an image. Photograph of a sectionalized Kodak Ektar lens forming image of T-shaped luminous object at left and throwing it on groundglass at right. Notice that top and bottom of the object are reversed in the image. Light beams made visible with the help of smoke

THE LENS

There are almost as many different types and sizes of lenses as there are types and sizes of cameras, but here again, in spite of all their apparent differences, all lenses have certain fundamental properties in common, and they all follow the same basic optical laws. Studying characteristics and behavior of one lens will enable us to work successfully with all of them later when making photographs.

Modern lenses are complicated optical precision instruments. We have seen pictures made with the simplest type of lens—a double-convex magnifier lens—and they were rather crude and unsatisfactory (pages 19-20). The unsharpness and distortion we noticed in those photographs were the combined result of six different lens faults: chromatic aberration, spherical aberration, coma, astigmatism, curvature of field, and curvilinear distortion. Before a lens can produce a sharp and undistorted picture, these faults have to be "corrected," which is done principally by making two faults similar in character but opposite in value compensate for each other. The barrel-shaped distortion of the rectangular window casing in the picture on page 20, for instance, is the result of "curvilinear distortion." This fault is found in all simple positive lenses, and produces an outward-curving of straight lines if the diaphragm was in front of the lens, and an inward-curving of the same straight lines if the diaphragm was behind the lens; by constructing a composite lens consisting of two meniscus lenses and putting the diaphragm between the two this fault can be almost completely corrected.

Similarly, all the other faults can be eliminated more or less completely by using glasses with different refraction coefficients and curvatures of opposite character. But the higher the degree of correction becomes, the more different lens elements have to be used—especially in the case of "highspeed" lenses with large apertures. Merely to make the necessary calculations for a new lens of this type may take a specialist a full year, a fact which makes it easier to understand why quality lenses are so very expensive. Despite all the efforts of experts, however, even our best lenses are about as far from "ideal" as are our cameras, since with present means it appears to be impossible to correct completely every one of the six basic lens faults in one and the same lens. Consequently, even the finest of lenses are only compromises, in which traces of certain faults had to remain so that others could be corrected more completely. In order to get the utmost in sharpness, for instance, speed and a wide angle of view have to be sacrificed, with the result that our sharpest lenses (process apochromates) always are relatively slow and cover only a narrow angle of view.

On the other hand, to get a maximum of "speed" (lenses with apertures of *f* 1.9 to *f* 1.5) we have to accept a certain loss of definition and sharpness in depth, since the special construction of this type of lens makes a certain softness unavoidable and often bars the use of small diaphragm openings, thus making such lenses unsuitable for all-around work. And in most of the faster wide-angle lenses remains a trace of curvilinear distortion—the price that must be paid for an extreme angle of view in connection with speed and sharpness. And so on. To be familiar with facts like these is all-important when selecting a lens for any special purpose (or even an all-around lens, for that matter!) in order to get a maximum of useful qualities and to avoid disappointments. Many a photographer who bought a minicamera with an *f* 1.5 lens and thought he had the finest available outfit that money can buy found to his sorrow that actually he had acquired a lemon, as he couldn't get a single perfectly sharp picture—while on the other hand he hardly used the full speed of the lens more than once or twice a year. . . . For little more than half the price he paid for this camera he probably would have gotten exactly what he needed.

Regardless of other special qualities, all lenses have certain fundamental properties in common. The most important ones are: focal length; aperture ("speed"); covering power ("angle of view"); and definition ("sharpness"). Before a photographer goes out to buy a lens he ought to be familiar with the meaning of these terms, if he wants to get full value for his money.

Light is refracted by a prism. At left is the condenser that concentrates a beam of light into a pencil point.

Light is refracted by a lens which can be imagined to consist of innumerable minute prisms with different angles.

How a lens forms an image by refraction of light

A simple lens (double-convex lens) forms an image in space of an object consisting of three tiny sources of light (to the left of the lens). Rays of light made visible with smoke.

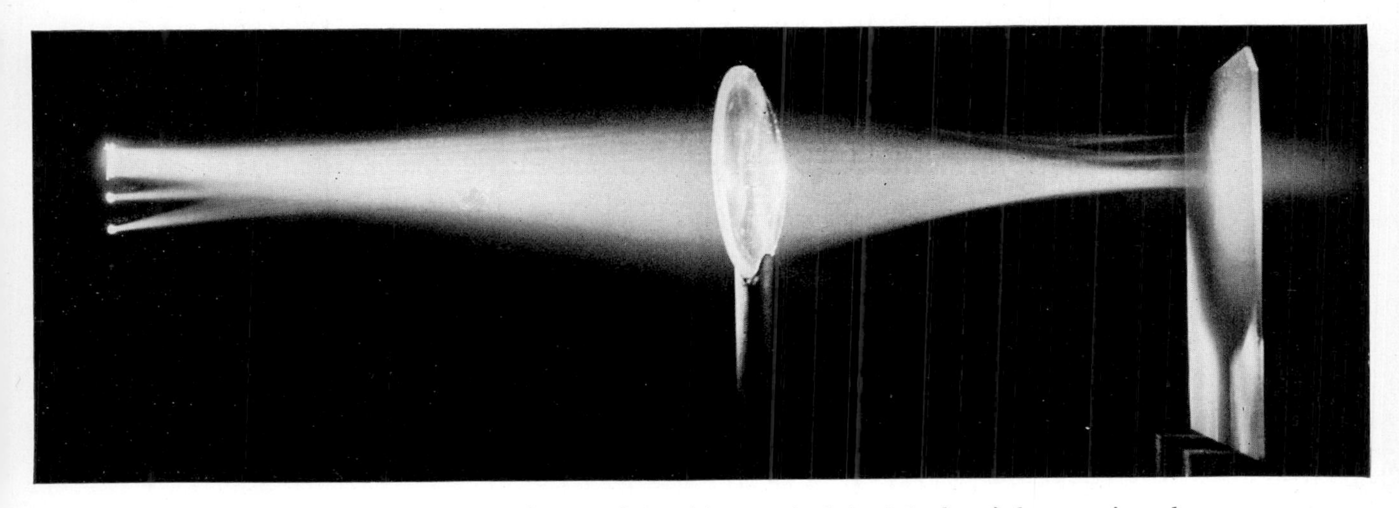

Instead of being lost in space, the image of the object to the left of the lens is here projected onto a piece of groundglass, just as in a camera. For taking a picture, this groundglass would have to be replaced with a piece of film.

Properties of lenses

The focal length

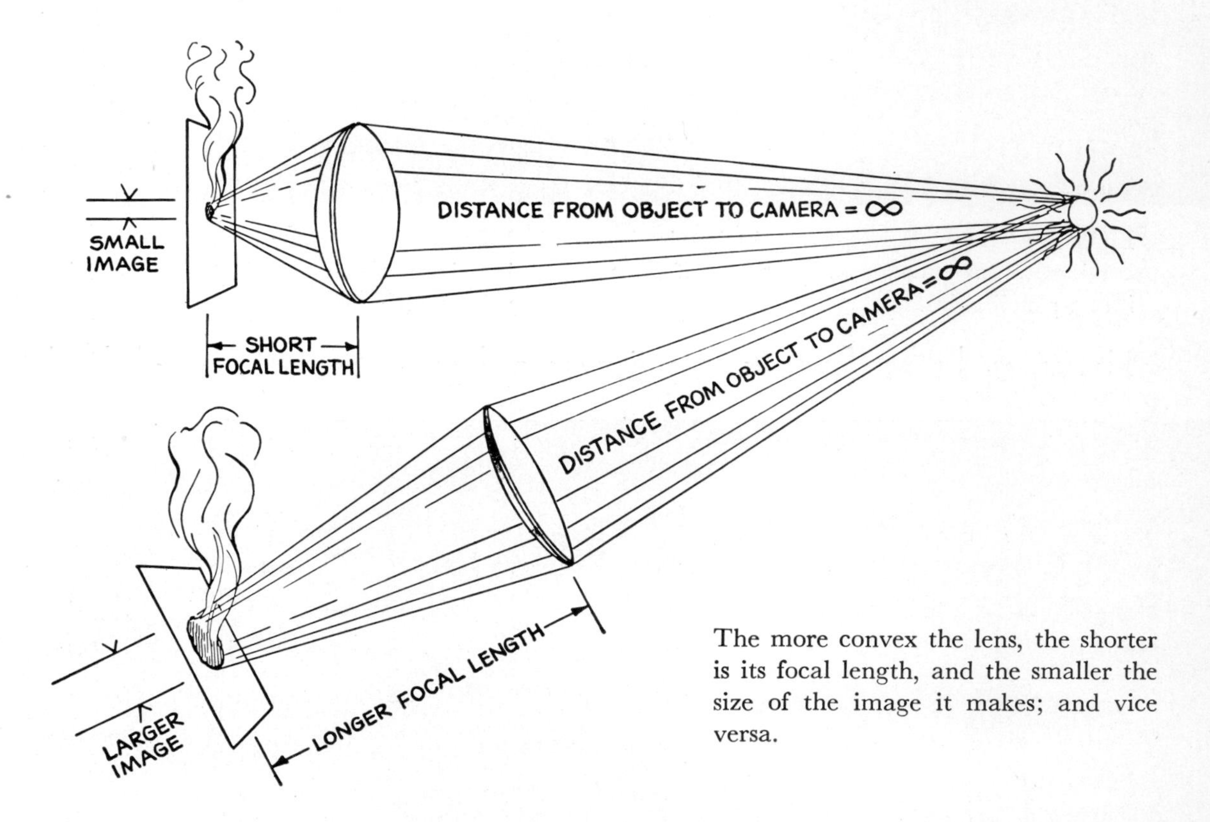

The more convex the lens, the shorter is its focal length, and the smaller the size of the image it makes; and vice versa.

You can get a pretty good idea of the focal length of a lens by holding it up to the sun and finding the distance from which it makes the sharpest, smallest, and hottest image of the sun on your hand or on a piece of paper.

The focal length of a lens is roughly the distance between the optical center of the lens and the film, measured when the lens is focused on "infinity" (the optical center of genuine telephoto lenses lies at a considerable distance in front of the lens; see page 45). It is the shortest possible distance between lens and film at which the lens will still make a sharp image of an object.

The focal length is measured in inches, centimeters, or millimeters and is usually engraved on the mount of the lens. Otherwise (in the case of some old-fashioned lenses) it can be determined very accurately in the following manner: mount the lens on a camera with groundglass and double or triple bellows extension (temporarily on a cardboard lens board, if necessary) and focus on a far-away object (a mile, or farther); mark the position of the pointer or the front edge of the lens board on the stationary camera bed; then rack the lens way out and focus on a ruler, etc., in such a way that the image of the object on the ground-glass has exactly the same size as in reality (i.e., you have to get an image in natural size); finally, measure the distance between the stationary mark on the camera bed and the new position of the pointer or the front edge of the lens board, respectively, and you have the exact focal length of your lens.

The focal length determines the scale of the rendering: the longer the focal length of a lens, the larger will be the image on the negative, and vice versa, regardless of size of film or camera. A lens with a focal length of ten inches renders the image of an object twice as big as a lens with a focal length of five inches; if used in the same camera on the same size of film, however, the effective angle of view of the lens with the five-inch focal length will be twice as wide as that of the ten-inch lens. Consequently, if a photographer wants to get a relatively large picture of a faraway object he can increase the image size by using a lens with a longer-than-average focal length ("telephoto lens"); on the other hand, if he wants to cover an unusually wide angle of view in order to show as large an area as possible in his picture, he has to use a lens with a shorter-than-average focal length ("wide-angle lens"). A "standard" lens should have a focal length approximately equal to the length of the diagonal of the negative size it has to cover. In that case, the angle of view is somewhere between 45 and 55 degrees, which experience has shown results in pictures with the most natural-appearing perspective.

The relative aperture

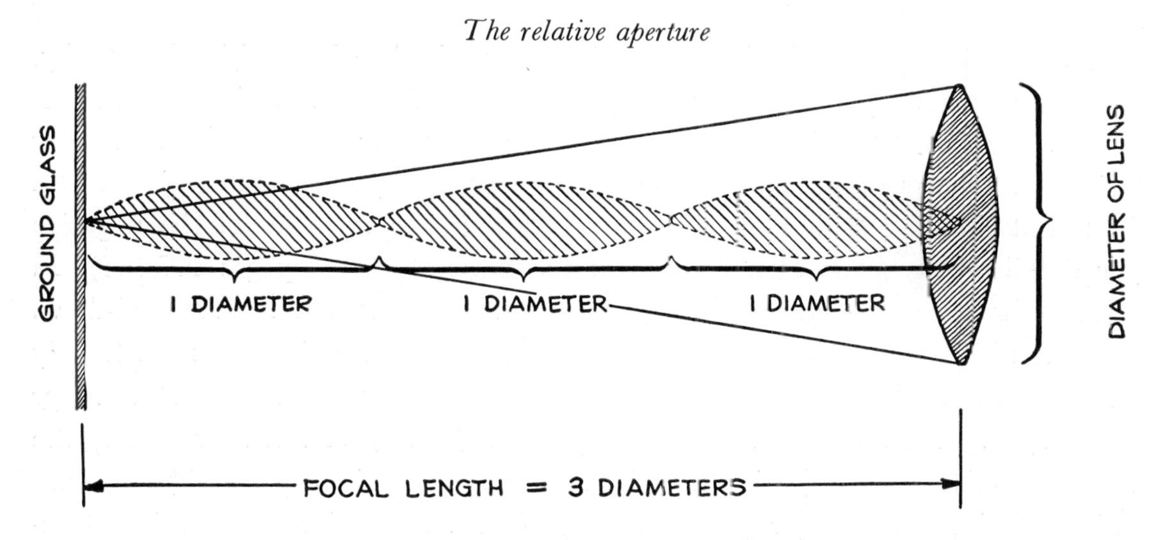

The measure of the "speed" of a lens—which plays an essential part in determining proper exposure time when taking the picture—is the ratio of the effective diameter of the lens opening to the focal length of the lens. It is called the "relative aperture" of the lens and is commonly expressed in terms of "*f* numbers." In the sketch on page 37, for instance, the ratio between diameter and focal length of the lens is 1:3, which would give this lens a relative aperture of *f* 3 (most European lenses would be engraved 1:3 instead of *f* 3).

The diameter of a lens alone is insufficient to indicate its speed (or its relative aperture, which means the same). In this respect, a lens can be compared to a window of a given size which may admit plenty of light to illuminate the opposite wall brightly if the room is shallow; but set into one end of a long corridor it would only dimly illuminate the opposite end of the much deeper room. Similarly, the larger the diameter of a lens in *relation* to its focal length, the brighter would be the illumination that reaches the opposite end of the room, which in this case would be the groundglass or the film at the other end of the camera, i.e., the higher would be the "speed" or "relative" aperture of such a lens. Expressed in terms of *f* numbers, a lens with a relative aperture of *f* 2 would be faster than a lens with a speed of only *f* 3.5, which again would be much faster than an *f* 11 lens. The speeds of lenses with different relative apertures are directly proportional to the squares of their *f* numbers. To find out, for instance, how much faster an *f* 3.5 lens is than an *f* 11 lens, square both *f* numbers, and you get the proportions of their speeds: $3.5^2:11^2 = 12.25 : 121$ or approximately 1 : 10. In other words, the *f* 3.5 lens is ten times as fast as the *f* 11 lens, and when it comes to exposing the negative, the man with the *f* 11 lens has to expose ten times as long as the man with the *f* 3.5 lens if both are shooting under identical conditions with their lenses "wide open."

The relative aperture indicates the highest speed a lens is capable of. Actually, most of the time a photographer doesn't need the full speed of his lens and prefers to "stop down the diaphragm" of the lens to a greater or lesser extent in order to improve sharpness in depth (see page 110) or simply because there is so much light that shooting "wide open" would result in overexposure of the negative (for detailed information on the use of the diaphragm see pages 107-115). In order to have control over the "effective speed" of a more or less stopped-down lens, the diaphragm is calibrated in *f* numbers, too, and their values are exactly the same as the "speeds" of lenses with corresponding relative apertures. For instance, an *f* 3.5 lens that has been stopped down to *f* 11 has now exactly the same "effective speed" (which now is called the "effective aperture") as a lens with a relative aperture (or greatest speed) of *f* 11. For easier computation of exposure times when switching from one *f* stop to another one, diaphragm stop numbers (as engraved on the mount of the lens) are calculated so that closing the lens one stop (from one *f* number to the next higher one) necessitates doubling the exposure time, and opening the lens one stop (from one *f* number to the next lower one) necessitates halving the exposure time, if the result is to remain the same.

Sometimes old-fashioned lenses are calibrated according to a system different from the *f*-number system. In order to use such lenses in connection with *f*-number calibrated exposure meters, they have to be recalibrated, which can be done as follows: mount the lens in a camera, focus on infinity; replace the groundglass with a piece of cardboard, prick a large pinhole into it exactly opposite the lens; take the camera into a darkroom, cut a piece of sensitized paper to fit into the lens cap (or fasten it tightly somehow against the front of the lens) and put the cap on the lens; finally, take a strong flashlight and throw its beam through the pinhole in the cardboard and the lens onto the sensitized paper (make sure that the diaphragm is wide open), wiggle the light to get a fully exposed circle; then develop the sensitized paper. The resulting black circle is the "effective diameter" of the lens and will usually be found to be slightly larger than the actual diameter. Next, determine the focal length of the lens as described on page 36, divide it by the effective diameter of the lens, and the result will be the relative aperture according to the *f*-number system. If, for instance, the effective diameter of the lens was 23½ mm, and its focal length 150 mm, dividing 150 by 23½ would give 6.8, which means that this lens would have a relative aperture of *f* 6.8. Similarly, intermediate diaphragm stops can be found. To find the indicator position for *f* 11, for instance, divide the focal length (here: 150 mm) by the *f* number (here: 11) and you get 150 : 11 = 13.6; stop your lens down until you find by trial and error the position in which the black circle on your sensitized paper has an exact diameter of 13.6 mm, and you will have found the indicator position for *f* 11; and so on.

Strictly speaking, the *f*-number values are correct only as long as the lens is focused on infinity. In order to bring nearer objects into focus we have to rack out the lens, i.e., we have to increase the distance between lens and film—the more so, the closer the object is to the camera. For instance, if with a lens that has a focal length of 150 mm and an effective diameter of 23½ mm, we photograph an object that is so close to the camera that in order to bring it into focus we have to increase the distance between lens and film to 200 mm, then actually the effective aperture of our lens would be no longer 150 : 23½—or *f* 6.8—but 200 : 23½, or *f* 8.5, and this in spite of the fact that we haven't touched the diaphragm and haven't stopped down the lens! Remembering our comparison between lens and window, such an increase in distance between lens and film could be compared with an increase in the depth of the room, which naturally would make the illumination of the wall opposite the window proportionally less intensive. Such a loss in light intensity (loss in effective speed of the lens) has of course to be compensated for by a proportional increase in exposure time, or underexposure would result. This problem will be discussed more exhaustively in the section on the diaphragm (page 116), where it belongs.

The covering power. If we mount a standard lens with a three-inch focal length on a 4x5 camera, focus it on infinity, and have a look at the groundglass, we find that only the center of our image is clear and sharp, that definition deteriorates rapidly into increasing fuzziness toward the edges of the picture, and that the corners are entirely black and seem to get no light from the lens at all. However, if we would make the same experiment with a three-inch wide-angle lens, the picture would look entirely different and we would get a sharp and well-illuminated image extending over the entire field of the groundglass. The reason for this difference: the covering powers of the two lenses are different, despite the fact that their focal lengths are the same, for these two lens properties have nothing to do with each other. The first lens was a "standard" lens, designed to cover only a circle

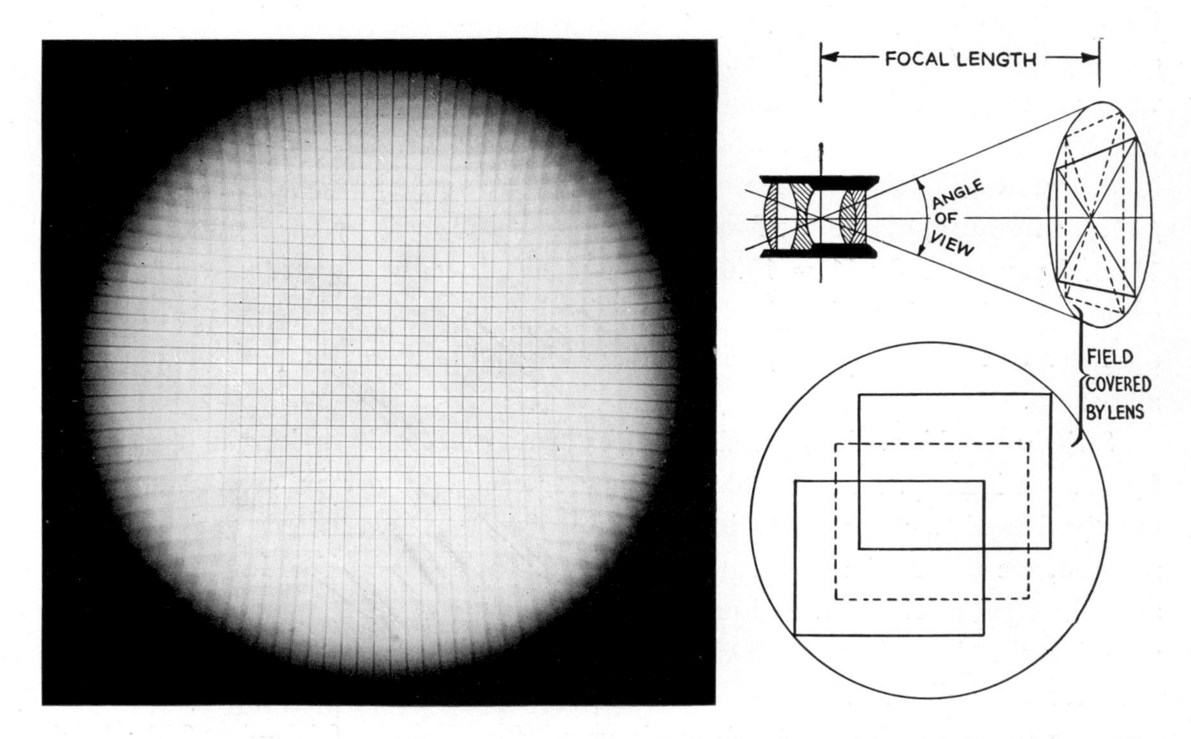

Left: Demonstration of the covering power of a lens. Definition is good enough for picture-taking purposes only within a limited, sharply defined circle. *Right, top:* Largest negative size to be covered sharply by any lens has to fit within this circle; its diameter should never be shorter than the diagonal of the rectangle corresponding to the negative size. *Right, bottom:* Only if the diameter of the circle sharply covered by a lens is larger than the diagonal of the negative size can the different swings of a camera really be used to fullest advantage. If covering power of the lens is too small, part of picture will fall outside the sharply covered circle when swings are used.

with a diameter approximately equal to its focal length, while the second lens was a "wide-angle" lens, especially designed to cover a proportionally much larger field than a standard lens. The fact that the first lens covered a smaller field than the second doesn't reveal anything about its quality; actually, it might have been a much faster, sharper, and more expensive lens than the wide-angle . . . but it could as well have been an inferior type of cheap and simple lens.

The minimum field a lens should cover sharply is a circle with a diameter as large as the diagonal of the negative size it will be used on (see illustrations on opposite page). As long as a negative fits within this circle, it can have any shape from very long and narrow to a full square (*top right*, on opposite page), and will still be covered sharply. The moment we use such a lens on a camera with swings, however, and raise (for instance) the front, the sharply covered zone will slide upward, too, and part of our image would be formed outside the sharply covered field of the lens with resulting blurredness along one of its sides. To avoid this it is essential that lenses used in cameras with any kind of swings have covering power enough to give sharp images even when in extreme position. Using as a "standard lens" on a 4x5 camera a lens designed as a wide-angle for 5x7 camera (which in this case would have a focal length corresponding to that of a standard lens designed for a 4x5 camera), is the best way to insure enough covering power to guarantee perfectly sharp pictures even when all the swings of the camera are in use simultaneously.

Stopping down increases the covering power of almost any lens, often to quite a considerable extent. Wide-angle lenses especially are commonly designed to be used with rather small stops only and have larger apertures merely to help in focusing and composing—a large stop makes the image on the groundglass brighter. Likewise, racking out the lens increases its covering power, and consequently, any lens that wouldn't nearly cover a given negative size if focused on infinity, will more than cover this same size if used for an extreme closeup shot. Actually, the best lenses for super-magnifying closeups with 4x5 cameras are 16 mm movie- and 35 mm miniature-camera lenses. A lens with a focal length of only one inch, for instance, that would just cover a 16 mm moving-picture frame when focused on infinity, will perfectly cover a 4x5 negative at a distance of ten inches from the film, giving an image of about eight and one-half times magnification.

Sharpness and definition. Stopping down increases sharpness and definition of any lens to a greater or lesser extent. The higher the correction of a lens, the less it has to be stopped down in order to reach its maximum of sharpness, which must not be confused with "sharpness in depth" (depth of field, see page 112), which increases proportionally the more a lens is stopped down. Average lenses give a maximum of sharpness if stopped down somewhere between *f* 8 and *f* 11. Stopping down below *f* 22 often decreases definition and sharpness again, a danger that is the greater the higher the initial speed of the lens is. This should be kept in mind especially when taking super closeups or telephotographs, where the need for extreme depth of field often tempts a photographer to use the smallest available stops.

Types of lenses

To combine all good and desirable qualities in one single type of lens is impossible for technical reasons. Consequently, a number of different more or less highly specialized types of lenses have been developed for use in cameras that provide interchangeability of lenses. The following are the most important:

Standard lenses offer the best possible compromise between wide-angle and telephoto, high speed and perfect definition, in order to give best results in the greatest number of cases. The ideal all-around lens has a focal length approximately equal to the length of the diagonal of the negative it has to cover, an angle of view of 45 to 55 degrees, a relative aperture of from *f* 3.5 to *f* 6.8, is sharpest when stopped down to somewhere between *f* 8 and *f* 11, and when used in cameras with swings has enough covering power to insure good definition even when most of these swings are in use (provided a small stop is used for taking the picture). Typical representatives are among others the B. & L. Tessar and the Kodak Ektar lenses.

Convertible lenses combine two or more different focal lengths within one lens unit. The complete lens has all the properties of an ordinary "standard" lens except its speed, but its front and rear elements can be used individually by themselves and have longer focal lengths (but less speed) than the combine. If front and rear elements are of equal focal lengths, the lens is called "symmetrical" and offers a choice between two different focal lengths; if front and rear elements have different focal lengths, the unit is called "unsymmetrical" and can have three or five different focal lengths, since in certain instances (for instance, the Meyer Satz Plasmat lens) the front element used behind the diaphragm has a different focal length from the front element used in front of the diaphragm, while similarly, the rear element, too, can be used in two different positions resulting in two different focal lengths.

The price for this advantage over the regular standard lens is lower speed (these lenses start with relative apertures of *f* 6.8 or smaller) and sometimes less critical definition. Typical representatives are the Zeiss Protar (extremely sharp, but rather slow) and the Meyer Satz Plasmat (somewhat faster, but softer rendering, preferred for portraits).

Comparison between images made (from left to right) by standard lens, wide-angle, and telephoto lenses. The wide-angle shows most, but everything is very small. The telephoto shows things very large and near, but has a limited field of view. The standard lens makes a photograph that is somewhere in between.

Different uses for telephoto lenses: Left—to magnify objects that are too far away to photograph well with standard lenses because their images would be too small on the film. *Right—to preserve proportions and avoid exaggerated perspective* by voluntarily increasing the distance between camera and object. Magnifying power of telelens still guarantees fair-sized images.

Different uses for wide-angle lenses: Left—to cover the widest possible angle where distance between object and camera is limited because of lack of space. *Right—to make the best use of limited bellows extension* for getting closeups in as large a scale as possible.

Telephoto lenses have longer than "standard" focal lengths compared to the size of film they have to cover. Consequently, they magnify like telescopes and produce images in proportionally larger scale than standard lenses. They will be used wherever objects are so far away from the camera that a standard lens would give an image too small to be useful. Typical for "genuine" telephoto lenses is the fact that actual extension between lens and film is always considerably shorter than the effective focal length of the lens: the 32 cm Zeiss Tele-Tessar, for instance, needs only about 20 cm extension when focused on infinity, while any "regular" 32 cm lens giving the identical telephoto effect would need all of a 32 cm extension. Constructively, any genuine telephoto lens consists of a positive front component and a negative rear component, and its "optical center" lies at a considerable distance in front of the lens, which accounts for the shorter-than-normal extension telephoto lenses need. As usual, however, this desirable compactness has to be paid for with a disadvantage: because of their peculiar, space-saving construction, telephoto lenses can never be as fast and are often not quite as sharp as regular lenses with correspondingly long focal lengths. Typical representatives of the true telephoto lens are the Zeiss Tele-Tessar and the Dallmeyer Dallon and Grandac lenses.

Wide-angle lenses are designed to cover a greater angle of view than "standard" lenses (from 65 to 140 degrees). They are used wherever space is too limited to get enough distance between camera and object to show all of it with a standard lens, or when an unusually wide angle of view has to be covered for some other reason. Compared to standard lenses, wide-angle lenses have shorter focal lengths with regard to the film size they have to cover, and consequently produce images in proportionally smaller scale (they show more, but everything is smaller). Their relative apertures are smaller (beginning with *f* 6.8; only a few minicamera wide-angle lenses are faster), and some of the faster types show traces of curvilinear distortion, the inevitable price that has to be paid for the advantageous combination of greater angle of view, sharpness, and fair speed. When selecting a wide-angle lens for a specific camera, make sure that bellows, etc., extensions can be kept short enough (in most reflex cameras, the mirror prevents use of wide-angle lenses because it needs too much space to swing upwards), or that the camera bed can be dropped out of the way so it will not cut off part of the picture. Typical representatives are the Schneider Angulon, and the Goerz W. A.-Dagor and Hypergon lenses.

High-speed lenses are constructed with only one goal in mind: to get the utmost in speed. Consequently, other features have to be sacrificed, and compared to standard lenses, high-speed lenses usually are less sharp, cannot be stopped down as far (with resulting limitation of depth of field) and are more likely to produce flares and halations (see page 176). Their relative apertures range from *f* 1.5 to *f* 2.8, which makes the fastest of them exactly nine times as fast as a standard *f* 4.5 lens ($1.5^2 : 4.5^2 = 2.25 : 20.25$ or $1 : 9$). However, the depth of field at *f* 1.5 is proportionally smaller, too, and focusing with the lens wide open has to be done extremely carefully if sharp pictures are to result. High-speed lenses are very highly specialized instruments and cannot be recommended for use as all-around lenses even if their focal lengths and angles of view are more or less identical with those of standard lenses. Typical representatives are the Kodak *f* 1.9 Ektar, the Zeiss *f* 1.5 Sonnar, the Schneider *f* 1.5 Xenon, the Leitz *f* 2 Summar, etc., for 35 mm miniature cameras, and the Zeiss Tessar *f* 2.7, etc., lenses for larger cameras.

Soft-focus lenses give images in which contrasts between sharp and unsharp are less abrupt than in pictures made with ordinary lenses, and transitions from the plane in focus to the plane out of focus are softer and less brutal. This is accomplished by a special construction which makes use of remnants of spherical aberration to "stretch" the extension of the depth of field with the result that nowhere in the whole picture is there any absolute sharpness; but out-of-focus areas, on the other hand, are never quite as fuzzy as in photographs made with ordinary lenses. A picture showing this effect is reproduced on page 328. Often, the degree of softness can be controlled by means of a special diaphragm. Sometimes the center element of the lens can be adjusted to different positions, producing any degree of rendering from sharp to very soft and diffused.

Soft-focus lenses are used mostly by "pictorialists" of the Misonne school, and for certain types of portraits; they are unsurpassed for the rendering of sun-glittering water, but otherwise, their usefulness is extremely limited. Typical representatives are the Leitz Thambar for the Leica, and the Hermagis and Perscheid lenses for large cameras; the two last-mentioned lenses have not been made for many years and are difficult to get.

Slip-on lenses (supplementary lenses) change the focal length of standard lenses, permitting limited wide-angle and tele-effects with cameras with permanently attached lenses. They are simple lenses that slip over the lens mount like filters, shortening the focal length of the permanent lens if they are positive, and lengthening it if they are negative, in which case they demand quite a considerable bellows extension and groundglass focusing. When using supplementary lenses, small diaphragm stops have to be used for getting best definition, but even so, sharpness is never quite as good as in pictures taken with real wide-angle or telephoto lenses. Typical representatives are the Kodak Portra and Telek, and the Zeiss Proxar and Distar slip-on lenses.

Buying and testing lenses

When buying a new lens of a well-known make from a reputable dealer, you can be pretty sure of getting full value for your money, and all you have to watch out for is to see that you get the right type of lens with regard to focal length, relative aperture, and covering power. The quality of the lens as such ought to be beyond doubt. Remember, however, the following: speed alone is not a sign of high quality or general usefulness; relatively slow lenses are usually considerably sharper than high-speed lenses; they are lighter and definitely much cheaper. Slower lenses don't produce flares as easily as the more complicated high-speed lenses with their greater number of elements, and they can be stopped down farther, thus covering a greater zone of sharpness in depth. Generally, the more a lens is curved, and the more free air surfaces it contains, the more likely it is to produce flares; on the other hand, the less curved a lens is and the more cemented elements it contains, the less likely it is to break out in flares. Flares can be minimized or eliminated completely by coating lenses.

Many of the less common lenses—especially German lenses—are almost impossible to get new and have to be acquired secondhand. This is perfectly safe as long as you stick to reputable dealers. But I advise you to steer clear of pawn shops! I have invariably found their prices outrageous.

When buying a secondhand lens—especially an older type—examine it carefully for the following possible defects: *scratches and chips* (a slightly chipped edge, or a small scratch that is not exactly in the center of the lens, usually has no influence whatsoever on the sharpness of the picture, but abrasion-like hair scratches are bad; how bad, only a test picture can reveal). *Dented mounts* mean that the lens has been dropped and that its elements may be *off center or loose*. Hold the lens close to your ear and shake it. Loose elements will rattle, but don't be deceived by a rattling shutter or diaphragm. Off-center elements have to be centered by the manufacturer before the lens can be expected to give sharp pictures. Hold the lens against the light and look through it. Air bubbles in the glass are unavoidable in many of the special glasses used for making fine lenses and are a sign of quality rather than a defect; they have no detrimental effect on the quality of the picture. Brownish or blueish discoloration is often found in older lenses, and doesn't seem to do any harm; some experts claim that it actually improves speed by reducing surface reflection the same way as "coating" does. A pattern resembling water squeezed between two glass plates indicates that the *cementing between the elements* is defective and has to be mended by the manufacturer before satisfactory pictures can be expected.

COLOR FILTERS

Color filters are pieces of colored transparent material interposed between the scene or object we want to photograph and the film. Their purpose is to regulate the amount of light of certain colors (wavelengths) that is permitted to reach the film with the ultimate goal of controlling and improving the transformation of colors into shades of gray.

For further information on the use of color filters see page 223.

The colors of color filters

Color filters are available in over a hundred different shades and densities, but for ordinary photographic purposes less than half a dozen are sufficient. Filters usually are designated by a letter or a combination of number and letter; see the following table of Wratten filters:

Color of Filter	Light Shade	Medium Shade	Dark Shade
Yellow	K1	K2*	G*
Red	E	A*	F
Green	X1	X2	B
Blue	80		C5

*Asterisks mark the three most important filters.

Filters do not restrict transmission of light of their own color, but retard or even prevent the passage of light of other colors—the more so, the more complementary ("opposite") to their own color the color of such light is. Yellow filters, for instance, transmit yellow light, but retard blue light—the more so, the darker yellow they are. This, for example, is the reason why yellow filters improve the rendering of white clouds in a blue sky: by partially absorbing the blue they make the sky appear darker in the picture and thus increase the contrast between clouds and sky. For specific purposes, select the proper filters according to the tables on pages 226 and 227.

The filter factor

Since filters absorb part of the light that otherwise would reach the film through the lens, underexposed negatives would result if we didn't make allowances for this loss of light by increasing the exposure time accordingly. The number of times by which the exposure has to be multiplied if a given filter is used depends on color and density of the filter, the type of negative material, and the kind of illumination. This number is called the "filter factor" of that particular filter and will be found in the table on page 232.

Types of color filters

Color filters are made either from colored glass, or from colored gelatine. Since gelatine is much easier to dye in colors that have to conform to rigid spectroscopic specifications, the number of different available gelatine filters is many times as great as the number of different glass filters. From the viewpoint of optical and mechanical quality, the best available filters are made of the same heavy optical glass as fine lenses, ground and polished to the same extremely low tolerances as optical precision instruments, and are consequently very expensive.

For normal photographic purposes, however, gelatine filters are perfectly adequate. Usually, they come cemented between two pieces of flat, colorless glass. Only for unusually critical work with regard to sharpness of the picture, or when working with lenses of very long focal lengths, is it necessary to use gelatine filters unmounted as films, either in special holders in front of the lens, or inserted directly between the elements of the lens. In this way, possible defects of the glass mounts cannot exert harmful influences on the definition of the picture. That such can actually be the case is proven by the fact that occasionally cemented gelatine filters which gave perfectly satisfactory results when used on lenses with relatively short focal lengths, suddenly produced unsharp pictures the moment they were used in connection with long-focus lenses, which because of their magnifying power enlarged the normally invisible defects of the filter to a degree where they became visible and manifested themselves in unsharpness.

Cheap filters made of ordinary colored glass cannot be recommended. Their optical qualities usually are so low that they prevent production of negatives with satisfactory definition.

Care of color filters

Even the best color filter will produce unsharpness in a negative if it isn't painstakingly clean, free from dust and fingerprints. Unmounted gelatine filters are so sensitive that touching them with the hands is enough to leave indelible traces. Hold them only by the edges, the same as you would hold a precious negative. When cleaning glass or cemented gelatine filters, be careful not to scratch them. Breathe on them and polish them lightly with lens tissue. Don't use cleaning fluid or water on cemented filters; if it gets between the glasses it will destroy the cementing, swell the gelatine, and spoil the filter. Keep filters away from moisture, heat, and unnecessary light, since some dyes are apt to fade if exposed too long to bright light.

EXPOSURE METERS

The basis of every good photograph is a well-exposed negative. Too short an exposure leads to excessive contrasts and to loss of detail, especially in shadows, while too long an exposure results in graininess, loss of all-over contrast, and lack of detail in the highlights of the picture. To insure correct exposures even under the most difficult light conditions—at dusk, at night, and indoors—several types of exposure meters have been designed, which, if properly used, provide reliable protection against incorrectly exposed negatives.

To guess exposure times is amateurish, and photographers who boast of being able to get correctly exposed negatives without ever using an exposure meter are either working under always identical conditions (for instance, in a studic), or lying. The human eye is a very poor instrument for estimating brightness values, and is easily deceived by small changes in light intensity. It accommodates itself so automatically to such changes that the individual is not aware of them. The majority of professional photographers use exposure meters because they cannot afford to muff an exposure, and personally I would rather spend my money on a less expensive camera and a first-rate exposure meter, than on a more expensive camera and no meter at all.

Exposure tables, guides, or charts don't actually measure light intensities. However, they interpret light conditions in terms of everyday experience and, because of their simplicity, often prove more useful to the beginner than exposure meters. They cost no more than ten cents or a quarter.

Extinction-type exposure meters can be used to measure any kind of illumination, but their accuracy depends to a rather high degree on the skill and experience of the user. While the meter is aimed at the object to be photographed, the photographer looks through an eyepiece and by rotating a gray wedge determines the exact moment at which the scene as seen through the aperture becomes extinct. The calculator will then indicate the correct data for diaphragm stop and shutter speed. Extinction-type exposure meters are about the size of a pocket watch and relatively inexpensive.

Photoelectric exposure meters are completely automatic and when properly used are the most accurate and reliable of all types of light meters. When the meter is pointed toward the object to be photographed, light reflected from the object strikes a photoelectric cell where it generates an electric current in proportion to its own intensity. This current acts upon a measuring unit that indicates light values, which in turn have to be transferred to a calculator where they are evaluated automatically and translated into diaphragm stops and shutter speeds.

Photoelectric exposure meters are precision instruments which, if properly guarded against shock and excessive heat, will last a lifetime. In order to get the utmost in value out of them, careful study of the always accompanying instruction booklet is urgently recommended. Prices range around $25.

TRIPODS

One of the main prerequisites for sharp negatives is perfect steadiness of the camera during the exposure. The longest exposure times that still can be hand-held without too great a danger of shaking the camera and blurring the negative are between 1/50 and 1/25 second. At slower speeds, cameras should be hand-held only if circumstances require it, as there is bound to be some sacrifice in sharpness.

The best, simplest, and safest support for any camera is a sturdy tripod. Actually, possession of a tripod more than doubles the scope of a photographer's work, and opens to him some of the most exciting fields in photography: time exposures at dusk and at night; interior shots under poor light conditions; telephotographs with long-focus lenses; closeups where fractions of an inch more or less between camera and object make all the difference between a sharp and an unsharp negative—these are only a few of the more important instances where a tripod is absolutely indispensable for successful picture-taking.

The most important quality of any tripod is rigidness. When buying a tripod, pull out the legs to their greatest extent, put your hand flat on the tripod head, press downward hard and try to twist the tripod sideways. The better it is, the less it will give. You will be surprised to find how few really sturdy tripods there are on the market. . . . Next to rigidness, the weight of the tripod is important to the photographer who has to carry it on assignments. Pay further attention to the height to which the tripod can be extended. Especially in industrial photography, great height is invaluable in making difficult over-all and downward-angle shots. The pan and tilt-head of the tripod should permit full 90-degree tilt downward for easy copy work. If the head can be locked into position with one twist of the handle instead of two adjustments, it will be a further advantage. Rubber-tipped legs are generally more useful than spike-tipped ones, which slide more easily, scratch floors indoors and are quickly dulled outdoors.

A tripod with an adjustable centerpost is particularly useful for close-up work in which fine adjustments in height are constantly necessary; they can be made by a simple turn of a crank, instead of the cumbersome readjustment of the three legs. Such "elevator tripods" are available in different models for lighter or heavier cameras and are well worth their higher price.

LIGHTING EQUIPMENT

Knowledge of the different types of lights and their effects is the first essential for arranging effective illumination. Many photographers have rather hazy conceptions of "spots" and "floods," of "Kleig" lights (which are open arc lights) and "Fresnel" lenses (which are spotlight lenses with concentric rings for more even distribution of the light), etc., and are easy prey for smooth and voluble salesmen when it comes to purchasing lighting equipment. . . Too late, they will realize how unbalanced a set of lights they have acquired.

The following survey should help to clarify this confusion:

Spotlights give the most "sunlike" illumination, a hard and contrastful light with sharply defined deep-black shadows. They concentrate the light by means of an optical system consisting of a parabolic mirror and a condenser lens, and can usually be "focused," which means that the spread of the light beam and diameter of the field of illumination can be adjusted wider or narrower as the case may warrant. Spotlights come in all sizes, from tiny 150-watt "baby spots" which are ideal for the traveling photo-reporter to illuminate closeups, to giant 5,000-watt "sun spots" big enough to illuminate the largest setting in a studio. Spotlights, or "spots" as they are often called for short, are used either as the main source of illumination because of their sunlike effect, or as auxiliary "accent lights" to put accentuating highlights into a picture.

Floodlights give much softer illumination than spots, with less sharply defined, more diffused and detailed shadows. They come in different sizes from 250 to 1,500 watts, and the larger the diameter of their reflector, the softer their light will be. If used with a "diffuser" in front of the reflector (consisting of oilcloth or glass-fiber cloth in a frame), they give practically shadowless light and are ideal for lightening shadows cast by the spotlight main light that otherwise would appear too black and too detail-less. "Floods," as they are often called, cannot be focused, and the intensity of their light has to be varied by changing their distance from the object.

Flashbulbs give a light softer than spots but harder than floods, and have the invaluable advantage that they can be used to take instantaneous exposures as fast as the shortest shutter speed of the camera permits, regardless of "local" light conditions (by means of a "synchronizer," see page 58). This advantage, however, is partially offset by the disadvantage that they flash and are gone, i.e., flashbulbs can be used only once, their light lasts only a fraction of a second and cannot be used for focusing or composing. If several flashbulbs are used simultaneously, an exact prediction of the all-over light effect and the position of the different set of shadows cast by each one of the flashbulbs is almost impossible. . . . To offset this serious disadvantage, many photographers balance their lighting, compose, and focus by floodlights, and after everything is set, replace the floodlight bulbs with flashbulbs without changing the positions of the lights, start the action and flash the picture at a fast shutter speed. However, in my opinion, the complexity of this operation makes it advisable to limit the use of flashbulbs to those occasions where, for technical and journalistic reasons, other means of illumination cannot be used (as, for instance, lack of electric current, moving objects that have to be photographed at a high shutter speed, etc.). Flashbulbs come in different sizes with different light intensities from low to high, which can be used simultaneously. Combinations of flash with floods or spots, however, are only occasionally possible, when the special effect of a combined time and instantaneous exposure is desirable.

For further information on flash equipment and bulbs, see pages 57 to 63 and 332-337.

Balanced lighting equipment is absolutely essential for the creation of balanced light effects. A spotlight, that is too weak or too powerful with regard to the floodlights used in connection with it, is practically valueless, even if it was ten times as expensive as all the floodlights together.

Purpose and necessity, and nothing else, should determine the type and number of lights a photographer buys. But unfortunately it is often price, or appearance, or prestige, or a glib salesman which influences the selection. . . . Naturally, the needs of a studio operator are different from those of a traveling magazine photographer, and a man who specializes, for instance in architectural photography with predominantly motionless settings will need a different type of lighting equipment from a man doing nothing but industrial photography involving almost constant movement. Such differences in purpose obviously make it impossible to establish more than a few general rules for the selection of lighting equipment. The most important ones (in the opinion of the author):

1. Buy the best you can afford. A few first-class lights are better than twice as many "second bests." The most expensive lights usually are the cheapest ones in the long run.
2. If you have to travel with your lights, watch their weight and bulk. Buy reflectors that can be stacked tightly. Then half a dozen reflectors will take hardly more space than a single one. Use lightstands made from aluminum instead of steel tubing.
3. If you need a spotlight, select one that takes a bulb of about the same wattage as the average flood it is to be used with. A baby spot, which is one of the most useful lights for closeups, should have no less than 200 watts.

The minimum equipment for a studio is four lights: a 1,000-watt spot for main light, a 500-watt overhead spot ("boom light") for accent light, and two 1,000-watt floods for fill-ins. A man who knows his business can do an amazing number of things with these few lights. From there on, the sky is the limit. . . . However, the next two lights could advantageously be a 500-watt spot, and another 1,000-watt flood.

An architectural photographer needs mostly floodlights. Six clamp reflectors, four of them taking No. 2 Photoflood bulbs of 500 watts and two smaller and narrower ones for No. 1 Photofloods of 250 watts will do nicely to begin with. Altogether they would draw 2,500 watts, which is about as much as ordinary home wiring can carry, provided this load is distributed over at least two, better three, different circuits with different fuses, and no other electric appliances are in use at the same time (electric refrigerator, flat iron, vacuum cleaner, heater, toaster, etc.). Before taking interior photographs in offices, public buildings, or plants, the house electrician should be consulted in order to avoid embarrassing blowouts of fuses.

Some industrial photographers can take the most wonderful pictures with only three floodlights of 500 watts each. For they know how to make use of the "local" illumination, take short time exposures of "posed action" (see page 371), and use their lights merely for accentuation and background separation. . . . Others use one 5,000-watt spot plus some smaller spots plus several 1,000-watt floodlight fill-ins—and still cannot guarantee first-class pictures. Here, more than almost anywhere, it is ingenuity and resourcefulness that count—imagination and an eye for the photogenic, and not the number of lights, or the amount of wattage burned. . . . For unposed action shots, flash equipment is essential. A main light on an extension and one smaller fill-in at the camera are the minimum. For large over-all shots of busy industrial interiors up to 20 and more flashbulbs on separate extensions, all synchronized to the camera, will occasionally be necessary.

For indoor fashion photographs an equal number of spots and floods—with a minimum of two of each—is usually required.

For sculpture photography one spot and two floods is the minimum. Their size depends on the size of the objects to be photographed. For small pieces of sculpture up to about 15 inches high, a baby spot makes an ideal main light.

A magazine photographer's lighting equipment theoretically should combine all the possibilities and good features of the more specialized photographer's various lights, with a minimum of weight and bulk. A good magazine photographer has to be a photographic Jack-of-all-trades, able to take a portrait closeup today, to shoot a complete story on steelmaking tomorrow, to cover a sculpture exhibition next; he should have the ability and the equipment to photograph fashions and girls as easily as the inside of an electron tube in action, and closeups of biting mosquitoes as well as the rotunda of the United States Capitol. . . . And finally, he should be able to lug all of his equipment himself whenever necessary, carrying it with his own two hands without the help of a truck or a procession of porters and assistants. . . .

I know this sounds impossible. But I know that it can be done, for this is just one of the "impossible" feats one performs as part of the routine of working for a national picture magazine. And now I am going to divulge my "secret," learned in nine years' experience with *Life*. Actually, it is hardly a "secret," but rather a "system" for lighting: wherever it is possible, and sometimes even where it seems impossible, I make use of the "local" illumination—daylight coming in through windows and skylights, worklights, desklamps, ceiling lights, etc.—to provide the "main light" of my lighting scheme, and use my own portable lights only for accentuation, background separation, and shadow fill-ins. This is the whole "secret" of the "natural" appearance of the lighting in my pictures, which people sometimes think could have been done only with batteries of big and expensive lights. I don't know whether to be ashamed or proud of the fact, but never in any of my stories have I used more than eight lights simultaneously, either 500-watt floodlamps or flashbulbs, in clamp reflectors costing less than three dollars apiece.

I arrived at this system the hard way. When first I started to work for *Life*, I was duly impressed by the multitude of lights and the amount of equipment most of the other photographers carried with them on assignments. I believed that this was the only way to get results, and started to acquire more and more lights. Soon transportation became a problem, and I had to hire porters wherever I went. I became dependent on the help of others, and I loathed it. And in spite of all the lights I carried, I always found I could have used twice as many, and still would have been short somewhere. . . . The pay-off came when I did a story in an airplane factory on the production of heavy bombers. There I met another photographer, one of the commercial big shots, whose lighting equipment consisted of a number of 5,000-watt spots and a score of 1,000-watt floods, who had to travel with his own power generator in a special truck, who disrupted production for hours (the one unforgivable sin for an industrial photographer, especially in wartime), and who still complained to me that he didn't have enough lights to get a "natural" effect in his over-all shots! Then and there, the bottom dropped out of my conception of the value of portable lights. That settled it: the whole system must be wrong if not even an incredible expenditure of lights such as that could lead to natural-looking pictures. I started thinking, and eventually found a remedy of my own: natural light, or local artificial illumination, may sometimes need a little help—an accent may be necessary here, a shadow may be a little bit too black there and need to be filled in with a small amount of light—but basically, such illumination cannot be improved by any number of auxiliary lights! Actually, the opposite is true. The less extra light we use, the fewer portable lights used to balance the illumination (which is all we ever ought to do!), the better and the more "natural" will be the lighting in our pictures.

For several years now, I have not taken more than eight 500-watt floods in clamp reflectors out on an assignment—and often only from four to six—and thanks to my "system" have never found myself short of lights. Besides these floods, I use two baby spots for closeups. I use flashbulbs in the same reflectors used for floods wherever flashbulbs are unavoidable (instead of having special flash reflectors with quick-change sockets which are heavy and bulky). My synchronizer has a four-cell battery case for positive synchronization, but if extensions are long or more than three bulbs have to be fired simultaneously, I flash them with house current of 110 volts and an Abbey multi-flash. Instead of a few long cables and heavy spider boxes for distribution, I use a larger number of short lengths of wire with female T-plugs at one end, so I can plug in branch wires without wasting cable. I carry only two lightstands to save weight and use clamp reflectors that are easily attached to any protruding corner, piece of furniture, or machinery, etc. My whole lighting equipment fits into one large suitcase and weighs less than forty pounds. I am a happy man again, and I don't care if some people think I *am* nuts . .

Hints on the use of electric power

For the installation of any kind of big-scale lighting system, the assistance of a professional electrician is absolutely indispensable; ordinary house wiring is much too weak to carry the heavy electric loads that a battery of studio lights would draw, and a special cable will have to be installed that is connected directly with a main power cable in the street.

If you want to know how many lights you safely can use simultaneously on one and the same circuit, either in your home or somewhere on location, find out the voltage (V) of the power line you want to connect your lights with, and the amperage (A) the fuse of this particular line permits you to draw. Multiplying the voltage by the permissible amperage will give you the maximum number of watts (W) that you can use for lighting purposes, provided no other electricity-consuming appliances are connected to the same line at the time. For example, if your line carries current of 110 volts, your fuse permits a maximum load of 15 amperes, and you want to use floodlamps of 250 and 500 watts, you make the following calculation:

$$V \times A = W, \text{ or } 110 \text{ volts} \times 15 \text{ amperes} = 1{,}650 \text{ watts}$$

This means that the combined wattage you can safely use is 1,650 watts or less. Divided among your floodlamps it means that you may use simultaneously either three 500-watt bulbs, or two 500-watt and two 250-watt bulbs, or one 500-watt and four 250-watt bulbs, or six 250-watt bulbs. In any case, the combined wattage of these lights will amount to 1,500 watts, which leaves you 150 watts available for other purposes, as, for instance, ordinary room illumination with a 150-watt bulb.

On the other hand, if you want to use, for instance, 3,000 watts, you can find out the amperage (*A*) your power line and fuse have to stand safely with the help of the following formula:

$$\frac{W}{V} = A; \text{ for 110 volt current this would be: } \frac{3000}{110} = 27.2 \text{ amperes}$$

The fuse is the safety valve of a power line. It is an "artificial weak link" which will break if the line is overloaded for some reason (too many lights, or a short circuit) and thus will save the line itself from destruction. If you blow a fuse, never replace it with a stronger one in order to avoid future blowouts; because if you do, the next time it will be the power line that melts, and the resulting short circuit may easily start a serious fire. To repair a blown fuse by placing a penny in the socket is criminal and punishable by law. If you want to avoid the nuisance of blowing fuses in your studio, have them replaced with automatic switches, which will open an overloaded circuit like a fuse; having removed the cause of the overload, you just flip the switch, and the current will flow again.

Flash equipment

In order to make fullest use of the potentialities of flashbulbs or speedlamps the firing of the bulb and the exposure by means of the shutter have to happen simultaneously; the instrument that correlates these two actions is the flash synchronizer.

Flash synchronizers operate on battery current and use two, three, or four ordinary flashlight batteries. They fire the flashbulb, automatically compensate for the time lag between maximum light output of the flashbulb (usually reached in 20/1,000 second) and maximum shutter opening (usually reached in 5/1,000 second), and in many cases release the shutter itself—all this upon the push of a single button.

The last word in battery-operated flash guns is the "BC-synchronizer"—the "battery capacitor gun." It is powered by tiny 22½ volt hearing-aid batteries, and stores electricity in a small condenser (capacitor). When in use, only the exact amount of energy needed for firing the flash and tripping the shutter is released, while in conventional synchronizers the batteries are drained as long as the release button is pressed. According to their manufacturers, batteries in BC-synchronizers last for more than a year under average working conditions.

Speedlights ("strobes") are a kind of electronic super-flash, see p. 63.

Shutters with built-in synchronization are always in synchronization and require no battery current to trip the shutter. They are the latest and potentially most useful development in flash synchronization.

Mechanical synchronizers use battery current only for firing the flashbulb; this puts only a comparatively small load on the batteries which consequently last much longer than in electrical synchronizers. Mechanical synchronizers are operated by pressing a release which simultaneously trips the shutter and closes the switch that admits current to the flashbulb, while a mechanism within the synchronizer automatically compensates for more or less rapid operation of the release. It thus has no influence on the accuracy of the synchronization. Some of our finest synchronizers operate on the mechanical principle.

Electrical synchronizers both fire the flashbulb and trip the shutter with battery current. A "tripper" working on the electromagnet principle is attached to the lens board or the front of the camera and trips the shutter the moment the release button of the synchronizer is pressed, which simultaneously closes the circuit to the flashbulb and fires it. Since the electromagnetic tripper uses a considerable amount of current, batteries have to be checked quite frequently; ten amperes is the absolute minimum for positive and accurate synchronization.

Focal-plane shutters demand special synchronizers as well as special flashbulbs. Such synchronizers can either be attached to, or permanently built into, the camera; in the latter case, a cord from the battery case is simply plugged into a socket built right into the camera, making this a very neat-looking job; available for Leica, Contax, Speed Graphic, etc.

Multi-flash equipment should be used whenever more than three bulbs have to be fired simultaneously with an electrical synchronizer, since positive synchronization is otherwise impossible in such cases because of the limited amperage of the batteries. With the help of a multi-flash device, flashbulbs are fired with 110-volt house current and the batteries are merely used to trip the shutter. Hence, practically any number of flashbulbs (up to 20 or more) can be synchronized accurately to the shutter, even if very long extensions have to be used.

Exposure times in connection with synchro-flash vary between 1/50 and 1/1,000 second (provided, of course, that the camera shutter permits speeds as fast as that). The shorter the exposure, however, the less light will reach the emulsion, the

TROUBLE-SHOOTER CHART FOR FLASH PHOTOGRAPHERS

WHAT'S THE TROUBLE?	SYNCHRONIZER	BATTERIES	WIRES	CONNECTIONS	SHUTTER	LAMPS
Nothing happens when you press the switch	Switch or release button doesn't make contact	Batteries may be dead or inserted wrong side up, or case isn't closed tightly	Wire is broken somewhere, or not connected	Worn-out plug doesn't make connection		Faulty bulb (try different bulb)
Flash fires, but shutter doesn't work		Weak batteries (Very common)	Faulty tripper cord	Tripper wire not connected, or worn-out tripper plug	Maybe you forgot to cock the shutter	
Shutter works only after flash has fired	Synchronizer out of synchronization	Weak batteries (Very common)		Check tripper connections		
First few shots all right, then shutter clicks after flash or not at all		Load gets too heavy for batteries; use more cells, or fresher batteries, or booster				
Shutter clicks all right, but flash doesn't fire	Flash not pushed deep enough into socket		Broken wire	Bad connection		Faulty bulb (try different bulb)
Flash fires too late, after shutter has clicked	Corroded socket contacts			Corroded connections		Solder on base corroded; rub base on emery cloth
Adding extensions causes shutter, which so far worked all right, to click after flash		Weak batteries; use fresher or more cells, booster, or flash with house current		Corroded connections		
Adding extension causes both shutter and flash at camera, previously O.K. to go before extension flash		Weak batteries; use fresher or more cells, booster, or flash with house current	Try using heavier gauge wire	Corroded connections		
Extension flash doesn't fire		Weak batteries	Wire is broken	Extension not connected, or switch is off		Faulty bulb
Correctly exposed and developed negatives too thin in spite of apparently perfect working of flash	Synchronizer out of synchronization					Slow burning bulbs that go off like fireworks are "leakers" due to cracks or untight bulb-socket connection. They give off very little light only, cause underexposures
Correctly exposed and developed negatives are blank in spite of apparently perfect working of flash and shutter					Forgot to cock shutter, to remove slide, to open *the other* shutter, to remove lens cap	
Flashbulb goes off the moment you insert it into the socket	Short circuit		Wire plugged into remote-control outlet, or short circuit	Short circuit		

larger the diaphragm stop that will have to be used, and the closer to the object should be the flashbulb—but the faster the movement and action that can be "stopped" in the picture. For determination of correct exposure data consult the exposure charts prepared by the different flashbulb and film manufacturers. For further information on flash exposure, see pages 332-337.

Reflectors in a great variety of shapes are available for use with flashbulbs. Flat reflectors give a more diffused light with softer shadows than deep reflectors, which throw a much more concentrated beam of light. Midget bulbs need special reflectors for highest efficiency; some of these reflectors can be focused for maximum illumination at different object-camera distances and for softer or harder light. Many photographers use ordinary floodlight reflectors for flashbulbs on extension in order to save the bulk and weight of special reflectors. For back light and side light, flashbulbs can often be used to best advantage without any reflector at all, if only they are properly hidden from the camera. See pages 334-337 for more detailed information.

Extension cords should have soldered connections in order to keep electrical resistance as low as possible and to save battery current. For the same reason, all contact surfaces (plug prongs and holes, switches, the bases of flashbulbs) should be kept free from corrosion at all times (use fine emery cloth; make it a habit to draw every flashbulb with its base over a piece of emery cloth before you stick it into your reflector; I have a piece of fine emery cloth glued into the lock of my lighting equipment case just for this purpose). The longer the extensions, the more battery current will be needed to overcome internal resistance and to guarantee positive synchronization. As a rule, a total of 15 feet is the maximum for three batteries, 25 feet is maximum for four batteries, and 40 feet for five batteries. Beyond this, a booster battery or multi-flash apparatus has to be used (these figures apply to 18-gauge wire, simultaneous use of two or three flashbulbs, and synchronizers operating with electrical trippers; slightly larger footage is permissible for 16-gauge wire; extension length can be doubled if mechanical synchronizer or shutter with built-in synchronization is used). The Bright Star Battery Company manufactures batteries that are designed especially for flash and synchronizer service; I have always found them dependable.

Flashbulbs

The great variety of flashbulbs made today gives the photographer considerable choice when selecting the right bulb for the right occasion. On the other hand, using the wrong type of flash may occasionally result in complete failure.

The shutter type of the camera is the first thing to consider when selecting a flashbulb for taking a synchro-flash picture (for "open flash" any type of flashbulb may be used). Flashbulbs used in connection with between-the-lens shutters (as, for instance, Compur shutters) should have a rather short flash duration (a "short peak"), while bulbs to be used with focal-plane shutters have to have a comparatively long flash duration (a "long peak")—long enough to expose all of the negative while the shutter opening passes across the film. Using a long-peak flashbulb with a between-the-lens shutter is a waste of light intensity that may lead to underexposure, while using a short-peak bulb with a focal-plane shutter would result in a partially unexposed negative. Intensity and duration of the flash can be illustrated by means of a graph which contains complete information on the characteristics of a bulb: the amount of light it produces, the length of time during which brightness is most intense, and the time required after we press the switch before the light output reaches its "peak." Two typical curves are reproduced here. Since manufacturers' pamphlets always contain the curves of their products, it is advisable to become familiar with this form of graph, which tells everything a photographer must know in order to choose the best bulb for his purpose.

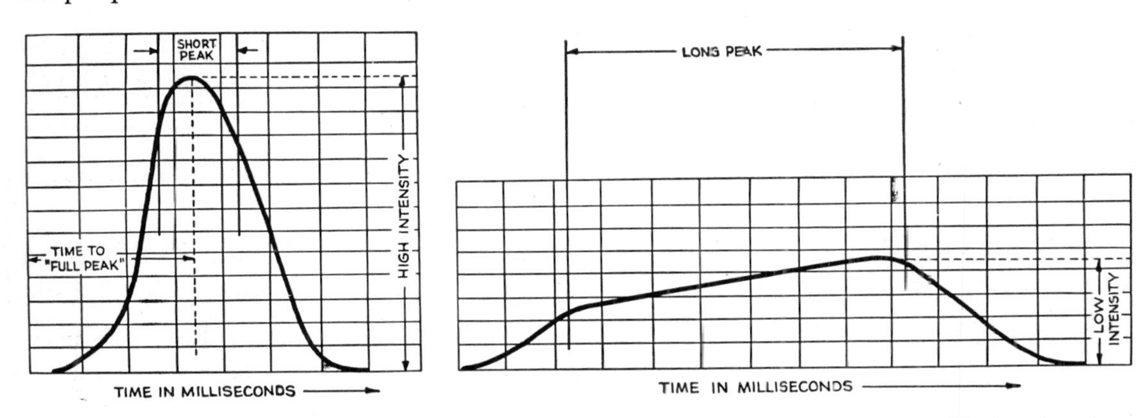

Left: Characteristic curve of a flashbulb intended for between-the-lens shutters. Notice the short peak and the high intensity of the flash. *Right:* Characteristics of a flashbulb intended for focal-plane synchronization. Notice the very long peak, indicating a long duration of the flash at uniform intensity, which, however, is generally much lower than that of the flashbulb at left. Instead of being concentrated in one quick punch of tremendous intensity, the light output of flashbulbs for focal-plane shutter synchronization is spread out over a relatively long time with corresponding decrease in intensity per time unit.

The light output of a flashbulb depends on its size, or rather on the amount of light-producing material it contains. Small bulbs should be used for closeups, larger bulbs for long shots and occasions where greater areas have to be illuminated evenly. The light output of a flashbulb can be learned easily by looking at its characteristic curve: the higher the peak, the greater is the intensity of the light.

The effective light output of a flashbulb depends only partly on its size. Much depends on the way this actual light output is used. A lot of light can be lost by using the wrong type of reflector, or a badly designed reflector; both waste a lot of light by spreading it outside the picture area which should be illuminated. This is especially important if small flashbulbs, or "midget flashbulbs" ("peanut bulbs") are used. Their light output is so low that nothing ought to be wasted; on the other hand, if this relatively small light output is concentrated by means of a "focusing reflector," a much greater proportion of the light is utilized than in the case of much larger bulbs in ordinary reflectors. The result is that in actual use space-saving "peanut bulbs" compare very favorably with flashbulbs three and four times their size.

Interval to full peak. Flashbulbs are fired with electric current which heats up a "primer" which in turn ignites the light-producing material. This process, of course, takes a certain time, and the length of this interval from the moment we press the switch to the moment the light is at its highest peak is important for the synchronization of the flashbulb. Most bulbs reach their peak in from 20 to 23 milliseconds, but a few bulbs take only five milliseconds and some others 28 to 30 milliseconds. Bulbs that need 28 or 30 milliseconds will usually synchronize if the shutter speed is relatively low (from 1/25 to 1/50 second), but in order to use five-millisecond bulbs the synchronizer has to be specially adjusted. The "time to full peak" a flashbulb needs can be learned from its characteristic curve: the closer to the left the highest point of the peak is, the less time the bulb needs before it fires.

The voltage. All flashbulbs need a minimum of three volts before they fire (use two dry cells or more). Some flashbulbs, however, can be fired with any voltage from 3 to 125 volts, which is important when multi-flash equipment has to be used in order to synchronize a great number of flashbulbs on extensions. In such a case, make sure you use only bulbs that will stand this high voltage. Consult the manufacturer's charts to avoid exploding bulbs and blown-out fuses.

The light-producing material. Wire-filled flashbulbs synchronize much more reliably than foil-filled ones, which ought to be used only for "open flash." A tiny lump of solid material produces light in the Speed Midget SM flashbulb, which reaches its peak in only 5 milliseconds and demands special synchronization.

Speedlights

The latest developments in flash equipment are the so-called speed- or strobo-lights. Their advantages over the conventional flashbulbs are: repeating-type flashtube that will produce from 10,000 to 25,000 flashes before it has to be replaced (change of flashbulbs after every shot becomes a thing of the past!); extremely short flash duration of 1/1,000 to 1/10,000 second (short enough to "freeze" motion as fast as that of a bullet leaving the muzzle of a rifle!); and a "flash" that because of its extremely short duration is almost invisible to the eye (which puts an end to the annoying glare of ordinary flashbulbs, especially annoying when photographing in night clubs, churches, or in court). These valuable qualities, however, have to be paid for with comparatively high weight (7 pounds or more for flashgun and powerpack) and relatively low light output comparable to that of an ordinary No. 5 flashbulb. Furthermore, since the units operate on high voltage (ca. 2,000 volts), careful handling is vitally important in order to avoid dangerous shocks.

A speedlight unit consists of four basic parts: the gun with reflector and flash-tube, the powerpack containing the condensers (and batteries in portable units), the trip cable with push button for firing, and the synchronized shutter cord between shutter and gun. Two different types of speedlights are available: portable units containing their own power supply in the form of batteries, and batteryless units that have to be plugged in on an AC-current wall outlet (intended mainly for use in studios). Batteries usually are good for 100 to 150 flashes before recharging becomes necessary; battery chargers that plug into 115-volt, 60-cycle AC outlets are available or build directly into the powerpack.

Maximum flashing rate for most speedlights is from four to ten flashes per minute (condensers need from 5 to 15 seconds to build up their charge). They work best when used in connection with internally synchronized shutters like the Kodak Supermatic, the Ilex Synchro-, or the Wollensak Rapax shutters. Compur shutters can be used after proper synchronization. For determination of the correct exposure a flash-guide number of 200 is usually recommended. For more exhaustive information on guide numbers consult manufacturers' pamphlets.

Some of the better-known speedlight manufacturers are Strobo-Research; Sylvania Electric; Heiland; Wilcox Photo Sales; etc. For each flashtube, a separate powerpack should be used for maximum light output. For multiflash shots, several units can be flashed simultaneously either by interconnecting cables or with the help of photoelectric cells (no cable connections necessary, the distant "slave units" will be set off by the flash produced by the "master unit").

CHAPTER 3

THE MATERIALS OF A PHOTOGRAPHER

NEGATIVE MATERIAL

MODERN negative material is almost as highly specialized, and is available in as great a variety of different types with different characteristics, as cameras or lenses. A man who would ask a clerk in a photo shop to sell him "a film" without further specification as to type, speed, color sensitivity, gradation, graininess, etc., would act as foolishly innocent as somebody wanting to buy "a camera."

To be familiar with the above-mentioned basic properties of photographic negative material doesn't mean that a photographer has to take a course in sensitometry before he can (*A*) select the right type of film for a specific occasion, and (*B*) make good photographs. As a matter of fact, nowhere in photography has a relatively simple issue been clouded in greater mystery than just here, where for some obscure reason textbooks frequently present basic facts in scientific form involving logarithms and mathematical equations instead of just stating them in ordinary plain language. As a consequence, photographers often become scared and try to get along without closer study of these important facts, and their pictures suffer for their ignorance. Or they become fascinated by the mathematical problems involved, get stuck with them, and—as so frequently happens with photographers—remain more interested in the means than in the ends, becoming gadgeteers and collectors in the realm of knowledge.

On the following pages, only information that is essential for the making of good pictures—helpful in selecting the right kind of film—will be found, presented in a form that can be understood without more than ordinary mathematical knowledge.

Apart from a basic knowledge of the properties of negative emulsions, certain rules concerned with the handling, storing, etc., of photographic materials have to be observed as essential conditions for successful picturemaking. The most important ones will be found on the opposite page. Their observance ought to become a habit with every beginner right from the start.

Some DO'S and some DON'TS

Generally: Never let your fingers touch the emulsion of a film or a plate, because the omnipresent acid moisture would cause indelible marks like the one illustrated at right. . . . . →

When handling negatives, always hold them at the edges only, in the way illustrated at the left; this is the only way of avoiding destructive and indelible fingermarks.

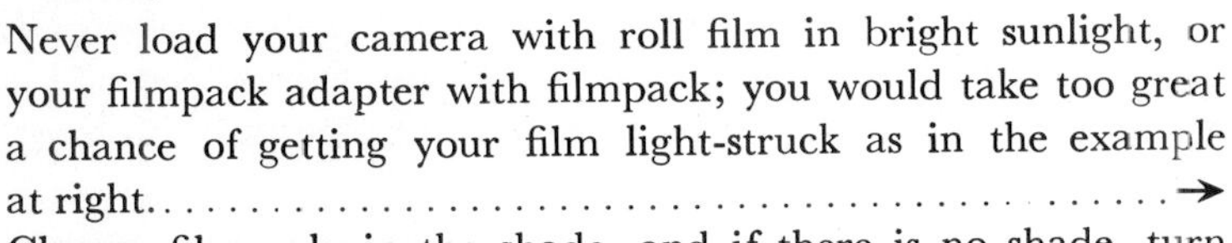

Never load your camera with roll film in bright sunlight, or your filmpack adapter with filmpack; you would take too great a chance of getting your film light-struck as in the example at right. . . . . →

Change film only in the shade, and if there is no shade, turn away from the light and use the shadow cast by your body.

When buying film, watch the expiration date on the package; it is your guarantee of freshness. Refuse film that is overage, be skeptical about film that shows no expiration date stamped on the package.

Store your film supply only in a dry and cool place, away from the radiator, from steampipes, moisture, and dampness which would cause the emulsion to deteriorate in a relatively short time by causing more or less dense over-all fog. ("Tropical-pack" film is available for use in damp climates.)

Roll film: Watch out that your rolls are always wound tight. When loading the camera, thread the endpaper carefully into the empty spool, fold it over sharply so it doesn't make the film bulge —or your negatives will get light-struck like the one at right. . →

On the other hand, never tighten a loosely wound roll by pulling the end of the paper strip tight—you would only scratch the emulsion and get "cinch marks" across the pictures.

Filmpack: Filmpacks are very delicate things. Always hold them by the edges only, never squeeze them by pressing on the flat sides because that would partially open them and permit light to strike the film sheets inside.

The right way and the wrong way of holding a filmpack are illustrated at right. . . . . →

Always pull the tabs straight and slow when changing film, or you may scratch the emulsion. Don't rip off the papers until you take the film out for development (in the darkroom)—and you will have eliminated one possible source of light streaks across your pictures.

Sheet film: When loading sheet-film holders, be sure the emulsion side is facing the lens. In perfect darkness (panfilm), you recognize the emulsion side by the position of the notchings that indicate the type of film: if you hold the film sheet vertical, and the notches are in the upper right corner, then the emulsion side will be facing you; see illustration at right. . . . . →

Certain cameras permit the alternative use of several types of negative material; and sometimes a photographer may have a preference for a certain type of negative material and will select his camera accordingly. Characteristics of the different types of negative material are listed in the following survey:

Large-size negative material is always easier to process than small-size material. The film grain doesn't show up so easily; normal developers demanding no increase in exposure time can be used; occasional specks of dust aren't too conspicuous in an enlargement and can easily be spotted (retouched). On the other hand, the cameras are larger and slower to operate, and depth of field is always shallower with any given stop than if the picture were made with a smaller camera using a lens of shorter focal length. Besides, large-size material is more expensive than material of smaller size. Large sizes can be recommended for the slow and careful worker who wants to get the utmost in print quality and is prepared to pay for it by accepting the inconveniences connected with large-size cameras (weight, bulk, and relative slowness).

Small-size negative material is cheaper than larger sizes, and small cameras are faster to operate than larger ones. Pictures taken with small cameras have greater depth of field with any given stop than photographs taken with larger cameras using lenses of longer focal length. Smaller negative sizes have three disadvantages, which are intensified the smaller the film size: (1) danger of film grain showing up in the print and spoiling sharpness and uniformity of tone; (2) consequent necessity of using finegrain emulsions of slower speed and finegrain developers which demand further increases in exposure times; (3) more time and care required in processing both negatives and prints to get high-quality results.

Small sizes can be recommended for the photographer who values the inherent advantages of the small camera more than technical perfection in the print, who wants to travel light and work fast and is interested more in action and candid shots than in slow or motionless subjects.

Roll film is faster and easier to use than any other kind of negative material, simple to load into the camera, and simple to process; it is the most compact form of negative material. Its disadvantages are the impossibility of processing individual shots individually, of changing from one emulsion type to another without sacrificing unexposed frames on the roll (exception: the Swedish Hasselblad 2¼ x 2¼″ camera which provides self-contained, interchangeable backs), and the necessity for sacrificing unexposed frames if only a few shots have been made on a roll which must be processed right away.

Rollfilm adapters are available for quite a number of sheet film and filmpack cameras.

Sheet film permits making and processing individual shots individually and changing from one emulsion to another without wasting film; it has a heavier base than any other type of negative material, a feature which facilitates handling.

Its disadvantages are the necessity for loading it sheet for sheet into individual filmholders in a darkroom, and the considerable weight and bulk of the filmholders; material for only half a dozen shots takes almost as much space as the camera itself.

Filmpack combines most of the advantages of roll film and sheet film and avoids their disadvantages: it can be loaded into the adapter in daylight, permits switching from one emulsion to another without wasting film (by using different adapters), can be processed individually, and single exposed sheets can be taken out of the adapter without sacrificing the rest.

On the other hand, it is the most expensive form of negative material, and occasionally sheets buckle in the adapter and don't always stay as flatly in the plane of focus as sheet film. This causes partial unsharpness when shooting with relatively large diaphragm openings.

Glass plates are used today only for making positive transparencies and color-separation negatives and for certain scientific purposes and making photoengravings.

The speed of an emulsion

To make accurate determination of exposure data possible, every emulsion type has been assigned an individual speed rating which provides the basis for setting the dial of the exposure meter. Unfortunately, today there are five or six different systems for measuring the "speed" (the light sensitivity) of films, but only three of them are really important: the ASA (American Standards Association) system and the Weston and General Electric systems. Speed ratings for certain types of negative material should be determined from the pamphlets and charts prepared by the manufacturers of exposure meters or film, since film manufacturers change the speeds of their products once in a while, and ratings given here probably would be partially outdated before this book is published.

Practically speaking, the speed of an emulsion is not a constant factor. Until the introduction of ASA speed values, most listed ratings indicated the maximum of speed that could be obtained under favorable conditions, i. e., if objects of medium to low contrasts were photographed and negatives were fully developed in a rapid developer. ASA ratings include a safety of two, comparable to one full stop. However, extreme object contrasts and use of genuine finegrain developers still necessitates certain increases in exposure times which in effect are identical with proportional reductions in film speed. We will hear more about these influences in the discussion of exposure, pages 119-123.

The higher the speed rating of an emulsion, the shorter the possible exposure time, and the smaller the possible diaphragm stop, with resulting increase in depth of field (see page 112). Consequently, fast films will give well-exposed negatives even under conditions where slower emulsions would fail—in poor light, in stopping fast action, and in obtaining extension of sharpness in depth with relatively short exposure times. This would seem to make it advisable always to use the fastest available type of film. Actually, however, just the opposite is true for the following reasons: the faster an emulsion, the more pronounced will usually be its grain (see page 73)—especially undesirable when working with a miniature camera, and the softer its gradation (see pages 69-73). On the other hand, the slower an emulsion, the finer is generally its grain, and the more brilliant its gradation. Consequently, speed may often be an unavoidable necessity (as was the case with lenses, remember?), but from the point of technical picture quality, the best results will always be achieved with the *slowest* film that still permits the use of the diaphragm opening and shutter speed prescribed by pictorial considerations.

Color sensitivity of emulsions

In black-and-white photography, the natural colors of objects are transformed into gray tone values. In order to obtain as natural-looking a picture as possible, the brightness values of these gray shades should generally correspond as nearly as possible to the brightness values of the original colors, so that, for instance, a bright red is represented in the final photograph by a lighter shade of gray than a medium blue. This depends greatly upon the color sensitivity of the negative material (and the filter used, see page 226) on which the picture was taken. In this respect, we have to differentiate among the following three groups of emulsion types:

"Color-blind" emulsions are sensitized only for blue—which because of oversensitivity they render as white—but are not sensitive to red and yellow, which colors consequently would appear as black in the final photograph (see picture on page 225). Naturally, such emulsions can only be used for reproduction of black-and-white objects.

Orthochromatic emulsions are sensitive to all colors except red, which in the final photograph would appear as black. They are oversensitive to blue, which they render too light (see picture on page 225). Their only rather questionable "advantage" is derived from their insensitivity to red, which permits developing such emulsions under a red safelight—and checking on development from time to time by visual inspection. As we will see in the section on development (page 141), however, this can hardly be considered an advantage any more, and is certainly not worth the loss of one important color—red—and the disadvantage of not being able to use a red filter for darkening a blue sky or for haze penetration in a telephotograph (see page 289). The only reason for the existence of orthochromatic emulsions is conservatism on the part of a large group of amateurs who are still shy of the "professional" panchromatic films. Most orthochromatic emulsions have medium speeds.

Panchromatic emulsions are sensitive to all colors, permit the use of any kind of color filter and are the only type of negative material that can be recommended for serious creative work. We will see later (page 228) how pan films can be made to transform practically any color into any desired shade of gray in a picture, thus giving the imaginative photographer an opportunity to create as freely as any other artist.

Panchromatic emulsions usually have medium to very fast speeds, especially in artificial light. They have to be developed in complete darkness according to the "time and temperature" method; see page 141.

According to their degree of sensitivity for red and blue we have to differentiate between two subgroups of panchromatic emulsions, which for perfectly true color transformation into gray values need different color filters (see table on page 226): Type B emulsions, which are oversensitive to blue and slightly oversensitive to red, and Type C emulsions which render blue approximately correctly but are considerably oversensitive to red. A few of the more common films belonging to these two groups are listed below:

Type B	Type C
Ansco Supreme	*Ansco* Superpan Press
Isopan	Triple-S Panchromatic
Finopan	SS Panchromatic
Kodak Panatomic X	*Kodak* Tri-X Panchromatic
Plus X	
Super XX	
Super Panchro Press, Type B	

The gradation of emulsions

Contrasts between light and dark as we find them in nature have to be transferred via the negative to the final photograph in such a form that their original character is either preserved, or—if possible—improved. This sounds simple but actually can be rather difficult since in nature contrast ranges of 1 to 1,000 are common, while the average print has a contrast range of only 1 to 30. Consequently, it will often be necessary to reduce the natural contrasts—proportionally without changing too greatly their internal relationship—to such a degree that the lightest as well as the darkest parts of the object still show tonal differences and detail in the final print instead of merely being pure white and black. On the other hand, if natural contrasts are relatively low—say only 1 to 30—further reduction of these contrasts would result in a flat and gray print without any clean whites and blacks; under such conditions, contrasts have to be preserved as they are. And, to take a third, extreme case, contrasts that are too low in nature to look good in a photograph if transferred "literally," may actually have to be increased before we get an impressive picture, as, for instance, in many telephotographs where actual object contrasts are extremely low because of distance and atmospheric haze.

The easiest way for conscious reduction, preservation, or increase of contrasts is through selection of negative material with the proper gradation. How to choose the right type of emulsion with regard to gradation for a certain purpose can be told laboriously in scientific form, or it can be compressed into a few simple sentences based on practical experience. In the excellent photo encyclopedia *The Complete Photographer*, for instance, the chapter on "contrasts" dealing with this problem contains no less than 15 pages, crammed full with gradation curves, logarithmic and Greek-letter equations. Their essence, however, is nothing but the following:

With regard to gradation, we must differentiate among three basically different types of emulsions which are called hard (high contrast), medium (normal), and soft (low contrast). This has nothing to do with the speed or color sensitivity of an emulsion, and there are panchromatic emulsions that are slow and hard, and others that are fast and soft, etc. If we should take three identical photographs of an object with medium contrasts, develop the films under identical conditions, and print the negatives on the same type of paper, the picture taken on an emulsion with a hard gradation would show the object with greater contrasts than it actually had; the picture taken on an emulsion with a soft gradation would show the object less contrastful than it appeared to the eye; while the picture taken on an emulsion with a medium gradation would probably preserve the object contrasts very much as they actually were.

Consequently, if a photographer has to photograph a very contrastful object (for instance, dazzling-white adobe houses with deep-black shadows), he would have to reduce contrasts artificially by using a film with a soft gradation in order to preserve detail and tonal differences in the brightest as well as in the darkest parts of the final picture. If he has to take a telephotograph over miles of distance and through layers of blueish haze, he would have to increase contrasts artificially by using a film with a hard gradation in order to get differentiation and detail. And, if he has to photograph objects of average contrasts, he would use a normal emulsion with medium gradation in order to get the best results.

This is the whole secret of proper selection of the right gradation; it really is quite simple when told in plain language, isn't it? For different occasions, a film with the right gradation can be selected from the following chart listing the more important panchromatic films:

Hard Gradation	Medium Gradation	Soft Gradation
Kodak Contrast Process Panchromatic	*Ansco Finopan* Isopan *Kodak Plus-X* Panatomic-X	*Ansco Superpan Press* Ultra Speed Pan SS Pan *Kodak Super-XX Panchromatic* Tri-X Panchromatic

To become thoroughly familiar with the characteristics of different gradations, the following experiment can be recommended (instead of negative emulsions—films—we will use sensitized paper, because it is less sensitive and exposures can be controlled much easier; the visual results will be exactly the same).

In the darkroom take a sheet of sensitized paper of soft gradation and an equally large or slightly larger piece of cardboard. On the sensitized paper mark off eight or ten strips of equal

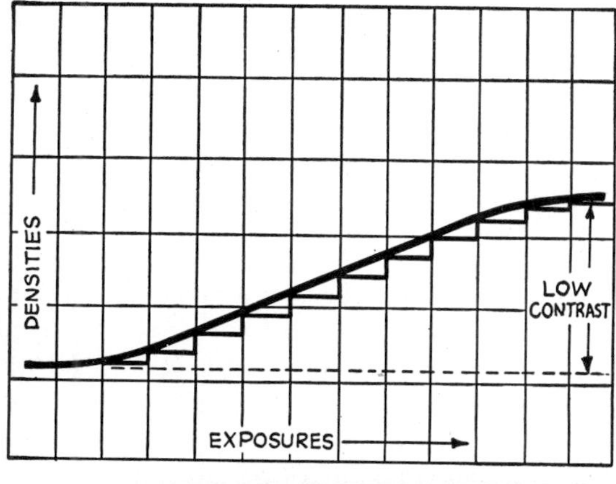

Example of a "soft" (or long) gradation. Notice abundance of well-differentiated half-tones, the slow and gradual increase in density under uniform increase of exposure.

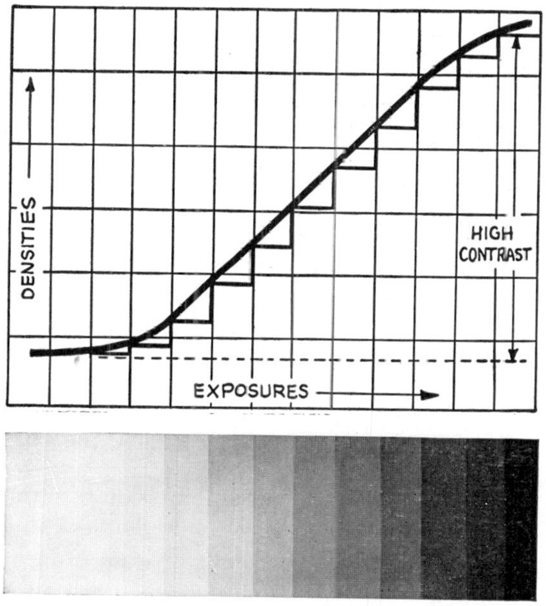

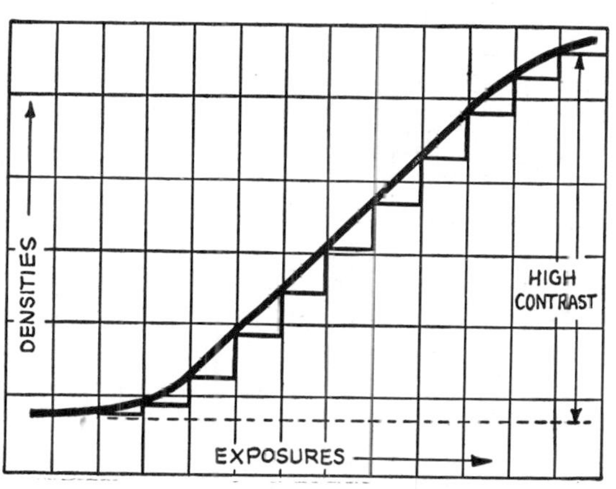

Example of a "hard" (or short) gradation. Number of different half-tones between white and black is small, abrupt increase in density under uniform increase of exposure.

width, and expose the whole sheet under the enlarger for a very short, predetermined time (stop down the enlarger lens so as to permit reasonable exposure times, for instance, ½ second for the first exposure). Then take the cardboard and cover the first strip of the sensitized paper and expose the rest for the same time as before. After this, move the cardboard until it covers the third strip and expose for twice the length of the second exposure; move the cardboard one section and expose for twice the length of the third exposure; move the cardboard another section and expose for twice the length of the fourth exposure, and so on. Each consecutive exposure should be twice as long as the previous one, resulting in a gradation scale with exposures in the proportions of 1 : 2 : 4 : 8 : 16 : 32 : 64 : 128 : 256, etc. After development, the first step on the scale should be practically white, while the next to last should be just a trifle lighter than the last one.

Next, take a piece of sensitized paper of hard gradation and repeat the performance, using the same exposure times and light conditions as before. Compared to our first gradation strip, this new strip made on paper of hard gradation will show a much shorter scale of gray steps, with a long white beginning and a long black ending, while in between the differences between the various shades of gray will be greater than they were in the strip made on the paper of soft gradation.

The more or less abrupt increase in density resulting from a uniform increase in exposure can be expressed in the form of a graph, and in order to get reliable comparisons between emulsions of different gradations, conditions under which such gray scales should be made and evaluated have been standardized: the exposures are standardized in candle-meter-seconds and plotted logarithmically on the axis of abscissae (the horizontal), log $i \times t$ representing exposure intensity multiplied by exposure time. The resulting densities (in the exposed film) are measured step for step with a densitometer and plotted on the axis of ordinates (the vertical).

To facilitate understanding, we could imagine each consecutive exposure to add a uniform layer of thickness to the gray scale, which thus would assume the appearance of a row of steps: the smaller the increase in density from step to step, the lower would be each individual step; and the greater the increase in density from step to step, the higher would be each individual step. The

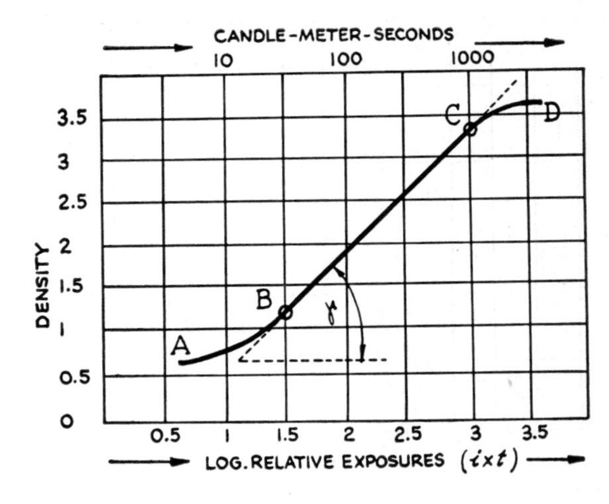

Typical gradation curve of a normal emulsion: *A-B* is called the toe of the curve; *B-C* is called the straight-line portion; and *C-D* is called the shoulder of the curve. The angle included between the straightline portion and the horizontal is called Gamma (the Greek letter).

first case could represent an emulsion of rather soft gradation, where each consecutive exposure results in only a slight increase in density, while the second case could represent a more contrastful gradation, where each consecutive exposure results in a comparatively great increase in density.

Finally, by connecting the edges of all of the steps with a line, we get a curve that in character corresponds closely to the actual gradation curves illustrated on the previous page: the softer the gradation of an emulsion, the flatter would be the sequence of steps, and the flatter would be the ascent of the curve (previous page, *left*); while the harder the gradation of the emulsion, the steeper the sequence of steps, and the steeper the ascent of the curve (previous page, *right*).

Manufacturers of negative material usually show the gradation curves of their various products in their pamphlets, giving the photographer who is familiar with these symbols a very accurate idea of the characteristics of the respective films. To read and understand gradation curves, he has to know the following (compare illustration and caption above):

A very short exposure has no effect on an emulsion—the curve doesn't start at zero, but a little bit to the right at *A*. This point is called the threshold value, and some speed-rating systems start from here.

From *A* to *B* (the "toe" of the curve), density increases slowly and out of proportion to the increase in exposure. Here begin the first delicate traces of an image, the deepest blacks and darkest shadows, which are difficult to reproduce but nevertheless essential to prints which require a full range of dark tones.

The straight part of the curve between *B* and *C* represents the most valuable qualities of the emulsion. Here, densities increase in proportion with exposure times, and as long as the contrasts of our negative are within this range we can rest assured of a faithful rendering.

From *C* to *D* densities increase less rapidly than exposure times, and beyond the highest point of the curve, further increase in exposure actually results in a decrease of the densities in the negative, a process called "solarization."

The angle between the straight part of the curve and the horizontal—the gamma—represents the character of the gradation for that particular degree of development. The smaller this angle is, the softer is the gradation, and vice versa. An angle of 45° is called gamma 1, representing a "normal" gradation. For most negatives, a slightly lower gamma of 0.7 to 0.8 is preferable in the interest of better printing.

Instructions for altering the gradation of an emulsion will be found on the opposite page.

The gradation of a negative emulsion as expressed in its characteristic "curve" is not unalterable. As already stated, such curves are always computed under strictly standardized conditions—just because change of conditions would lead to different results. Quite often, however, a certain negative emulsion must be used for one reason or another despite the fact that its gradation is not very suitable for the specific purpose. For instance, a photographer may have to use a high-speed panchromatic film like Kodak Tri-X Pan, either because at the moment no other film is available, or because he needs a film of the highest possible speed. But since the contrasts of the object he has to photograph are comparatively low, he is handicapped by the comparatively soft gradation of this particular film. In such a case, the gradation of the emulsion can be changed to a certain degree by exposing and developing the film in an "abnormal" way. A slightly shortened exposure (yet not an underexposure) combined with greatly prolonged development will make the gradation of any emulsion harder, increasing the contrasts; while on the other hand, an increase in exposure time (which may be a considerable overexposure!) in connection with a radical decrease in the time of development, will make a gradation softer in any desired degree, decreasing the contrasts—the more so, the more the times of exposure and development deviate from the "normal." However, an emulsion can always be made softer much easier, and to a much greater degree, than it can be made harder. We will hear more about this in the chapter on "Contrasts and How to Control Them" (see page 207).

The grain of negative emulsions

In the developed photographic emulsion, the image is built of innumerable tiny particles of metallic silver. These grains are so infinitesimal that they can be seen only under a microscope. However, they give the image a heterogeneous character, which under certain conditions shows up in an enlargement as "graininess." Gray shades that previously were smooth will now break up and look coarse, showing a sandpaper-like texture. Contours that appeared sharp and cleanly defined in the negative will become fuzzy and blurred. Consequently, in the interests of picture quality and clearness, the graininess should always be kept as low as possible—especially important when working with small-size films which must be greatly enlarged. The factors which influence "graininess" are discussed on the following page.

As a rule, the speed of a film and the size of its grain are very closely related: the higher the speed, the larger will be the size of the grain, and vice versa. The largest grain is always found among the super-fast panchromatic emulsions, while the extremely slow-process films and microfilms are practically grainless. Avoiding excessive and unnecessary graininess was one of the reasons for recommending on page 67 the use of the slowest possible film, instead of an unnecessarily fast one.

Graininess, like so many other emulsion qualities, is not an unalterable factor. It can be influenced in several different ways, among which the following are the most important:

Film grain always increases with the time of development. Consequently, relatively short development will help to keep the grain small, while overdevelopment will make it excessively large.

As we will see later in the discussion of development (page 129), contrasts, too. increase with the time of development. Consequently, a comparatively short development may result in contrasts that are too low, a fact which can be compensated for (*a*) by using a film of relatively hard gradation that doesn't have to be developed very long before it gives sufficient contrasts, and (*b*) by lighting the object so contrastfully (or by waiting for such light) and exposing it so long that comparatively short development will produce negatives of sufficient contrast and density.

The type of developer plays an important role with regard to graininess of the negative. Rapid developers produce a much larger grain in the same film than slower and less forceful developers, while special "finegrain developers" keep graininess down to a minimum. Such finegrain developers, however, have the disadvantage of requiring an often considerable increase in exposure time in order to produce well-exposed negatives of sufficient density, a fact which—as already mentioned in the discussion of film speed (page 67)—is identical with a more or less serious loss in emulsion speed.

Contrasty printing papers always emphasize the grain, while soft papers reduce the apparent graininess in a print. Consequently, when developing a film, avoid negative contrasts that are so low that the negative has to be printed on contrasty paper in order to get pictures with sufficient contrasts.

Graininess increases with increasing density of the negative, and is always most pronounced in overexposed films. Intelligent use of a good exposure meter (page 50) is indispensable for the production of thin but not underexposed negatives, in which graininess always shows least.

Hints for the selection of negative material—a summing up

Only panchromatic emulsions—films that are sensitive to *all* the colors in the spectrum—can ever satisfy the creative photographer. There is no earthly reason why he should voluntarily limit himself to truthful rendering of only a fraction of all the colors that surround him, or deny himself the use of some important color filters, when a long and diversified list of highly perfected, all-color-sensitive films is at his disposition for the asking.

Next to color sensitivity, the most important quality of a film is its speed. A film that is too slow to do a certain job is practically valueless. On the other hand, excessive speed usually will result in unnecessary graininess, and sometimes in flat and inferior gradation. The best film is always the one that is just fast enough to permit the use of the shutter speed and diaphragm opening necessary to do a perfect job. The photographer should not be forced to shoot faster or to stop down further merely to avoid overexposure.

The faster an emulsion is, the coarser is usually its grain, and the softer its gradation; and vice versa.

Neither speed, nor gradation, nor graininess are unalterable factors. Each of them will change or can be changed, under certain circumstances:

The effective speed rating of an emulsion has to be reduced by increasing exposure (*a*) when very contrastful objects are to be photographed (prolonged exposure permits shortening time of development, resulting in reduction of excess contrasts to printable stage; gives deep black shadows time to register on the film)—so open up the diaphragm from one to two stops, or alter the shutter speed accordingly; (*b*) when the film has to be developed in a finegrain developer (reduction of effective film speed, i.e., increase in exposure, depends on type of developer; consult manufacturers' charts).

The gradation of an emulsion can be made more or less contrasty by changing the times of exposure and development: decrease in exposure time and increase in time of development always make an emulsion more contrasty, while increase in exposure time and decrease in time of development make it less contrasty; see page 129.

The grain of an emulsion will be the larger, the more rapid-acting a developer is used, the longer the film is developed, the more the negative is overexposed, and the faster the film is dried; and vice versa. Grain always shows up more annoyingly if the negative is printed on contrasty paper than if a paper with a softer gradation is used.

Photographers on location assignments, who cannot carry a full line of films with different emulsions for reasons of space and weight, have to standardize on one or two types of film. Personally, I have found it entirely possible to do practically all my work with the help of only a single type of high-speed panchromatic film, the characteristics of which I adapt to the requirements of different occasions by accordingly selecting the times of exposure and development, and sometimes the type of the developer, too. Naturally, success in such a case depends to a great extent on accurately kept notes with regard to exposure times and contrasts of object and illumination—and their deviations from the "normal," so that afterward, when it comes to developing the film, we know exactly what type of developer to use, and how much longer or shorter the negatives have to be developed than "normal."

> Once you have found a film that you like, *stick to it!* Today, all films made by nationally known manufacturers are of practically the same high quality, and as long as you use the right kind of film with regard to color sensitivity, speed, and gradation, you shouldn't worry much about the make of the film. In your hands, the best film will then be the one with which you are most familiar.

SENSITIZED PAPERS

When selecting the most suitable paper for printing a certain negative, two factors have to be considered above all: gradation and surface texture of the paper. Compared to these two, other qualities like sensitivity, weight, and tint are of only minor importance.

After exposure, modern "developing-out" papers have to be developed and fixed, etc., very much like negatives (see page 155). Their emulsions differ from negative emulsions mostly insofar as they are not color sensitized and less sensitive in general, as a result of which photographic papers can be processed in comparatively bright yellow-greenish light (see pages 92-93, on safelights).

The gradation of papers. Similar to negative emulsions, paper emulsions are manufactured with different gradations from very contrastful (hard) through medium (normal) to very contrastless (soft). Usually, a certain type of paper is available in from four to six different gradations, proper selection of which enables a photographer to make drastic correction of undesirable negative gradations. If, for some reason or other, a negative is so contrastful that if printed on a normal paper the image would consist mostly of blacks and whites with very few half-tones in between, printing this negative on a soft paper will considerably improve its tone-rendering and bring out the previously lacking half-tones. On the other hand, if a negative is so soft that if printed on normal paper the image would consist mostly of muddy grays without any clean blacks and whites, printing such a negative on hard paper will considerably improve the gradation of the image by increasing its contrasts. Negatives of "normal" gradation, of course, would have to be printed on "normal" paper.

Surface textures of papers. The type of subject and the purpose of the picture determine the surface texture of a photographic paper. Principally, the smaller a print is, the smoother ought to be the surface of the paper, since otherwise its texture would obliterate the finer detail of the picture. Larger prints—especially if they don't depend on fine detail for their effect, may be printed on correspondingly rougher surfaces. Prints made for reproduction, however, should always be printed on glossy paper, no matter what their size or subject may be, in the interest of good reproduction.

When it comes to discussing surface textures of photographic papers, opinions usually are sharply divided, and final decisions rest with the personal taste of the photographer. Personally, I print all my negatives on glossy paper—regardless of size of picture or character of motive—for the following reasons:

1. A glossy surface is the most typically "photographic" one. In no other art form is glossy paper commonly used. On the other hand, matte and rough surfaces are widely used for drawings in pencil or ink, aquarelles, lithographs, etchings, etc.; thus these surfaces, when used for photographs, always suggest—to a greater or lesser degree depending on the treatment of photograph and subject—these other forms of art. When seeing prints on matte and rough surfaces I always have a feeling that the photographer who made them was a frustrated "artist" at heart, suffering from an inferiority complex and secretly trying to imitate one of the "finer" arts as far as his medium permitted. . . .

2. Glossy papers have a far greater tone range than papers with rougher surfaces. Their whites are whiter and their blacks are deeper. A picture printed on glossy paper always has more sparkle, and its tonal values approximate more closely the original values of the subject—giving it a more lifelike appearance—than if it had been printed on a rougher surface.

3. Most of my photographs are taken for reproduction, which for best results necessitates printing the negative on glossy paper.

4. Confining myself to only one type of surface—the photographically most impressive one—permits me to keep my paper stock small and promotes economy.

Degrees of sensitivity of papers. Photographic emulsions are made with different speeds for contact-printing and enlarging purposes. Use of the slower chloride or chlorobromide papers facilitates exposure control in the fast contact-printing machines, while the faster bromide and bromochloride papers help to cut down exposure times in the comparatively slow projection printers (enlargers).

The weight of the paper stock. Most photographic papers are manufactured in two different weights: singleweight, which is best for ordinary use and print sizes up to and including 8x10 inches; and doubleweight, which is preferable for larger prints from 11x14 inches up. Singleweight stock is cheaper, washes and dries more rapidly, is easier to mount and less bulky in quantity than doubleweight stock, which, however, doesn't curl so easily and can stand a lot more rough handling.

Hints for selecting the right type of paper—a summing up

The method of printing determines the speed of the paper, which should always be in proportion to the light intensity of the printing machine: if the paper is too fast, exposure times will result that are too short to be measured accurately, and "dodging" (local print control, see page 216) becomes virtually impossible. On the other hand, if the paper is too slow, the negative may get too hot during exposure and start to curl and to move, causing blurredness in the print. For enlargements, exposure times not shorter than 10 and not longer than 25 seconds are ideal. If a paper is unusually fast, or a negative unusually thin, stopping down the diaphragm of the enlarger will prolong exposure times.

The gradation of the negative determines the gradation of the printing paper; see instructions on page 76. A soft paper gradation is often designated by the number 1, a normal one by the number 2, a hard one by the number 3, and an extra hard one by the number 4 (sometimes, there is an ultra-hard paper with the number 5, too).

The size of the print determines (*a*) the coarseness of the paper surface (see discussion on page 76), and (*b*) the weight of the paper stock (see page 77).

The purpose of the print should be considered when selecting a paper surface. I have already mentioned that prints intended for reproduction should be made on glossy paper. Glossy paper, however, easily catches the light and then shines like a mirror; consequently, photographs intended as wall decorations or for exhibition purposes, etc., had better be printed on semi-matte or matte paper which makes it easier to see the picture from every angle.

The character of the subject influences choice of surface texture and tint. An industrial photograph, for instance, always looks best on glossy paper, while most people prefer to see a portrait printed on a paper with a dull surface. A white surface is the normal one for a photograph, and as long as you use white paper stock you cannot go wrong; papers with an ivory or buff tone more often than not make either a dull and stuffy impression, or look just plain "arty."

For final selection of all but glossy papers (which to the eye look all alike) consult the manufacturers' sample books at your dealer's. When ordering a specific paper you have to indicate: the name of the manufacturer, the trade name of the paper, the type of surface, the weight of the stock, the gradation of the emulsion, and the size of the paper. Here is an example: Ansco Brovira—glossy—doubleweight—normal (No. 2)—11x14 inches.

PHOTOGRAPHIC CHEMICALS

While it is advisable for the beginner to buy his developer, hypo, etc., ready-mixed, the more advanced photographer will usually prefer to mix his solutions himself for the following reasons:

Economy. Self-mixed developers, fixers, etc., are less expensive than those bought ready-mixed from the manufacturer. This is particularly true of finegrain developers.

Versatility. Only a comparatively few basic chemicals are necessary for mixing a great number of formulas with different properties, simply by altering the number and proportions of their components accordingly. Sometimes, a very slight change in the properties of, for instance, a developer is desirable for accomplishing a specific purpose; self-mixed formulas are easily adjusted to fit such special occasions (mainly because we know their exact composition), while monkeying with ready-mixed ones is a sure-fire way to invite disaster.

Availability. Certain formulas, especially some developers and correction baths are so unstable that they are not available in ready-mixed form. Unless a photographer wants to deny himself the benefit of these sometimes extremely useful formulas, he has to prepare them himself every time he wants to use them.

The equipment needed for self-preparation of solutions is simple and not expensive; savings made through self-mixing will soon amortize its initial cost. We need:

One large and one small graduate

One large and one small glass funnel

One laboratory balance ("trip scale") accurate to within 0.1 gram, and a set of weights from 1 to 100 grams (formulas in this book will be given in metric form)

Several glass spoons for taking chemicals out of their containers; wooden or metal spoons are unsuitable because they are not chemically inert and are difficult to clean

Two glass rods with flat ends for stirring solutions and crushing remaining crystals

A mortar for pulverizing coarse crystals

A filter stand with heavy base to hold the funnel when filtering solutions, and several sheets of filter paper

Glass beakers in different sizes for dissolving and mixing chemicals (up to 1 gallon)

Wide-necked bottles in different sizes, with plastic screw tops for storing chemicals

Ordinary quart and gallon bottles of brown glass for storing mixed solutions

How to buy chemicals. The price of chemicals constitutes only a tiny fraction of the cost involved in making a photograph, way out of proportion to their actual importance for ultimate success: chemicals that are not pure enough can throw a developer so much off balance that negatives will be spoiled beyond hope. . . . Consequently, only chemicals of guaranteed quality and uniformity should ever be used, even if they actually are a few cents more expensive than unguaranteed store brands. . . . Manufacturers with enviable reputations for producing photo-chemicals of highest quality and uniformity are, among others, the Mallinckrodt Chemical Works and Eastman Kodak Company.

When ordering chemicals, certain expressions, symbols, and abbreviations will be found to be in common use among chemists and manufacturers. The most important ones are the following:

"Technical"—comparatively low grade

"Purified"—medium quality

N.F.—meets the requirements of the National Formulary

U.S.P.—meets the requirements of the United States Pharmacopoeia

C.P.—chemically pure

A.R.—analytical reagent purity

The ending "ate" means that the chemical contains a comparatively high degree of oxygen (for instance, sulfate)

The ending "ite" means that the chemical contains a small degree of oxygen only (for instance, sulfite)

The ending "ide" signifies a hydracid salt (for instance, sulfide)

How to store chemicals. The majority of chemicals used for photographic purposes are sensitive to either air or light or heat or cold or moisture, and will deteriorate if exposed to these influences for a greater or shorter length of time, depending on the particular chemical. The best way to store chemicals is in glass containers—wide-necked jars with plastic screw tops for substances in powder or crystalline form, and ordinary corked bottles for solutions. Glass stoppers, now widely used, have a tendency to get stuck. To loosen them, heat the neck of the bottle all around (one or two matches should do the trick; don't crack the glass by applying too much heat); knock lightly against the sides of the stopper with a piece of wood; and try to twist the stopper counterclockwise; it usually comes out easily then. Don't forget to grease the stopper with Vaseline before you put it back into the bottle. Never store chemicals in paper bags or cardboard containers. Observe the few following rules, and you will experience no trouble.

Rules for storing chemicals

Use only chemically inert glass containers; brown ones for developing agents and the other light-sensitive chemicals mentioned below.

Store chemicals only in a dark, cool (but not cold), dry place. Keep ammonia water, ammonium sulfide, and sodium sulfide separated from the rest of your stock because they release fumes that have a deteriorating influence on most other chemicals.

Never store sensitized material (films and paper) together with chemicals; some chemicals give off fumes that would fog your emulsions.

Make sure that all containers are properly labelled to avoid disastrous mistakes.

Never leave chemicals exposed longer than necessary. Keep containers tightly stoppered at all times.

Always keep bottles with stock solutions of developers filled up to the neck as much as possible, to keep out air which would oxidize the developer. If you have a bottle that isn't quite filled, fill up the empty space by dropping glass marbles right into the solution until it reaches the neck of the bottle.

If preparing a large amount of developer stock solution at a time, store it in a number of smaller bottles (quart bottles) rather than in a single big one. Whenever you withdraw solution you thus have to open and expose to air only one bottle containing a small amount of liquid (which probably will be used up within a short time anyway), and the bulk of your stock remains undisturbed.

Don't store finegrain developer stock solution in bottles that for a long time held alkaline liquids. Remaining traces of alkali retained by the glass may change the alkalinity of the developer and considerably alter its activity.

The following chemicals need special attention with regard to the way they are stored:

Unusually sensitive to moisture are the following chemicals, which in spite of glass-stoppered bottles should be stored only in a perfectly dry and moisture proof place: Amidol—ammonium persulfate—caustic soda—pyrocatechin—glycin—hydroquinone—metol—potassium carbonate—pyrogallol.

Unusually sensitive to light are the following chemicals, which in spite of brown glass bottles should be stored only in a dark place: potassium ferricyanide—ferric oxalate—gold chloride—potassium permanganate—silver nitrate—potassium iodide.

Unusually sensitive to heat are the following chemicals, which should be dissolved only in cold water, and their solutions added only to other cold solutions: ferric oxalate—potassium metabisulfate—sodium bisulfate.

Poisonous, or at least damaging to skin or lungs (vapors!) are the following chemicals, which should always be kept locked away in containers clearly marked POISON:

Caustic soda is an alkali for developer solutions that because of its corrosive poisonous effect on the skin should never be touched with bare hands.

Potassium bichromate, used for intensification, is intensely poisonous if it gets into wounds or cracks of the skin, causing ulcers.

Sulfuric acid, used to clean developer trays and tanks, gives off poisonous vapors and will cause bad burns.

Uranium nitrate, used for toning and intensifying, is poisonous.

Pyrogallol is a rarely used, but highly poisonous, developing agent.

General rules for mixing solutions

When you buy developers, fixers, etc., in ready-mixed form, instructions concerning the correct way of dissolving the chemicals are usually included. Otherwise, or when preparing solutions yourself, observation of the following rules will help to prevent disappointments:

Never add a new component to a solution before the previous one has been *completely* dissolved.

When preparing a certain formula, dissolve the chemicals in the order they are listed.

When weighing chemicals, never pour them right onto the pan of the balance. Instead, put a piece of paper on each one of the pans (so you don't disturb the balance) and pour the chemicals on the paper to avoid contamination with other chemicals weighed. However, you may use the same paper for weighing all the components that go into one and the same formula before discarding it.

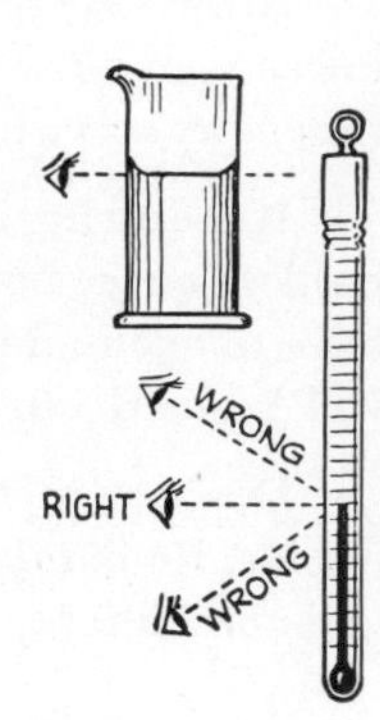

When mixing formulas (especially finegrain developers) where minute quantities of certain chemicals are being used, be sure to measure them accurately. Keep the points of your balance free from corrosion (more expensive balances have knife edges made from agate, which is corrosion-proof, but brittle if handled roughly), so your balance keeps its accuracy. When measuring liquids, hold glass graduates so the surface of the liquid is level with your eye, take the reading at the bottom of the curve formed by surface tension at the top of the liquid; see sketch. When taking a thermometer reading, too, keep your eye level with the top of the mercury, or your reading may be off as much as two degrees because of the refracting effect of the cylindrical magnifier built into the thermometer rod; see sketch.

Use containers made only of glass (laboratory beakers) or stainless steel for mixing and dissolving chemicals. Hard rubber absorbs certain chemicals and may contaminate solutions subsequently prepared. Enameled containers sometimes give off alkali (especially undesirable when preparing finegrain developers), while glazed stoneware sometimes has flaws into which chemicals may penetrate.

Always pour dry chemicals into water; don't pour water on dry chemicals. Desiccated chemicals would cake immediately and take a very long time to dissolve; this applies especially to ready-mixed acid fixing salts.

To speed up dissolution, stir chemicals vigorously while pouring them slowly into the water or solution, but be careful not to whip air into the solution when mixing developers, since oxygen has a very corrosive effect on all developing agents.

When mixing a developer, dissolve the preserving agent (for instance, sodium sulfite) before you dissolve the developing agent (hydroquinone, pyro, etc.). Otherwise the developing agent will probably start to oxidize (indication: brownish discoloration of the solution), and its activity will be impaired before addition of the preserving agent can stop further disintegration of the developer. However, Elon (Metol) can be dissolved more easily in water containing a small pinch of sulfite. After complete dissolution, balance of sulfite should be added.

After you prepare a solution, write the date on the bottle with a grease pencil; it will aid you later in estimating its freshness. If you pour used developer back into the bottle for later re-use, mark the number of films developed in it with grease pencil on the bottle to keep track of the degree of exhaustion of the solution, important for determination of necessary increase in subsequent developing times.

When preparing (or using!) a fixing bath, be especially careful not to spill hypo crystals or solution on floor or table of the darkroom. Hypo acts like poison on all developers! Spilled hypo solution will dry and the powder will contaminate the whole darkroom, leaving white dots wherever some of it settles down on, or comes in contact with, undeveloped film or paper. Many times, tiny white dots on prints—blamed on "air bubbles"—actually result from spilled hypo.

Water and its influence on the preparation of solutions

In general, all *developer stock solutions* should be mixed with boiled water only. Boiling drives out most of the free air contained in water, the oxygen content of which would tend to oxidize the developing agent, and precipitates nearly all suspended impurities, besides eliminating a large percentage of the calcium and magnesium salts.

Finegrain developers should be mixed with distilled water that has been boiled shortly. Distilled water is chemically free from impurities but contains much free air which has to be eliminated by boiling.

Fixers and acid hardeners can be made with any water that is pure enough for drinking purposes.

Intensifiers are extremely sensitive to chemical impurities and should be made only with distilled water.

Reducers should preferably be made with boiled water, but ordinary tap water will usually do.

Toners are the most sensitive of all photographic solutions and have to be prepared with chemically pure distilled water, except sulfide and thiosulfate sepia toners which can be made with boiled and filtered water.

Impurities in water may have the following effects: calcium and magnesium may form soluble salts with other chemicals which would dry on emulsions in the form of fine crystals or white scum, showing as spots in the print. Or they may form insoluble salts that settle down at the bottom of the tank; they should be eliminated by filtering the solution, since otherwise, if stirred up, they may settle on emulsions and dry there, causing spots in the final prints. Iron in the form of rust should be eliminated by filtering; there are special water filters available that can be attached directly to the faucet. Iron increases the rate of oxidation of the developer, and causes rust spots on negatives and prints. Sulfur, usually in the form of hydrogen sulfide, forms silver sulfide with the silver of the emulsion and interferes with proper developing and fixing.

Filtering the developer before each use eliminates the danger of getting spotty negatives and prints; it takes considerably less time than it would take to spot and retouch spotty prints from spotty negatives.

Temperature and its importance in preparing solutions

In general, increasing the temperature increases the rate of chemical reaction (we will hear more about this in the discussion of developing, page 129). Consequently, all chemicals dissolve more readily, and in greater amounts, in warm than in cold water. However, certain chemicals are sensitive to heat, which changes their chemical properties to such a degree that they become useless for photographic purposes; see page 81.

For mixing developers, the water can be as hot as 125° F., but should not be hotter; before use, however, such a bath has to cool down to normal temperatures of 68 or 70° F.

When mixing fixers, the hypo may be dissolved in water as hot as it comes out of the tap without any damaging effects. Pouring the hypo crystals into the hot water will almost instantaneously lower its temperature to somewhere around 50° F.

The acid-hardener component of an acid fixing bath should always be dissolved separately from the hypo. Acid hardener is sensitive to excessive heat and decomposes at temperatures above 125° F. Mix hypo and hardener after both have cooled down to normal temperatures of 68 to 70° F., or the bath may turn milky white as a result of the formation of free sulfur.

The percentage of solutions

There are two different ways of indicating the strength of a solution: one gives the degree of concentration in percentages and is used mostly when speaking of solids dissolved in a liquid; the other gives the degree of concentration in the form of a ratio and is used mostly when speaking of a mixture of a solution and water.

A 5 per cent solution of acid sulfuric, for instance (used in making up shortstop baths), means that 100 cc of the solution would contain 5 grams of acid sulfuric, which expressed in graphic form would look like this. . . . . →
To mix a *5 per cent* solution it is accepted practice to proceed as follows: dissolve 5 grams of acid sulfuric in 95 cc of water; however, since the volume of the chemical is smaller than that of water, we get less than 100 cc of solution; consequently, we now have to add some more water until we get a total of 100 cc. This gives us a solution, 100 cc of which contain exactly 5 grams of acid sulfuric.

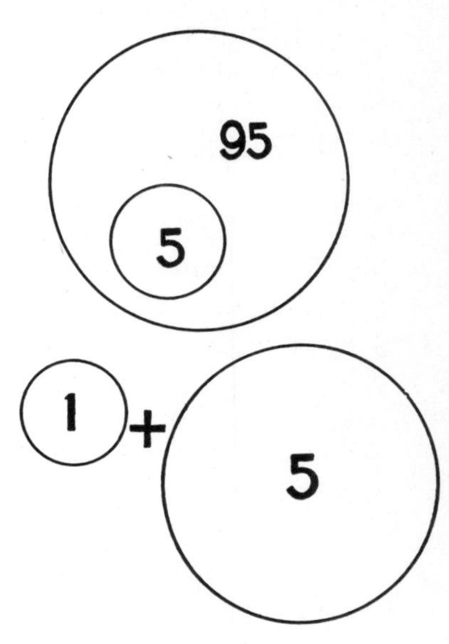

A solution of 1:5—of a developer, for instance—means that one part of concentrated developer stock solution should be mixed (diluted) with five parts of water, which expressed in graphic form looks like this. . . . . →
The total amount of this solution 1:5 consists now of six equal parts (5 parts water, 1 part concentrate); in order to convert this ratio into per cent, we have to divide 100 by 6 and get as the result 16.7 per cent; in other words, a solution of 1:5 is the same as a 16.7 per cent solution.

Often it will be found necessary to dilute a stock solution of high concentration in order to get a working solution of lower percentage. The easiest way to do this is by means of the crisscross method as illustrated on the opposite page: Write the percentage strength of the solution that has to be diluted at *A*; write the percentage strength of the solution you want to dilute with at *B* (if you want to dilute with water, your percentage naturally will be zero); write the percentage strength you want to get at *W*. Then, subtract *W* from *A* and write the result at *Y*; subtract *B* from *W* and write the result at *X*. Finally, take *X* parts of *A* and mix them with *Y* parts of *B*, and you will get the desired solution of *W* per cent strength.

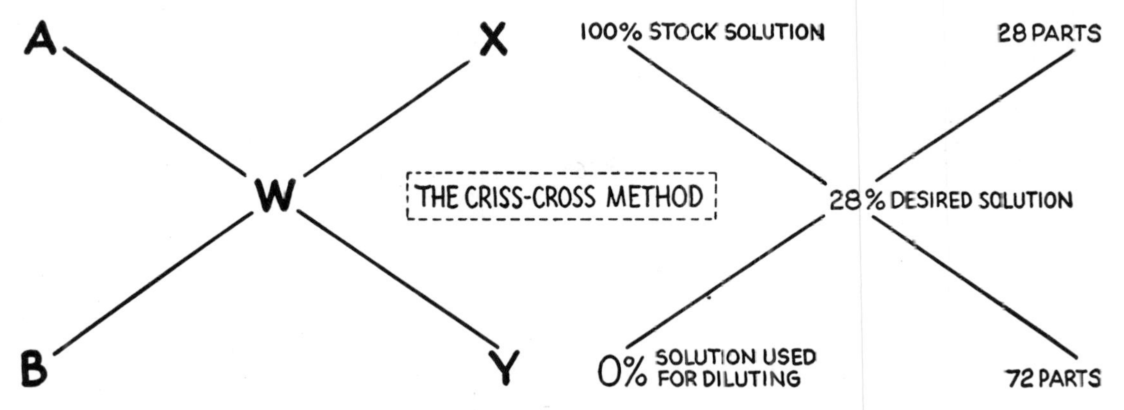

The crisscross method for diluting stock solutions. Left: See explanation on opposite page. Right: As an example, 100 per cent glacial acetic acid stock solution is diluted to 28 per cent acetic acid working solution. Write the percentage of the stock solution (100 per cent) in upper left corner; write the percentage of the solution you want to dilute with in lower left corner (in this case 0 per cent, since you dilute with water which contains 0 per cent acetic acid); write the percentage of the desired working solution in the center of the cross (28 per cent); subtract center from upper left and write the result (72) in the lower right corner; subtract lower left from center and write the result (28) in upper right corner; finally, take upper right parts (28) of upper left (100 per cent glacial acetic acid) and mix with lower right parts (72) of lower left (water), and you will get the desired solution of center per cent (28 per cent).

The keeping properties of solutions

For getting results of highest quality, uniformity, and greatest permanency when processing photographic material, it is important that solutions are not exhausted beyond a certain point. When developing negatives and prints, the increasing degree of exhaustion of the developer manifests itself in increasing sluggishness with regard to its activity, producing increasingly softer gradations in negatives (to the point of useless flatness) and discoloration of tone toward brown in prints (to the point of sickly muddiness). Fixers that are exhausted are even more dangerous because they will still clear a negative emulsion or make a print insensitive to light, even if it takes a longer than normal time, but such negatives and prints are not permanent and will in time discolor and fade.

To prevent premature exhaustion of developers from oxidation it is important that solutions after use either be poured back into the bottle (which always should be filled up to the neck; see page 81 for methods), or that developer in deep tanks be protected from the air by a thin sheet of Kodaloid floating on its surface in the form of a shallow boat and a tank cover. Re-use of small amounts of diluted paper developer (working solution) is definitely not advisable.

To get a rough idea of how long certain solutions will last, see examples given on the following page; they represent averages based on average working conditions and may not always fit your case.

Kodak Developers	Will Keep Unused in:				Capacity per Gallon in:	
	Tray	Gallon Tank	Stoppered Bottle		Tray	Deep Tank
			Full	Half Full		
For Negatives						
DK-20	24 hrs.	1 mo.	6 mo.	2 mo.	20 rolls No. 120	30 rolls No. 120
DK-60a	24 hrs.	3 wks.	6 mo.	2 mo.	20 rolls No. 120	40 rolls No. 120
D-76	24 hrs.	1 mo.	6 mo.	2 mo.	20 sheets 8x10	30 sheets 8x10
For Prints					Diluted 1:2	
D-72	24 hrs.	2 wks.	2 mo.	3 wks.	100 sheets 8x10	

One roll of film No. 120 is equivalent (in terms of emulsion surface for determination of useful life of developer and fixer solutions) to one roll of 35 mm film (36 exposures), or one sheet of 8x10 film, or four sheets of 4x5 film, or six sheets of 3¼x4¼ film.

Use of replenisher prolongs useful life of developers in deep tanks considerably. See page 130, or manufacturers' instructions.

If only a few films, or individual films, are developed at a time and solutions have to stand unused for some time in between developments, only a smaller quantity of film than recommended above can be developed with good results.

If developers are used only once for development of a maximum number of films at one time, a slightly greater quantity of film or paper can be developed than indicated in table above.

In one gallon of acid fixer about 100 rolls of No. 120 (or equivalent quantity of other film), or 100 prints 8x10 (or equivalent number of prints of other sizes) should be fixed.

How to clean trays, tanks, and hands

Absolute cleanliness is one of the first conditions for successful work with chemicals and is the only way to prevent contamination of solutions. But in spite of all efforts at cleanliness, most developers leave stains on trays and tanks after a time, which, if not removed periodically, will flake off, settle on the emulsions, and cause spots. The best remedy for removal of such residues is the following solution, which, however, should not be used on non-acidproof enamel trays:

Potassium Bichromate . . . . 3 oz.
Water . . . . 32 oz.
Sulfuric Acid . . . . 5 oz.

Dissolve the potassium bichromate in the water and slowly (!) add the sulfuric acid to the solution. Reversing the process would cause a minor explosion.

The best way to remove developer stains from hands and fingernails is as follows: soak the hands in a 20 per cent solution of potassium permanganate; this will leave a brownish stain which will disappear when you rinse your hands in 5 per cent solution of sodium bisulfate. Sometimes, milder stains will disappear when rubbed with a slice of lemon.

Never leave your equipment dirty overnight. . . . Make it a habit to clean up right after you are through, using brush and cleanser and plenty of water.

Weights and measures

Unfortunately, the cumbersome and antiquated system of measuring in fluid ounces, drams, grains, pounds, etc., is still more widely used in this country when publishing photographic formulas than the simple and efficient metric system (gram, cubic centimeter, liter), the advantages of which are so obviously evident that it will be used exclusively in this book when specific formulas for different solutions are given. However, sooner or later it will become necessary to transform weights indicated in avoirdupois into the metric form, or vice versa. This can most easily be done by using the following table:

CONVERSION TABLE FOR UNITS OF VOLUME AND WEIGHT*

To Convert From:	Multiply By								
	To Fl. Oz.	To Pint	To Quart	To Gallon	To C. C. or G.	To Ltr. or Kg.	To Grain	To Oz. Av.	To Lb. Av.
Fluid Ounce	1.00000	.062500	.031250	.007813	29.5736	.029573	......	......	......
Pint	16.0000	1.00000	.500000	.125000	473.177	.473177	......	......	......
Quart	32.0000	2.00000	1.00000	.250000	946.354	.946354	......	......	......
Gallon	128.000	8.00000	4.00000	1.00000	3785.42	3.78542	......	......	......
Cubic Centimeter or Gram	.033814	.002113	.001057	$.0_{3}2642$	1.00000	.001000	15.4323	.035274	.002205
Liter or Kilogram	33.8140	2.11337	1.05669	.264172	1000.00	1.00000	15432.3	35.2739	2.20462
Grain	......	......	......	......	.064799	$.0_{4}6479$	1.00000	.002285	$.0_{3}1428$
Ounce Avoirdupois	......	......	......	......	28.3495	.028350	437.500	1.00000	.062500
Pound Avoirdupois	......	......	......	......	453.593	.453593	7000.00	16.0000	1.00000

*Courtesy of E. I. Dupont de Nemours & Co.

Note: The small subnumeral following a zero indicates that the zero is to be taken that number of times; thus, $.0_{3}1428$ is equivalent to .0001428.

For example: To convert 2½ av. oz. to grams, multiply 2½ by the factor 28.3495 or 70.87 grams.

In addition, the following factors will often come in handy when conversions have to be made (courtesy of Mallinckrodt Chemical Works, reprinted from "The Chemistry of Photography"):

Avoirdupois to metric:

grains per 64 oz. × 0.0342 = grams per liter
ounces per 64 oz. × 14.962 = grams per liter
pounds per 64 oz. × 239.40 = grams per liter

Metric to avoirdupois:

grams per liter × 29.22 = grains per 64 oz.
grams per liter × 0.0668 = ounces per 64 oz.
grams per liter × 0.00417 = pounds per 64 oz.

For conversion of centigrade to Fahrenheit (and vice versa), use the following table:

Centigrade:	17	18	19	20	21	22	23	24	25	26
Fahrenheit:	62.6	64.4	66.2	68	69.8	71.6	73.4	75.2	77	78.8

To convert Fahrenheit into centigrade: subtract 32, multiply by 5, divide result by 9.
To convert centigrade into Fahrenheit: multiply by 9, divide by 5, add 32 to the result.

The author's darkroom—New York's lightest—is an ordinary workroom.

CHAPTER 4

THE DARKROOM

AS A CONSOLATION to all amateurs who cannot afford the luxury of a permanent darkroom with running water and built-in sinks, I want to confess that during the thirty years I have indulged in photography, first as an amateur and later as a professional, I have worked only occasionally in "real" darkrooms, but have had to do the majority of my work in ordinary rooms, the windows of which I had to make light-tight every time I wanted to do some developing or printing. And still, I have managed to do my regular work for *Life* and *Fortune* magazines and have illustrated and published several books on photography. So I hope you will believe me when I say here that exactly the same kind of work can be done in an ordinary room that can be darkened, as in a "permanent" darkroom which is specially fitted with running water, built-in sinks, and similar conveniences. Admittedly, these can simplify operations considerably, but lack of them certainly shouldn't be detrimental to your work and should never be used as an excuse for failure.

Transformation into a darkroom takes less than two minutes: Masonite panels on wooden frames fit tightly into the windows, trays replace the typewriter, running water is available in the near-by bathroom.

Any workable darkroom has to fulfill three imperative demands:

1. *It has to be light-tight;* otherwise sensitized material will be fogged and spoiled.
2. *It has to possess an outlet for electric current* for the operation of safelight, printer, and enlarger.
3. *Its temperature should be constant between 68 and 75° F.;* otherwise temperatures of solutions have to be raised or lowered artificially which not only is a nuisance, but is rather difficult, too.

In summer, some kind of a ventilating system will help considerably to keep temperatures from rising too high.

Other agreeable, but not strictly necessary, features are:

4. *Running water and built-in sinks;* otherwise negatives and prints have to be rinsed in the bathtub. Several layers of newspaper underneath the trays will effectively absorb occasionally spilt solution. But a careful worker hardly ever spills a drop, mainly because he doesn't fill his trays so high that he spills solution while carrying them to and from the nearest faucet and sink.
5. *Light-colored walls.* As long as our safelight is really "safe" (tested, see page 92), it can and should be really bright, and the lighter colored the walls are, the better they will reflect the light, improving the efficiency of the darkroom illumination and facilitating operations. Nobody can do accurate and critical work unless he can see what he is doing.
6. Anyone who needs a waterproof floor in his darkroom must be such a sloppy worker that he will never make a good photographer.

If you are fortunate enough to have the run of a whole house, finding a place that can be devoted exclusively to photographic purposes should not be difficult; otherwise, makeshifts will have to do, which may mean a little more work for you, but never has to mean inferior results. Arranged according to their merits, here are a few suggestions for permanent and improvised darkrooms:

The basement of a private house. An unused corner can nearly always be found. Advantages: fairly even temperature in summer and winter, electricity and running water usually near, privacy and seclusion, permanent setup possible, as a rule.

The attic of a private house. Here, too, an unused corner should not be too difficult to find. Disadvantages compared to basement: likely to be too hot in summer and too cold in winter, often remote from running water and electricity, in which case an electric cable would have to be drawn from the nearest line. Advantage: the privacy of a room exclusively and permanently devoted to photography.

As a tenant, unless real darkrooms are provided by the landlord as in the case of a very few ultramodern apartment houses in big cities, the choice will usually be among the following possibilities:

A big closet, usually found only in older types of apartments. Its greatest disadvantage is lack of air; otherwise it isn't bad. Maybe the landlord will give permission to install a ventilator (with light-trap) into the wall above the door. Advantages: even temperature the year round, permanent setup possible.

The bathroom. Its advantages are: running water, electricity, light-colored walls. All you have to do is to provide cover for the window (a Masonite panel on a wooden frame) and to build a wooden grill which put across the bathtub will provide you with a working table. If space conditions permit, a drop-leaf table that folds flat against the wall when not in use is even better. Disadvantages, and rather serious ones, are: permanent setup impossible; members of your family may want to use the bathroom when you like it least; steam and moisture spoil equipment, chemicals, and sensitized material, which should never be kept in the bathroom longer than necessary and will have to be stored elsewhere.

An ordinary room, the windows of which have to be covered every time you start to work. The simplest way is to install light-tight roller curtains of heavy black felt of the kind used in projection rooms in schools and lecture halls. Cheaper, but less convenient, and bulky when not in use, are solid blinds made of Masonite on wooden frames that fit tightly into the window casings.

The efficiency of any darkroom—especially a small one—depends to a very high degree on rational organization, and the first step in furnishing the place should be the creation of a "dry zone" and a "wet zone." Usually the left-hand side would be "dry" and the right-hand side "wet." Ranging from left to right, this would be a good layout for any darkroom: negatives, paper, printer, enlarger on the "dry" side; developer, shortstop, hypo, water on the "wet" side. This way, the negatives, which are the most valuable and vulnerable objects in the darkroom, are as remote as possible from water and chemical solutions, and the various steps in processing follow each other logically in smooth succession.

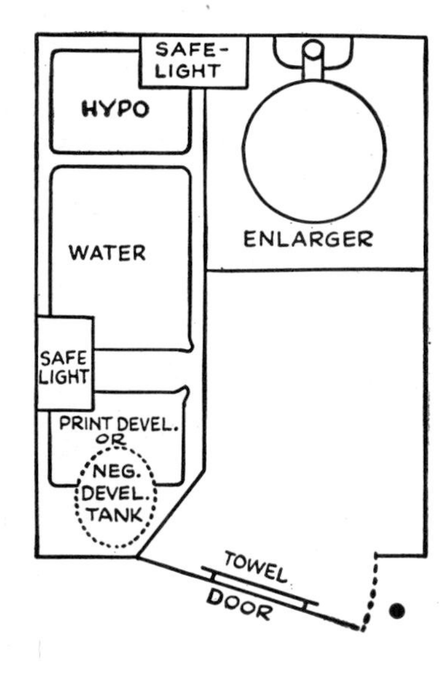

BASIC LAYOUTS
FOR DARKROOMS

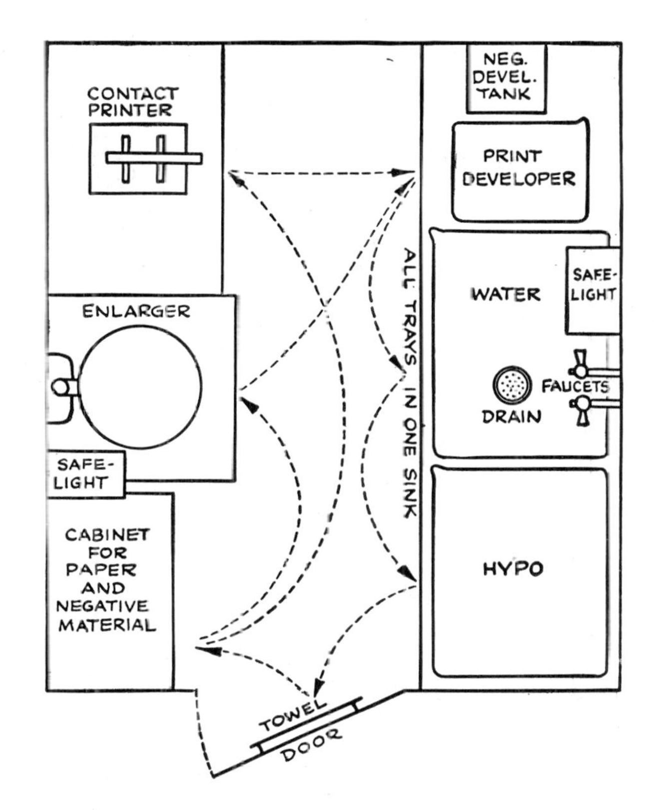

Left: The apartment darkroom in a 3x4-foot closet. Negatives and papers are kept underneath the enlarger (in drawers or small cabinet), together with the contact printer (or printing frame) which has to be used on the enlarger baseboard (enlarger head raised all the way up). Chemicals and bottles are stored underneath developing table.

Wet zone separated from dry zone by a 3-inch-high partition.

Space restrictions permit use of only three trays, for developer, water, and hypo.

In my opinion a shortstop bath is unnecessary if acid fixer is used (which will stop development immediately the moment the paper hits the fixer); in the *Life* darkrooms, for instance, no separate shortstop bath is ever used.

Two safelights: one to the left of the enlarger, the other one above the developer tray. Negatives and prints have to be washed in the bathtub.

Right: The homeowner's permanent darkroom in basement or attic. Clear separation of dry and wet operations. All trays should stand in one common sink with drain, preventing spilled solutions from running down to the floor and contaminating the darkroom with chemicals after drying. Exhausted solutions are simply poured out of their trays into the sink and down the drain.

The towel should hang on the inside of the door, handy after negatives or prints have been deposited in the water.

Three safelights for highest efficiency: one over-all illumination with indirect safelight from lamp suspended from ceiling in center of darkroom (directed against the white painted ceiling); one safelight near enlarger, connected by two-way foot switch with light inside enlarger so that safelight goes out the moment enlarger light goes on; one safelight above developer tray.

White light above water tray; see page 93 *top*.

Shelves for bottles and chemicals above developing sink.

Ventilation built into wall above the door, fan with light-trap.

Variations of these two basic layouts can easily be made to fit any imaginable situation.

DARKROOM EQUIPMENT

Depending on how much money he intends to spend, a photographer can set up a workable darkroom with the help of comparatively few basic pieces of equipment, or he can fill it with an almost limitless number of accessories, gadgets, etc., without, however, any guarantee that they will broaden the scope or improve the quality of his work. In the following survey, only items actually necessary for successful operation of a darkroom have been mentioned; beyond this, it is up to the individual photographer to decide how much further he may want to go, and what else he may want to acquire.

General equipment

Darkroom illumination. Depending on the type of negative material being used, three to four different colors of light are necessary: white for over-all room illumination when cleaning up or mixing solutions, etc., and above the water tray (see later recommendations); dark red (ruby) for processing orthochromatic negative material, or dark green for processing panchromatic emulsions; yellow-green for printing and enlarging.

Only safelights with color filters should be used (Eastman Kodak, Ansco); colored incandescent bulbs usually are far from "safe" and are likely to fog sensitized material. To test a safelight for "safety," take a piece of the sensitized material for the processing of which the safelight is to be used; place a few coins on it; expose it to the safelight for about the length of time it would be exposed during actual processing; develop it in perfect darkness for the regular length of time, and examine it after fixation. It should be perfectly clear (if negative is used) or white (if paper is used). A grayish tone, even if it is ever so slight, with clear or white circles where the coins had been, indicates that the safelight wasn't really "safe," and under actual conditions would have fogged the film or paper. If the gray tone was only very light, repeat the test with the safelight farther away from the sensitized material. If it still produces fog, it has to be discarded; otherwise, use it at the thus-determined "safe" distance.

Negative processing should be done as much as possible in complete darkness according to the "time-and-temperature method" (see page 141) since our modern, extremely sensitive emulsions are too easily fogged during visual inspection. But for successful printing it is absolutely essential to see as well as possible. Most efficient visibility will be achieved as follows: have one large safelight in the center of the darkroom suspended from the ceiling, its light turned upward and illuminating indirectly (reflected from the white ceiling) the whole darkroom

Have another safelight next to the enlarger, coupled with the lamp inside the enlarger via a two-way footswitch in such a way that the safelight is on for adjusting the paper on the easel, but goes off the moment you step on the footswitch for focusing or exposing the print. This makes critically sharp focusing, correct calculation of exposure time, and proper dodging (see page 216) much easier than if the safelight were on all the time and its light weakening the visual image projected onto the easel. A third safelight should be suspended directly above the developer tray, its light directed downward onto the print so progress of development can be followed closely. Finally, a white light (with a 15-watt bulb) should be suspended above the fixer or water tray, its light directed downward and shaded carefully (by means of a deep and narrow reflector) to prevent it from spilling beyond the fixing bath and fogging developing prints. It should be operated by means of a footswitch and should normally be out. After a print has been in the fixer for about ten seconds, you may safely turn on this white light by stepping on the switch and may examine the print at leisure. Judging the correct degree of lightness or darkness of a print is almost impossible in yellow light, which always tends to make a print appear lighter than it actually is; if it looks just right in yellow-green light, you can be pretty sure that it will look too dark in daylight after it has been dried.

Ventilation and temperature control. In winter, an electric heater is the simplest means of warming a darkroom that is too cold. In summer a simple ventilating system consisting of a fan built into the darkroom wall and connected with the outside by means of a "light trap" will not only contribute considerably to your personal comfort but will also help you to get better results, and prevent your negative emulsions from melting off their bases.

The ideal temperature in a darkroom is between 68 and 72° F., which is the standard temperature at which all photographic solutions operate best. Solutions that are colder than 68° or warmer than 72° have to be warmed up or cooled down, respectively, before they can safely be used: fill a small vessel with very hot water, or with cracked ice, respectively, and dip it into the solution until the proper temperature is reached. There are special immersion heaters on the market for heating up solutions, but most of them are rather flimsily made and will sooner or later cause trouble; using hot water is so much simpler.

An apron and a towel belong in every darkroom. Certain developers cause indelible stains, and a single drop can often spoil a pair of perfectly good pants—an apron is so much less expensive. The towel should always be at hand because wet fingers leave permanent marks on negatives and sensitized papers. Its relative dampness furnishes a rough guide to the skill of the photographer: an experienced craftsman never wets his fingers voluntarily; instead, he uses film hangers and print tongs for handling negative material and papers.

A thermometer and a clock are as indispensable to a darkroom as a compass to a ship or radar to a night fighter plane. Together with the exposure meter, they are the three essential control installments that every photographer needs—simple to operate, easy to use—and as important as the camera itself for producing technically perfect pictures.

The thermometer (for measuring the temperature of solutions) should be accurate to within one-half degree (for instructions on how to read a thermometer correctly, see page 82). Instruments that have their scales etched directly on the stem are most reliable in the long run; separate scales to which the stem is not firmly anchored are likely to slide up or down in time—even if ever so slightly—and make such thermometers valueless for accurate work.

The clock (for timing the development of negatives) should be of the preset type that rings when the indicated time has elapsed. Excellent timepieces for darkroom use are sold by General Electric and Eastman Kodak Company.

A large graduate and stirring rod for measuring a definite quantity of developer stock solution and diluting and mixing it with water in the prescribed proportions. Glass graduates are preferable to enameled or porcelain ones which, because of their opacity, are more difficult to "read" accurately (see page 82).

Equipment for negative development

Film developing tanks, different in type for roll film, sheet film, and filmpack. Some rollfilm tanks can be loaded with film in daylight, eliminating the necessity for a darkroom, since printing and enlarging can be done in any ordinary room after dark (photographic paper isn't sensitive enough to be fogged by the rays from street lights and passing cars that inevitably will penetrate the drawn curtains). Before loading with film, tanks or sheet-film holders have to be absolutely dry, or the film will stick. This can be especially disastrous when loading roll film onto a reel and can ruin a whole film. Filmpack and rollfilm tanks and reels of stainless steel are preferable to those of bakelite which break easily when dropped or knocked about. Sheet-film hangers made of plastic are better left alone. . . . Some rollfilm developing tanks have adjustable reels that will accommodate several different widths of film—something for the man with cameras of different sizes.

Negative developer, see pages 135-139.

Hardening fixer solution, see page 139.

A viscose sponge. After washing, every negative has to be wiped off carefully on both sides before it is ready for drying, for thorough elimination of water drops and foreign matter which otherwise would dry on the emulsion and cause spots in the print.

Film clips of stainless steel, to hang up processed films to dry. Two clips are needed for each roll of film, one at the top and the other to weight the bottom of the strip so as to prevent the end from curling up and sticking to the film, scratching the emulsion with its sharp corners. For sheet film and filmpack, hangers of stainless steel consisting of clips attached to a rod are more practical than individual clips, permitting drying of 12 sheets of film on each hanger.

Equipment for printing and enlarging

A printing frame or a contact printer for making contact prints. The best way to make contacts for record purposes from No. 120 roll film is to cut the film into three strips of four frames each 2¼x2¼, or four strips of two frames each 2¼x3¼, and to print them side by side on an 8x10 sheet of paper; for this, an 8x10 printing frame is needed. Besides 8x10, it permits printing any smaller-size negative, or four 4x5 negatives together.

A tray 8x10 or larger for the developer. Smaller trays are impractical, even if smaller prints have to be developed. The best material for all trays is stainless steel, which outlasts any other material and in the long run is cheaper than enamel, which chips easily the moment a tray is knocked around a little bit, preparing the way for corrosion and premature discard.

Two deep trays 11x14 inches or larger for fixing bath and water. Here, too, stainless steel is unsurpassed as material. If acid fixer is used, a special shortstop bath becomes unnecessary since the acid content of the fixer interrupts development instantaneously.

Two print tongs for transferring prints from one tray to another. Handling developing prints with fingers usually leaves brown spots and stains on the paper. Print tongs made of stainless steel or of bakelite are easier to keep clean than wooden ones. Cover the tips of steel tongs with rubber tubing to prevent scratching. Since fixer acts like poison on most developers, never dip your fixer tong into the developer. Mark fixer and developer tongs differently to prevent mix-ups.

Paper developer, see page 155.

Acid fixing bath, see page 139.

Electric print dryer for perfect rapid drying and ferrotyping of prints. Different sizes available, but sizes too small to take a print 11x14 inches are not practical. The best models are "double-sided," permitting drying two large prints simultaneously by making use of top and bottom of the dryer. Make sure thermostatic heat control for prevention of overheating is provided.

A squeegee or a print roller for forcing prints into firm contact with the ferrotype tins.

The enlarger. An enlarger is nothing but a camera in reverse. The negative is projected by the lens onto sensitized paper to form a positive image, whereas in a camera an object is projected by the lens onto the film to form a negative. Like any ordinary camera, an enlarger has a lens that has to be focused in order to give a sharp image on the sensitized paper, and a diaphragm that can be stopped down, if this image is too bright, to permit reasonable exposure times, while the scale of the image (the size of the print) is directly proportional to the distance between enlarger lens and paper.

The character of an enlarger depends on its lighting system, of which there are three basically different types:

Condenser and clear-glass lamp (specular enlargers) give sharpest and most brilliant prints with shortest exposure times, but have the disadvantage of emphasizing the film grain and minute scratches on the film in a very disagreeable way, besides increasing the contrasts of the negatives quite considerably. They can be recommended if unusually large enlargements have to be made (photomurals, photoposters, etc.), or exceptionally contrastless negatives have to be printed.

Diffusion enlargers have a lighting system consisting of parabolic reflector and opal diffusion glass between light source and negative. They suppress emulsion grain and accidental abrasion marks in the film to a remarkable degree, but demand comparatively long exposure times and decrease the contrasts of the negative to such an extent that they are unsuitable for enlarging films with subaverage contrasts. They can be recommended for larger-size negatives from 5x7 up.

Semi-condenser enlargers represent a good compromise between both previously mentioned systems, having a lighting system consisting of condenser and milk-glass bulb. They give enlargements with good but not excessive contrasts without unduly emphasizing the film grain or abrasion marks. The majority of commercial enlargers belong in this category, which can be recommended for all negative sizes up to and including 4x5 inches.

Before buying an enlarger, the following points should be considered:

The size. If you have two or more cameras with different negative sizes, you can buy an enlarger that will take them all, provided their sizes don't differ too much; enlarging a 35mm negative with an enlarger made for handling 5x7 film can be done, but is somewhat awkward. . . .

To get the utmost in efficiency when selecting an enlarger that will accommodate different sizes of film make sure that it provides for interchangeable lenses and condensers. Otherwise the sizes of your prints will be all the more restricted, the smaller the negative that has to be enlarged.

Manual focusing versus automatic. Any enlarger has to be focused exactly like a camera before you can get a sharp enlargement. With the majority of enlargers, this focusing has to be done by hand—by racking the lens in or out while checking the sharpness of the image on the easel with the eye. Some of the more expensive enlargers, however, have automatic focusing, and the image on the easel is always sharp, regardless of the position of the enlarger head; lens focusing is coupled mechanically with the vertical movement of the enlarger.

Auto-focus enlargers save time, make composition easier, and are—naturally—considerably more expensive than enlargers with hand-focusing. Sometimes, however, focusing is not quite as accurate as with visually controlled hand-focusing, a fact which gave some low-minded amateurs a pretext to call such enlargers "out of focus."

If the cost of an enlarger doesn't matter to you, auto-focus enlargers are fine. But if you want the greatest value for your money, be conservative and stick to one of the traditional, always reliable enlargers with manual focusing.

Distortion control. Uncontrolled perspective distortion—the apparent converging of verticals in a negative taken with the camera tilted backward—can be corrected while enlarging by projecting the image on an easel that is not horizontal, but more or less tilted; see instructions on page 163. In such a case, however, the enlarger lens has to be stopped down all the way to insure enough sharpness in depth, and yet, sometimes even the smallest stop (with correspondingly enormous exposure times) may not be enough to give all-over sharpness in the print. All this can be avoided if the enlarger permits tilting the negative by means of a tilting negative carrier, or if the enlarger lens can be tilted sideways, in which case the image on an easel tilted in the opposite direction will be sharp all over even with the diaphragm of the enlarger lens wide open.

Enlargers featuring either one of these two devices for correction of perspective distortion are almost indispensable for any kind of really creative photographic work.

The negative carrier. You can take your choice between two types. Glass plates hold the film perfectly flat, but offer four surfaces for dust and dirt to collect on, and sometimes produce "Newton-rings," irregularly shaped, concentric forms in all colors of the rainbow. These can drive a photographer crazy because they are real enough to be projected onto the print and to register there; they are especially disastrous when appearing in the delicate medium grays of enlargements made from miniature negatives.

Glassless negative carriers avoid all these nuisances, but they don't hold the film as flat as is always desirable and may thus give cause to partial unsharpness in the print.

Generally, glassless negative carriers are preferable for the smaller sizes up to 3¼x4¼; beyond that glass plates will more effectively curb the tendencies of larger negatives to buckle, while occasional specks of dust and lint will not be quite as objectionable because such negatives are usually not enlarged as much as the smaller sizes.

The light distribution of some enlargers is not always as even as desirable. Make a test by exposing a sheet of extra-hard paper (No. 4 or No. 5) without a negative in the enlarger. Try to get a medium-light, grayish tone in the print; develop, and check for uniformity of tone. If the center of this test sheet is visibly darker than the edges—showing a "hot spot"—light distribution is uneven and will cause you trouble later.

Diaphragms of enlarger lenses that have special catches for each stop position are much easier to handle in comparatively dark darkrooms than those that have no notches and have to be adjusted visually.

An easel that can be adjusted for different sizes of paper is the best means of holding your paper flat on the enlarger baseboard.

CHAPTER 5

THE FUNCTIONS OF THE CAMERA

EVERY good photograph is a blend of equal parts "Art" and "Technique." This means that artistic conception and composition is neither more nor less important to the final photograph than perfection of technique of execution.

We call a photograph "technically perfect" if it is sharp (or unsharp!) in the right places and if its tone values and contrasts are such that they truly and effectively represent the subject. And, of course, it must be clean, without spots, specks, streaks, smears, etc., of any kind.

A technically perfect photograph starts with a technically perfect negative. And —apart from cleanliness, which should be a matter of course—a technically perfect negative is the result of proper balance among the following factors:

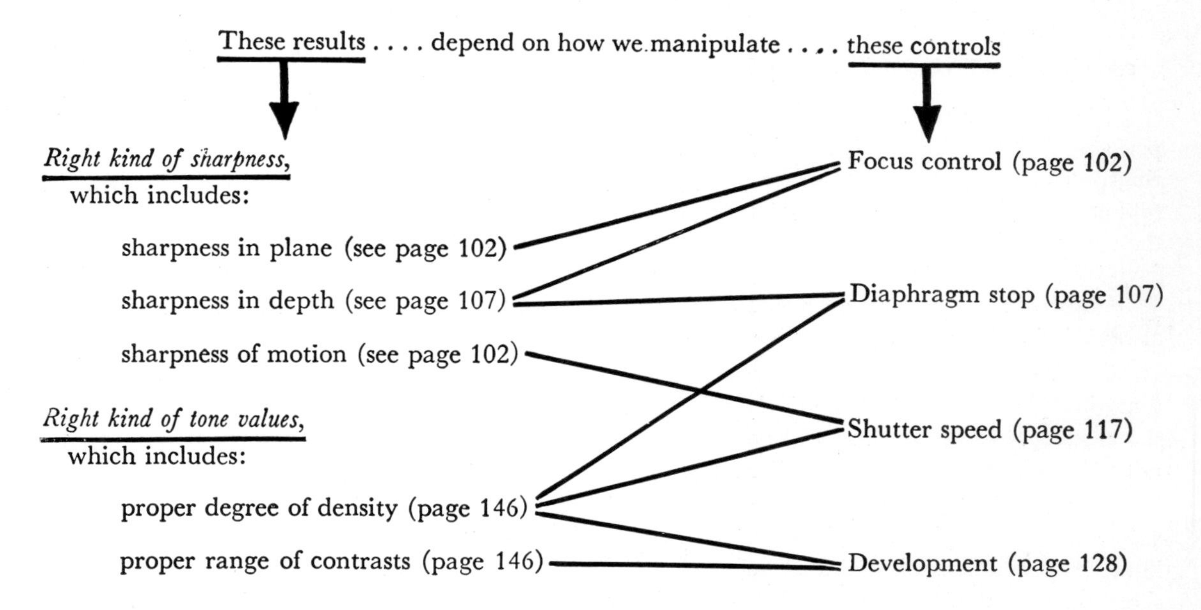

From this diagram it should be clear that each one of the camera controls has a double function: it doesn't merely do one thing, but two. . . . For example, the way in which we focus the lens determines not only (*a*) the position of the plane of sharpness in the picture, but also (*b*) the plane from which sharpness in depth will extend toward and away from the camera. The diaphragm setting affects not only (*a*) extension of sharpness in depth, but also (*b*) the density of the negative. The shutter speed decides (*a*) the degree of sharpness with which moving objects will be rendered and influences (*b*) the density of the negative. Finally, the way we develop a negative will manifest itself (*a*) in the density and (*b*) in the contrast range of the negative.

Further study of the functions of the different camera controls (including development) will reveal that some of these functions have detrimental effects on the ultimate goal, the technically perfect negative. For instance, the more we stop down the diaphragm, the greater the extension of sharpness in depth, but the less the amount of light that reaches the film during exposure and the more likely becomes the danger of underexposure. Or the higher the shutter speed, the sharper the rendering of objects in motion, but the smaller the amount of light that reaches the film during exposure, and again, the greater the possibility of underexposure. And so on.

Consequently, the best way of setting and operating the different camera controls can, in the majority of cases, only be a compromise. For instance, when adverse light conditions prohibit the combined use of small diaphragm opening and high shutter speed, the photographer has to decide which one of the two is more important: degree of extension of sharpness in depth or degree of sharpness with which an object in motion will be rendered. Sometimes, a different mode of attack may solve the problem, for instance, in the following example where selection of a film with greater "speed" permits the use of considerably smaller stops; or following the moving object with the camera like a gun (see page 353) might result in a sharp rendering of the moving object in spite of a relatively long exposure. And so on. Once more, resourcefulness and ingenuity play a decisive part in producing the "perfect photograph," and, by compromising more or less successfully the photographer proves whether he really is a creative and imaginative artist, or merely a practicing photo-technician.

The basic factors for setting the camera controls are *light intensity* and *film speed.* The first thing a photographer should do when considering the best possible "compromise" for setting his camera controls is to adjust his exposure meter according to the speed of the film he intends to use, and to take a meter reading of the brightness of the illumination. Let's imagine, for example, that the speed of his film is 24 Weston (he uses a finegrain film in his minicamera), and that he gets a light reading of 100 Weston. Under these conditions, he has the choice between the following combinations of diaphragm stop and shutter speed, with subsequent effects with regard to manner of focusing, extension of sharpness in depth, and degree of sharpness of objects in motion:

Diaphragm stop numbers	1.5	2	3.5	4.5	5.6	6.3	9	11	16	22	32
Corresponding *shutter speeds*	1/1200	1/800	1/250	1/150	1/100	1/80	1/40	1/25	1/12	1/6	1/3
Focusing	← Increasingly accurate, because of decreasing depth of field.				Increasing sharpness in depth compensates for less accurate focusing. →						
Extension of *sharpness in depth* . . .	very limited — limited — medium — increasingly extensive →										
Rendering of *objects in motion*	very sharp — sharp — slightly blurred — increasingly blurred →										
Conclusions	← The faster the action, or the motion of the object, the faster shutter speeds are necessary for getting sharp pictures.					The greater the depth of the subject, the smaller diaphragm stops must be used for getting the necessary sharpness in depth. →					
	← Exposure times short enough to be handheld.						Tripod must be used. →				

Regardless which one of these different combinations of diaphragm stop and shutter speed he may choose, a photographer will get negatives that are identical in densities and contrasts—provided they were developed under identical conditions—and so far he will get "technically perfect" pictures. So his next question is: which one of these possibilities will give me the best result in this case? The answer is given in the table under "conclusions": the more important it is to "stop" motion and action in a picture, the farther to the left is the answer; and the greater sharpness in depth required, the farther to the right is the answer. The chart opposite shows in graphic form the relationship of all the questions involved.

Summing up, we draw the following conclusions:

Light condition is the first factor. An underexposed negative is valueless, and if the light is poor, depth of field has to be sacrificed by opening up the diaphragm in order to insure sufficient exposure if time exposures are not feasible. Consulting the exposure meter should always be the first step before taking a photograph. Its dial will at one glance show you all the possible combinations of diaphragm opening and shutter speed that can be used under given circumstances. All you have to do is to select the one combination that fits your present requirements best.

Focusing, either on the groundglass or by means of a rangefinder, is so simple that nothing can go wrong, provided it is not forgotten completely in the excitement of shooting. For critical work use magnifier on groundglass. Unless the rangefinder is built right into the camera (Ektra, Leica, Contax, etc.), occasional checkups are necessary since rangefinders are delicate instruments that easily get out of adjustment.

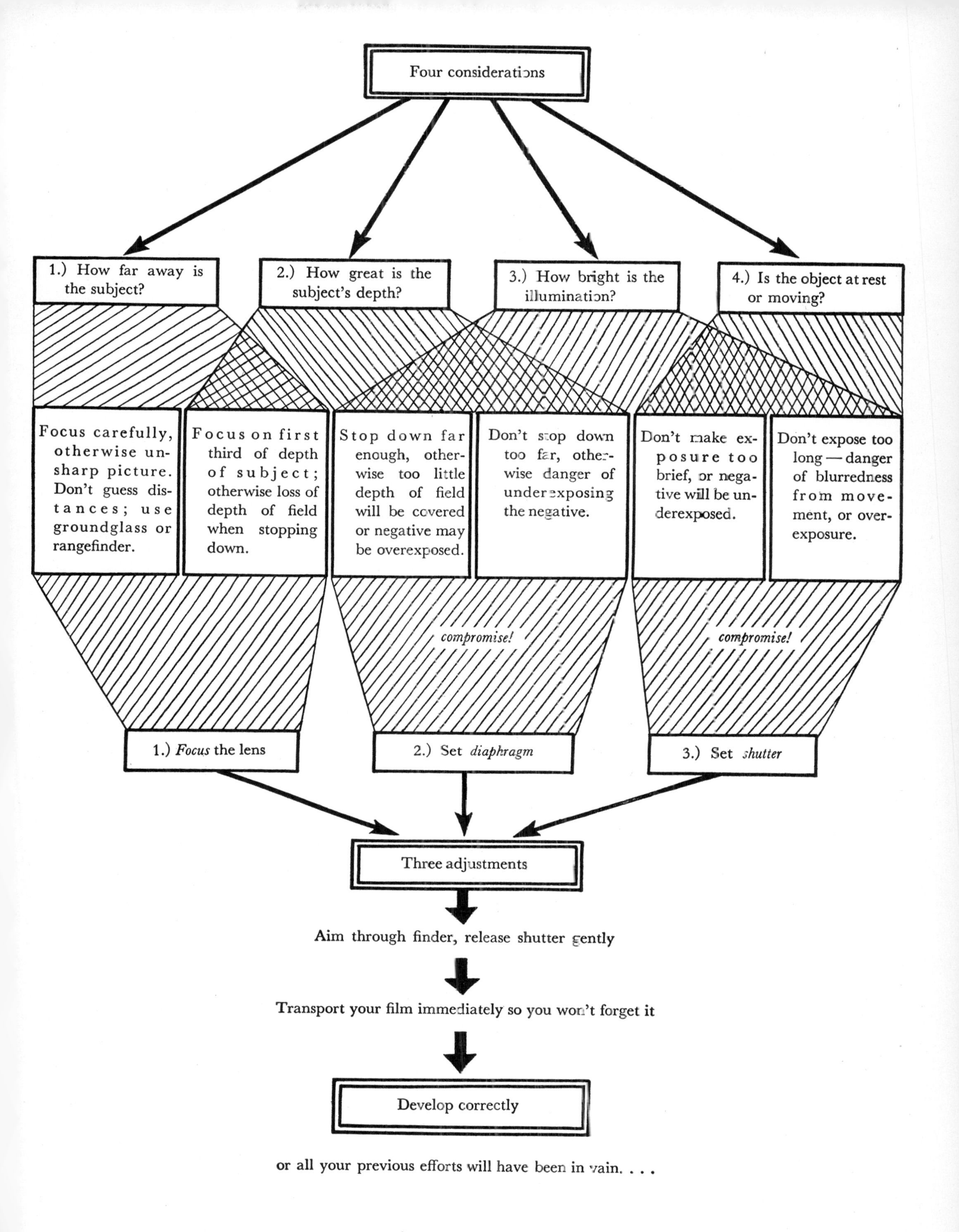

Four considerations
1.) How far away is the subject?
2.) How great is the subject's depth?
3.) How bright is the illumination?
4.) Is the object at rest or moving?
Focus carefully, otherwise unsharp picture. Don't guess distances; use groundglass or rangefinder.
Focus on first third of depth of subject; otherwise loss of depth of field when stopping down.
Stop down far enough, otherwise too little depth of field will be covered or negative may be overexposed.
Don't stop down too far, otherwise danger of underexposing the negative.
Don't make exposure too brief, or negative will be underexposed.
Don't expose too long — danger of blurredness from movement, or overexposure.
compromise!
compromise!
1.) *Focus* the lens
2.) Set *diaphragm*
3.) Set *shutter*
Three adjustments
Aim through finder, release shutter gently
Transport your film immediately so you won't forget it
Develop correctly
or all your previous efforts will have been in vain. . . .

Depth of field is the distance between the nearest and farthest parts of a subject that must be rendered sharp. To insure greatest possible depth of field with the least amount of stopping down, focus on a point in a plane approximately one-third within the depth zone you want to render sharp, and stop your diaphragm down accordingly (consult depth-of-field ring on camera lens, or chart, or check on groundglass). Stopping down the diaphragm increases sharpness in depth about twice as fast beyond the plane on which the lens is focused, than toward the camera.

Movement of object or photographer results in blurred negatives unless "frozen" with a shutter speed fast enough to "stop" the motion. Slowest "safe" exposure time for handheld shots is 1/50 second (1/25 if you are really experienced and know how to "brace" yourself). For longer exposures, tripod or other firm support for camera should be used whenever possible. The faster the movement of an object, the shorter is the exposure time necessary to "stop motion" in the negative. The longest permissible shutter speeds that will still give sharp pictures of various moving objects will be found in the following table. Notice influence of direction of motion on shutter speed, a factor that is helpful whenever poor light conditions or lack of high enough shutter speed make reduction of apparent speed desirable.

The following is a simplified table of shutter speeds necessary for getting sharp pictures of objects in motion. A more complete table will be found on page 353.

Object	Distance From Camera:	Direction of Motion		
		↓ ↑	↙ ↘	⇄
Children playing, pedestrians, slow-moving animals, ocean waves, brooks, wind-swayed trees and fields, etc.	25 ft.	1/25	1/50	1/100
Bicycle riders, trotting horses	25 ft.	1/50	1/100	1/200
Cars and vehicles moving at 20-30 mph.	50 ft.	1/50	1/100	1/200
Cars, trains, speedboats at 40-60 mph.	100 ft.	1/100	1/200	1/400

The technically perfect negative is mostly the result of a happy compromise!

FOCUSING THE LENS

In order to get a sharp picture of the subject to be photographed, the lens of the camera has to be "focused" on the subject, i.e., the distance between lens and film (or groundglass) has to be regulated until the image projected there by the lens appears perfectly sharp—until it is "in focus." This can be done in three different ways: (*a*) by visual observation of the image on the groundglass of the camera (Rolleiflex, Graflex, or view camera); (*b*) by means of a lens-coupled rangefinder, where the moment of coincidence of two identical images of the subject (or the joining of the two halves of a split image) indicates the moment when this object is in focus (Speed Graphic, Ektra, Leica, Contax, etc.); and (*c*) by measuring or guessing the distance between object and camera and using the result for focusing the

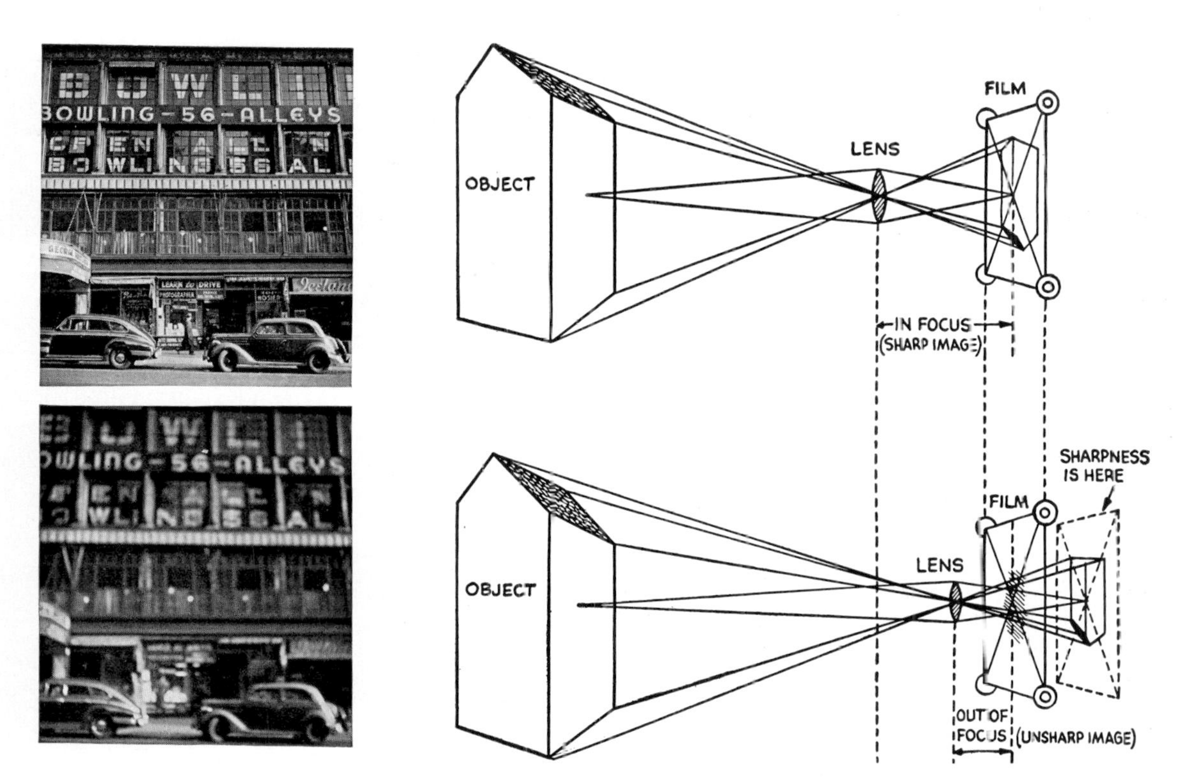

Top: Lens focused correctly, resulting in sharp image. *Bottom:* Lens focused incorrectly; image is "out of focus," i.e., unsharp. The actual position of the sharp image is in this case behind the plane of the film where it doesn't do the least bit of good.

lens by means of the foot scale attached to the camera bed (this is the only way of focusing a simple rollfilm camera that has neither groundglass nor rangefinder; it is a slower and less accurate way of focusing than either (*a*) or (*b*).

Accuracy in focusing is a decisive factor in the production of sharp pictures. Especially when shooting with a high-speed lens at a large diaphragm stop, focusing must be done extremely carefully, since the zone of sharpness in depth is almost incredibly shallow in such a case. On the other hand, focusing may be done rather sketchily when shooting with the diaphragm stopped down relatively far, and the object probably will still be rendered sharp, since in such a case the zone of sharpness in depth is comparatively extensive. We will see later (page 113) how to make use of this phenomenon for establishing a "preparedness system" that is invaluable for taking unexpected action photographs and snapshots.

In spite of the most careful focusing, pictures occasionally turn out unsharp. There are many different reasons for this, but the most common are the three following: (1) camera movement during the exposure; (2) rangefinder out of adjustment, which happens especially frequently with rangefinders not built directly into the camera; (3) filmpack sheets sometimes buckle slightly, causing partial or all-over unsharpness when shooting with comparatively large diaphragm openings.

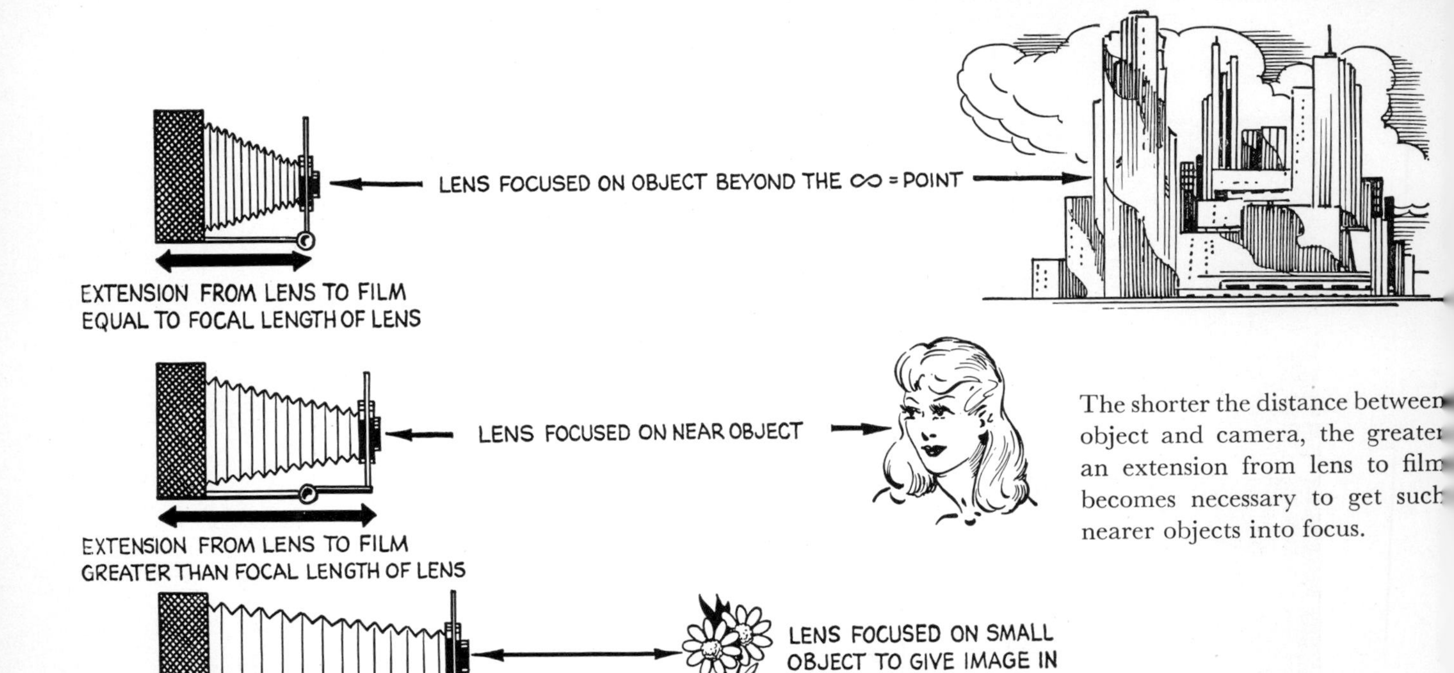

The shorter the distance between object and camera, the greater an extension from lens to film becomes necessary to get such nearer objects into focus.

When focusing on objects at various distances from the camera, we will find that the shorter the distance is between object and lens, the longer must be the extension between lens and groundglass (or film) in order to result in a sharp image, and vice versa. But while we always will have to rack out the lens more, the nearer the object is, the opposite is true only up to a certain point: when focusing on objects beyond a certain distance from the camera, extension between lens and film cannot be farther decreased without causing total unsharpness. The shortest distance between lens and film at which a lens will still give a sharp image is equal to the focal length of the lens (see page 36), and in this position the lens is focused on "infinity," often expressed by the symbol ∞. When focused on ∞, a lens will give sharp images of all objects beyond a certain distance from the camera—a distance which varies with the focal length of the lens and its relative aperture: the shorter the focal length of the lens, and the smaller its relative aperture, the closer to the camera will this ∞-point be, and vice versa. For a lens with a focal length of two inches and a relative aperture of *f* 3.5, for instance, infinity begins at a point approximately 100 feet from the camera, while infinity for a six-inch lens with the same speed of *f* 3.5 would begin at approximately 300 feet from the camera. When focused on infinity, all objects beyond 100 or 300 feet, respectively, would be rendered sharp when photographed with these two lenses, and no refocusing would be necessary to get objects at different distances beyond these ∞-points into focus.

With decreasing distance between object and camera (necessitating racking out the lens), the ratio between the aperture of the lens and the distance from lens to image changes with the result that the effective values of the stop numbers change, too. As long as the difference between focal length of the lens and actual extension from lens to image is only small it can be neglected; otherwise, however, the decrease in effective lens speed resulting from an increase in distance between lens and image when photographing objects close up has to be taken into consideration when calculating the exposure time. For instance, a lens with a focal length of six inches and a relative aperture of two inches would have a "speed" of 6 : 2, or 3 : 1 = *f* 3 when focused on infinity, since then the extension between lens and image actually would be six inches. When focused on an object that is closer to the camera than ∞, however, distance between lens and image would be greater than six inches, while the diameter of the relative aperture naturally would remain unaffected. For example, when taking the picture of a small object in natural size with the six-inch lens, the distance between lens and image would be equal to two focal lengths, and the ratio between actual lens-image extension and relative aperture wouldn't be 6 : 2 any more, but 12 : 2, or 6 : 1 = *f* 6! In other words, by increasing the distance from lens to image twofold we automatically decrease the effective speed of the lens at full opening from *f* 3 to *f* 6—without even touching the diaphragm. Naturally, such a serious loss of speed has to be compensated for by a corresponding increase in exposure time if disastrous underexposure is to be avoided. In this case, we have to expose *four times as long* as the exposure-meter reading tells us, since the effective speed of our lens isn't *f* 3 any more, but *f* 6—in spite of the fact that the diaphragm is still set at *f* 3—and if we consult the dials of the exposure meter we find that *f* 6 needs four times as long an exposure as *f* 3.

Naturally, such a decrease in effective speed resulting from an increase in distance between lens and image happens regardless of the diaphragm stop at which the lens is used. When taking pictures in natural size, for instance, exposure times have *always* to be increased four times regardless of the stop used. Such increases can easily be determined with the Effective Aperture Kodaguide made by Kodak. More detailed information on how to calculate such increases in exposure time will be found on page 116.

Ordinarily, focusing a lens correctly is one of the easiest operations in photography; however, there are four different occasions that are interesting enough to deserve special mention here:

When using infrared-sensitized negative material, focusing presents a problem because infrared light waves are not only invisible, but focus at a different point from visible ones—and a visual check on the sharpness of the image on the groundglass is impossible. Only a very few lenses are specially calibrated for infrared as, for instance, some of the Leica lenses, and the Kodak, Ektra, Medallist, and some other Ektar lenses. If working with an ordinary lens, it is accepted practice to increase the distance between lens and image by one-fourth per cent to two per cent of the focal length of the lens beyond the visual focal plane, depending on various factors like type and focal length of the lens, diaphragm stop, lens-object distance, etc. According to experiments conducted by Wabash, racking out a six-inch Tessar lens one millimeter (1/25 inch) beyond the visible focus gives acceptable sharpness at medium object-lens distances from eight to fifteen feet. To make doubly sure that the infrared image is in focus, such pictures should only be taken with the lens stopped down to at least *f* 8 or more.

Using a dark-red color filter may produce unsharpness with certain not-too-well-color-corrected lenses—especially some old-fashioned lenses with comparatively long focal lengths—if the filter is put on the lens after focusing or a rangefinder is used. In such a case, visual focusing on the groundglass with the filter in place on the lens will usually result in sharp pictures.

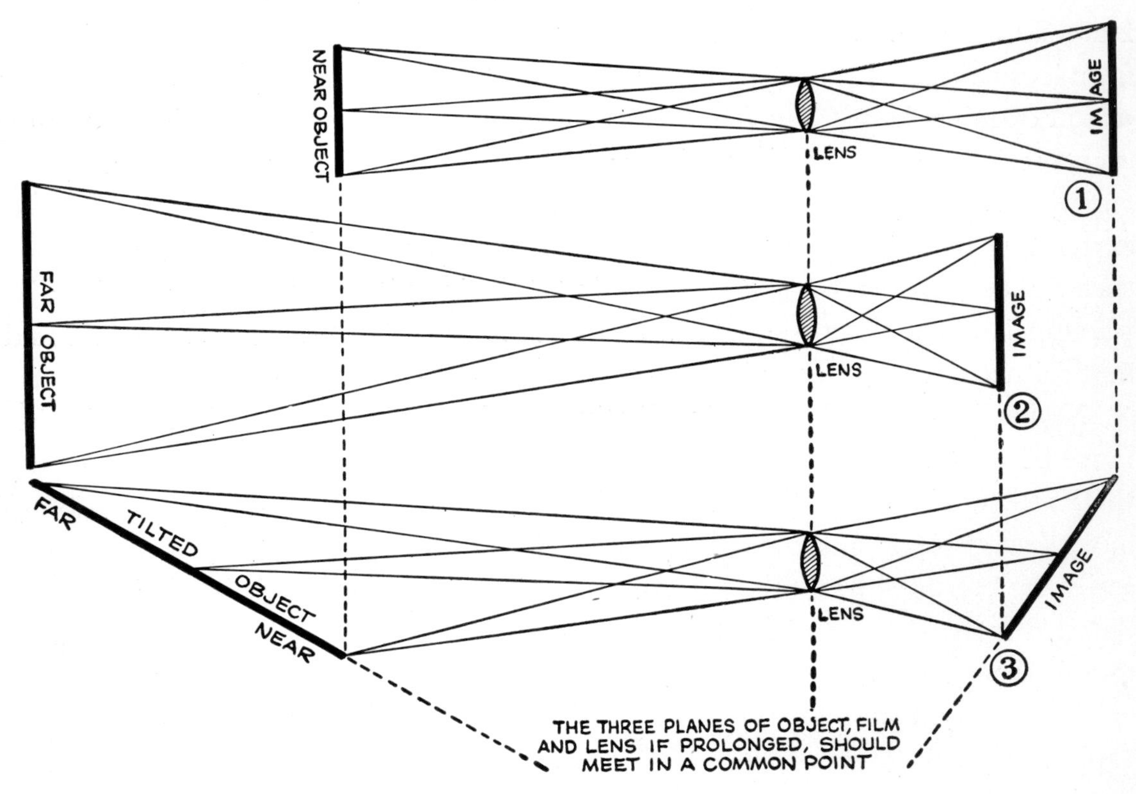

Extension of the zone of sharpness in depth (depth of field) can be increased considerably in oblique angle shots by making use of the swing back of the view-type camera. The sketch above illustrates how to proceed: (1) shows the position of a lens focused on a near object; distance from lens to image is comparatively large; (2) shows the same lens focused on an object farther away; distance from lens to image is much shorter; (3) shows a combination of (1) and (2)—a lens taking a photograph of an object tilted at an angle. Both the near and the far ends of the object are brought into focus simultaneously by tilting the negative accordingly with the help of the back swing of the camera, resulting in an image that in spite of the considerable depth of the object is in perfect focus all over, even with the diaphragm of the lens wide open. Using this method of near-far focusing will result in much shorter exposure times when taking oblique downward or sideways shots than if the necessary sharpness in depth had to be created with the help of small diaphragm stops.

A few high-speed lenses are afflicted with the fault of "focus-difference," i.e., if focused with the diaphragm wide open and then stopped down for taking the picture, they give unsharp negatives. Such lenses have to be focused visually on the groundglass, using the stop with which the picture will be taken, in which case they usually will produce perfectly sharp photographs.

THE FUNCTIONS OF THE DIAPHRAGM

The diaphragm has a double purpose: it determines the extension of sharpness in depth in a photograph, and it plays an important role in regulating the amount of light that passes the lens during the exposure, thus directly influencing the density of the negative. As a rule, these two functions have opposite effects on the picture, since usually it is (*a*) desirable to have the zone of sharpness in depth extend as far as possible in a photograph—which means use of as small a stop as possible—while on the other hand it is (*b*) advantageous to keep exposure times as short as possible to avoid unsharpness resulting from movement of either object or photographer—which demands the use of as large a stop as possible.

Making the best possible compromise between these two contradictory demands will be easier if the photographer is familiar with the "how" and "why" that lie behind the simple operation of turning the diaphragm ring of the lens one way or another.

The diaphragm as regulator of sharpness in depth

If we set a number of objects at different distances from the camera, focus the lens on each in turn and watch the groundglass image while slowly closing the diaphragm, we see something very much like the pictures on the following pages. Such an empirical experiment demonstrates the following important facts:

Extension of sharpness in depth increases proportionally the more we reduce the diaphragm opening, i.e., the smaller a stop with the higher a stop number we use.

The brightness of the groundglass image decreases the more we reduce the diaphragm opening, necessitating proportionally longer exposure times in order to avoid underexposure of the negative.

With a given stop, extension of sharpness in depth is greater if the lens is focused on a far-away object than if the lens is focused on a near-by object; when the lens is focused on near panel No. 1 (pictures, opposite page), stopping down the diaphragm all the way increases sharpness two intervals, bringing No. 3 into focus; but when focused on far-away No. 9, stopping down all the way extends sharpness in depth four intervals, bringing No. 5 into focus.

Stopping down the diaphragm increases the zone of sharpness in depth in both directions from the plane on which the lens is focused—toward and away from the camera. Consequently, focusing on either the near end or the far end of the depth zone that has to be rendered sharp is wasteful, since in such a case extension of sharpness is utilized in only one direction. Sharpness in front of or beyond the zone that has to be rendered sharp is useless. The same diaphragm opening (*f* 22) that in the first ex-

Focusing your camera on a bank of lights, this is what you would see on the groundglass: *Left:* With the diaphragm wide open, the image on the groundglass appears comparatively bright, but its sharpness in depth is limited to the zone on which the lens was focused. *Right:* "Stopping down" darkens the groundglass image and simultaneously increases extension of sharpness in depth in direct proportion with the narrowing of the diaphragm.

1. Lens focused on No. 1. Stopping down the diaphragm pulls No. 3 into focus, extending the zone of sharpness in depth for two intervals away from the camera.

2. Lens focused on No. 9. Stopping down the diaphragm extends zone of sharpness in depth four intervals toward the camera, bringing No. 5 into focus.

3. Lens focused on No. 5—halfway between 1 and 9. Stopping down the diaphragm extends sharpness in depth three intervals toward the camera and all the way back, bringing Nos. 2 and 9 into focus.

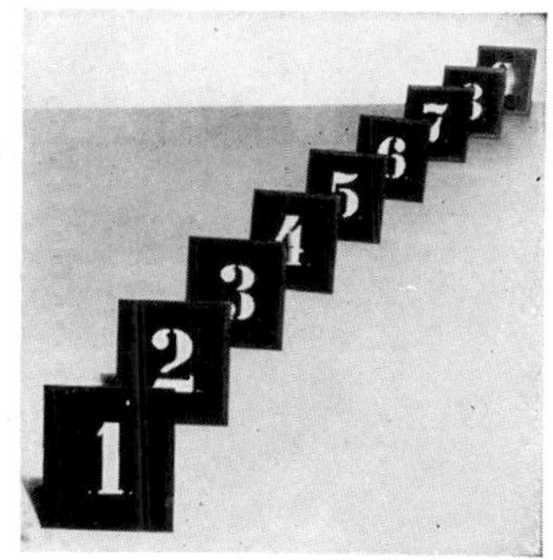

4. Lens focused on No. 4. Stopping down the diaphragm extends zone of sharpness three intervals toward camera and all the way back, bringing Nos. 1 and 9 into focus

ample with the lens focused on panel No. 1 increased sharpness in depth "one way" for two intervals (from 1 to 3), increases sharpness in depth in the last example with the lens focused on panel No. 4 eight intervals (from 1 to 9) because the increase in sharpness in depth was put to use "two ways," both toward and away from the camera.

Stopping down the diaphragm increases the zone of sharpness faster beyond the plane of focus than toward the camera. The only way of bringing all the panels into focus simultaneously is by focusing the lens somewhere near panel No. 4 and stopping the diaphragm down all the way. This increases the zone of sharpness three intervals toward the camera and five intervals away from the camera, counted from the plane on which the lens was focused.

Greatest extension of sharpness in depth with the least stopping down will be produced if the lens is focused on a plane about one-third within the zone of depth that has to be rendered sharp. In such a case, sharpness in depth created by stopping down the lens will be used most economically and completely, extending "two ways" in both directions from the plane on which the lens was focused, toward and away from the camera.

NOTICE: The transition from sharp to unsharp is almost imperceptible, and it is more or less a matter of personal opinion to decide where sharpness ends and unsharpness begins. Obviously, such delicate nuances will be more or less lost in reproduction—the reason why there is little visible difference among the stopped-down components of each picture pair shown here. For this reason it is recommended that the reader repeat these experiments himself and personally study the changes caused by different diaphragm openings in conjunction with different ways of focusing.

The shorter the focal length of a lens, the greater is the extension of the sharply rendered zone in depth with any given stop—equal distances between object and such lenses of different focal lengths provided. This fact explains the superior depth of field observed in minicamera photographs compared to pictures taken with larger-size cameras.

Too small a diaphragm opening will result in loss of definition. While the zone of sharpness in depth increases proportionally the more the diaphragm is stopped down, the optimum in definition is reached with most lenses somewhere around *f* 8 or *f* 11. Stopping down beyond this will always increase the zone of sharpness in depth but will eventually have a deteriorating influence on the definition of the picture. This should be kept in mind especially when taking closeups of small objects in more than natural size. In such cases the abnormally long lens-image distance can easily decrease the effective value of the lens stop beyond the point where deterioration of definition begins; see pages 39 and 116.

Creation of sharpness in depth

To illustrate why stopping down the diaphragm increases the extension of sharpness in depth (the "depth of field"), let's imagine two luminous points at different distances from the camera (see following sketches). Naturally, if we focus the lens on point *A*, point *B* is out of focus and rendered unsharp in the negative, appearing no longer as a sharp point, but unsharp in the form of a disk—scientifically called the "circle of confusion."

Actually even the sharp parts in a photograph are composed of innumerable tiny circles of confusion, so small that they appear to the eye as points—similar to the dots that make up a half-tone reproduction—while the unsharp parts are composed of overlapping larger circles of confusion—the greater their diameter, the more pronounced is the unsharpness in the photograph. Obviously, to increase sharpness, we must reduce the diameters of these larger circles of confusion, which we can do by stopping down the diaphragm with the effect illustrated opposite:

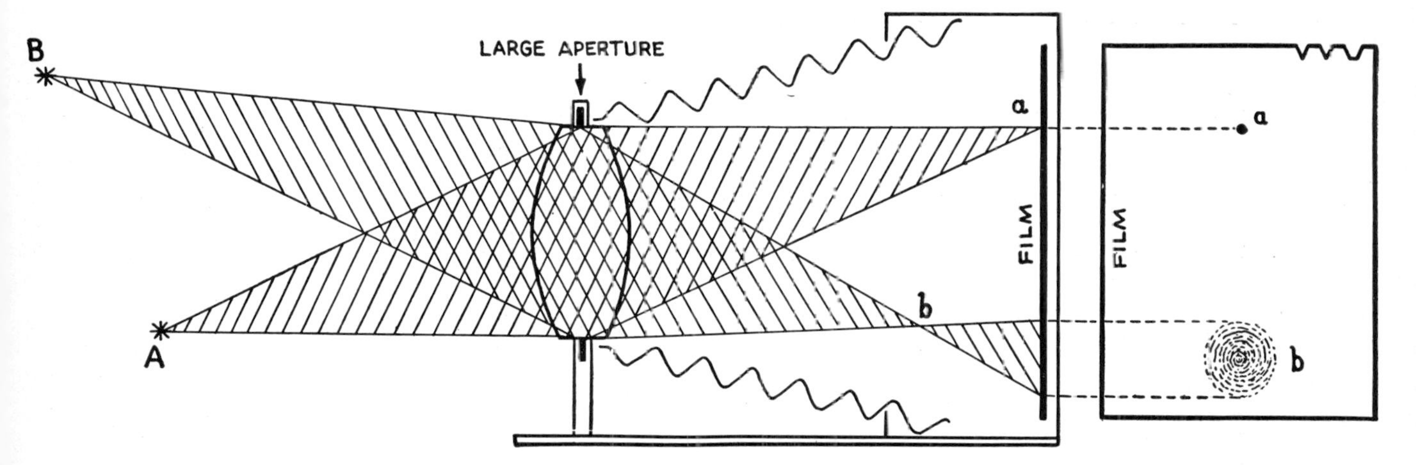

Lens focused on point *A* gives point-sharp image on film at *a*, while image of point *B* would be created in space at *b* and projected on the film in form of an unsharp circle—the "circle of confusion"—shown in this sketch in the head-on view of the negative to the right of the camera.

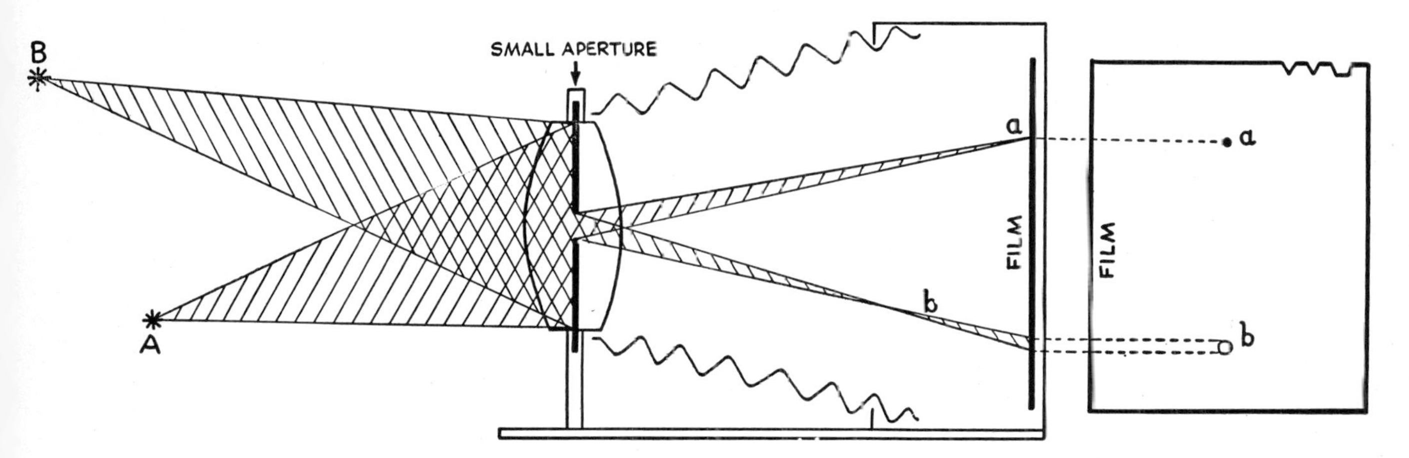

Stopping down the diaphragm reduces the angle of the cones of light that pass the lens, thus directly reducing the diameter of the circle of confusion formed by the out-of-focus point *B* with the result that this point now appears practically sharp—extension of sharpness in depth has been increased.

Definition of "sharpness" in a photograph

We know now that sharpness in a negative depends on the diameter of the circles of confusion that compose the picture. If these circles are so small that they appear to the eye as points, the negative appears sharp; however, such sharpness is always only relative and may dissolve into unsharpness the moment we enlarge the negative—and with it the circles of confusion. Consequently, the necessity for sharpness differs with negatives of different sizes and demands are more rigid for miniature-camera negatives which must stand considerable enlarging than for large-size negatives which are usually enlarged proportionally less. Generally, depth-of-field scales and tables are calculated on the basis that, in negatives from 2¼x2¼ inches on up, a circle of confusion with a diameter of 1/1,000 of the focal length of the standard lens for the particular film size is still permissible, while for smaller-size negatives diameters of 1/1,500 of the focal length of the standard lens are deemed maximum. In the case of 35 mm miniature negatives this corresponds to a circle of confusion with a diameter of 1/30 mm (1/750 inch).

Difference between "depth of field" and "depth of focus"

Two of the most constantly confused terms in photography are "depth of field" and "depth of focus." Depth of field is the distance between the nearest and the farthest point of the depth zone that is rendered sharp in a photograph, while depth of focus, which is of little practical use, designates the distance which the groundglass can be moved forward or backward without decreasing the sharpness of the image beyond a certain degree, which depends upon the largest permissible diameter of the circles of confusion; see illustration below:

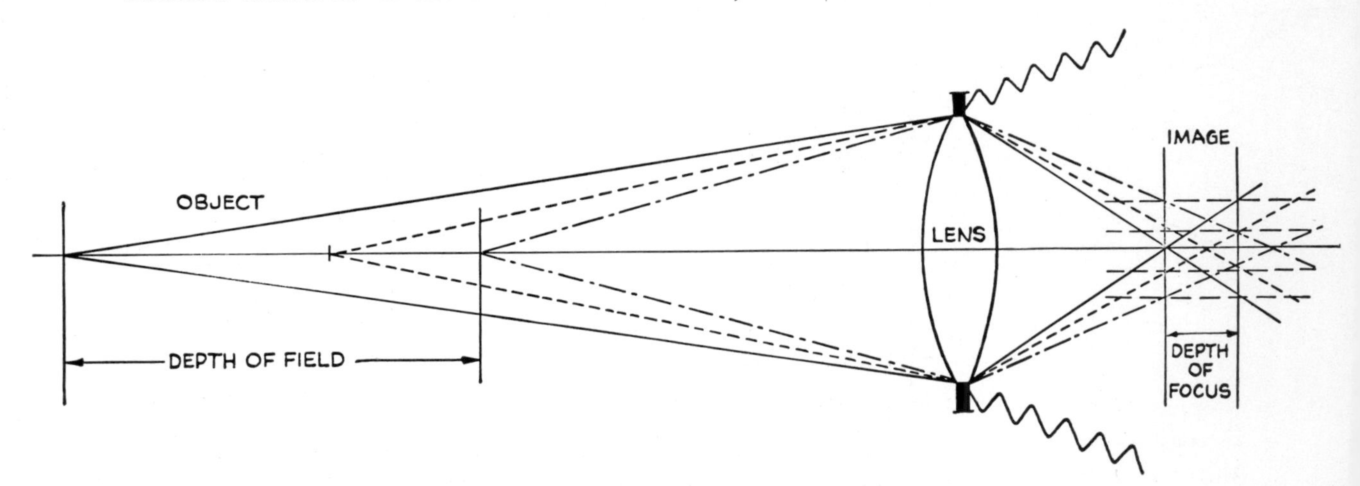

Determination of the depth of field

To avoid wasting lens speed through use of unnecessarily small diaphragm stops, focusing and stopping down have to be correlated intelligently, which can be done in several different ways:

By using the depth-of-field scale engraved on the mounts of most minicamera lenses. Focus on near and far ends of the zone you want to render sharp to determine their distances from the camera. Remember these two values on the foot scale of the lens mount and refocus your lens until identical stop numbers on the depth-of-field scale appear opposite the two numbers marking the beginning and the end of your desired zone of sharpness in depth on the foot scale. Leave the lens focused that way. Stopping down the diaphragm to this stop number will then give you the required sharpness in depth with the largest possible diaphragm opening.

By using a depth-of-field table or calculator, indicating the extension of sharpness in depth for lenses with different focal lengths at different diaphragm stops for different lens-object distances. Available at your dealer's for a few cents; instructions for use are included.

By visual inspection of the groundglass image, which usually is the fastest and easiest way—provided the camera is equipped with a groundglass.

Preparedness for unexpected action situations and snapshots can be increased considerably by presetting the camera according to the following simplified but accurate depth-of-field chart:

Focal Length of Lens	Focus Lens at	Stop Lens Down to	Resulting Zone of Sharpness
	CAMERA SETTINGS FOR MEDIUM CLOSEUP SHOTS		
5 cm (2 in.)	12 ft.	*f* 5.6	9-20 ft.
		f 8	8-30 ft.
7½ cm (3 in.)	12 ft.	*f* 6.3	9-20 ft.
10½ cm (4 1/5 in.)	12 ft.	*f* 8	9-18 ft.
15 cm (6 in.)	12 ft.	*f* 11	9-17 ft.
	CAMERA SETTINGS FOR MEDIUM DISTANCES TO INFINITY		
5 cm (2 in.)	30 ft.	*f* 8	15 ft. to ∞
7½ cm (3 in.)	40 ft.	*f* 8	20 ft. to ∞
10½ cm (4 1/5 in.)	60 ft.	*f* 11	30 ft. to ∞
15 cm (6 in.)	100 ft.	*f* 12.5	50 ft. to ∞

These data are useful to you only when available at the moment of taking the picture. Since you can hardly take this book with you any time you go out shooting, I recommend that you copy the data that concern you right now into your camera case with India ink. There they are always handy when you need them, and after presetting your camera accordingly, all that remains to be done is to set the shutter speed according to light-meter reading—and to snap the picture.

By calculation. This is the slowest but most accurate way of producing greatest extension of depth with the least stopping down. The most useful formula is reprinted on the following page. With its help, degree of sharpness can be varied according to the requirements of the occasion by varying the diameter of the permissible circle of confuion.

The hyperfocal distance, and its use

If a lens is focused on hyperfocal distance, all objects that are between infinity and half the hyperfocal distance from the lens will be in focus simultaneously, and consequently will be rendered sharp, provided the diaphragm is stopped down accordingly.

If, for instance, the hyperfocal distance for a certain lens is 50 feet at f 8, everything from 25 feet to infinity will be rendered sharp if the lens is focused on 50 feet and stopped down to f 8. The hyperfocal distance can be determined for any lens and diaphragm stop by the following formula:

$$\text{Hyperfocal distance in inches} = \frac{F^2}{f \times C} \text{ inches}$$

In this formula F = focal length of lens in inches
f = diaphragm stop number
C = circle of confusion in fractions of an inch

For example: We want to find the hyperfocal distance for a Contax lens with a focal length of 2 inches stopped down to f 8. The permissible diameter of the circle of confusion is 1/1,500 of the focal length of the lens or 1/750 inch. We then get the following equation:

$$\frac{2^2}{8 \times \frac{1}{750}} = \frac{4 \times 750}{8} = \frac{750}{2} = 375'' = 31'3''$$

Thus, under these conditions the hyperfocal distance would be 31 feet 3 inches. Focused for this distance and stopped down to f 8 our lens would give sharp images of all objects from half this distance or 15 feet 7½ inches on to infinity.

With the help of this formula, anyone who is interested and has half an hour or so to spare, can easily compute a chart of hyperfocal distances for his pet lens at different stops. It may come in very handy when light conditions are poor and a maximum depth of field has to be covered with a minimum of stopping down—thus preserving maximum lens speed.

Focusing for maximum depth of field with minimum stopping down

We have seen how important a role proper focusing plays when lens speed has to be conserved by covering a maximum of sharpness in depth with a minimum of stopping down. As long as the extension in depth of the zone that has to be rendered sharp is known, the most advantageous plane in depth on which to focus can be found with the help of the following formula:

$$\frac{N \times F \times 2,}{N+F}$$ in which N = distance between lens and nearest plane
F = distance between lens and farthest plane

If, for instance, we want sharpness to begin 15 feet from the lens and to end 25 feet from the camera, the most advantageous distance on which to focus would be:

$$\frac{15 \times 25 \times 2}{15+25} = \frac{750}{40} = 18'10''$$

Thus, focusing on a plane 18 feet 10 inches from the camera, and stopping down the lens according to depth-of-focus scale or table, will cover the desired zone of depth with the least possible amount of stopping down.

The diaphragm as light regulator

As the diaphragm is closed down to increase the depth of field, there is a parallel decrease in the brightness of the groundglass image which naturally must be considered when calculating the exposure time. To simplify this operation, diaphragm stops are calibrated in such a way that stopping down from one *f* number to the next higher one necessitates doubling the exposure time, while opening up the diaphragm from one *f* number to the next lower one necessitates halving the exposure time.

The American stop-number system:

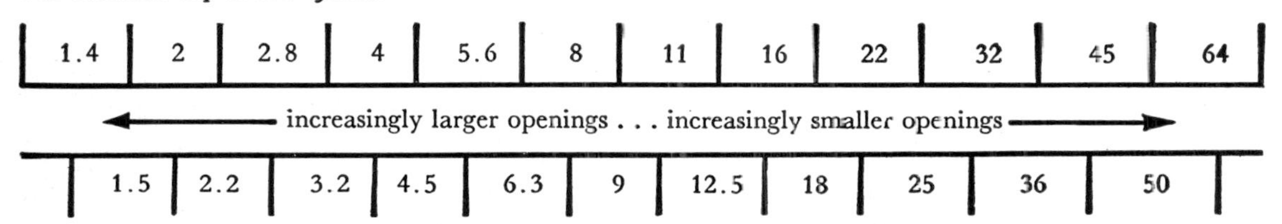

The Continental stop-number system.

For example, if according to the exposure meter we should expose 1/50 second at *f* 11, but want to stop down to *f* 16, we would have to double the exposure time and expose for 1/25 second; on the other hand, if we want to open up the diaphragm one stop to *f* 8, we would have to expose for only half the time or 1/100 second.

> The smaller the stop number, the larger the diaphragm opening, and the shorter the corresponding time of exposure. And the larger the *f* number, the smaller the diaphragm opening, and the longer must be the corresponding time of exposure.

Notice that doubling the diaphragm stop number necessitates quadrupling the exposure time, because the diameter of the diaphragm opening is halved, and its effective opening is reduced to only one quarter. Thus, while closing the diaphragm from *f* 8 to *f* 11 (from one stop to the next smaller one) necessitates doubling the exposure time, closing down from *f* 8 to *f* 16 (two stop numbers) necessitates quadrupling the exposure time. See sketch below:

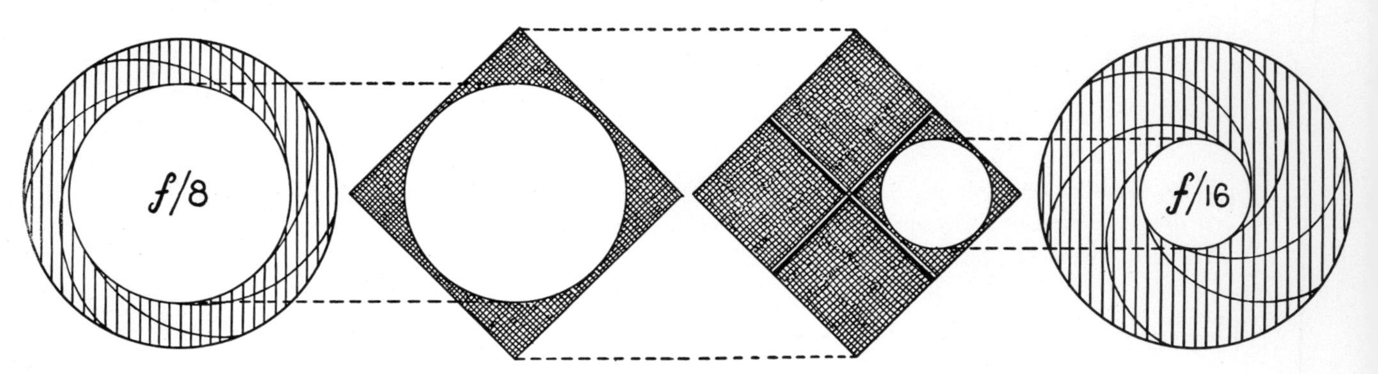

Determination of the exposure increase for closeups

As stated in the section on focusing (pages 102-107), the values of the diaphragm stops as indicators for the amount of light reaching the film change with the lens-image distance. They are correct with regard to exposure-meter readings as long as the lens is focused on infinity, but decrease in proportion to increasing lens-image distance. In other words: the closer to an object we go with the camera, the more we have to increase exposure. As long as we don't go too close with the camera, however, resulting increases in exposure times are so small that they will be absorbed by the exposure latitude of the film and consequently can be neglected. In practice, only when taking pictures of objects closer than approximately four feet from the camera do we have to worry about increasing the exposure beyond the normal value indicated by the exposure meter. For genuine closeups, the necessary factor by which the "normal" exposure has to be multiplied when taking closeups at various distances between camera and object can be found with the help of the following formula:

$$\frac{\text{lens-to-image distance} \times \text{lens-to-image distance}}{\text{focal length of lens} \times \text{focal length of lens}}$$

For example: We want to take a closeup of a flower with a six-inch lens. The distance between lens and image (bellows extension) after focusing measures ten inches. This gives us the following equation:

$$\frac{10 \times 10}{6 \times 6} = \frac{100}{36} = \text{roughly } 3$$

Consequently, we get 3 as the factor by which to multiply exposure, and if the meter reading is 2 seconds at *f* 32, we either have to expose for $2 \times 3 = 6$ seconds at *f* 32, or open diaphragm accordingly, in order to get a correctly exposed negative.

THE FUNCTIONS OF THE SHUTTER

Like the diaphragm, the shutter, too, has a double purpose: it plays an important role in regulating the amount of light that passes the lens during the exposure and thus directly affects the density of the negative; and its higher or lower speed decides the degree of sharpness with which objects in motion are rendered on the film. Again—as in the case of the diaphragm—these two functions sometimes conflict. On the one hand it is all-important that a negative be sufficiently exposed—which often demands comparatively long exposure times—while on the other hand, blurredness from movement should normally be avoided, which often demands comparatively short exposure times. However, it is generally easier to compromise on a shutter speed than to compromise on an aperture.

The shutter as light regulator

Diaphragm opening and shutter speed together regulate the exposure of the negative. If we compare the light that passes the lens to water, we could say that the diaphragm represents the water pipe, while the shutter represents the valve that releases and shuts off the flow of water through the pipe. To get a certain predetermined amount of water (a certain quantity of light, predetermined by means of an exposure meter as necessary to produce a sufficiently exposed negative), we can either (1) adjust the length of time the valve is open and accept the diameter of the water pipe as it is (whenever depth of field is more important than fast exposure)—or (2) accept the fact that the valve can be opened only so long (if fast exposure is more important than depth of field)—and adjust the width of our water pipe (diaphragm) accordingly. The basic relationship between the size of the diaphragm opening and the speed of the shutter is demonstrated in the table on page 100. Similarly, corresponding values of diaphragm openings and shutter speeds can be found for any imaginable occasion with the help of any exposure meter, and all a photographer has to do is to decide which one of these different combinations will fit his present needs best. Remember, however, the following elemental rules:

> In general, too much light is better than too little; so when in doubt, increase, rather than decrease, your exposure. An underexposed negative is valueless, but modern film emulsions can stand very considerable overexposure. You cannot intensify something that isn't there, but you can usually reduce the density of your negative if you should happen to overexpose.

The shutter as means for "stopping motion"

In order to get sharp pictures of objects in motion, the shutter speed has to be so high that the object moves only an unnoticeable distance during the exposure of the film. Generally speaking, the faster the movement of the object, the higher must be the shutter speed if motion is to appear "frozen." Consult the table on page 353 or the simplified table on page 102 for the longest shutter speeds permissible to stop the motion of various traveling objects and read the discussion of movement and action beginning on page 344 for suggestions on different ways of representing "movement" in a photograph before you snap your picture at the fastest possible shutter speed. Not always is "freezing" of motion the best and most expressive way of rendering movement and action in a still photograph. . . .

Motion is motion, regardless of where it manifests itself, and often the images even of perfectly stationary objects will appear blurred in a photograph—because the photographer was moving when he made the exposure. To avoid this rather embarrassing cause of blurredness it is necessary that the photographer brace himself and his camera before he releases the shutter, and that he use a tripod or other improvised but rigid camera support for all shutter speeds longer than 1/25 second. For taking teleshots, the camera should always be supported because the telelens magnifies not only the size of the image, but the slightest and otherwise most harmless vibrations, too. . . .

Object speed is not an unalterable factor, as far as the photographer is concerned. The take-off speed of a plane, for instance, may be over 100 mph, but to a person standing far away on the runway looking at the oncoming plane this same speed will appear practically nil—at least until the plane is comparatively close and about to pass over his head. Wherever reduction of apparent object motion is desirable in order to shoot the picture at a lower shutter speed—because of poor light conditions, because great depth of field is essential, because the shutter doesn't have a high enough speed, etc.—try to make use of the following rules for decreasing the apparent speed of moving objects:

Follow the moving object with the camera the way you would follow it with a gun, releasing the shutter while you swing the camera with the object (see page 353). This is the only instance where the camera *should be moved* during an exposure.

Avoid photographing fast-moving objects sideways; take them at an angle coming toward or going away from you. Notice the difference in shutter speed necessary to stop identical movement under different conditions, as indicated in the tables on pages 102 and 353.

THE EXPOSURE

The climax in the making of a picture is of course the instant a photographer presses the proverbial little button that releases the shutter. Up to this moment, everything was up to him; he was the sole director who decided, arranged, composed, elected, or discarded—artist and master-craftsman in one person. But with the clicking of the shutter most of his controls have ended, and what remains to be done is mainly mechanical processing and finishing that any intelligent apprentice should be able to do. . . . The really important decisions are unalterably made, the result is in the bag—or rather in the filmholder—for better or for worse, waiting for its final resurrection to testify to the artistic and technical qualifications of the "man behind the camera."

The instant *before* he releases the shutter is the moment a photographer should utilize to make a final quick checkup on all the various factors, artistic and technical, that influence the outcome of his picture. In addition to satisfying himself regarding such aesthetic matters as the distribution of light and shadow, the balance of illumination and contrasts, the appearance of the background and its relationship to the subject proper, perspective and possible distortion, etc.—all of which are discussed in Part II—he should quickly check again all the following factors, which influence the exposure from the technical point of view:

Film speed
Type of developer to be used
Brightness of illumination
Movement of object or photographer
Extension of the subject in depth
Color filter and filter factor
Contrast range of object
Color shade of object
Bellows extension
Slip-on lens

On the following pages, these factors will be discussed one by one.

Remember that an exposure meter provides only the basic data for setting the camera controls, which have to be interpreted intelligently and modulated in accordance with the requirements of the particular circumstances before they can be used successfully.

The film speed. Adjust the exposure meter according to the speed of the film you are going to use (see page 67). For information on the properties of films and suggestions for the selection of the "best" type of film, see pages 64 to 75.

Type of developer. Film speed ratings are based on development with standard rapid developers. All finegrain developers demand certain increases in exposure—different in degree depending on the type of developer. Generally, developers that produce the finest grain necessitate the longest increases in exposure. See pages 135 to 139, or consult manufacturers' charts and pamphlets for developers not mentioned there.

The simplest way to calculate necessary increases in exposure is to deduct the corresponding amount of film speed when setting the dial of the exposure meter. For instance, if a film with a Weston speed of 100 has to be processed in a developer that necessitates doubling the exposure in order to produce fully exposed finegrain negatives, set the dial for an effective speed of 50 instead of the theoretically correct 100, and all your diaphragm-shutter speed combinations will automatically be computed for processing in that particular finegrain developer.

Brightness of the illumination. Always measure the light intensity with an exposure meter (page 50); don't "guess." . . . The eye is a very poor instrument for measuring light intensities because of its capacity for rapid and unconscious adaptation to changes in brightness.

Wherever possible, go close to the object proper for taking a light reading. Take measurements from distances of only a few feet; when doing portraits, take your meter reading from a distance of only a foot or so from the head, but be careful not to cast a shadow on the face.

When taking meter readings in open landscapes, point the meter slightly downward to prevent excessive sky light from getting into the electric eye and falsifying your meter reading, resulting in exposure settings that would cause underexposure. Protect the photocell from direct light by shielding it with your flat hand from above. For exposure hints on flash pictures, turn to pages 58 and 333.

For subjects that are too dark to produce a meter reading consult charts on the following page. Notice, however, that if pan film with a Weston tungsten rating of 32 is being used instead of Super XX film, exposure times have to be doubled, while they can be halved if super-speed pan film of the new sports type is being used. For development in finegrain developers the usual increases in exposure have to be considered.

EXPOSURE TABLE FOR OUTDOOR NIGHT SHOTS (*Computed for Super XX film developed in DK-60a*)

Subject	*f* 1.5	*f* 2	*f* 3.5	*f* 4.5
Movie entrances with people. .	1/150 to 1/50 sec.	1/100 to 1/30 sec.	1/30 to 1/10 sec.	1/20 to 1/6 sec.
Brightly lighted main streets, etc.	1/25 to 1/5 sec.	1/15 to 1/3 sec.	1/5 to 1 sec.	1/3 to 1½ sec.
Ordinary city streets, neither exceptionally light nor dark. . .	4 to 10 sec.	6 to 15 sec.	20 to 45 sec.	30 to 75 sec.
Very dark streets and corners, only occasional street lights. .	25 to 60 sec.	35 to 90 sec.	2 to 5 min.	3 to 8 min.
City skyline with lighted windows, long shots at ¼ mile distance.	2 to 3 sec.	3 to 4 sec.	10 to 15 sec.	15 to 25 sec.

EXPOSURE TABLE FOR CANDID THEATER SHOTS (*Computed for Super XX film developed in DK-60a*)

Brightness of Stage Lighting	*f* 1.5	*f* 2	*f* 2.8	*f* 3.5
Dim.	1/10 to 1/5 sec.	1/5 to 1/3 sec.	1/3 to 2/3 sec.	1/2 to 1 sec.
Medium.	1/40 to 1/25 sec.	1/25 to 1/15 sec.	1/12 to 1/8 sec.	1/8 to 1/5 sec.
Bright.	1/150 to 1/75 sec.	1/100 to 1/50 sec.	1/50 to 1/25 sec.	1/30 to 1/15 sec.
Brilliant.	1/200 to 1/100 sec.	1/130 to 1/60 sec.	1/60 to 1/40 sec.	1/40 to 1/25 sec.

Since accurate determination of degree of illumination is subject to personal judgment, it is advisable to make several exposures with different shutter speeds or diaphragm settings to make sure of getting the best possible results.

Movement of object or photographer. Objects at rest can be exposed for any length of time provided the camera is supported firmly during the exposure. For the exposure of objects in motion consult the chart on page 353 or the simplified table on page 102. Decide whether the exposure has to be made with the camera hand-held, or if a tripod can be used. In the first case, a shutter speed of 1/25 second or faster has to be used to prevent blurredness due to unavoidable motion on the part of the photographer; if this is impossible for one reason or another, try to use a tripod or similar camera support. For complete information turn to the discussion of movement and action beginning page 344.

Extension of the subject in depth. In general, the greater the extension in depth of the zone that has to be rendered sharp, the smaller must be the diaphragm stop, and the longer will be the corresponding exposure time. Intelligent focusing aids considerably in securing the maximum depth of field with the minimum amount of stopping down; see pages 106 and 114. Finding the best possible compromise between as short as possible a shutter speed and as great as possible a depth of field will in the majority of cases lead to the technically best solution.

Color filter. Color filters are often necessary to improve the transformation of colors into gray tone values; see pages 48 and 223-232. However, since all color filters absorb a certain amount of light that otherwise would pass the lens and be available for the exposure, corresponding increases in exposure have to be made in order to prevent underexposure of the negative. Filter factors—the number by which an exposure, as determined with the help of an exposure meter, has to be multiplied when a certain filter is used in connection with a certain type of film—will be found on page 232. Compensation for the loss of light due to the filter action can be made either by prolonging the time of exposure, or by opening up the diaphragm a corresponding amount. If, for instance, we should expose according to the exposure meter 1/100 second at *f* 11, but want to employ a yellow filter with a factor of two, we would have to revise our exposure data and would have to shoot either at 1/50 second at *f* 11, or at 1/100 second at *f* 8.

Contrast range. If object contrasts are unusually great, an ordinary over-all meter reading would give exposure times that are too short to produce negatives with well-exposed shadows, since in such a case the photoelectric cell is affected almost exclusively by the bright parts of the subject and disregards the shadows, which consequently will be underexposed. Under such conditions, separate readings for the brightest and darkest parts of the subject should be taken and an intermediate exposure time should be computed. This is especially easy when using the Weston exposure meter with its markings for under- and overexposure. All a photographer has to do is to take a reading for the lightest and the darkest parts of the subject and to set the calculator so that the *O*-mark and *U*-mark (marking beginning of over- and underexposure, respectively) are at equal distances from the light-value numbers as determined for the lightest and darkest parts of the object. For example: let's imagine we are using a film with a speed of 100 Weston and get a meter reading of 6.5 for the darkest and 200 for the brightest part of our subject. In such a case we would have to turn the calculator until the *U* and *O* markings are at equal distances from 6.5 and 200, respectively (in this position, the arrow of the calculator would point at 50), and our dials would be set for the best possible combinations of diaphragm openings and shutter speeds for this particular case. As a rule it will be found that contrasty objects need at least twice as long an exposure as an ordinary over-all meter reading would have indicated.

On the other hand, objects with lower than normal contrasts should always be exposed a relatively short time, since then the resulting thinner negatives can be developed a little bit longer than normal to increase their contrasts if necessary. Remember, a comparatively short exposure increases, and a comparatively long exposure decreases, the contrasts of an object in the negative, especially when later combined with a correspondingly prolonged or shortened time of development, respectively. See discussion of contrast control beginning on page 207 for complete information.

Color shade. Exposure meters are calibrated to give correct readings for medium-colored to light objects. To get fully exposed negatives of dark-colored objects the indicated exposure times have to be doubled.

Bellows extension. Increase in lens-image distance beyond the focal length of the lens decreases the effective value of the diaphragm stop; see page 105. Information on when and how this loss of lens speed has to be compensated for in order to avoid underexposure will be found on page 116.

Slip-on lenses change focal length and diaphragm values of permanently attached "standard lenses" (see page 46). The simplest way to determine the effective stop value for any lens-object distance is to focus sharply; then to measure the distance from diaphragm to film and the diameter of the diaphragm stop that will be used to take the picture, and finally divide the first by the second. The result will be the effective *f* value of the combination of slip-on lens and permanent lens.

Conclusions: Just to show how much the initial exposure data as found by an over-all meter reading have to be revised occasionally, let's take an example: We want to make a closeup of a white rhododendron with dark-green leaves, illuminated by blue reflected sky light (in the shadow), and we want to develop the negative in a finegrain developer. Let's assume we got a meter reading of one second at *f* 32.

However, we would have to multiply this one second by the following factors: two for finegrain development; two for a medium yellow filter to improve the contrasts within the white flower (blue sky light); two because we have here an object with excessive contrasts between the white and the dark green; four because we want an image in natural size on the negative necessitating a bellows extension equal to two focal lengths of the lens. Altogether, we have to multiply our original one second by $2 \times 2 \times 2 \times 4 = 32$, arriving at a final exposure of 32 seconds at *f* 32. Which, of course, makes the whole project impractical!

CHAPTER 6

THE PROCESSING OF NEGATIVES AND PRINTS

ONCE your films are exposed you can take them to the nearest drugstore or photofinisher for processing—which is convenient and cheap and quite unexciting. Or, you can give yourself the treat of developing them yourself, which today is about as difficult as boiling eggs: anybody who can read a watch and a thermometer can do it, for duration of the development for a given film is normally determined by the temperature of the developer. Generally speaking, if the developer is warm the time of development must be shorter than if the developer were cold (the terms "warm" and "cold" here covering temperature ranges from approximately 55 to 80° F.). Naturally, different types of film, as well as different types of developers, may require different times of development (the "ideal" temperature is always the same: 68° F.); but these can be learned easily enough from the convenient little charts that manufacturers of film provide. Outstanding in this respect is the Kodak booklet *Kodak Films* which gives complete and easily understandable information on all the different types of Kodak film and the best methods of processing; it is available at every photo-dealer's for 50 cents. Charts for processing Panatomic-X 35 mm film are reprinted here for demonstration purposes:

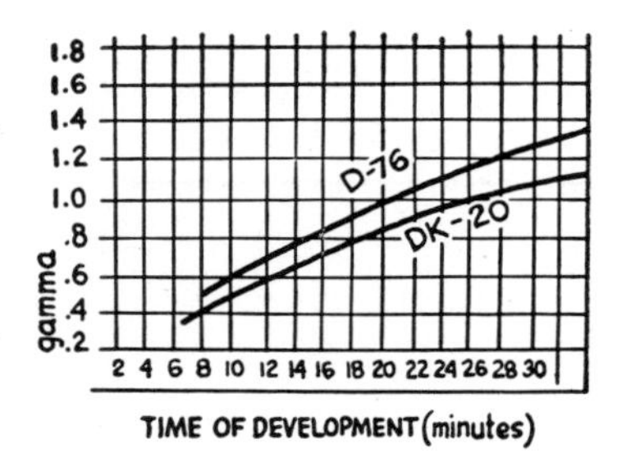

Time-gamma curves for developing in D-76 or DK-20, intermittent agitation at 68° F.

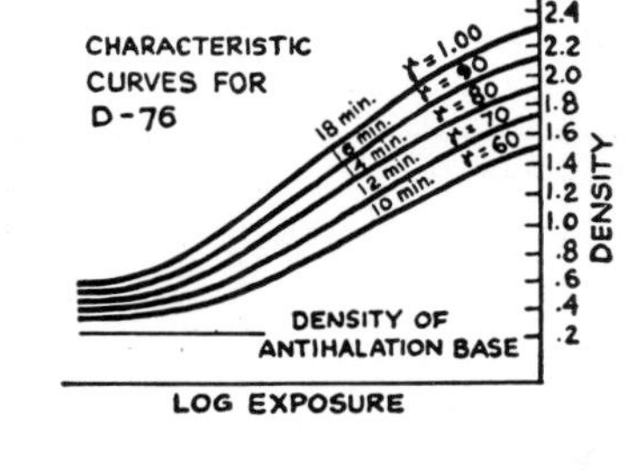

Characteristic curves for D-76 developer and different times of development.

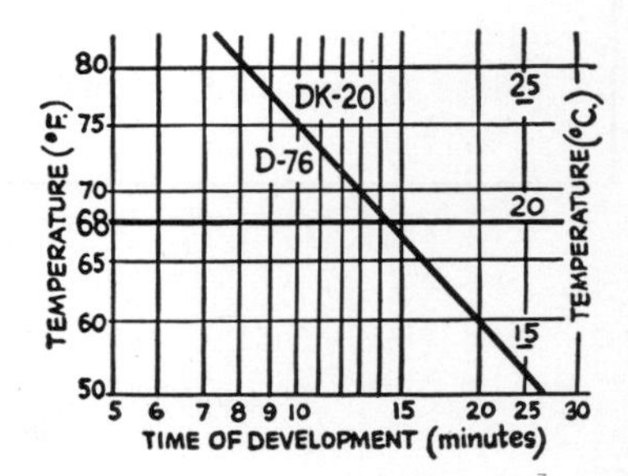

Time-temperature curve for D-76 and DK-20 developers.

To use these charts, decide on the gamma (i.e., contrast range, gradation; see pages 70-73) to which you want to develop your film, find necessary developing time at 68° F. in chart at left. If your developer is either warmer or colder than 68° consult chart at right to find corresponding developing time which will give negatives of the same gradation (gamma) as the time necessary for development at 68° F. Chart in center shows how different times of development in D-76 at 68° F. will change the gradation (gamma) of this film.

General suggestions and principles for successful developing and printing

Neatness, order, and cleanliness everywhere and at any time are first conditions and best guarantees for success.

Wherever possible (and it is almost always possible in photography) do the same thing in the same way. Develop a "system" for every step in processing negatives and prints and stick to it. Standardize wherever you can; try to master *one* method, *one* type of film or developer, etc., completely before you try a different one—if you feel you must try something different at all. . . .

Never jump from one thing to another simply because "somebody told you about it." There are about as many rumors in photography as there are in politics and war—and most of them are as unfounded. . . .

Always remember that photography is as much a matter of individuality as any other art. Methods suited beautifully to someone else may be entirely wrong for your own temperament, your own way of working. Be critical, don't be gullible. . . .

If you are about to give up after comparing your own production to the superior work of more famous and experienced photographers, remember that even men like Steichen or women like Bourke-White were once beginners—depending on the friendly advice of their betters, or compelled to make their own sad mistakes. . . .

Without gauges and instruments, no airplane could fly, no car could be driven safely for any length of time, no battleship maneuvered. . . . The same applies to photography if you want to bring it under control and are dissatisfied with accidental success. . . . These are the control instruments of our craft: EXPOSURE METER, TIMECLOCK, THERMOMETER. There are only these three, but they are indispensable, invaluable. . . . Use them constantly and rather too often than not often enough. Don't rely on your senses alone—they will deceive you most thoroughly when you can least afford it. . . .

Don't be a miser, especially with chemicals. Most chemicals are very cheap anyway, so even *before* your developer, hypo, etc., show signs of exhaustion, replace them with freshly prepared baths. "Saving" on chemicals is one of the surest ways to waste much more valuable things, such as irreplaceable negatives, irrevocable opportunities, precious time. . . . It often means that things will have to be done over—if there is a chance to do them over at all—and the waste will always surpass the meager initial saving. . . .

Buy only products of well-known, reputable manufacturers. "Nameless" films and chemicals as sold by certain chain stores might be cheaper but are often outdated stock bought up cheaply in bulk for resale to suckers. . . . or are so much inferior in quality as to be practically valueless. After all, what percentage is there in spending a lot of time and energy only to find it was all in vain because your materials let you down?

THE CHEMISTRY OF DEVELOPMENT

The moment a photographic film or paper is exposed to light, chemical changes occur within its emulsion: a "latent" (i.e., invisible) image is formed, its character depending on the intensity of the light that produced it, manifested in a more or less pronounced reduction of the light-sensitive silver halides to metallic silver. (This process is not completely understood by science, and opinions differ as to what actually occurs within the emulsion under the influence of light). To transform the latent image into a visible one, the exposed emulsion has to be "developed," i.e., reduction of the light-affected silver salts has to be completed by treating them with chemicals that separate the silver from the salts and deposit it in the form of minute, irregular grains of metallic silver—of which the image is composed. Such chemicals are called "reducing agents." To make the resultant image permanent and impervious to light, the undeveloped (unexposed) silver salts must be changed to soluble form (so that they can be removed during washing). This is done in a "fixing bath." Finally, these undeveloped salts as well as all chemicals used in developing and fixing have to be eliminated completely by washing the film in water to make the negative permanent and to prevent its otherwise unavoidable deterioration within a comparatively short time.

The basic components of developers

Regardless of how simple a developer formula is, it has—with very few exceptions—to contain among its ingredients the following four basic components:

The reducing agent. Its purpose is to reduce as completely as possible the exposed silver halides to the metallic silver that forms the image without attacking the unexposed silver salts; if they, too, were affected, the whole emulsion would turn uniformly gray or black and an image could not be formed. Only a few substances are known that possess those delicate selective qualities necessary for differentiating between exposed and unexposed silver salts, among which hydroquinone, Metol (Kodak "Elon" or Mallinckrodt "Pictol"), glycin and para-phenylene diamine are the most commonly used.

The activator. It is a peculiarity of photographic reducing agents that they operate properly only in alkaline solutions. Consequently, alkaline activators (or accelerators, usually sodium carbonate, borax, or sodium or potassium hydroxide) have to be part of the solution. The higher the alkali content of the developer, the more energetic, rapid and contrasty will be its development, which can go so far that the reducing agent may begin to attack the unexposed silver salts, too, producing all-over fog in the negative.

The restrainer. To prevent the reducing agent from attacking parts of the unexposed silver salts and to counteract the effects of possible overexposure, a restraining agent, most often potassium bromide, is usually added to the developer solution. It minimizes the tendency of overactivated reducing agents to produce fog. Also, it permits speeding up development by making it possible to add greater quantities of alkali without harmful effects. Too much restrainer, however, slows down the effective speed of an emulsion (the film speed) and necessitates prolongation of exposure times.

The preservative. All reducing agents have a natural affinity to oxygen. Since water always contains a large amount of free oxygen resulting from air dissolved in it, and also because of contact with surface air, reducing agents in developer solutions would oxidize rapidly—forming brownish oxidation products that would stain negatives and prints—unless a preservative, usually sodium sulfite or potassium metabisulfite, were added to the developer. These two chemicals have an even greater affinity for oxygen than reducing agents, which they protect from premature oxidation by combining with the free oxygen in the water, exhausting the supply before the reducing agents have had time to oxidize noticeably. Apart from this, such preservatives have no influence on the development.

To keep the initial oxygen content of a developer as low as possible, boiled water should be used for the preparation of stock solutions, especially where pyro is involved (boiling drives most of the air out of the water). Care should be taken not to whip air anew into the solution when stirring it. Notice, however, that distilled water contains at least as much free oxygen as ordinary tap water and consequently should be boiled, too, before use in developers.

The five basic rules for proper preparation of developer solutions:

1. Always dissolve chemicals in the order they are listed in the formula.
2. Always dissolve one chemical completely before you add a new one—if you want to avoid discoloration of the solution and oxidation and precipitation of the chemicals.
3. Always dissolve the preservative before the reducing agent which it has to protect. Exception (see page 82): developers containing Elon. Elon should be dissolved in water containing a pinch of sulfite, balance of sulfite added later.
4. Always add the alkali to the solution after you have dissolved preservative and reducing agent since alkali increases the natural affinity of the reducing agent for oxygen and would accelerate its rate of oxidation unless prevented by the preservative.
5. Never use water of more than 125° F. for dissolving a reducing agent.

For further information—especially with regard to self-mixing of developer—see the discussion of photo-chemicals beginning page 79.

Controls of development

Despite the fact that the type of film emulsion and the amount of light it receives during the exposure play the most important role in determining the character of a negative, the final result nevertheless depends to a large degree on the way in which such a negative is developed and can be influenced in different directions through appropriate selection and modulation of one or several of the following factors:

The type of developer. Generally speaking, the choice is between "ordinary" developers and "finegrain" developers. Ordinary developers permit the photographer to make use of the full listed speed of a film, but they produce negatives with comparatively coarse grain and medium to high contrasts. Finegrain developers demand certain increases in exposure times—equivalent to a more or less serious loss in film speed—in order to produce sufficiently dense negatives of usually low to medium contrasts, but compensate for this disadvantage by keeping the film grain so fine that enlargements of very considerable magnification can be made before the grain becomes noticeable in the print.

Consequently, ordinary developers are preferable in the following instances: (1) for the development of larger-size films where graininess is no problem because enlargements of only moderate magnification have to be made; (2) whenever utilization of the full speed of an emulsion is necessary for one reason or another; (3) whenever object contrasts are relatively low and have to be increased or at least preserved in the negative. On the other hand, finegrain developers have definite advantages: (1) when it comes to processing small negatives which have to stand considerable magnification as enlargements; (2) whenever negatives with a maximum of sharpness are desired; (3) whenever object contrasts are comparatively high and need to be reduced in the negative.

The boundaries between ordinary and finegrain developers, as well as between contrasty and soft developers, are not always clearly drawn because some developers show characteristics of several types without going to extremes. Since the character of a developer depends entirely on the character of its reducing agents and activator, and since different reducing agents and activators have different characters, it is easily possible to compose developers consisting of two different reducing agents with opposite qualities (as, for instance, hydroquinone and Metol), and by mixing the two in different proportions with either a mild or an energetic activator, to modulate one type of developer in any desired direction, making it produce any desired type of negative gradation from very contrasty to very soft.

The time of development. Density and contrasts in negatives increase gradually during development—the longer developed, the denser and more contrastful the negative. Consequently, observation of the correct developing time is all-important for producing negatives of desired contrast and density (this is why a clock is absolutely essential in a darkroom). Since these times may vary from two to 60 minutes and more—depending on the type of developer and film, the temperature of the solution, and the desired density and gradation of the negative—no general rules can be given; instead, follow the directions accompanying ready-mixed developers, or consult the manufacturer's charts and tables for developing different types of film.

In general, a comparatively short development—especially in connection with a longer than normal exposure—will produce negatives of lower than average contrast while a comparatively long development—especially in connection with a slightly shorter than normal exposure—will produce negatives of higher than average contrast. Whenever necessary, these facts can be used to decrease or increase the natural contrast of the subject to quite a considerable degree in the negative.

The temperature of the developer. As in all chemical reactions, the rate of development depends upon the temperature of the developer. Heat speeds up development; cold retards development or stops it completely (this is why a thermometer is absolutely essential in a darkroom). The best temperature for all developers is 68° F., but some developers will still work at temperatures as low as 55° F. or as high as 90° F. (for special "tropical" developers, see page 136). Naturally, deviations from the normal temperature of 68° F. have to be compensated for by corresponding increases or decreases in developing time if under- or overdevelopment is to be avoided. Consult the manufacturer's time-temperature charts in all cases where you have to develop under abnormal temperature conditions; see page 124.

Apart from changing the rate of development, abnormal temperatures may have the following undesirable effects: Cooling down certain highly concentrated solutions may produce crystallization and precipitation of chemicals, changing the properties of the solution. Temperatures that are too high make the gelatine of the emulsion swell dangerously; soften it so that it is easily damaged; loosen it from the film base or make it wrinkle and shrivel and produce "reticulation" (see page 180). Differences in temperatures between different solutions (developer—hypo—water) are the most common cause of reticulation. If work has to be done under abnormal temperatures, not only special developers but special hardening fixers must be used.

Agitation during development. To insure uniform and controllable development over the entire surface of the negative, the developer has to be agitated to bring fresh solution into contact with all parts of the negative from time to time. If we leave a negative undisturbed in the developer, the rate of development slows down more and more as the power of the developer becomes increasingly exhausted; furthermore, bromide liberated from the emulsion during the development then remains stagnant. And since its quantity increases with the density of the negative, it would be more concentrated near dense parts than near the thin parts of the negative, spreading slowly over the dense parts into the thin parts, where in its capacity as a restrainer it would even further retard development of those already thin parts, besides causing unevenness and streaks.

Naturally the more we agitate the developer, the faster will be the rate of development (within reason). Consequently, if rate and degree of agitation during development are not specified and standardized, recommended developing times are meaningless. All developing times given later on in connection with different developer formulas are based on recommendations for agitation made by Kodak as described in the discussion of practical development beginning on page 141.

Longevity of the developer. Within a certain quantity of developer only a certain quantity of film can be developed; see table on page 86. But even so, the developer will become increasingly exhausted the more films are developed in it, resulting in a decreased rate of development that has to be compensated for by an increase in developing time in order to prevent underdevelopment. Accurate factors for such increases cannot be given since they depend on too many different conditions, like number of films developed simultaneously, time intervals between uses of the developer, stability of the solution formula, etc. All that can be said is that such increases in developing times are very small to start with but become increasingly large with increasing exhaustion of the developer.

To eliminate the uncertainty connected with more or less hypothetical increases in developing time, so-called "replenishers" can be used to keep the activity of a developer constant throughout its entire useful life, which, incidentally, can thus be prolonged from five to ten times. The basic idea of replenishing is to replace the amount of developer solution absorbed by the film emulsions or otherwise lost (spilled) with developer concentrate mixed according to specific formulas. However, this very good method works better for deep-tank development where larger quantities of developer are involved (from approximately four gallons on up) than in cases where comparatively small amounts of solution are used. Eastman Kodak recommends the use of approximately one ounce of replenisher for every 80 square inches of film developed (equal to one roll No. 120 or one roll of 35 mm film with 36 exposures, or four sheets of 4x5 film, etc.); if this is more than the amount of solution lost during development, enough developer should be taken out of the tank to make space for the replenisher. If the suggested amount of replenisher doesn't keep the tank filled to normal level, the difference should be made up with ordinary developer solution. To make sure that the replenisher doesn't change the rate of development, occasional checks on density and contrasts of the processed negatives have to be made.

A developer's life cannot be prolonged indefinitely through replenishment. Sooner or later the solution will become unreliable. Silver sludge, gelatine particles, and dirt will accumulate, a tendency to stain or fog will be noticeable, and the bath will have to be discarded.

Fixation of the negative

After development is completed, the negative has to be "fixed" in a fixing bath, which serves a triple purpose: it interrupts development instantaneously; it removes from the emulsion the unexposed and hence undeveloped silver salts, which otherwise would darken in time and obscure the image, and it clears the negative and makes it transparent so it can be printed easily. Usually, a fixing bath consists of the following four components:

Sodium thiosulfate, or "hypo," which dissolves the undeveloped silver salts out of the emulsion by combining with them to form water-soluble thiosulfates of silver and sodium which can easily be washed out when fixation is completed.

Acetic acid, the purpose of which is to neutralize whatever alkali the emulsion carries over from the developer. Since developing agents can reduce silver halides only in alkaline solutions, continued development resulting from developer remaining in the gelatine is thus made impossible.

Sodium sulfite which acts as a preservative and prevents the acid from decomposing the hypo into free sulfur and sodium sulfite, which would turn the bath milky, stain the gelatine, and bleach out the image.

A hardening agent—white potassium alum or potassium chrome alum—which takes care of excessively softened emulsions due to prolonged soaking in developing and fixing solutions. It tans the gelatine and thus makes it less vulnerable to accidental damage—especially necessary in hot weather when solutions become abnormally warm.

BASIC RULES FOR PREPARATION AND USE OF FIXING BATHS

Dissolve the sodium sulfite first, then add the acetic acid.

Add the hardener (alum) to the sulfite-acid solution. Don't mix sulfite and alum directly with each other, because they would form aluminum sulfite which would precipitate as white sludge.

Dissolve the hypo by itself in hot water; let it cool down.

Never mix hypo and acetic acid directly with each other or the acid will decompose the hypo and turn the bath milky.

Acetic acid is activated by heat; don't add it to solutions with temperatures over 85° F. Mixed with hypo in solution over 85° F. it begins to decompose the hypo and to liberate free sulfur, even in the presence of sodium sulfite, spoiling the bath.

After they have cooled down below 85° F. mix the sulfite-acid-alum with the hypo solution.

A fixing bath that has turned milky is spoiled and has to be thrown away.

An exhausted fixing bath will still clear a negative, but such a negative won't be permanent and will deteriorate within a comparatively short time. In one gallon of acid fixer not more than 75 rolls of No. 120, or 75 rolls of 35 mm film of 36 exposures each, or 75 sheets of 8x10 film, or 300 sheets of 4x5 film, should be fixed.

Generally, a fixing bath is exhausted when it takes twice as long to clear a film as it took when the bath was freshly prepared.

Leave the negatives about twice as long in the fixing bath as it takes to clear the emulsion.

The safest way of fixing negatives (and prints) is to use two fixing baths: fix first in one bath for the prescribed time, then put the negatives (or prints) for one or two minutes into a second bath that is used only for this purpose and thus will always be guaranteed to be fresh and strong. Then, when the first bath begins to show signs of exhaustion, discard it, replace it with the second bath, and prepare an entirely new bath for the second fixing.

To insure uniform fixation, watch out that your negatives don't stick together in the fixer. Move them around occasionally; agitate the bath.

The temperature of the fixing bath should always be the same as that of the developer. Differences in temperature between different solutions (including the washing water) are apt to cause reticulation of the gelatine. Fixing baths below 60° F. are sluggish and unreliable.

Leaving negatives (and prints) more than twice the time they need for clearing in the fixer usually doesn't do any harm, but leaving them in the bath excessively long (over 20 minutes) may result in a slight bleaching of the image and may cause the gelatine to swell too much, unless the bath contains sufficient hardener, especially in warm weather.

Washing and drying of negatives

When fixation is completed, all the chemicals used in processing have to be washed out of the emulsion in order to make the negative (or print) as permanent as possible. This, and all the following rules for washing, also applies to prints. The thoroughness with which this is done determines the degree of permanency of the negative (or print), since even slight traces of remaining chemicals, and especially hypo, will in time decompose the image and make it fade. Proper washing is based on the fact that hypo is heavier than water and will sink to the bottom of the vessel. Simply letting negatives (or prints) soak in a tray under the faucet will never remove the hypo as thoroughly as necessary for a permanent job; all it accomplishes is to swell the gelatine to the danger point and to let the negatives (or prints) soak in an increasingly heavier syrup of hypo concentrate.

Basic rules for proper washing and drying:

Since hypo is heavier than water and sinks to the bottom, negatives (and prints!) should be kept suspended in the water and should never lie flat at the bottom of the vessel.

Leave roll films on the reel and keep the reel suspended in the water; or take them off the reel and keep them free-floating by fastening two or three cork clips to their edges. Make the cork clips yourself by splitting a bottle cork lengthwise and holding the halves together with a rubber band; see illustrations on the following page.

Wash sheet film (and prints) by keeping the individual sheets separated and suspended in the water on cork clips.

In my opinion the *only* proper way of washing negatives (and prints!) is in a specially built tank with overflow which removes the hypo-loaded water *from the bottom;* see the picture and sketch on the following page. Any tinsmith will build such a tank to specifications for a few dollars. Its mode of operation is greatly superior to any syphon arrangement, and infinitely more effective than the merely "symbolic" way of washing in a tray under the faucet.

The duration of the washing depends on the method employed. Here the three important factors are agitation, separation, and rate of replacement of the water in the tank. In a tank such as that described above, negatives will be washed properly within 30 minutes; if tray and syphon are used, washing should be continued for one hour; negatives washed in a tray under the faucet will never become completely free of hypo, no matter how long they "wash."

The duration of the washing should be measured from the moment the last negative has been put into the tank, since partly washed negatives absorb hypo anew each time negatives are brought in from the fixer.

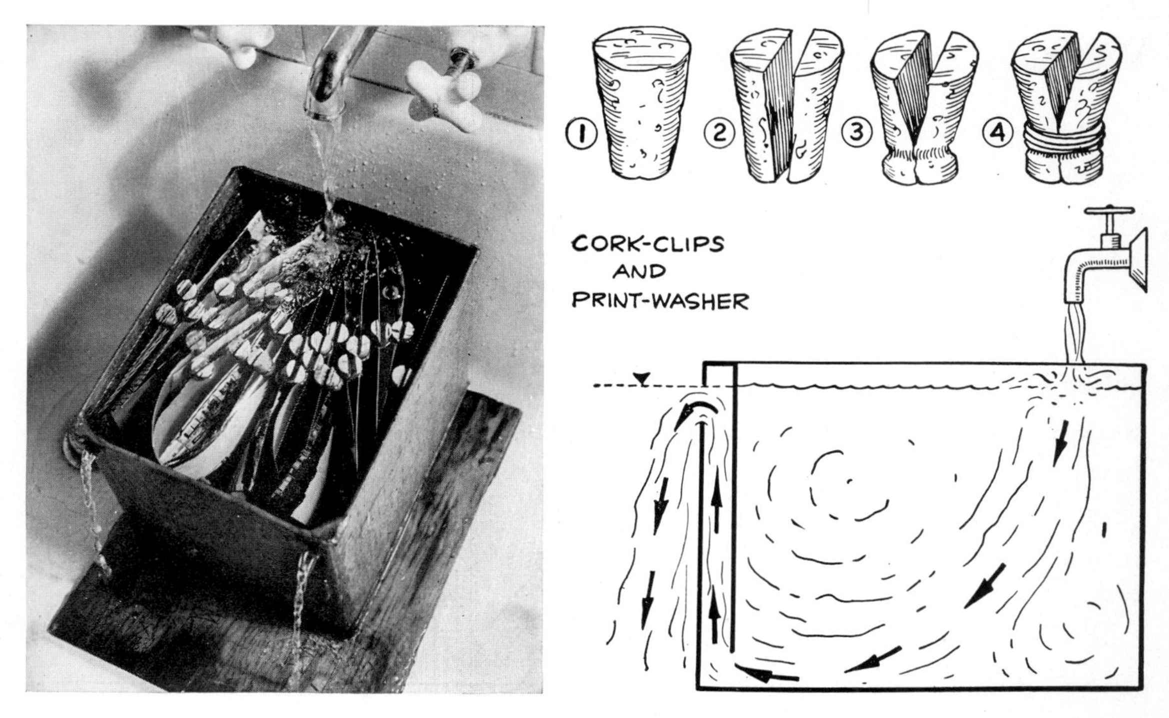

Left: Print washer in use under faucet in bath tub. To prevent the galvanized metal from marring the enamel of the tub, tank is put on a sheet of waterproof plywood. The prints, floating in vertical position suspended from cork clips, stay well separated from each other. The dissolving hypo, heavier than water, slowly sinks to the bottom of the tank from which it is removed via two overflow-pipes built into the front corners of the tank (see cross-section drawing at right).

Top right: Make cork clips by splitting bottle cork (1) into halves (2), shaping and grooving them (3), and joining finished halves with rubber band (4).

After washing is completed, each negative should be wiped off carefully on both sides with a soft and well-soaked chamois leather or a viscose sponge in order to eliminate gelatine and dirt particles carried out of the water.

Hang negatives in a *dust-free* place to dry, carefully wiping off all remaining drops of water which otherwise would leave indelible traces after drying (see picture on page 181). Never remove drying negatives to a different place or indelible streaks from unevenly dried emulsions will result. Attach a clip to the lower end of each roll film to prevent curling.

Negatives should be dried slowly in order to keep the film grain small. Rapid drying with heat is possible if emulsions are well hardened but will produce a somewhat larger grain. Using a fan usually blows into the emulsion dust that will cause spots in the final print.

Developer and fixer formulas

The number of published photographic formulas is so great that a photographer can easily get confused when trying to make a selection, unless he systematically cuts down this abundance to a few likely possibilities from which it should be simple to pick "the winner." The following suggestions will help.

Wherever possible, follow the film manufacturer's recommendations with respect to type of developer and method of development. He made the film, he ought to know it best, and it is certainly as much in his interest as in yours that *you* get the best possible results. After all, the man wants you to be satisfied, to come back and buy more of his film.

Beware of all formulas that claim to produce a film grain "as fine as other finegrain developers or finer" while simultaneously retaining the full speed of the emulsion. Such things simply don't exist. Believe me, if such developers were possible, Ansco, Kodak, or any other of the big manufacturers would have made them long ago. Don't waste your money or risk your films.

Don't overestimate the capacities of finegrain developers. They can produce only comparatively (!) fine grain if they are used properly (overdevelopment increases the size of the grain even with finegrain developers); if the initial emulsion grain wasn't too coarse; and if the negative was exposed correctly.

On the other hand, finegrain developers have very definite disadvantages: they demand certain increases in exposure times, and they produce negatives of lower contrasts than ordinary developers. Only occasionally is this desirable, and often it has to be compensated for by using a paper of harder gradation which emphasizes the grain.

Laboratory tests have shown that many standard developers recommended by reputable manufacturers will produce a film grain that is practically as fine as that produced by special finegrain formulas, provided developing time is shortened and negatives are developed to the same low contrasts as those processed in finegrain developers. The real advantage of finegrain developers is the fact that they make it much more difficult to overdevelop than do standard developers.

Most of the formulas reprinted on the following pages are recommended and produced by America's leading manufacturers. Quite a number of them are available in ready-mixed form. The two Windisch formulas are valuable European contributions.

Ansco Developer Formulas for Development of Ansco Film	Water, 125° F. Warm	Metol	Sodium Sulfite (Anhydrous)	Sodium Bisulfite	Hydroquinone	Borax	Sodium Carbonate (Monohydrated)	Potassium Bromide	Water
Ansco 47, *standard developer* for tray and tank development	750cc	1.5 gm.	45 gm.	1 gm.	3 gm.	....	6 gm.	0.8 gm.	Fill up to make 1 liter
Ansco 47-A, replenisher for Ansco 47	750cc	3 gm.	45 gm.	2 gm.	6 gm.	....	12 gm.	....	as above
Ansco 17, *fine grain developer* for tray and tank development	750cc	1.5 gm.	80 gm.	....	3 gm.	3 gm.	....	0.5 gm.	Fill up to make 1 liter
Ansco 17-A, replenisher for Ansco 17	750cc	2.2 gm.	80 gm.	....	4.5 gm.	18 gm.	....	....	as above
Ansco 64, *tropical developer* for high temperatures	750cc	2.5 gm.	25 gm.	....	6.5 gm.	....	16 gm.	1 gm.	Fill up to make 1 liter
Ansco 90, *high-contrast developer* for process films	750cc	5 gm.	40 gm.	....	6 gm.	....	40 gm.	3 gm.	Fill up to make 1 liter

Dissolve all chemicals in the order they are listed. If negatives are to be developed in Ansco 17 finegrain developer, increase exposure times by 30 to 50 per cent beyond "normal" as indicated by exposure meter. Do not dilute any of the above developers.

The following table shows normal developing times for Ansco developers at 68° F.:

Developer	Tray, Continuous Agitation	Tank, Intermittent Agitation
Ansco 47	5 to 7 min.	6 to 8 min.
Ansco 17	8 to 12 min.	10 to 15 min.
Ansco 64	3 to 4 min. at 68° F.; 2 to 3 min. at 85° F.*	
Ansco 90	4 to 6 min.	......

*When development is necessary at temperatures above 75°F., the use of a chemical such as sodium sulfate, which acts as a "swelling suppressor," is advisable.

Developing times depend on the type of film and the desired contrast and density of the negative. For best results make test or consult manufacturer's charts. Usually, shorter development should be given film with a comparatively contrastful gradation (usually in conjunction with low film speed) or if negatives of lower contrasts are desired. The softer the initial gradation of the film, or the higher the negative contrast desired, the longer the development necessary.

Use of replenisher: add between one-half and three-fourths ounce of replenisher to the developer for each roll of No. 120 film (or equivalent; see page 86) developed. Maintain original volume of developer even if it means discarding some of the original solution. Under these conditions developing times will remain constant throughout the useful life of the developer.

Kodak Developer Formulas for Development of Kodak Films	Water, 125° F. Warm	Elon	Sodium Sulfite (Anhydrous)	Hydroquinone	Sodium Carbonate (Monohydrated)	Kodalk	Borax, Granular	Sodium Thiocyanate (Sulfocyanate)	Potassium Bromide	Sodium Sulfate (Anhydrous)	Water
Kodak D-76, *standard developer* for tray and tank development........	750cc	2 gm.	100 gm.	5 gm.	......	....	2 gm.	.....	....	......	Fill up to make 1 liter
Kodak D-76R replenisher for Kodak D-76...	750cc	3 gm.	100 gm.	7.5 gm.	......	....	20 gm.	.....	....	......	as above
Kodak DK-20, *fine grain developer* for tray and tank development........	750cc	5 gm.	100 gm.	....	......	2 gm.	......	1 gm.	0.5 gm.	......	Fill up to make 1 liter
Kodak DK-20R, replenisher for Kodak DK-20	750cc	7.5 gm.	100 gm.	....	......	20 gm.	......	5 gm.	1 gm.	......	as above
Kodak DK-15, *tropical developer,* medium to high contrast..	750cc	5.5 gm.	90 gm.	....	......	22.5 gm.	......	.....	2 gm.	45 gm.	Fill up to make 1 liter
Kodak DK-15A, *tropical developer,* low to medium contrast..	By reducing the Kodak contents of the DK-15 developer to 5 gm. per liter, less contrastful negatives will be produced. Otherwise, formula and processing instructions remain unchanged.										
Kodak D-11, *high contrast developer.*	500cc	1 gm.	75 gm.	9 gm.	30 gm.	......	......	....	5 gm.	....	Fill up to make 1 liter

Dissolve all chemicals in the order they are listed. Do not dilute any of the above developers. If negatives are to be developed in DK-20, increase exposure times by 30 to 50 per cent beyond "normal" as indicated by exposure meter.

The following table shows average developing times for Kodak developers at 68° F.:

Developer	Tray, Continuous Agitation	Tank, Intermittent Agitation
Kodak D-76............	10 to 13 min.	14 to 17 min.
Kodak DK-20...........	9 to 12 min.	12 to 15 min.
Kodak DK-15...........	10 min. at 68° F., 2 to 3 min. at 90° F. for tank; 20% less for tray	
Kodak D-11............	4 min.	5 min.

Developing times depend on the type of film and the desired contrasts and density of the negative. Further instructions on time-temperature development methods are on page 141.

Use of replenisher: Add enough replenisher to the original developer to keep the volume constant, but notice recommendations by Eastman reprinted on page 130. Under these conditions, developing times will remain approximately constant throughout the useful life of the developer.

Pyrocatechin developer (*Windisch*). Pyrocatechin is a compensating developer for extreme light contrasts which prevents overdevelopment of overexposed highlights while getting the most out of underexposed shadows. This is not a genuine finegrain developer, but produces a fairly fine grain. No increase in exposure time is needed. Preparation from two separate stock solutions simplifies modification for special purposes.

STOCK SOLUTION I

Water (boiled) . . . . 1000 cc
Pyrocatechin . . . . 80 gm.
Sodium sulfite cryst. . . . . 25 gm.
(This solution will keep up to six months in bottle filled to the top)

STOCK SOLUTION II

10% solution of sodium hydroxide (caustic soda)
(This solution will keep up to two months in bottle filled to the top)

Recommended Use	Water	Solution I	Solution II	Developing Time
For use as standard developer. .	500cc	12cc	7cc	15 to 20 min.
For unusually contrastful negatives.	500cc	20cc	5cc	12 to 20 min.
For under-exposed night and theater shots, to get the utmost out of a negative	500cc	15cc	15cc	3 to 8 min.

Use the shorter developing times if negatives of softer gradation are desired; develop longer for greater contrast. Because of the caustic soda component, constant agitation of the developer is essential for even and uniform development, regardless whether tray or tank is used. This is probably the best developer for getting the utmost out of badly underexposed negatives. The diluted developer should be used only once and then discarded.

Ultra-finegrain developer (*Sease III*). This was one of the first, and still is one of the most successful, finegrain developers. Compared to other finegrain formulas, this one has the advantage of great simplicity, and of actually producing an extremely fine grain. Exposure has to be increased from two to three times.

Para-phenylene diamine . . . . 10 gm.
Glycin . . . . 6 gm.
Sodium sulfite (anhydrous) . . . . . 90 gm.
Water to make . . . . 1,000 cc

Dissolve all chemicals separately, mix afterwards. Use only distilled and boiled water. The glycin will dissolve only after mixing. Filter solution before use. Be careful when handling the para-phenylene diamine because it stains hands badly and clothes permanently.

Developing time at 68° F. is from 10 to 15 minutes, depending on the initial contrast of the film emulsion and the desired contrasts of the negative.

CAUTION: para-phenylene diamine may cause skin irritation. Avoid contact with it.

Ultra-finegrain developer (*Windisch 665*). Compared to the Sease III formula, this developer has the advantage of containing a nonstaining reducing agent, ortho-phenylene diamine, while at the same time producing a grain as fine as Sease III. Further advantages are: exposure factor is only 2 (instead of from 2 to 3); somewhat better shadow rendering than Sease III; very economical (up to 15 rolls of 35 mm film of 36 exposures each can be developed in 600 cc developer solution).

Water (boiled) . . . . 600 cc
Ortho-phenylene diamine . . . . 7 gm.
Metol . . . . 7 gm.
Sodium sulfite (anhydrous) . . . . . 55 gm.
Potassium metabisulfite (cryst) . . . 6 gm.

Dissolve all chemicals separately in small amounts of lukewarm water. The orthophenylene diamine and the Metol will dissolve completely only after the two solutions have been mixed. Add the sulfite solution and then the metabisulfite solution to the developer solution. Stir until clear and filter.

Developing time at 68° F. is from 12 to 18 minutes depending on the gradation of the film and the desired contrast of the negative. After the negatives have been fixed, rinse for a few minutes in three per cent acetic acid bath as this developer produces so-called "semi-physical" development, i.e., silver is dissolved and partially redeposited on the developing molecules. If this coating is later removed in the acid bath, an extremely fine grain will result while at the same time any possible lime deposits (from the water) will be removed.

Up to 15 rolls of 35mm film can be developed in 600cc solution; determine developing times for the second to the fifteenth rolls by multiplying developing time of the first roll by the following factors: 1.06–1.13–1.19–1.25–1.31–1.38–1.44–1.5–1.56–1.62–1.7–1.79–1.89–2.

Stop Bath, Hardening and Fixing Baths	Water	Potassium Chrome Alum	Sodium Thiosulfate (Hypo)	Sodium sulfite (Dessic.)	Acetic Acid (28% Pure)	Kodak Balanced Alkali	Potassium Alum	Water
Ansco 210 *shortstop bath* for negatives and prints	1,000cc	. . . . . .	. . . . . .	. . . . . .	45cc	. . . . . .	. . . . . .	. . . . . .
Ansco 216 *hardening bath*	1,000cc	30 gm.	. . . . . .	. . . . . .	. . . . . .	. . . . . .	. . . . . .	. . . . . .

In hot weather or for tropical development, use the above bath instead of Ansco 210 to give additional hardening to the film emulsion. Bath has to be prepared freshly before each use. Treat films for about 3 minutes between development and fixation; agitate constantly.

Kodak F-6 *acid-hardening fixer* for negatives and prints	600cc	. . . . . .	240 gm.	15 gm.	48cc	15 gm.	15 gm.	Fill up to make 1 liter
Kodak F-6a hardener, stock solution for preparing Kodak F-6 fixing bath	600cc	. . . . . .	. . . . . .	75 gm.	235cc	75 gm.	75 gm.	as above

Add one part of the cool stock hardener solution (F-6a) slowly to 4 parts cool 30% hypo solution (2½ pounds hypo per gallon of water) while stirring the hypo rapidly.

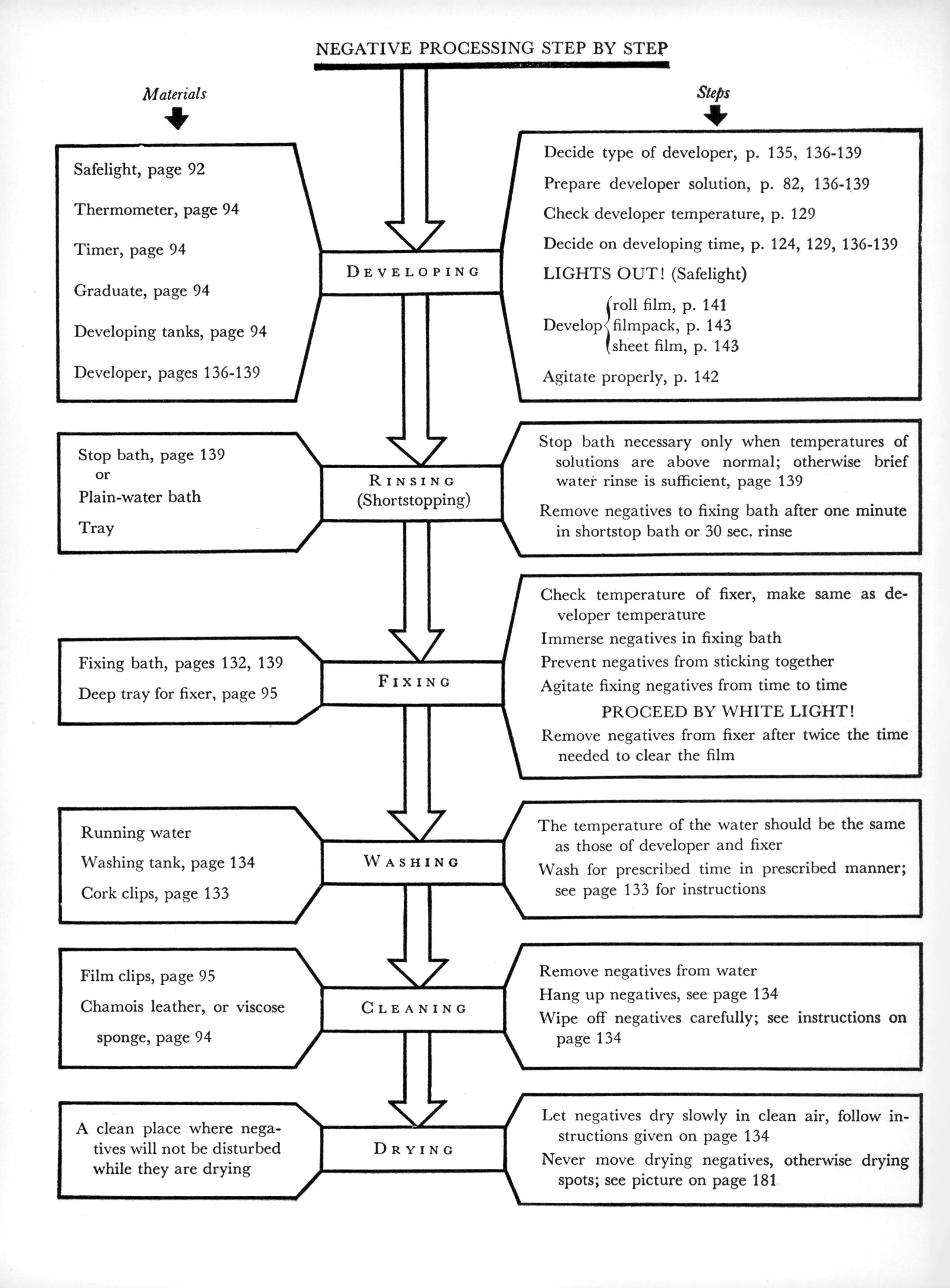
NEGATIVE PROCESSING STEP BY STEP
Materials
Steps
Safelight, page 92
Thermometer, page 94
Timer, page 94
Graduate, page 94
Developing tanks, page 94
Developer, pages 136-139
DEVELOPING
Decide type of developer, p. 135, 136-139
Prepare developer solution, p. 82, 136-139
Check developer temperature, p. 129
Decide on developing time, p. 124, 129, 136-139
LIGHTS OUT! (Safelight)
Develop
roll film, p. 141
filmpack, p. 143
sheet film, p. 143
Agitate properly, p. 142
Stop bath, page 139
or
Plain-water bath
Tray
RINSING
(Shortstopping)
Stop bath necessary only when temperatures of solutions are above normal; otherwise brief water rinse is sufficient, page 139
Remove negatives to fixing bath after one minute in shortstop bath or 30 sec. rinse
Fixing bath, pages 132, 139
Deep tray for fixer, page 95
FIXING
Check temperature of fixer, make same as developer temperature
Immerse negatives in fixing bath
Prevent negatives from sticking together
Agitate fixing negatives from time to time
PROCEED BY WHITE LIGHT!
Remove negatives from fixer after twice the time needed to clear the film
Running water
Washing tank, page 134
Cork clips, page 133
WASHING
The temperature of the water should be the same as those of developer and fixer
Wash for prescribed time in prescribed manner; see page 133 for instructions
Film clips, page 95
Chamois leather, or viscose sponge, page 94
CLEANING
Remove negatives from water
Hang up negatives, see page 134
Wipe off negatives carefully; see instructions on page 134
A clean place where negatives will not be disturbed while they are drying
DRYING
Let negatives dry slowly in clean air, follow instructions given on page 134
Never move drying negatives, otherwise drying spots; see picture on page 181

PRACTICAL DEVELOPMENT OF FILMS AND PLATES

Today, exposure and development of negatives have been brought under control so completely that the best results will be achieved by the most thoroughly scientific methods. Today, intelligent use of the three control instruments, exposure meter, thermometer, and watch (timer) enables a photographer to produce negatives technically far superior to those obtainable with any other method, especially a method based on our own subjective senses. In my opinion, exposing negatives "by experience" and developing them by "visual inspection" is as antiquated today as the horse-and-carriage: you may still find this in use in some parts of the country, but the majority of citizens consider it "old-fashioned."

General preparations. Regardless of the type of film to be developed, the preliminary steps are the same (consult chart on the opposite page as you go along):

Decide on the type of developer. Before choosing a finegrain developer, make sure that exposure times were increased accordingly when the pictures were taken.

Mix the developer solution; if previously prepared and stored in a bottle, check its temperature. If it is somewhere between 65 and 72° F., consult the film manufacturer's time-temperature chart for correct time of development. If the developer is below or above this temperature range, its temperature should be raised or lowered before it is used; see instructions on page 93.

Prepare the fixing bath, or, if already mixed, check its temperature. If it varies more than three degrees either way from that of the developer, reticulation of the film emulsion may result; see page 129.

In hot weather, prepare an acid stop bath; otherwise have a vessel filled with water of the proper temperature ready for rinsing the film between development and fixation.

Finally, arrange everything so you can easily find it in the dark. Set your timer, get your exposed film, and turn off the light—the safelight too, for modern panchromatic films must be processed in complete darkness.

Rollfilm tank development. Roll films can be developed either on reels in small tanks which take from one to three films—the method best suited for development of a few rolls at a time—or they can be developed suspended in deep tanks, which is a more economical way of processing large quantities of film but of practical interest only to professional photofinishers. I will confine myself here to a description of the first method.

The only operation during the whole business of rollfilm development that may cause trouble is winding the film on the reel. To prevent this, make sure that the reel is absolutely dry before you start to wind your film on it. Otherwise the film would stick to the reel and get water spots, kinks, and scratches resulting in a complete mess. Sacrifice a roll of unexposed film and practice winding it on the reel, first in full daylight and then in darkness, before you start with your first exposed film.

Immerse the loaded reel slowly in the developer-filled tank and start the timer. Tap the reel gently several times against the tank bottom to free air bubbles clinging to the film, and put the cover on the tank. Now you can safely turn on the darkroom illumination and proceed by white light.

As already stressed (page 130), proper agitation during the entire period of development is of utmost importance for uniformly developed negatives of correct density. The main thing to avoid is mechanical uniformity of agitation which might cause uniform streakiness in the negative. This is the reason why I have avoided mentioning mechanical agitators before; their action is too even and is more likely to cause trouble than to help. Start to agitate the film after it has been in the developer for half a minute by vigorously moving the tank backward and forward while tilting and rotating it simultaneously for about five seconds. Repeat this at half minute intervals during the entire period of development. If using a daylight loading tank, or a tank which permits turning the reel inside by means of a rod inserted through the top of the tank, rotate the reel counterclockwise for about one minute from the beginning of development, and thereafter for about five seconds at two-minute intervals until development is completed.

The moment your timer starts to ring, indicating completion of the development, pour the developer out of the tank back into the bottle, fill the tank with water, empty it, fill again, and repeat this three or four times. If temperatures of solutions are above normal (higher than 72° F.), use shortstop solution instead of water and agitate the film for about 30 seconds.

This done, pour out the water or shortstop bath and fill the tank with fixer. Agitate as before for half a minute, and repeat agitation several times during fixation.

After ten to fifteen minutes pour the fixer back into its bottle and wash the film for half an hour or more in running water with the top of the tank removed. Empty the tank completely at five-minute intervals to insure thorough washing.

If you have a larger number of films to process you can save time by taking the developed film off the reel (in darkness, naturally), fixing it in a separate tank or deep tray and washing it in the tank described on page 133. This way, your developing tank will be ready for re-use much sooner—as soon as you have washed and dried the reel after you peel off your film.

Take the thoroughly washed film out of the water, put a film clip on one end, and hang it up. Wipe both sides carefully with a well-soaked chamois or a viscose sponge to remove gelatine particles, foreign matter, and water, and hang the film up to dry in a place where it can remain undisturbed, where the air is free from dust and is neither too cold nor too hot, and where the sun cannot shine on it and cause drying streaks. Put a second film clip at its lower end to prevent it from curling up.

Thirty-five-millimeter films have to be cleaned especially carefully because even the smallest specks of foreign matter will show up big and ugly in an enlargement; especially if the emulsion is very soft, it is almost impossible to rid the film completely of tiny gelatine paritcles, because wiping it with the viscose sponge only loosens more particles from the edges of the perforation holes. In such a case, rinse the film briskly from both sides under the faucet, then immerse it for about two minutes in a one to two per cent solution of a wetting agent like, for instance, Aerosol-OT (observe instructions which come with different wetting agents), take it out and hang it up to dry without touching the emulsion again. The water will then run off smoothly with no drops remaining, and the film will dry perfectly clean. (NOTICE: since Aerosol will be precipitated by hard water, prepare solution with distilled water only.) Have another look at the film after about ten minutes: if a few drops have formed (not very likely but still possible), remove them, not by wiping, but by soaking them off with the corner of a moist viscose sponge.

Filmpack tank development. In general, proceed exactly as when developing a roll film but insert the filmpack-sheets into the compartments of a special "cage" instead of into a reel. Some types of film are liable to stick to the walls of the cage. This can be prevented by leaving the paper backing on the film instead of tearing it off prior to development. Leave this paper behind the film when inserting the sheets into the cage, thus separating the film from the cage walls. Pound the loaded tank a few times on the table to dislodge air bubbles from the film, then agitate at intervals of half a minute by once turning the tank slowly end over end. After development is completed, take the sheets out (in complete darkness, naturally), tear off the backing papers, and fix the negatives in a tray. Don't let them stick together. Agitate at least once every minute. Finally, wash the fixed films suspended on cork clips in the tank described on page 133 for at least half an hour. Take them out, wipe them carefully from both sides and hang them up to dry, following instructions given on page 134.

Sheet-film and plate tank development: In perfect darkness, load the developing hangers, start the timer, and lower the hangers smoothly into the developer-filled tank. Strike the hangers down hard two or three times to dislodge air bubbles, then agitate vertically for about five seconds. Leave the hangers undisturbed for about one minute, then lift the whole rack completely out of the solution, let the developer drain from one corner for a second or two, and put the hangers back into the tank. Repeat this operation once every minute for the whole duration of the development, draining the hangers alternately from different corners.

After completion of development, lift the whole rack out of the tank, drain, and remove to the water tank for rinsing—or, in warm weather, to the acid stop bath. Lift and drain four or five times, then transfer hangers to the fixing tank. Agitate the negatives vertically below the fixer surface for half a minute after immersion, then lift and drain hangers once every two minutes for the whole duration of fixation. From here on, proceed by white light.

After fixation is completed, wash negatives in their hangers for at least half an hour, wipe them carefully from both sides with a damp chamois leather or viscose sponge and put them up to dry, following instructions given on page 133.

Filmpack and sheet-film tray development. If up to six filmpack or sheet-film negatives have to be developed in a hurry, the following method will give excellent results, provided (*a*) that the operator is careful—and has short fingernails! (*b*) that the temperature of the developer is not higher than 68° F. because otherwise the gelatine would soften too much, and (*c*) that the alkali content of the developer is not too high—for the same reason.

Immerse the exposed films one after another into a tray of water not warmer than 68° F., emulsion side up, but make sure that the first film is completely immersed before you put the next one on top of it; otherwise they may stick together for good. After the last film is immersed, carefully draw the bottom one out and put it on top of the pile, touching it at the extreme edges only and watching that its corners don't scratch any of the other films. Similarly, take one film after another off the bottom and put it on top until the whole stack has been leafed through twice.

Start the timer and remove the films to the developer tray, pulling them one at a time from the bottom of the water tray. Repeat the operation of leafing slowly through the films from bottom to top for the entire duration of the development, turning the negatives sideways once in a while but always keeping the emulsion side up.

After completion of development, remove the films individually to the acid stop bath, leafing them through twice as described above. Finally, transfer the negatives one by one to the fixer and repeat the performance of leafing through the pile two or three times right after immersion, and once every two minutes until fixation is completed. Finally, wash for at least half an hour in the tank described on page 133, then clean and dry the films as usual.

In the same way, single films or plates can be developed, only the method of agitation is slightly different: start the timer and slide the film or plate smoothly into the developer from the right, while simultaneously lifting the left side of the tray just enough to make the developer flow evenly over the film or plate. Lower the left side of the tray and lift the near side slightly, lower it and repeat the performance with the left side, and so on. Keep on agitating like this during the entire period of development, then transfer the negative to the rinse or shortstop bath, and from there to the fixer, always agitating as described above. Finally, wash, clean, and dry the negative as usual; see page 133.

Recognition of mistakes

Everybody occasionally makes a mistake, but in order to avoid repeating such a mistake one has to be able to recognize its cause. Determination of the cause of faulty negatives, however, is not always easy because actually they may be the result of two different kinds of mistakes: faulty exposure, faulty development, or both. And sometimes, a mistake made during exposure can be obscured or partially compensated for by a mistake made during development, as, for instance, underexposure and overdevelopment, two of the most common mistakes made by beginners, which together can produce negatives that are apparently right in density and contrast, but which nevertheless will only give unsatisfactory prints, lacking quality and shadow detail. On the following pages are shown combinations of different mistakes made during exposure and development, together with a survey of their characteristics and recommendations for possible correction. To distinguish between mistakes caused by faulty exposure and by faulty development consult the following table. (It is assumed in this table, that either exposure *or* development are faulty, but not both of them together; for such cases, consult the more exhaustive survey on page 147):

Appearance of the Negative		Cause of the Mistake	
Too thin	and too contrasty	= Exposure	too short
	and too contrastless	= Development	
Too dense	and too contrastless	= Exposure	too long
	and too contrasty	= Development	

← EXPOSURE →

Too short | Correct | Too long

← DEVELOPMENT →

Too short

Normal

Too long

Underexposed and underdeveloped:

All-over—density extremely low

Contrasts—much too low

Shadow detail—completely lacking

Highlights—much too weak

Remedy: None. Such negatives are total losses

Correctly exposed but underdeveloped:

All-over—density too low

Contrasts—too low

Shadow detail—present but thin

Highlights—too weak

Remedy: Print on paper of hard gradation

Overexposed and underdeveloped:

All-over—density almost normal

Contrasts—too low

Shadow detail—abnormally strong, highlights not strong enough

Remedy: Print on paper of extra-hard gradation

Underexposed but normally developed:

All-over—density too low

Contrasts—too great

Shadow detail—practically lacking

Highlights—rather transparent

Remedy: None. No intensifier can produce shadow detail that is not there

Correctly exposed and correctly developed:

All-over—density normal

Contrasts—normal

Shadow detail—is present

Highlights—strong but still transparent

Negatives intended for enlarging should generally be slightly thinner, more transparent, than those intended for contact printing

The *ideal* negative

Overexposed but normally developed:

All-over—density too high

Contrasts—too low

Shadow detail—abnormally strong

Highlights—too dense, graininess rather pronounced

Remedy: If negative is very dense, reduce in Kodak R-4a reducer (page 169). Print on paper of hard gradation

Underexposed and overdeveloped:

All-over—density about normal

Contrasts—much too high

Shadow detail—too weak

Highlights—rather dense and black

Remedy: If extremely dense, reduce carefully with Kodak R-15 reducer (page 170); print on paper of soft or extra-soft gradation

Correctly exposed but overdeveloped:

All-over—density too high

Contrasts—somewhat higher than normally desirable

Shadow detail—strong

Highlights—very black and blocked, pronounced graininess

Remedy: Reduce in Kodak R-15 reducer (page 170); print on paper of soft gradation

Overexposed and overdeveloped:

All-over—density extremely high, negative appears practically black

Contrasts—about normal

Shadow detail—much too strong

Highlights—perfectly black and detailless, graininess extremely pronounced

Remedy: Reduce in Kodak R-5 reducer (page 170), print on paper of normal gradation

PROCESSING THE PRINT

We have to differentiate between "contact prints" and "projection prints" (enlargements, blowups). Contact prints are made directly from the negative and their size is always identical with that of the film, while projection prints are enlargements and can have practically any size. To make contact prints we need a printing frame or a contact printer (page 95); to make projection prints we need an enlarger (pages 96-97). Other differences between these two types of prints are: contacts are usually made on the slower chloride or chlorobromide papers (pages 77-78) in order to get exposure times that are not too short, while enlargements usually are made on the faster bromide or bromochloride papers (pages 77-78) in order to get exposure times that are not too long. Contacts are true positive replicas of negatives with most of their merits or faults. Enlargements can be controlled to a very high degree and extensive corrections of undesirable features or faults of the negative can be made; see pp. 161-163.

Apart from this, processing of contacts and enlargements is identical: both have to be exposed, and in both cases a latent image has to be developed, fixed, washed, and dried very much like a negative. However, operations can now be performed by comparatively bright yellow-greenish safelight illumination (pages 92-93) because of the relatively low sensitivity of printing papers.

Contact Printing Step by Step

In the darkroom or a darkened room.......—	
put negative into printing frame or contact printer, emulsion side up.................—	by white room illumination
select a printing paper of suitable grade according to density range of negative (page 150)...................................—	by yellow-green safelight illumination
place printing paper on negative, emulsion side down, close frame or printer..........—	as before
expose the print (page 152)..............—	with white light; but first make sure that your paper supply is wrapped light-tight
take the paper out of the frame or printer and develop it (page 155)...................—	by yellow-green safelight illumination
rinse the print in the shortstop bath (page 139)—	as before
fix the print in the fixing bath (page 139)...—	white light can be turned on after ten seconds
wash the print (page 133)................—	by white light, any light, or in darkness
dry the print (page 158)..................—	as before

In the darkroom or a darkened room.......—	
make sure your negative is clean and free from dust.......—	by white room illumination
put the negative into the negative carrier of the enlarger, emulsion side downwards, facing the lens.......—	by white room illumination
turn on the enlarger light.......—	turn off the room illumination
adjust the size of the image by raising or lowering the enlarger head; focus image sharply on easel.......—	in darkness—you will see better(!)
turn off enlarger light.......—	turn on the yellow-green safelight
select a printing paper of suitable grade according to the density range of the negative (page 150).......—	by yellow-green safelight illumination
(unless you are experienced, make test exposure with paper strip, see page 153).......—	(turn off safelight during exposure, and you will see your projected image better; use two-way foot switch as described on page 93)
(develop and fix this test strip, determine correct exposure for your print)	
insert your printing paper of correct gradation into the enlarger easel.......—	by yellow-green safelight illumination
expose the print according to test strip (page 153).......—	turn off safelight during exposure for reason mentioned above
develop the print (page 155).......—	by yellow-green safelight illumination
rinse print in shortstop bath (page 139).......—	as before
fix print in fixing bath (page 139).......—	white light can be turned on after ten seconds; make sure your paper supply is safe from light
wash the print (page 133).......—	by white or any light
dry the print (page 158).......—	by white or any light

The negative

A good print starts with a good negative. And "good" means not only well exposed and well developed, but CLEAN, too. . . . So before you put your negative into the printing frame or the enlarger, brush off dust particles and lint with a camel's-hair brush. And make sure that the glasses in the printing frame and negative carrier are clean, too. . . . Fingermarks can sometimes be removed by wiping a negative with a carbon-tetrachloride-soaked cotton tuft. Minor scratches and abrasion marks disappear often after treating them with "scratch-patch"; a fine film of Vaseline rubbed into the scratches does the same job equally well but has to be wiped off afterwards with carbon tetrachloride

While for contact printing it doesn't matter very much if a negative is thin or dense, negatives that are very dense have to be reduced before they will make good enlargements, because otherwise exposure times would become so long that stray light from the enlarger may fog the paper. A negative is "too dense" for enlarging if it would necessitate an exposure time of more than one minute. Before you reduce a dense negative, examine its gradation: if it is too contrasty (overdevelopment), reduce with Kodak R-15 (page 170); if it is too contrastless (overexposure), use Kodak R-4a reducer (page 169). If a negative is too thin, try stopping down the enlarger lens and printing on slow chloride paper before you attempt intensification (page 170), which always involves hazards that had better be avoided . . . .

> The first condition for successful printing and enlarging is clean negatives of proper density and contrast!

The gradation of the printing paper

Unfortunately, not every negative is "technically perfect"—whether from an exposure a little too long or too short, a developer too warm or too cold, an incorrect developing time, or simply because the contrasts of the subject were excessively high or unusually low. In all such cases negatives with "abnormal" gradations result, but fortunately these faults can usually be corrected when making the print by selecting a paper with an appropriate gradation:

Character of Negative Gradation:	Extremely Contrasty	Contrasty	Normal	Soft	Extremely Flat
Recommended paper gradation: (contrast grade numbers in parentheses)	Extra soft (No. 1)	Soft (No. 2)	Normal (No. 3)	Hard (No. 4)	Extra hard (No. 5)

(NOTICE: Manufacturers usually designate their No. 2 paper gradation as "normal"; actually it will be found, however, that most normally developed negatives will have to be printed on No. 3 paper when snappy prints are wanted—especially if negatives have been finegrain developed—which is the reason why I here call No. 3 papers "normal.")

When judging a negative with regard to the printing paper gradation it may require, don't confuse gradation with density. The two have nothing to do with each other, and a very thin negative, for instance, can be extremely contrastful (underexposed and overdeveloped) as well as extremely flat (overexposed and underdeveloped), and the same goes for very dense negatives. When in doubt,

← PAPER GRADATION →

Too soft | Correct | Too hard

Paper too soft—print underexposed

Paper right—print underexposed

Paper too hard—print underexposed

Too short

← EXPOSURE →

Paper too soft—exposure correct

Paper right—exposure correct

Paper too hard—exposure correct

Correct

Paper too soft—print overexposed

Paper right—print overexposed

Paper too hard—print overexposed

Too long

make a print on normal paper and compare it with the pictures on the preceding page; if necessary, make corrections accordingly.

> The second condition for successful printing and enlarging is selection of a printing paper of the correct gradation with regard to the gradation of the negative.

The exposure of the print

The only operation during the whole printing process that is likely to cause the beginner trouble is determination of the correct exposure time for the printing paper. Unlike negatives, which can stand considerable overexposure and even some underexposure and still turn out all right, printing papers have to be exposed "on the nose." Negatives are only an intermediate step in the process of picture-making, and mistakes made at this stage can be corrected to a certain degree during the following step, printing. But the print is final, and mistakes made during its execution cannot be corrected any more. Partially, this is because the emulsion of a printing paper is infinitely thinner than that of a negative and consequently doesn't have the "reserve"—the "exposure latitude"—of the thicker emulsion much richer in silver. Besides, a negative is an original and as such valuable enough to warrant elaborate measures to save it if something goes wrong; a print, however, is merely a positive reproduction of a negative and can be remade very simply at any time. And since printing paper is comparatively cheap, it is much more economical to remake an unsatisfactory print than to waste time trying to correct it. In the case of underexposure and selection of the wrong gradation it is hopeless anyway, and in the case of overexposure it could never match the quality of a correctly exposed print. Consequently, the beginner should remember right from the start:

> A wrongly exposed print belongs in the garbage can!

The simplest way of finding the correct exposure time is by trial and error. There are some exposure guides and meters for prints on the market, but they are either too complicated to use and too expensive, or too much depends on the subjective judgment of the operator, to make them of real practical value. And after he has successfully exposed only a few prints any beginner will rapidly acquire enough experience to judge the density of a negative correctly.

Contact-print exposure determination. If you use a contact printer, follow the directions of the instruction booklet. If using a printing frame, exposure times depend on several factors: they will be the shorter, the brighter and the closer to the printing frame your source of light is, the thinner the negative and the higher the speed of the printing paper, and vice versa. Standardize conditions as far as possible. Always expose with the same source of light at the same distance from the printing frame. Write down these data together with the resulting correct exposure times, the type and gradation of the paper used, and the density of the negative, so that later you can duplicate your results without having to start again from scratch. If your negative is relatively small, simply make a few test exposures until you get your answer. If negatives are larger, use only a strip of paper about one inch wide and as long as the negative for the test exposure in order to save paper. Develop such test exposures for exactly one minute (see pages 155-156), fix, and examine the result by white light: if the image is too light, exposure was too short; if the image is too dark, exposure was too long.

Projection-print exposure determination. Generally, enlargements are exposed exactly like contact prints, but exposure determination is slightly more complicated by virtue of the fact that two new variables have to be considered: aperture of the enlarger lens and degree of magnification of the image. The more the lens is stopped down, and the greater the distance between lens and paper, the longer the exposure time, and vice versa.

The simplest way to determine the correct exposure time for an enlargement is with the help of a test strip that has been exposed step by step; see picture and caption below:

Exposure determination for enlargements: Cut a strip of sensitized paper of the correct gradation and place it on the enlarger easel so that the most important parts of the image will be projected onto it, containing light as well as dark sections. Cover the strip with a piece of cardboard and expose it gradually with different exposure times by pulling back the cardboard step by step. Develop, fix, and examine it by white light. In the strip above, for instance, exposure time for the first step was 40 seconds, for the second 20 seconds, the third 10 seconds and the fourth 5 seconds. Consequently, the steps received totals of 40, 20, 10 and 5 seconds, of which the one exposed for 20 seconds appears best. Use this exposure time for making the final print. Naturally, the correct exposure time may fall between two steps, but then it shouldn't be difficult to interpolate and make the necessary corrections when exposing the final print.

This method of test strips, simple as it may be, has one serious disadvantage: we have to compare different images, images which may sometimes be light (parts of the sky in the picture) and which may sometimes be dark (parts of the foreground in shadow). The method described in the following avoids this complication, giving four different exposures of identical parts of the negative and thus facilitates comparison of the results of different exposure times.

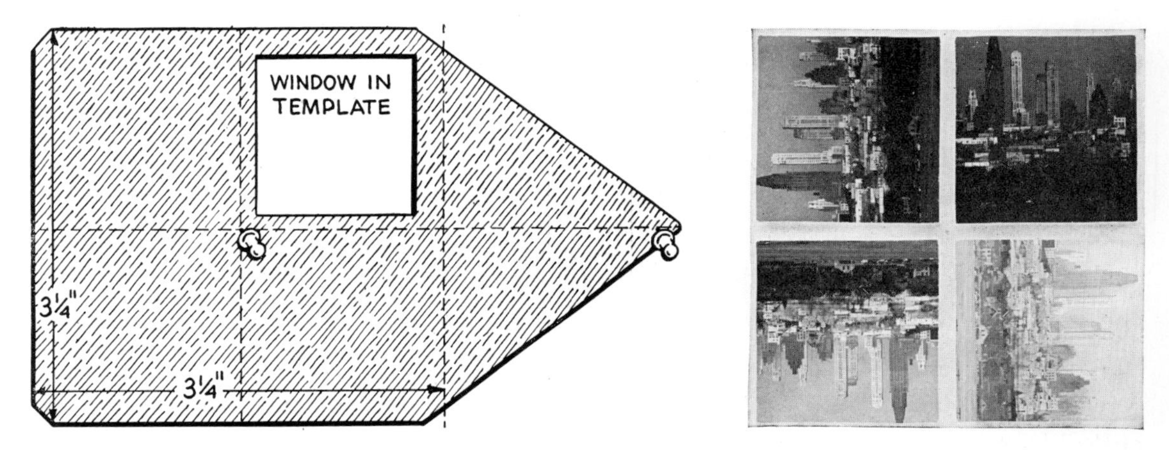

Exposure determination for enlargements: Cut template from thin, hard cardboard according to figure at left. Cut a piece of sensitized paper of correct gradation to size, place it underneath the template so that the most important part of the image appears projected onto it through the window in the template. Fasten template with two push-pins on enlarger easel so that the sensitized paper underneath can be rotated around one pin. Expose test paper four times with four different exposure times through template window, rotating the paper 90° for each consecutive exposure. Develop, fix and examine under white light. In the case above, exposure times were 5, 10, 20 and 40 seconds, of which the 20-seconds exposure appears best. Use the so-determined exposure time for exposing the enlargement.

The best test for the correctness of the exposure time is the behavior of the sensitized paper in the developer. If after one minute of development the image is still too light, with chalky highlights and grayish shadows, exposure was too short; and if the image appears within a few seconds and grows rapidly too dark, exposure was too long. In both cases the print is a total loss. In the first instance prolongation of development would only produce all-over grayishness resulting from fog, and yellow stain resulting from oxidizing developer. In the second instance pulling the paper prematurely out of the developer would only result in a brownish, discolored print with uneven and streaky tone values. Hence, our third rule for successful printing:

> The third condition for successful printing and enlarging is correct exposure of the paper!

Development of the print

Exposure of the sensitized paper produces a latent image which has to be developed exactly like a negative, except that the type of the developer and the time of development are slightly different. The following formula can be recommended for the development of any type of sensitized paper:

KODAK DEVELOPER D-72
(*Stock solution*)

Water (about 125° F.)	500.0 cc
Elon	3.0 gm.
Sodium sulfite (desiccated)	45.0 gm.
Hydroquinone	12.0 gm.
Sodium carbonate (monohydrated)	80.0 gm.
Potassium bromide	2.0 gm.
Water to make	1000.0 cc

Dissolve the chemicals in the order in which they are listed. For use, dilute one part stock solution with two parts of water; maintain a temperature of 70° F.; time your exposures so the prints will be fully developed in about 60 seconds.

This developer is available in ready-mixed form, together with a number of other good paper developers made by various manufacturers.

The temperature of the developer solution has a certain influence not only on the duration of the development, but on the tone of the print as well. Developers that are relatively cold develop sluggishly, producing prints that look underexposed, with chalky highlights and weak shadows; developers that are too warm produce prints of brownish and often outright muddy tones resembling the results of overexposure. Generally, however, developer temperatures for print development should be slightly higher than those for negative development in order to produce snappy prints with clean neutral black tones. Hence:

> The fourth condition for successful printing and enlarging is a developer temperature of 70° F.!

The time of development. As previously mentioned, sensitized papers have to be fully developed within a certain time—usually from 45 to 120 seconds—if prints rich in half-tones, with pleasant contrasts and clean tone values are to result. The only way of regulating the developing time is by adjusting the time of exposure accordingly; see pages 152-154. Prints that appear fully developed before this time, and prints that haven't acquired full strength within this time, are wrongly exposed, and nothing can be done to save them. Consequently, we make a mental note:

> The fifth condition for successful printing and enlarging is maintenance of a developing time of not less than 45 and not more than 120 seconds!

Practical print processing

Developing. Prepare and arrange your developer, fixer (shortstop), and water baths, maintaining temperatures from 70 to 72° F. Take the exposed paper carefully, without touching the emulsion side with hands or fingers, and slide it edgewise into the developer, emulsion side up. Make sure you immerse the paper smoothly without interruption, otherwise developing marks may result (picture on opposite page, *top right*). Develop the print for 60 to 90 seconds; agitate continuously. If the developer tray is relatively small, agitate by gently rocking the tray alternately from side to side and front to back. If the tray is large, agitate by moving the print around in the developer with print tongs. Don't dip your hands into the developer; handle prints with tongs only. This way, you will save many a print from getting fingermarks on it resulting from wet or developer- or hypo-stained hands.

Mistakes. If the image comes up very fast and seems ready after only half a minute or less, take the print out and throw it away. It was overexposed, and premature interruption of development would only give you a brownish muddy-looking print without sparkle or snap (picture on opposite page, *bottom right*). If after a minute and a half the print seems still too light, take it out and throw it away. It was underexposed, and further prolongation of development will produce nothing but an anemic-looking, grayish, and possibly yellow-stained print (picture on opposite page, *bottom left*). If after one minute in the developer the lightest parts of the image have already turned gray while the darkest parts still seem not dark enough—in other words, if contrasts are too low—then the gradation of the printing paper was too soft for that particular negative (see picture on page 151, *center row left*). And, if after one minute in the developer the lightest parts of the image are still chalky and without detail while the darkest parts are perfectly black and half-tones are more or less missing—in other words, if contrasts are too high—then the gradation of the paper was too hard for that particular negative (see picture on page 151, *center row right*).

Fixing. The well-exposed print will appear ready after 60 to 90 seconds in the

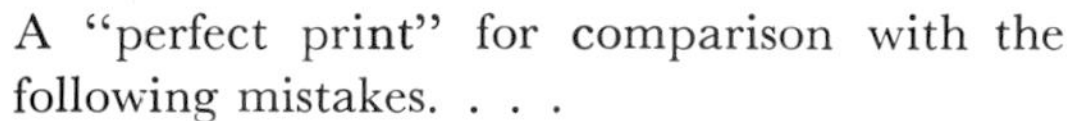

A "perfect print" for comparison with the following mistakes. . . .

When putting the exposed paper into the developer, make sure that it is being covered evenly, or marks like these may result. . . .

THE THREE MOST COMMON MISTAKES MADE DURING THE PROCESSING OF PRINTS

Forcing an underexposed print in the developer nets nothing but an anemic-looking, flat, and grayish print like this. . . .

Pulling an overexposed print out of the developer prematurely will produce nothing but a muddy-looking, mottled print like this. . . .

developer, when it should be taken out (print tongs!), transferred to the shortstop bath (which can be omitted if a good acid fixing bath is used) for about 5 to 10 seconds (agitate!), and from there to the hypo (fixing bath), where it should remain for 10 to 15 minutes. Use the same fixing-bath formula that was recommended on page 139 for the fixation of negatives, or any one of the ready-mixed commercial fixing baths for printing papers as recommended and produced by various manufacturers, but avoid fixing negatives and prints in the same bath. Don't leave the print unnecessarily long in the hypo, especially if the bath has been freshly prepared, or the image may begin to bleach. Agitate fixing prints once every two or three minutes by turning them over. Since proper fixing is one of the main conditions for print permanence, a good way to insure thorough fixation is to use two fixing baths as described on page 132. Use separate tongs for handling prints in the developer and in the hypo—never mix them up (mark tongs to avoid mistakes). Hypo ruins both the developer and developing prints, taking the strength out of the developer and staining the prints.

Washing. After proper fixation, wash singleweight prints for at least one hour, and doubleweight prints for at least one hour and a half—in the tank described on page 133. Make test for thoroughness of washing as recommended on page 159.

Drying. The best way to dry prints of any size up to 16x20 inches is in an electric print dryer (page 95). This leaves prints perfectly flat and straight, and avoids the danger of lumps and bumps resulting from waterdrops that dried into the emulsion and distorted the paper stock. Before prints are put into the drier, wipe them from both sides with a damp lint-free cloth to remove excess water and to speed up drying. If you want prints with a high gloss, print on glossy paper and ferrotype the prints by squeezing them on ferrotype tins. They can then be dried in an electric dryer or simply by air-drying in a warm room. As soon as the prints are completely dry, they will come off the plate by themselves, or can easily be pulled off. To prevent sticking, wash ferrotype plates from time to time with plate polish as manufactured by Eastman Kodak and others.

Print permanence

If prints are expected to last for any considerable length of time without fading or developing stains and spots, they have to be processed much more carefully than usual. The practice of "washing" prints in a tray for 15 to 20 minutes, for instance, is a sure invitation to early fading and discoloration. I have seen prints that were treated in this way bleach and turn yellow all over within less than a year.

The most dangerous enemies of print permanence are chemicals remaining in the emulsion and paper stock, high humidity and temperature, and prolonged exposure to strong light. The groundwork for lasting print beauty has to be laid during fixation.

If the hypo is exhausted, it cannot completely dissolve all the unexposed silver halides, which in time will begin to decompose and stain the print. The surest way to guard against this is to use the two-bath fixing method recommended on page 132, followed by thorough washing (page 133). Even so, it is almost impossible to remove the last traces of hypo from the paper stock—especially from thick double-weight paper—and minute traces of hypo left in a print will in time act upon the emulsion and cause the image to fade. Guard against this by testing the wash water for traces of hypo, which according to Eastman Kodak can be done as follows:

KODAK HT-1A TEST SOLUTION FOR HYPO

Distilled water	180 cc
Potassium permanganate	0.3 gm.
Sodium hydroxide (caustic soda)	0.6 gm.
Add distilled water to make	250 cc

Add 1 cc of the above solution to 125 cc of distilled water. From this diluted solution, take 15 cc and pour it into a small clear glass vial or test tube. Take six 4x5 prints (or equivalent) out of the wash water and let water drip from them into the solution-filled test tube for about half a minute. If hypo is present, it will be disclosed by a discoloration of the test solution: within about half a minute, its initial violet color will turn to orange and will fade entirely within another half minute, making the solution appear clear again. A positive reaction like this would prove the presence of hypo, indicating that washing of the prints has to be continued. Make another test half an hour later: if it is positive again, continue washing. As long as the temperature of the wash water is not above 75° F., prints may be washed up to three hours without harmful effects, provided they were fixed in an acid-hardening fixing bath.

CAUTION! Water that is contaminated with oxidizable organic matter reacts on the test solution like hypo-contaminated water! To exclude erroneous results, test the water used for washing the prints as follows before you make the final hypo test: make up two samples of the above test solution with distilled water; add to one of them an amount of tap water equal to that drained off the prints into the second, and examine the colors of the samples. If the tap-water sample remains violet in color, no organic matter is present, and any discoloration of the other sample containing washing water drained from prints indicates the presence of hypo. If the tap-water sample becomes discolored, however, the colors of the two test samples made up from tap water and wash water have to be compared with each other; if they are different—if, for instance, the tap-water sample is pink and the wash-water sample is yellow—presence of hypo is proven; but if their colors are identical—if for instance both of them turned pink—the wash water is reasonably free from hypo, and consequently the prints, too . . . .

Ready-mixed solutions for testing the wash water for hypo are made by several laboratories. Your dealer probably has some of them in stock.

Absence of discoloration in the above test solution does *not* prove complete absence of hypo in the wash water or in the prints, but it proves that papers are reasonably free from hypo. To insure complete freedom from hypo, prints have to be treated with a hypo-eliminator solution: wash thoroughly (for at least 30 minutes in the tank described on page 133), then immerse the prints for about six minutes in a solution of the following hypo eliminator at 68° F., and continue to wash for another ten minutes before you dry your prints in the usual manner. (CAUTION: Prepare the solution immediately before use and keep in a special container during use. Do not store the mixed solution in a stoppered bottle, or the gas evolved may break the bottle.)

KODAK HE-1 HYPO ELIMINATOR

Water	500 cc
Hydrogen peroxide, 3% solution	125 cc
Ammonia, 3% solution	100 cc
Add water to make	1,000 cc

In 1,000 cc of this solution, one dozen sheets of 8x10 paper (or equivalent) can be treated.

Completeness of hypo elimination can be tested in the following way: together with your prints process a sheet of unexposed sensitized paper—which naturally will remain white—treating it in every respect exactly as you treat your prints, putting it through all the different steps of processing. After the final wash, cut this sheet in half, immerse one half of it for about three minutes in a one per cent silver nitrate solution, rinse briefly in water, and compare it while it is still wet with the other untreated half: if both look alike, hypo has been eliminated completely. If traces of hypo are still present, the portion treated with silver nitrate will appear brownish discolored, the darker in tone the more hypo it contained. Note, however, that contamination of the wash water with hydrogen sulfide or wood extracts may produce similar stains even in the absence of hypo . . . .

Use of the hypo eliminator may have the following effects:

Prints may acquire a tendency to stick to the belt on belt driers, which can be prevented by hardening the emulsions for about three minutes in a one per cent solution of formaldehyde before drying.

The print tone may change very slightly, which can be prevented by adding one gram of potassium bromide to 1,000 cc of the hypo-eliminator solution.

The whites in the prints may acquire a very slight yellowish tone, which can be minimized by treating the prints for about two minutes with a one per cent solution of sodium sulfite immediately after the hypo-eliminator bath, before they get their final washing.

To minimize the dangers resulting from exposure to air and light, prints that are expected to last as long as possible should be stored tightly packed in darkness. Framed on a wall and exposed to sunlight, any print may sooner or later begin to turn yellow. For additional protection, prints can be treated in the following gold solution, which covers the silver image with a protective layer of gold that is much less susceptible to atmospheric influences than silver.

KODAK GP-1 GOLD PROTECTIVE SOLUTION

Water	750 cc
Gold chloride 1% solution	10 cc
Sodium thiocyanate	10 gm.
Add water to make	1,000 cc

Dissolve one gram of gold chloride in 100 cc of water; take 10 cc of this solution and add it to 750 cc of water. Dissolve the sodium thiocyanate by itself in 125 cc of water; then add this solution slowly to the solution of gold chloride while stirring vigorously. The gold bath doesn't keep very well and should be prepared immediately before use.

In 1,000 cc of this solution, eight prints 8x10 inches (or equivalent) can be treated.

After thorough washing—and preferably treatment in hypo-eliminator bath—immerse the prints for about ten minutes in the gold bath at 70° F., or until you notice a slight change in tone of the image towards blueish black; wash for ten more minutes in running water and dry the prints in the usual way.

TIPS FOR SUCCESSFUL ENLARGING

The previous pages contained instructions and suggestions relevant to the customary processing of both contact prints and enlargements. Out of such routine, most photographers will sooner or later develop individualized methods of their own, based on improvements they have invented, short cuts they have discovered, personal preferences they have acquired—and the sum total of such deviations from, and additions to, the ordinary routine of print processing eventually becomes an important factor which greatly influences the outcome of their work. In this sense, the following hints and tips are offered as helpful additions to the ordinary routine of enlarging:

In cold and dry weather, removing dust from films and negative-carrier pressure plates can become quite a little problem; for the more we brush and rub, the more we increase their charges of static electricity, and the more stubbornly will particles of dust and lint cling to them. Under such conditions, brush only once and very lightly; then use a rubber syringe to blow off dirt with a series of short, sharp puffs.

Don't forget that you can make a full-size picture from only a section of a negative—one of the great advantages of projection printing over contact printing. Ruthlessly eliminate unsatisfactory parts of the negative, unsharp foreground, wires cutting through the sky, and superfluous detail and concentrate on the subject proper by blowing it up to an appropriate size in the pictorially most effective form.

When enlarging only small sections of a negative, mask off the rest of the film temporarily with thin black paper; by thus preventing stray diffuse light from fogging the paper you will considerably improve the contrasts of your print.

Watch out when making enlargements of great magnification: sometimes, light from the lens hitting the chromium-plated enlarger column is reflected back onto the sensitized paper where it manifests itself in the form of dark marks. Covering the column with black paper will prevent this.

If you work with a glassless negative carrier, heat may buckle the negative and snap it out of focus again before you are ready to expose the print, unless you work very fast. Give the negative a moment's time to warm up and to settle down into a more permanent position. Refocus just before you are ready to make the exposure.

If negatives are very dense, or if they don't contain any really sharp features, focusing may become difficult; in such cases, focus on one of the nearly always present minute blemishes—a scratch in the emulsion, the white mark left by a particle of dust, a tiny little "pinhole"—or use a magnifying focusing device of the type made especially for enlargers.

Use the diaphragm of the enlarger lens to best advantage: 1. To regulate the time of exposure; if negatives are very thin, exposure times would be too short to permit effective "dodging" or "burning-in" (see page 216) unless you stop down until you get exposure times from at least 15 to 25 seconds. 2. To improve the definition of the lens; especially in cheaper enlargers, lenses often don't cover the corners of the image sharply unless they are stopped down to somewhere around *f* 8. 3. To increase the depth of field when working with glassless negative carriers; in case the film should buckle under the influence of heat, stopping down the diaphragm will provide enough sharpness in depth to prevent partial unsharpness in the print.

Newton rings, irregularly shaped, concentric forms iridescent in all colors of the spectrum, are a pest that at times can make life miserable in a darkroom. They come and they go with the weather—here today and gone tomorrow. . . . The best way to prevent them entirely is to use a glassless negative carrier; sometimes, putting a piece of clear cellophane between film and pressure glass will help. Films that are very dry and have been rolled for a long time are more likely to produce Newton rings than films that have been kept flat and pliable—one definite reason for cutting up rolls of 35 mm film into lengths of six frames each and filing such negatives flat.

In older or lightly built houses, vibrations from passing trucks, etc., may shake the enlarger and—especially while enlargements of great magnification are being made—cause blurred prints. Under such circumstances, securing the upper end of the enlarger column to the wall with a bracket will minimize this danger by preventing the enlarger head from vibrating after the cause of the disturbance has passed.

When making a test strip for determination of the exposure (page 153), write the different exposure times you gave it with pencil on its back side before development. This way you can never forget them, which otherwise happens surprisingly often, forcing you to go through the whole rigmarole again. . . .

The best way to check the tone of the highlights or whites in a print is to bend a corner of the printing paper back and to hold it against the image. Since the back of the paper is always pure white (unless stained by old developer or fixing bath) even the slightest degree of grayishness in a supposedly white highlight can easily be discovered in this manner. Otherwise, a surprisingly dark shade of gray may stil pass unnoticed as white under the safelight, if the eye has nothing really white with which to compare it.

Remember that prints in the hypo or water always look lighter than after they are dry. A wet print that in the darkroom looked just right will probably appear too dark after it has been finished. Make allowance for this effect by developing prints slightly lighter than you want them finally to look.

An invaluable advantage of enlarging over contact printing is the possibility of redistorting or correcting "converging verticals" in the negative (or any other lines) to parallelism in the print. Simply tilt your easel according to the instructions below, stop down the diaphragm until the image is sharp all over again. Some enlargers have negative carriers which can be tilted independently of the enlarger head; with these, images that are sharp all over can be produced even with the diaphragm of the enlarger lens wide open (see page 97).

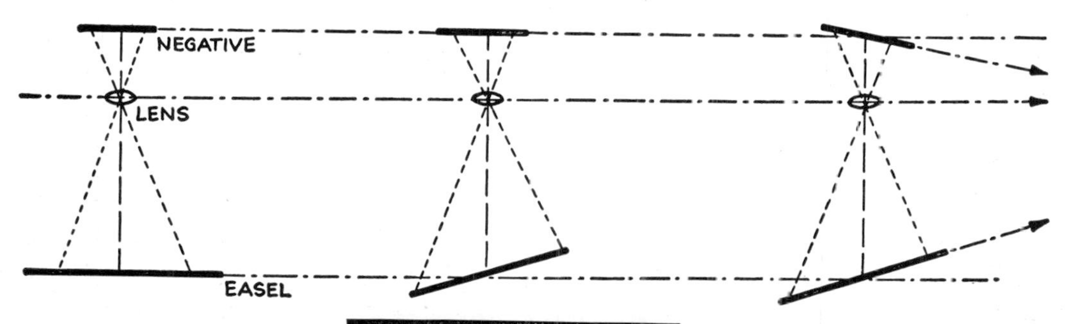

Straight enlargement—verticals converge, buildings appear to collapse. This impression can easily be corrected in the enlargement.

Tilting the easel restores verticals to parallelism; unsharpness has to be corrected by stopping the lens down accordingly.

Tilting easel and negative in opposite directions produces distortion-free image that is sharp all over, even with the diaphragm wide open.

Make the most of the possibilities of "dodging"—local contrast control (see page 216)—for improving range and distribution of contrasts in your enlargement, another unique advantage of the projection print over a mere contact print. . . .

FINISHING NEGATIVES AND PRINTS

As soon as our negatives and prints are dry we are faced with problems: How can they best be preserved? How should we file them so we can find them when we want them? How to display them to best advantage?

On all three counts, expert opinion is unanimous with regard to basic principles but divided when it comes to details of execution. Every photographer seems to have his own more or less personal system of keeping negatives and prints. The following suggestions are based on my own experience and on observations of the ways of others. . . .

Finishing and filing negatives

The first thing I do after taking down dry films is to trim the ends off roll films and to cut the edges that were punctured by the film clips off filmpack sheets and sheet films to prevent the rough edges of the small holes made by these clips from scratching the emulsions of other negatives. Next, I cut up No. 120 roll films into three lengths of four frames each, and 35 mm films into six lengths of six frames each. I am a great believer in filing and keeping films *flat* for the following good reasons: (1) flat negatives are much easier to print than negatives that have been rolled for any length of time; (2) films that have been kept flat don't break out in a rash of Newton rings as easily as rolled negatives; (3) when searching for a certain negative, stacks of glassine envelopes containing flat films can be leafed through easily without endangering valuable negatives; by contrast, tightly rolled rolls of film are tedious to look at; (4) short lengths of flat negative strips can be contact printed, filed, and catalogued much easier than multi-framed lengths of rolled film.

Immediately after cutting and trimming my negatives I number them on their edges with India ink and contact print them for the record (page 148). On one sheet of 8x10 paper I put either three strips of roll film No. 120 with four frames each or six strips of 35 mm film with six frames each—thus printing and recording one complete roll of film on a single sheet of paper. Of larger sizes, I print five negatives 3¼x4¼ inches or four negatives 4x5 inches on a single sheet of paper 8x10 inches. In order to compensate for unevenness in negative density and contrast when printing so many different negatives on a single sheet of paper—all of which have to be exposed at the same time—I use a paper with a soft gradation, giving it a full exposure and developing it relatively short. This way I get a sample chart of rather flat prints, which, however, are beautifully and delicately detailed in brilliant highlights as well as in deepest shadows, showing everything there is to be seen in the negative.

There is one great danger that I should like to point out to all photographers right here: don't postpone this important job of contact printing, recording, and cataloguing negatives "until tomorrow." . . . Unless this rather tedious business is disposed of right away—while interest in these particular negatives is still alive—it will never be done at all, and the photographer himself as well as his enthusiasm will slowly but surely be smothered by a steadily growing mass of unrecorded negatives—negatives that are slowly forgotten and can never be found when wanted. So do it right away and get it over with. The beginning is always hardest, but once you have started and built up a small collection of well-catalogued negatives, pride in your own achievement will keep you going, and soon future negatives will be recorded simply as a matter of course.

I have found it best to keep every single negative or single strip of negatives in an individual glassine envelope, and I collect all the glassine envelopes containing negatives from one roll of film—or from several rolls of film belonging to the same picture story—in one common larger envelope of "Kraft paper" (strong brown paper) on which I type the numbers of the negatives inside, and the name of the picture story, together with a short description of the contents of the negatives. These envelopes I keep in an ordinary steel filing cabinet with drawers 5x6½ inches. Such cabinets are available in all sizes, and in the form of boxes with only one or two drawers which are constructed so that two or any number of them will fit together and can be built into a single unit—ideal for harboring a growing negative collection. Keep these files in an ordinary room where temperatures are fairly constant and there is no danger from dampness or chemical fumes (as, for instance, in many darkrooms, basements, etc.).

In order to be able to find a certain negative in the shortest possible time I use a cross-index system: every negative is registered in two card index files, once alphabetically (name of the story or subject), and once chronologically, and all contact prints from the negatives in one Kraft-paper envelope are kept together in one envelope, 9x11 inches. Both Kraft-paper negative envelopes and contact-print envelopes are filed chronologically under corresponding numbers as soon as they come in from processing. So whenever I want to find a certain negative, I look it up in the alphabetical card index under the name of the story or the type of subject, find out its serial number and can lay my hands on either negative or contact print or both within a few seconds. Perhaps there is a simpler and more efficient system, but I haven't seen it.

Finishing, mounting and spotting prints

The impression a print makes on the beholder depends to a surprisingly great degree on the way in which it is presented: if it is perfectly flat or faultlessly mounted, trimmed evenly, clean, and free from dust specks and spots, then we are much more likely to overlook and excuse small faults of composition, contrast or definition than we would otherwise; somehow, subconsciously, we feel that the photographer painstakingly did his best—and everybody will give him credit for that.

On the other hand, a photograph may be really exciting subject-wise—but if the print is dried badly, full of buckles and bumps, marred by spots and specks from dust and dirt, we would conclude that it was made by a sloppy and careless person, and in criticizing its obvious faults would probably overlook its good features. . . . Even a sloppy person minds sloppiness in others.

The first thing to do with prints that come out of the drier is to trim them. If you want to preserve the white edge around the image, make sure that it is uniform all around. Personally, I think a print looks better without it since this pure white has a tendency to make the near-whites in the picture appear grayish by contrast. On the other hand, a white edge offers a certain protection to prints that have to be handled frequently: if it gets ragged after a while, just trim off a bit, and the print will look almost like new without the necessity of making it smaller.

Some papers have a tendency to curl. This can be overcome by dampening the back of the print with a cloth moistened in a mixture of equal parts of water and alcohol and by keeping such prints under pressure until they are perfectly dry. Separate them from each other with sheets of white blotting paper.

Prints can be mounted in many different ways—most of them bad (most editors, by the way, prefer to see unmounted prints). Water-solvent glues and pastes distort the paper stock, causing prints and mounts to buckle; only a professional bookbinder can do a perfect job with glue. Rubber cement is temptingly easy to use —but its aftereffect is disastrous: sooner or later the print will become discolored and stained, the cement will come through, and the photograph will have to be discarded. The only efficient and workmanlike way of mounting prints is with dry mounting tissue—not the rubber wax-base type, which doesn't last very long because of decomposition of the rubber component, but the resin-base type, which will last practically indefinitely and has the added advantage of protecting the back of the photograph from the deteriorating influences of chemically aggressive glues, unsuitable chemical components of the mount, and humidity from the air. Resin-coated dry mounting tissue is chemically absolutely inert; is not affected by humidity or water; doesn't buckle print or mount; and is applied by heat. The mounting process itself is very simple and can be done with an ordinary flat iron simply by following the instructions that go with any package of tissue.

The final thing you should do with a print is to "spot" it—to clean up small blemishes and marks left by dust and lint. The more carefully you cleaned the negative before printing, the simpler will be this job; you'll find out soon enough that cleaning a negative before it goes into the enlarger takes only a fraction of the time it takes later to spot the print.

Always start on the dark spots, which must be removed with an etching knife; if you overdo it and they become too light, you can later darken them again, together with the light spots. Hold the knife very loosely, and lightly shave the emulsion off layer after layer. Be careful not to penetrate through it to the paper base—a misfortune which would make the erasure ten times more obvious. . . . Practice on an old print before you start on a good one. Eventually you will acquire enough skill and "feeling" to remove even a very dark spot without breaking through the emulsion even if you may not believe this possible when you start.

Light spots have to be darkened with water color. Mix the right shade from black and white and apply it in very thin layers and as dry as you can with the tip of a fine camel's-hair brush. Water colors on a photograph always dry darker than they appear while wet, so keep the shade somewhat lighter than the surroundings of the spot you are obliterating. If necessary, apply a slightly darker coat after the first one has dried. If you overdid it, shave off the tone that was too dark before you apply a lighter one; otherwise you may have a bump of paint on your picture. . . . Be careful not to scratch the emulsion with the knife when shaving off this paint. . . .

While prints on matte paper can be spotted so that corrections are entirely unnoticeable, touching up glossy prints will always leave visible marks, even if special retouching colors that dry glossy are being used (available from your photodealers). But even so, a glossy print that is properly spotted will look much better than an unspotted one, especially since corrections are only visible when the print is held so that it catches a reflection, a position in which the image itself becomes obliterated by the gloss and which the spectator consequently will avoid.

CHAPTER 7

LEARNING FROM MISTAKES

TODAY, photographers can consider themselves fortunate. The materials at their disposition are technically of such high quality and uniformity that failures due to imperfect films, chemicals, sensitized papers, etc., are practically unheard of. It is easy and natural to try to put the blame for mishaps on somebody or something else—but out of hundreds of cases I have seen during recent years only two or three could positively be traced back to defective material. In all other instances the fault was obviously the result of incorrect processing or just plain carelessness. So, whenever something goes wrong with your pictures, believe me—the chances are overwhelmingly great that the fault was yours, and not that of the manufacturer.

Actually, honest mistakes are nothing to be ashamed of—we all make them occasionally—and very likely I have made some myself right in this book. The best (and maybe only) way to learn is from mistakes. As long as everything goes well we happily piddle along, unaware of possible pitfalls—until suddenly they catch up with us. Bang goes a picture. . . . But once this actually has happened, we not only know that it may happen again, but we usually discover the reason *why* it happened and, armed with this knowledge, can take precautions to prevent it from ever happening again. Considered in this spirit, every mistake a photographer makes is actually a blessing in disguise—another milestone on the well-known road to perfection.

Unfortunately, in photography the majority of mistakes one makes can never be corrected completely—if they can be corrected at all. A photographer should consider his mistakes the price he has to pay for final success. He would do well to preserve their manifestations as bitter souvenirs and reminders, learning from them all he possibly can. But it is futile to try to correct them and expect to get good pictures out of bad negatives or prints. It simply cannot be done. Consequently, I won't even attempt here to give advice for the correction of mistakes, with two exceptions: reducing negatives that are too dense and intensifying negatives that are too thin. Within reason, these two processes, and only these two processes, may make it possible to obtain good pictures from faulty negatives. Apart from this, all that usually can be done is to salvage what is salvageable—to enlarge the sections of a negative that are undamaged by spots, streaks, scratches, or whatever may be and to give up the rest as lost. Faulty prints, of course, should go directly into the waste can—with or without regrets. . . . It may hurt, but if a photographer "cannot take it," he will never make a good photographer. Self-discipline is not a quality to expect only in others. . . .

REDUCTION OF NEGATIVES THAT ARE TOO DENSE

Before a negative that is too dense can be reduced correctly, an examination of its contrasts has to be made (compare pictures on page 146) in order to determine the proper type of reducer. If contrasts are too low (overexposure), a "subtractive reducer" that strengthens contrasts should be used. If contrasts are too high (overdevelopment) a "flattening reducer" that weakens contrasts should be used. And in the rare cases where contrasts are about right (overexposure plus overdevelopment), treatment with a "proportional reducer," which leaves contrasts as they are, will give the best results. Since it is sometimes difficult to form a correct opinion about the contrasts of a very dense negative, it is advisable first to make a test print on a paper of normal gradation and to judge the contrasts of the negative from this print. Usually, negatives are best reduced in a clear glass tray with a weak light underneath so that progression of the reduction process can be watched more easily and stopped at the right moment.

The following reducer increases contrast:

KODAK FARMER'S REDUCER R-4a

Stock Solution A

Potassium Ferricyanide	37.5 grams
Water to make	500 cc

Stock Solution B

Sodium Thiosulfate (Hypo)	480.0 grams
Water to make	2.0 liters

For use, take 30 cc of Stock Solution A, take 120 cc of Stock Solution B, add A to B, then add water to make 1 liter. Pour the mixed solution at once over the negative that has to be reduced. Watch closely. When the negative has been reduced sufficiently, wash thoroughly before drying.

For less rapid reduction, use only 15 cc of Stock Solution A and mix it with 120 cc of Stock Solution B, then fill up with water to make 1 liter.

Solutions A and B should not be combined until they are to be used. They will not keep long in combination.

The following reducer decreases contrasts:

KODAK PERSULFATE REDUCER R-15

Stock Solution A

Water	1 liter
Potassium Persulfate	30 grams

Stock Solution B

Water	250 cc
*Sulfuric Acid (dilute solution)	15 cc
Water to make	500 cc

*To make, take 1 part of concentrated sulfuric acid and, with caution to avoid contact with the skin, add it slowly to 9 parts of water with stirring. *Never add the water to the acid* because the solution may boil and spatter the acid on the hands or face, causing serious burns.

For use, take 2 parts of Solution A, add 1 part of Solution B. Only glass, hard rubber, or impervious and unchipped enamelware should be used to contain the reducer solution during mixing and use.

Treat the negative in the Kodak Special Hardener SH-1 (p. 171) for 3 minutes and wash thoroughly before reduction. Immerse in the reducer with frequent agitation and inspection (accurate control by time is not possible) and treat until the required reduction is almost attained. Then remove from the solution, immerse in an acid fixing bath for a few minutes, and wash thoroughly before drying. Used solutions do not keep well and should be promptly discarded.

For best keeping in storage, the Stock Solution A should be kept away from excessive heat and light. Keeping life of Stock Solution A is approximately 2 months at 75° F.

The following reducer (Kodak formula R-5) preserves contrasts:

PROPORTIONAL REDUCER

Stock Solution I

Water	1,000 cc
Potassium permanganate	0.3 gm.
Sulfuric acid, 10% sol.	16 cc

Stock Solution II

Water	3,000 cc
Potassium persulfate	90 gm.

Prepare the 10 per cent acid solution by pouring one part concentrated sulfuric acid into nine parts of water. Never pour water into acid—it would boil and spatter hands and face.

For use, take one part of Solution I and mix with three parts of Solution II. After completed reduction, clear the negative in a one per cent solution of sodium bisulfite; wash for half an hour under running water and dry as usual.

As before, dry negatives have to be soaked for about ten minutes in water before they can be reduced. Agitate continuously while reducing; be careful not to carry reduction too far; interrupt shortly before you consider degree of reduction just right.

INTENSIFICATION OF NEGATIVES THAT ARE TOO THIN

Before you attempt intensification, remember that first of all there has to be something in your negative that can be intensified. Primarily, negatives are too thin for two reasons: underexposure and underdevelopment (see page 145). But while underdeveloped negatives usually show at least faint traces of shadow detail, and thus have something that can be intensified, underexposed negatives are characterized by more or less complete absence of shadow detail, thus lacking the elementary condition for successful intensification. No intensification magic can strengthen something that isn't there . . . and all an intensifier could do with such detail-less shadow sections would be to intensify the usual developer fog.

All intensification processes are extremely delicate and are not always reliable, and they frequently end with uneven negatives. Greatest purity of all chemicals is the first condition for success, and negatives must be perfectly free from even the slightest traces of hypo, which would invariably cause spots and stains.

Many different intensifier formulas have been published, but their effects are more or less alike. Some of them necessitate the use of deadly cyanide components and should be avoided—no negative is worth the risk of death from inhaling cyanide fumes. Others produce strong intensification, but the results are not very permanent. Still the best way of intensifying (indirectly) a weak negative is, in my opinion, to make a duplicate negative via a lantern-slide plate. At least, this method doesn't involve the risk of losing the negative because of uneven intensification and doesn't bring the photographer into contact with strong poisons. If your negative is comparatively large, contact print it, and if it is rather small, projection print and enlarge it, on a contrasty lantern-slide plate (or finegrain, contrasty process plate). Finegrain develop it approximately 20 per cent longer than normal in DK-20, fix, wash, and dry. Then contact print this lantern or process plate (which naturally will be a positive transparency) on a second lantern or process plate; process as you did the first one; and you will get a duplicate negative with greatly improved contrasts while still having your original intact. Try this before you try intensification.

Before intensification, harden negative in the following bath (Kodak formula SH-1) for three minutes:

Water	500 cc
Formaldehyde 40%	10 cc
Sodium carbonate, monohydrated	6 gm.
Add water to make	1,000 cc

After hardening, rinse, and immerse negative for five minutes in a fresh acid fixing bath, wash thoroughly and bleach in the following bath (Kodak formula In-4):

Stock Solution

Potassium bichromate	90 gm.
Hydrochloric acid, conc.	64 cc
Add water to make	1,000 cc

For use, take 1 part stock solution to 10 parts of water.

Bleach the negative thoroughly in the diluted solution at about 68° F.; wash it for about five minutes under running water and redevelop for about ten minutes (fully!) in D-72 (diluted 1:3) by either artificial light or daylight (but not in sunshine), rinse, fix for five minutes, wash for half an hour under running water, and dry as usual.

Repeating this process will produce even greater intensification.

COMMON FAULTS

The following pictures illustrate some of the most common faults and mistakes in photography. Instead of following the usual classification by characteristic manifestations (unsatisfactory contrasts—spots—mechanical injuries—stains—etc.), I have grouped them according to time and place of their origin—mistakes made while taking the picture—while processing the negative—while processing the print—since I believe that this will facilitate prevention of the fault in the future by connecting it more emphatically with its cause. Furthermore, mistakes are demonstrated in the final form of a positive print, *even if the mistakes actually happened in the negative*, and even if the print is just the innocent positive replica of a faulty negative. After all, negatives are only intermediate stages, and we are naturally less interested in how a mistake manifests itself at this point than in how it will appear in the final print.

One word of caution: If as a last resort you do decide to attempt to correct an unsatisfactory negative (some textbooks, magazine articles, etc., feature ways of removing stains, retouching, improving gradations, etc.), I strongly recommend making at least a few prints of as good a quality as possible from such negative—or if the negative is valuable, to make a duplicate negative on "direct duplicating film"—since there is always the risk that the operation will be unsuccessful and the negative will be spoiled completely. This is the main reason why here I don't even mention any other remedies for correcting negatives than those recommended on pages 169-171. These are safe so long as instructions are followed to the letter.

Mistakes that result in color stains in either negatives or prints cannot be demonstrated here in black-and-white reproductions. Usually, they can be traced back to contamination of the developer with hypo, exhaustion of the fixing bath, or incomplete washing. Stained negatives can sometimes be cleared with special stain-remover solutions (Eastman Kodak) followed by redevelopment. Stained prints should be thrown away. If such prints are valuable and cannot be remade because the negatives are not available, make a copy negative from such a print using a dark-yellow filter on the lens. Prints made from this copy negative will not show the effect of the stain.

Unsatisfactory gradation and density in negatives and prints (too hard, too soft, too light, too dark) are demonstrated in the pictures on pages 146 and 151, respectively. The causes of such faults and possible means of correction are mentioned in connection with those pictures.

MISTAKES MADE WHILE TAKING THE PICTURE

Carelessness or sloppiness are the sole causes of the three common mistakes illustrated below. While certain hazards are unavoidable in photography, and accidental breakdowns can happen to anybody, faults like those shown here can easily be prevented by careful and conscientious work.

Dirt on the film previous to exposure results in black marks like those in the sky of this picture (if such marks were white, they would have been caused by dirt that got on the negative after development; see page 182, *bottom left*). For future prevention, clean camera bellows regularly by extending it all the way, opening the back of the camera, holding camera vertically over a sheet of white paper and tapping the bellows gently on all sides. You probably will be astonished at the amount of dirt and lint that collects on the white paper.

Remedy: Retouching (see page 167).

Double exposure—two pictures on one negative—is not recommended for saving film. . . . Make it a habit to transport your film immediately after each exposure (unless, of course, film transport and shutter action are coupled and double exposures are impossible). Thus, you will also be better prepared to take unexpected snapshots. However, don't leave the shutter cocked for any great length of time because it is bad for the springs inside.

Remedy: None.

Parallel scratches on the film like these result frequently if roll film is wound while the camera is closed, and the emulsion rubs against the back rim of the lens mount. In the example shown here, sand inside the camera made matters even worse. When photographing at the seashore, never lay your camera in the sand, and never let it lie around open for any length of time or wind-blown sand may get inside.

Remedy: None.

MISTAKES MADE WHILE TAKING THE PICTURE

Unsharpness may have one or several of the following three causes: moving the camera while making the exposure, faulty focusing, exposing moving objects with shutter speeds that are not fast enough to stop motion.

Unsharpness caused by moving the camera during the exposure is probably the most common of all photographic faults, although often it goes unnoticed unless the negative is enlarged or examined with a magnifier.

Typical signs: No real sharpness anywhere in the picture, and everything appears slightly distorted in one and the same direction.

To avoid: Use tripod or shoot at higher shutter speed.

Remedy: None.

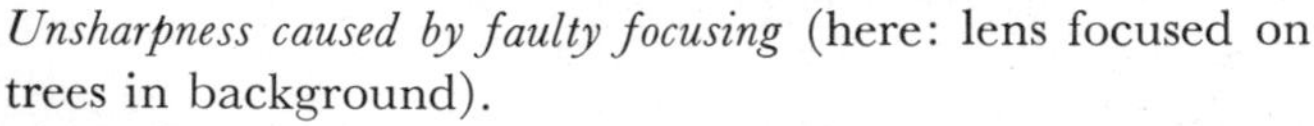

Unsharpness caused by faulty focusing (here: lens focused on trees in background).

Typical signs: Unsharpness usually confined to a certain zone of depth; parts of the picture may be perfectly sharp.

To avoid: Focus more carefully; check rangefinder for accuracy.

Remedy: None.

Unsharpness caused by shooting moving objects with insufficientl fast shutter speed.

Typical signs: Stationary objects appear perfectl sharp; only objects in motion are blurred.

To avoid: Consult table of permissible shutter speed on pages 102 or 353.

Remedy: None.

MISTAKES MADE WHILE TAKING THE PICTURE

Light striking the film accidentally can spoil a negative in many different ways. The most common causes of light-struck films are: light leaks in camera bellows or filmholders; loading the camera in bright light instead of retiring to a dark corner; incorrect handling of filmpacks.

Film was light-struck through holes in camera bellows. Typical signs: Light-streaks, which may appear anywhere on the negative, and usually have a well-defined direction.

To avoid: Insert small light into fully extended bellows, examine in darkness for holes which usually will be found where bellows fold. Repair damages with waterproof cement and tape—or install a new bellows.

Remedy: None, unless the light-struck parts can be cropped off without losing too much of the negative.

Filmpack negative light-struck because of incorrect handling of back; see page 65. Never squeeze the pack. Hold it at the edges only. Don't tear off the tabs after making the exposure.

Remedy: As above.

All-over fog caused by light admitted through a leak between camera body and bellows.

To avoid: Examine tightness of joints between bellows and camera front and back; if necessary, make repairs with waterproof cement.

Remedy: None.

Strong light striking the lens frequently manifests itself in form of flares and "ghost images" which can have almost any conceivable shape. Some of the more common forms are illustrated in the pictures below.

To a large extent, the danger of flares depends on the type and construction of the lens; see page 47.

If no sources of direct light have to appear in the picture (as in the photographs at the *top*), flares can be avoided by preventing direct light from striking the lens, either through use of a suitable lens shade or by keeping the lens in the shade of some other object. However, care has to be taken not to cut off part of the image by having such an object too near the lens; see picture on page 178, *left*.

If sources of direct light have to appear in a picture (as in the case of the night photographs reproduced here), flares will most likely be avoided by using a "coated" lens. If no such lens is available taking the shot with a simple type of lens will more likely result in a flareless picture than if a complicated high-speed lens is used; see page 47.

Remedy: None.

Above and *below: Raindrops on the lens*—while the pictures were taken—made these strange distortions of light, similar to those seen by wearers of spectacles when they walk around in the rain.

To avoid: Protect your lens with an effective lens shade, umbrella, etc., when taking photographs in the rain.

Remedy: None.

Above and *below: A stiff shutter*, which failed to close completely after the exposure because it was stiff from cold, caused these flukes. Winding the film with the lens partially open caused the lights to trace parallel lines, wavy (*below*) because camera was hand-held and moved during winding of film, straight (*above*) because camera was stationary on tripod. Remaining objects were too dark to leave visible traces on the film during the short moment of winding before shutter closed completely.

To avoid: If you have to take pictures in extremely cold places, have your camera "delubricated," since it is "sticky" oil which causes the mechanism to act so sluggishly.

Remedy: None.

Vignetting: Part of the image on the film was cut off by some obstacle within the field of view, and very close to the lens, as, for instance, a finger or the flap of an Everready camera case. Or the lens was raised so much that its covering power (page 40) was insufficient to make an image over the entire area of the film.

To avoid: Check covering power of lens on the groundglass (raise lens all the way, mark position when image begins to appear dark at the corners). Use lens shades that are not too long or too narrow; make sure that square or rectangular lens shades (for Rolleiflex and Contax, respectively) are slipped on parallel with the film. Sometimes, bellows of larger view cameras may sag at the center, cutting off part of the image with similar result. When shading lens from direct light with hand, hat, or other object, be careful not to cut off part of the view of the lens, in which case a similar effect would result.

Remedy: None.

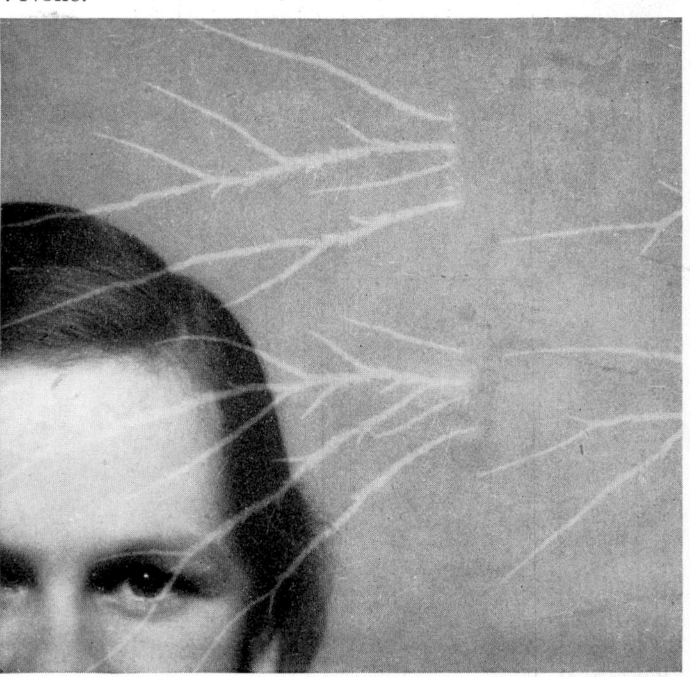

Static marks: When you are winding the film on a cold and dry day, friction easily generates static electricity on the film which, when discharged, leaves indelible black marks on the negative. These marks usually look like wavy short streaks, often branching into shapes resembling small trees, but occasionally appear in form of dots or stars, too.

To avoid: Wind film slowly and evenly (the danger exists only in cold and dry air) and keep the camera grounded. Wooden tripods, or rubber-tipped metal ones, for instance, prevent grounding and facilitate accumulation of static charges on the film.

Remedy: None.

Faulty development can irreparably ruin a negative, undoing all the time, money, and effort spent on getting the picture. . . . For examples of under- and overdevelopment, turn to page 146. Shown here are some results of faulty agitation. Because of their streaky unevenness they are even more useless—if possible—than the results of wrongly timed development.

Print from section of a 35 mm negative. Notice unevenness in sky—the dark streaks emanating from each one of the perforation holes—caused by mechanically even up-and-down agitation which, like a pump, forced developer under pressure through the film holes.

A similar effect often results when sheet films are developed in hangers and agitation is mechanically up-and-down, pumping developer through the holes in the sides of the sheet-film hangers.

To avoid such developer marks: Follow instructions given on pages 142-145, respectively.

Section of a rollfilm negative which was developed without sufficient agitation (during development—right side of picture was at the bottom of the tank). Notice the two dark streaks and the white right edge—results of stagnant developer of uneven strength due to lack of agitation; its components were permitted to separate slowly, causing this unevenness.

To avoid: Follow instructions given on page 142.

Excessive heat or solutions that were too warm caused these results. Read about the importance of correct temperatures on page 129, about ways of keeping temperatures constant on page 93, about thermometers on page 94. A method for controlling the effects of heat and putting them to use for the creation of stylized abstractions (Controlled Reticulation) is described on page 407.

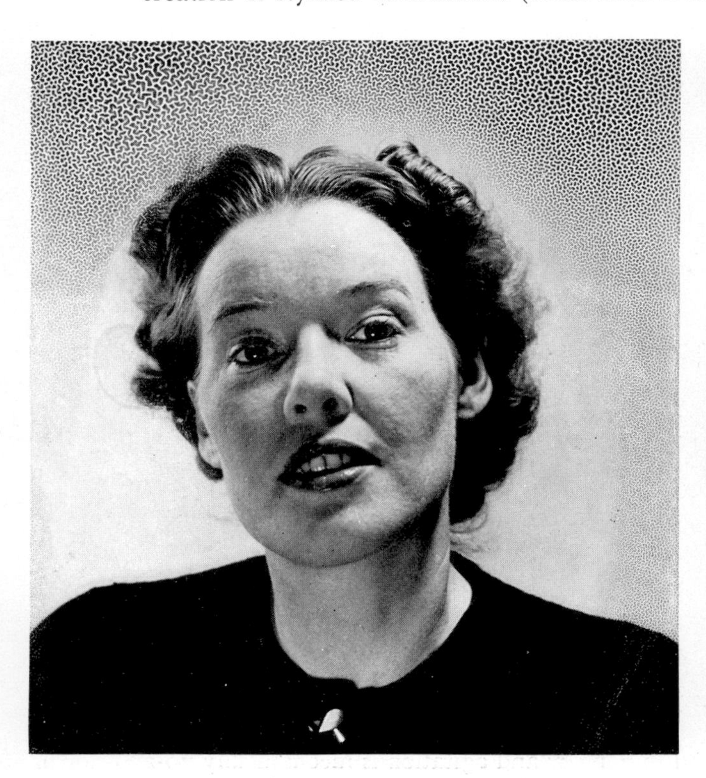

Above: Reticulation. Excessively warm solutions, considerable differences in temperature between different solutions or insufficient air circulation in hot-air drying cabinets, may cause the negative emulsion to wrinkle and shrink, producing this effect.

To avoid: Watch your temperatures which normally shouldn't be above 75° F.; make sure that the temperature of all your baths (including the wash water) is the same within 3° F.; use only fresh, strong hardening fixer.

Top right: Negative emulsion melted and ran off partially because film was dried forcibly on a radiator.

To avoid: Dry negatives in air not warmer than 90° F., use only strong, fresh hardening fixer which makes emulsion more heat resisting.

Right: Emulsion floated off its base and dried up wrinkled as the result of washing in water that was too warm. Especially in winter, the temperature of slow running water may rise occasionally above the danger point due to proximity of water and steam pipes.

MISTAKES MADE DURING NEGATIVE PROCESSING

Typical results of carelessness are shown in the three pictures below. Mistakes like these are unfortunately almost as common with beginners as they are unnecessary. . . .

Top left: Scars in the emulsion, left by fingernails or the sharp corners of other negatives.

To avoid: Keep fingernails short, be careful when agitating large numbers of fixing negatives that their corners don't dig into each other's emulsions. Weight down lower ends of drying roll films to prevent them from curling up and digging into the emulsion.

Top right: Marks left by waterdrops drying on the emulsion.

To avoid: Wipe negatives with damp viscose sponge from both sides before hanging them up to dry; follow instructions on page 134.

Bottom left: Fingermark. Never touch the emulsion of a negative—be it wet or dry—with hands or fingers; handle films by the edges only; follow instructions on page 65.

Pictures showing the results of faulty print exposure and faulty selection of paper gradation were reproduced on page 151; examples of faulty print development on page 157. The most common causes for stained prints were mentioned on page 172. Below are shown some typical examples of frequently made mistakes that with a little bit of caution can easily be avoided.

Unsharpness caused by film buckling during enlarging (glassless negative-carrier).

Typical signs: Only center of picture appears blurred while edges usually are sharp. Notice here that near and far objects (left and right side of picture) are sharp simultaneously, which would be impossible if faulty focusing were the cause.

Remedy: None. Next time use negative carrier with glass pressure plates.

Marks left by dust, lint, and dirt clinging to a negative in the enlarger, or to the glass pressure plates of the negative carrier. Similar marks may be caused by particles of dust and lint that dried into the negative emulsion. If such marks appear black in the final print, they were caused by dirt on the unexposed film; see picture on page 173, *top left*.

Marks from wet fingers that touched the emulsion side of the printing paper before development.

To avoid: Never touch the emulsion side of photographic papers with your hands before the print is safely in the developer. Even then, try to handle prints as much as possible with print tongs to avoid yellow or brownish stains.

PART TWO

The Art of Making a Photograph

CHAPTER 8

INTRODUCTION

THE first part of this book contains in concentrated form the fundamentals of photo-technique, bedrock knowledge essential for the production of technically sound photographs. Its application will enable the beginner to make successful pictures nine times out of ten.

BUT technical perfection alone means comparatively little in creative photography, where technique is nothing but a means to an end: the picture with purpose and meaning. Even though it may satisfy the average photographer to learn enough about photography to get recognizable images in nine cases out of ten, there will always be those who want to go further. Realizing that it is just that "tenth" photograph that hits the mark—the picture that is "different," more concentrated, packs extra punch—they are not satisfied until they know how to get it. It is for them—YOU—that the second and principal part of this book has been written.

As you work your way through the following pages, you will learn how to apply your technique to best advantage; how to select the means in accordance with the end. You will read about rendering contrasts most effectively, about treating colors in terms of gray, about creating illusions of space and motion within the flat plane of a "still," about the rules of lighting and composition. . . . Where previously you saw only one way to solve a certain photographic problem, you will soon see many—some better than others. You will learn to recognize and execute the most effective one. You will discover that so far you have merely scratched the surface; that you have controls at your command which previously you hadn't even suspected. . . . Photography will become a personal means of expression, and you will learn to use the camera—as the camera should be used: as an instrument for recording—documenting—educating—explaining—exploring—as a means of widening man's horizons through the medium of photography.

NECESSITY FOR CREATIVE CONTROL

Mastery of "technique" is the first condition for making good photographs. Without means of expression, no creative work is possible in any field. The painter who hasn't learned how to mix and apply his colors, the sculptor who hasn't learned properly to handle mallet and chisel, the writer who doesn't know how to build his sentences correctly—none of them will ever produce a work of art, no matter how talented he is, simply because he doesn't know how to express his ideas, how to execute them in paint on canvas, in plaster or stone or wood, in words and sentences. So it is only natural that this applies to creative photography as well; after all, creative photography is basically a means of expression, the same as painting, sculpturing, or writing. This neither proves, nor disproves, that photography is one of the Arts, for the same principle applies to the crafts as well. Without apprenticeship, nobody will ever become a master. But while a master does not necessarily have to be an artist, every real artist has to be a master, a master of the technique of expression in his own special field.

Let's take a practical example. Before I became a photographer, I had been an architect, so drawing a parallel between photography and architecture comes natural to me. A comparison between the erection of a building and the making of a photograph will clarify this point at once.

If we examine a building we find that it is made of bricks and concrete and steel besides many other materials. These bricks and steel beams, etc., are put together by skilled laborers according to certain rules that insure the stability of the building. Before these workers could do their jobs properly, they had to learn their crafts; they had to go through the stage of apprenticeship before they could qualify for the job. Applied to photography this means: before anybody can make a good photograph (which means: do a workmanlike job), he has to pass the stage of apprenticeship and learn to master his technique. If he does not, his work will fail as surely as the building will collapse if erected by workmen who don't know the technique of building construction. Mastering of technique marks the first stage of creation, signifies the skilled craftsman, the master, but not necessarily the artist.

Turning once more to our building we find that it has been erected in accordance with a certain plan. This is where the architect, the *artist*, comes in. There are many different types of buildings, some purely utilitarian, as, for instance, factories; others more decorative; some devoted to education; some to amusement; some to plain and simple living. And each separate building within one of these groups can again be planned differently, according to special circumstances and influences like surroundings, purpose, appropriated funds, climate, etc., and several architects competing for the same building will probably arrive at different solutions directed by their different personalities and conceptions. Exactly the same reasoning can be applied to photography:

First, there are different "types" of photographs, some purely utilitarian, as, for instance, technical photographs, others more decorative (we call them "pictorial"), or educational (news pictures, textbook illustrations), or amusing ("pin-ups"), or just plain and simple pictures recording our daily life (snapshots of purely personal interest).

For the moment, the categories are of no importance. The point is simply that every photograph, like every building, must be planned according to the peculiar requirements of its "purpose." (For instance: an educational picture should be instructive, a pictorial photo should be aesthetically pleasing, a "pin-up" picture is nothing without sex appeal, etc.)

Second, several photographers approaching the same subject will probably arrive at different solutions, according to their differences in personality and conception. This is where the artist enters the picture. For while there are certain laws and rules for the technique of erecting buildings as well as for the technique of making photographs, no fixed rules and laws exist *for the planning* of buildings and the planning of pictures. The circumstances influencing such planning are far too various to be covered by a finite number of rules. . . . Instead, we have to rely on instinct, imagination, and intelligence. Unfortunately, these qualities cannot be taught or learned like the rules and principles of technique; but their presence or absence makes all the difference between an artist and a mere craftsman.

It is significant that in judging a work of architecture, we usually confine ourselves to criticism of the plan and design, in other words to the work of the architect, the artist. And we notice "technique" only if something is badly executed, taking perfection of execution for granted. In photography, unfortunately, rather the opposite is the rule, and "technique" generally rates higher among critics than "planning" and "design." This misvaluation leads many people to believe that a photograph can never be a work of art. They forget the importance and the influence of conception, composition, and imagination, the fact that there are always innumerable solutions for one and the same problem. Paying too much attention to the "technical" side of a photograph, they overlook the fact that these same technical means are so manifold and so malleable that they allow the photographer freedom of expression nearly as great as that enjoyed by artists like painters or sculptors—as this book will attempt to prove. Nothing is more misleading than the old adage that "the camera cannot lie," or the slogan "you press the button, we do the rest," implying that the photographic process is singularly rigid, hopelessly matter-of-fact, merely mechanical.

Once this has been disproved, many commonly accepted "truths" about photography have to be reconsidered. The fact alone that the camera is perfectly capable of "lying" should hint that photography is anything but a mechanical and stereotyped process of reproduction, for an "untrue reproduction" is absurd. And when it is further shown that the ability of the camera to "lie" can be controlled and used in a creative sense, one must admit that photography does provide possibilities for doing artistic work. For the word "lie" used in connection with a photograph merely means "deviation from literal reproduction."

Such deviation can have either positive or negative value, and how it is used, either for dramatizing or for faking, is left entirely to the resourcefulness and imagination of the photographer, offering him an opportunity to prove whether he is really a creative artist or merely a mediocre craftsman.

"THE CAMERA DOES NOT LIE..."

That one of the greatest misconceptions about photography is expressed in the saying that "the camera does not lie," anyone who has ever been disappointed in a photograph should gladly agree. For what else is a photograph "that didn't turn out" but proof in black and white that the camera is eminently able to lie? Every single picture that doesn't come up to expectations, that doesn't do justice to the object it depicts, that doesn't look like "the real thing"—is nothing but a camera lie. And if we want to be really critical we have to admit that a vast proportion of the photographs produced today belong in this category.

On the other hand, it can easily be proven with the help of mathematical equations that every image produced by one of our modern, highly corrected lenses is always perfectly "true," regardless of how cockeyed it may appear to the eye of the beholder (as is often the case with wide-angle shots). And the same applies to the "chemical" side in photography: color transformation into shades of gray can look horribly wrong and yet may be entirely correct when checked with the densitometer; and vice versa.

The following diagrams and photographs should prove this conclusively.

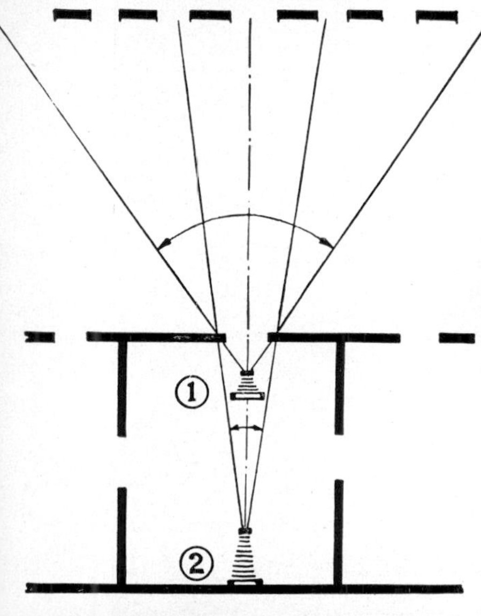

In order to give an "emotionally true" impression of space, the camera may have to be in a different position from the observer. Here, the picture at right (taken with a telephoto lens from deep within the room) renders narrow street as seen by observer standing at point *1*. A picture made from point *1* would have to be taken with a wide-angle lens in order to include the window through which observer sees the street, and space would appear much too deep.

Color scheme involving red, yellow, blue, and green.

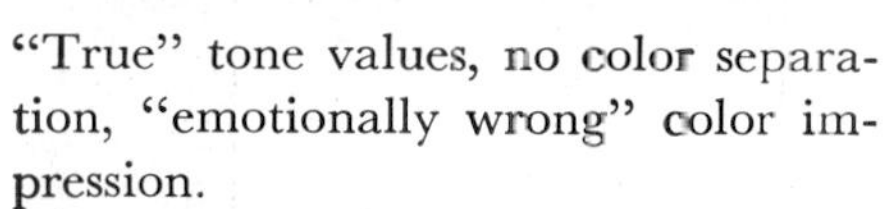

"True" tone values, no color separation, "emotionally wrong" color impression.

Good tone separation, "technical lie," but "emotionally correct" color impression.

Only conscious tone falsification can sometimes give an "emotionally true" rendering of different colors of equal intensity in a black-and-white picture; a "literally true" transformation into gray tones would render different colors of equal intensity as shades of identical gray.

Obviously, we have unearthed here quite a complicated problem, involving more than a simple choice between "truth" and "lie." And if a straightforward and "true" photograph can look wrong and "lying" (as proven by the above pictures), we may as well face the facts and consider the alternative—that in order to get a "truthful" impression, a photograph may sometimes have to "lie."

We don't have to go far to prove this to be correct; as a matter of fact, we have already shown it in the series of photographs and diagrams above, where "true" ones looked "wrong" (center pictures), and the "lying" ones appeared to be "emotionally true" (right-hand pictures).

One explanation of this paradox lies in the fact that camera and eye conceive their images differently. Even if reason convinces us that the center pictures above must be right and true, they nevertheless *appear* "wrong" and "lying." And in order to make them *appear true* we have to "improve" the theoretically true rendering our camera gave us—*by means of controlled lies*. This is the point where the artist has to enter the picture.

This is the way the brain conceives the image of a street; verticals appear vertical and parallel.

This is the way the "uncontrolled camera" conceives the image of a street; verticals appear converging, the picture does not look "true."

The angle of vision of the eye is very narrow. Contemplating a view down a street the eye builds up its image from many narrow sectors, corresponding roughly to the shaded parts of the different images above. This occurs very rapidly, and the brain transforms these different sections into one big impression, quite subconsciously. Instead of taking in a view "at a glance" we actually take it in "at a sweep."

To imitate the action of the eye a camera would have to function as shown here. We found above that within the narrow angle of vision of the eye (shaded areas), vertical lines appear vertical and parallel. In order to make them actually parallel over the entire width of the picture (as in picture at top, left), we have to rely on "controlled lies."

These three pictures explain in graphic form why vertical parallels appear to converge in a photograph, when the camera is tilted, unless perspective is "controlled" by means of "conscious falsification."

As a matter of fact, this convergence of verticals is the perfectly "true," geometrical manifestation of "perspective" toward height. It is as logical and as natural as the apparent convergence of railroad tracks in depth.

This is what happens when you take a photograph of a tall building and point your camera upward in order to get in the full height.

Obviously, the distance between B and B^1 is the same as the distance between C and C^1. However, the distance from A to $C\text{-}C^1$ is greater than the distance from A to $B\text{-}B^1$, and the farther objects are from the camera, the smaller will appear their image on film. Consequently, $C\text{-}C^1$ will be rendered shorter than $B\text{-}B^1$, and the result will be a picture looking like this:⟶

Technically, it is a perfectly "true" projection of the front of a building on a tilted sheet of film, illustrating "perspective in the vertical plane."

Emotionally, or artistically, however, it looks as if the walls were going to fall backwards. The whole picture looks wrong; it seems to "lie" unless we correct it by consciously introducing a "white lie," thus destroying the effect of perspective in the vertical plane, and making the verticals parallel once more.

The corrected photograph, the artistically "controlled" picture, would then look like this:⟶
Technically speaking, it is a "camera lie"; but emotionally it appears to be "true."

THE ART OF CONTROLLING CAMERA LIES

Once you are convinced of the camera's ability to "lie," the next step is to investigate in what respects, and to how great a degree, this fact can be brought under control. For if this can be done, such an apparent disadvantage automatically turns into an advantage of tremendous consequences, opening possibilities for creative work equal to those enjoyed by "recognized" artists like painters or sculptors or writers.

Later on (beginning on page 207), we will see in detail how the camera and its product, the print, can be controlled so as to produce almost any desired effect: how contrasts can be changed from soft to hard and back to soft again, how colors can be translated into gray shades from light to dark and from dark to light, how space can be depicted two-dimensionally in many different forms, how speed and action can be expressed graphically in a "still," and how time itself can leave its impression on sensitized paper. But before we learn how to create with the help of such "positive lies" we have to recognize the necessity for lying at all and to understand why a "straight" and "uncontrolled" photograph is often disappointing.

Generally speaking, photography is thought of as a "reproductive" process. This, however, is only occasionally literally true, even if we forget for a moment that lying is one of the outstanding features of the camera. A photograph of a page of newsprint, for instance, is truly a reproduction, for "reproduction" is derived from "re-produce," which means making a duplicate of something, or copying, the copy having all the properties of the original. This would be the case with the newsprint photograph, both original and copy (the photograph) being two-dimensional (flat), showing black letters on white background. A photograph of a landscape, however, could never be called a "reproduction" in the true sense of the word, regardless of how technically perfect it may be. Too great is the difference between the "original" (the real landscape) and the "copy" (the print). There three-dimensionality (space), color, movement (boughs and leaves of trees swaying in wind, people and animals moving)—here two-dimensional flatness, gray tones, lifelessness. A worse example for a "copy" is hardly imaginable.

No, the majority of photographs are not "reproductions," but rather "translations" from one medium (reality) into another medium (photograph) by means of a process of projection and abstraction. This necessitates a radical change in values, a result of the peculiarities of the process of transmutation: photography. Three-dimensionality, for instance, has to be changed into flatness (by means of projection), and color has to be changed into gray tones (by means of filters and the chemical properties of film emulsions), and so on. Because of the fact that during this process of changing values we always lose something (for instance, we lose one dimension while changing from three-dimensionality to two-dimensionality), the result of this change, of this transmutation from one medium into another, is bound to be inferior to the original—*unless we create new values*, artistic values, to compensate for the unavoidable loss experienced during the transmutation. As we have already learned in school, we cannot subtract from one side of an equation without adding a corresponding amount to the other side, if the product of the equation is to remain the same. But in spite of this early acquired wisdom, many photographers still seem to believe that they can with impunity take away from the subject its most important features, three-dimensionality, color and motion, its very life, *without* having to add to the other side of their equation—their picture—*equal but new values* of a creative nature. Their photographs are "substitutes" instead of "transmutations," and they are astonished and chagrined when later they have to admit that these substitutes are inferior to the originals in imparting beauty, mood, or whatever they liked in the subject.

If nothing else, considerations like these should prove that a "literal" translation is not only impossible, but undesirable as well, as undesirable as it is generally to translate "literally" from one language into another. Literal translations usually are clumsy and frequently even misleading, in speaking and writing as well as in the "picture language" of photography.

A parallel between spoken and written language and photography can reveal even more interesting things. Speech, for instance, is based on sounds, while writing is based on letters. Both sounds and letters are symbols that stand for something else: sounds (or rather combinations of different sounds) stand for spoken words, and letters are used to compose written words, which again symbolize sound combinations. Thus, both spoken and written words are nothing but *symbols* for objects, actions, values, properties, etc. Boiled down to fundamentals this means that both speech and writing are nothing but means of expression, based on a limited number of symbols that can be arranged in an unlimited number of combinations. By themselves these symbols mean nothing; properly used, they can be used to express anything.

The same reasoning can be applied to photography, which actually is nothing but "picture language," and is more often than not superior to ordinary spoken language when it comes to establishing facts. . . . Merely its symbols are different from those of language. In photography, space, for instance, is symbolized by the apparent convergence of receding parallels or the apparent decrease in size of objects with increasing distance from the observer, while color is symbolized by gray tones, motion by blurredness, seriousness by darkness, joy by lightness, strength by powerful contrasts between black and white, weakness by lack of contrast, and so on. And before anyone can express something successfully through photography he has to know and understand these symbols, their meaning and application; exactly as a speaker or a writer has to master the symbols of sound and letters, of speech and of the written word, before he can deliver his message.

Let's illustrate this with a few simple examples: pictures of children, for instance, can be taken in innumerable different ways. To express joy and happiness, however, the general keynote of the photograph should be bright and light, while to indicate squalor and misery (children in slums) it should be dark and gloomy. Slum pictures taken in sunshine and printed too light look picturesque and romantic and fail to convey the idea of poverty and misery, which would be expressed more adequately by a picture taken on a dull and rainy day. "Technical perfection" alone means absolutely nothing if it isn't directed by understanding of the subject at hand and of the particular problem it poses to the graphic medium of photography. Technical perfection can be achieved in sunshine as easily as during a rainstorm, in a light print as easily as in a dark one. But it can make all the difference in the world if a certain photograph, a picture that has to carry a certain message, actually was taken in sunshine or rain, or has been printed light or dark. Here again, the artist has the final word in deciding how to approach a certain problem, and in choosing the means necessary for achieving the most powerful form of presentation. Only after these decisions have been made do skill and craftsmanship enter the picture.

Another example: On page 190 we remarked on the unnatural appearance of converging verticals in the usual photograph of a street. But this is by no means always the case, for the apparent convergence of parallels is a form of perspective that graphically suggests "distance." Manifested in the horizontal plane, it occurs in a multitude of pictures and is so common a phenomenon that we are hardly conscious of its existence (the apparent convergence of railroad tracks, etc.). The same phenomenon applied to the vertical plane, introduces a powerful suggestion of "height," which is nothing but "distance in the vertical plane," and can be used successfully whenever tallness has to be emphasized as the outstanding quality of an object, regardless of whether the object happens to be a skyscraper, a tree, or even a person. Thus, if used in the right place and connection, the same converging parallels that looked wrong in the ordinary street picture will appear perfectly natural and true. The explanation is simple: only when looking upward consciously do we experience such a pronounced feeling of height as is expressed by converging verticals. Everyone who has ever stood at the foot of a skyscraper "rubber-necking" will know that certain feeling of dizziness that makes the building appear to fall upon him, the same feeling that is so strongly expressed in the apparent convergence of parallel vertical lines. However, if this feeling of height does not exist in reality—or in mood—the converging verticals will look ridiculous in a photograph. But in the right place they often make a Picture out of a picture.

Likewise, we showed (on page 189) why a scientifically correct translation of color is not always desirable. Admittedly, we photographers have reason to be grateful to an industry that has given us emulsions capable of rendering all colors simultaneously into corresponding tone values of shades of gray. But we should reserve the right to use this material according to *our own judgment*, which may often necessitate the transformation of colors, if need be, into *tone falsifications*, in order to separate *different* colors of equal intensity in our gray-tone photograph.

Still another example is found in the case of anti-halation properties of modern emulsions. These are invaluable for the vast majority of camera work, but may prove, in a few special instances (see pages 320 to 331), detrimental to the intentions of the creative photographer. As a result, special devices have to be used for the purpose of counteracting this laboriously acquired property of today's negative material. We simply cannot get away from the fact that camera and eye see differently, and that there never can be such a thing as an "absolutely correct" rendering, as long as the judgment of the result, the photograph, is dictated by feeling.

Considerations like these all point to one conclusion: that in photography, "truthfulness" and "naturalness" are anything but well-defined conceptions. What is right one minute may be wrong the next. As, for example, the converging verticals mentioned above, which in one case gave the impression of houses about to collapse, and in another instance evoked the feeling of height and soaring power. The relativity of photographic truth is perhaps the best explanation for the fact that there are good photographers and bad ones, impressive pictures and meaningless pictures. For, if photography actually were the faultless procedure it is said to be by those who sneer at creative intention and theory—those who demand nothing but "naturalness" of a stiff, flat, and colorless "photographic" kind—if it were just that, then, indeed, it would only be necessary to press a button to obtain good pictures automatically. The fact that not every buttonpresser is a good photographer should alone be enough to explode the myth of the infallibility of the camera.

Summing up we might conclude: through absence of color, three-dimensionality, and motion, the black-and-white photograph is *ipso facto* "unnatural." It expresses reality symbolically: gray tone values instead of color, two-dimensional projection (perspective) instead of space, blurredness or single-phase instead of constant motion. It is "symbolic" in the same sense that speech and writing are, where sounds (words) are symbols for objects and conceptions, and signs (letters) are symbols for sounds (words). Photography means "reproduction" only in the rare cases where the rendering of a two-dimensional, black-and-white object is the aim; otherwise it must be called *translation.*

We can translate from one language into another literally and stupidly or we can translate freely and true to the spirit and meaning of the language. Similarly we can translate nature into photographs in two different ways: either by a mechanical repetition or by free interpretation, using the camera to create an image *true to the feeling* of the subject. And which of these two roads will lead to the more impressive photographs I need not say again. At the same time, *free* translation must lead to the creation of *new values replacing* whatever is lost in "*naturalness*." Again, recall our equation: what we lose on one side involuntarily (because of the peculiar properties of photography), we must deliberately add on the other side. The balance of the equation "photograph = object" is thus safeguarded, and the *power of expression* of the picture need no longer suffer by comparison with that of the subject. And since human effort is not "natural," but "artificial," *nature can now be translated in terms of* "*Art*," assuming, of course, that the photographer has the necessary creative and imaginative powers.

Black-and-white photographs are graphic abstractions, whose artificially created symbols stand for natural forms and properties. Nobody would mistake a photograph of a forest for the forest itself, yet we refuse to consider the implication of the distinction, so accustomed have we become to "reading" a photograph as we would a letter. We know how to retranslate it into its original terms of nature; in this respect, photography merely takes over from drawing. But *if* we are forced to translate nature by means of symbols at all (as obviously we are), then we might as well be logical, make the most of it, and turn weakness into advantage. We should not proclaim ourselves satisfied with such symbolic forms as accident presents us with, but should try earnestly to make this process of translation as conscious and controlled as possible. The further a photographer can go in this respect, the stronger and the more convincing will be the message of his pictures.

THE MISSION OF THE CAMERA

No one will deny that a fundamental difference exists between eye and camera, even though the optical construction of the one may resemble the other. At first thought, the advantage may seem to be with the eye, an incredibly wonderful instrument for perceiving color, space, and movement, instantly, guided and supervised by thought and emotion. On second thought, however, severe limitations of its usefulness will be found: differentiation decreases rapidly beyond a distance of only a few score yards, and ceases completely at ranges shorter than half a dozen inches; haze, mist, and darkness cannot be penetrated; rapid movements cannot be dissolved into single phases; no picture conceived by the eye is ever registered in imperishable form; visual memory is deceptive. But none of these shortcomings, and others not mentioned here as well, exist for the camera, *if used with proper knowledge and understanding: as a means of intensifying, enlarging and enriching our powers of vision*, as an instrument which can enable man to progress beyond his congenital limits.

Up to now, only a few advanced photographers have exploited the possibilities of the camera to any great degree, while the majority have hardly scratched the surface. Perhaps the best examples of what the camera can do when really put to work have come so far from technical and scientific sources: air views made by cartographers, infrared long-distance views, high-speed photographs "freezing" the fastest moving objects. Stroboscopic "pattern" shots recording motions too rapid to be followed by the eye as a sequence of single phases, microphotographs, pictures taken with X rays or under polarized light, to name a few examples. Or take astronomical photographs, where the light-accumulating quality of the emulsion makes it possible to photograph otherwise invisible galaxies so far away that their light had to travel a million years to register the ghostly images of stars that may have been extinct for hundreds of thousands of years . . .

One of the reasons why so few photographers make use of the tremendous potentialities of photography may be the fact that exploiting them involves a certain amount of technical knowledge. Once again we must recognize that in order to be a good photographer one has first to master technique. For it is an indisputable fact that every top-notch photograph is a mixture of varying parts of "technique" and "Art." (This does not apply to purely scientific and technical photographs whose usefulness is solely determined by technical perfection and clarity of demonstration, while artistic considerations count for nought.)

The average person is usually gifted *either artistically or technically*, while a person who has both these talents is as rare as a Leonardo. Now, men of science are generally technically gifted too, which together with their interest in research and their talent for practical exploration of newly discovered methods explains their remarkable success in the photographic field. The artistically inclined amateur photographer, however, is usually interested only moderately in technical problems (as little as he can help). This is detrimental to his own interests because this lack of knowledge in technical matters will bar him from many of the more powerful forms of graphic expression in photography. Despite his artistic genius such a man is "technically" a baby. While he may see beyond the obvious, he is painfully powerless to express his advanced ideas. Anybody who ever saw the makings of a really fine picture spoiled from lack of proper execution will agree that in photography "technique" is a matter of fundamental importance. This is a fact that cannot be emphasized often enough.

But just because of its importance in photography, it should never be forgotten that "technique" is *nothing but a means to an end*, comparable in this respect to the grammar and vocabulary of a language one wishes to learn. But while mastery of grammar and vocabulary may be of the greatest importance to anybody who wants to speak a certain language, this ability by no means guarantees that what he will say will be important, learned, or witty.

Again, let me enlarge on this with the help of an example: let's imagine several photographers taking pictures of a very simple object, for instance a flower, and watch how differently they go to work. Lighter or darker filter, filters of different colors, emulsions of different properties, lenses of different focal lengths, top light, side light or back light, diaphragm wide open or stopped down—these are only a few of the various possible approaches, each of which can again be combined with any number of the others, all of them promising different results, each result being within the realm of "technical perfection." One photographer may see this flower as a pattern, another might be interested in its texture, a third may try to fit it into a carefully balanced composition, a fourth may fall in love with its gracefulness, the lovely outline and shape; and so on. Each photographer would select the camera, lens, filter, opening, etc., that are especially well adapted to express exactly the feature he wants to emphasize, and each may produce a "technically perfect" photograph. But while all these different pictures may be equally perfect with regard to technical execution, their content, the messages they are intended to convey to the beholder, may be as different as day and night. And some of them may be justified, beautiful, and clever, while others may be forced and shallow. An experiment like this would clearly demonstrate how little technical perfection means unless it is guided by artistic conception and inspired by imagination.

Now let's go one step further and imagine two arrangements of flowers: here yellow and red blossoms against a background of bright-green young leaves, there red and blue flowers against the white background of a wall. Translated by the orthodox, uncontrolled photographic process into black and white, the first arrangement would turn out gray on gray against gray, all colors being more or less of the same intensity. The second arrangement would appear as light gray and dark gray on white. Photogenically, the first arrangement would be rather disappointing, since only very superior photo-technique could prevent the complete merger of gray into gray, and even then could not greatly alleviate the flatness and general insipidity of the picture. In spite of all its natural colorfulness the first arrangement of flowers will never look well in black and white. The second arrangement, however, can be translated without difficulty into vivid contrasts of different grays; forms can easily be separated, and tension and interest of composition can be created. This subject would largely fulfill the photographic demand for contrasts and for separation of tones and forms, thus facilitating the process of translating terms of nature into terms of art. In short, this second flower arrangement is "photogenic."

This first condition for the successful creation of a photograph fulfilled, let's study the possibilities of the second phase of the work, that of artistic re-creation of the subject. For notwithstanding its generally good qualities, our "raw material" can be processed in a great variety of different ways. Orthochromatic film would show the blue flowers as very light gray and the red ones as near-black, thus providing for the very greatest contrasts, while a panchromatic emulsion with a light-yellow filter would render the blue as a medium gray, and the red as a lighter shade of gray. In the second case panchromatic material plus proper filter would satisfactorily separate these colors that in reality were of practically the same brightness, without violating their emotional value—as orthochromatic film would. Thus, we probably would settle for pan film. Now, the next step would be to decide what type of filters to use (without any filter, both red and blue would be rendered as practically the same medium gray, and contrast and separation would be lost). Here again, the artist has the last and decisive word. In this particular case, he might reason that red as the warmer, more aggressive color, should be rendered lighter, while for blue, as the cooler, more receding shade, a darker, more receding rendering would be indicated; hence, the yellow filter.

But fully as important as these subtleties, and here of even greater interest, would be the fact that it is possible in photography, not only to *separate* two different colors of equal intensity while translating them into black and white, but also *that it is left to the choice of the photographer to emphasize at will either the one or the other color*, through a proper selection of filters. And, what is of even greater interest, such freedom of creation is not limited to color rendering alone, but can be found throughout photography, permitting the re-creation of space, contrast, motion, and light in practically any desired way. It is knowledge and proper command of possibilities like these that enable a photographer to formulate his artistic conception and ideas.

So it all boils down to this: the main requisite for success in photography is understanding of typically photographic properties. This begins with the recognition that the lens perceives things differently from the eye. Again and again we find that objects that in reality were beautiful and stimulating look stale and insignificant when translated into a photograph, and vice versa. The vast expanse of the sea or the sweeping magnificence of rolling open country, for instance, will nearly always make a sadly disappointing photograph, unless dressed up with fancy clouds, interesting foreground matter, people, or something else; while apparently unimportant and in reality quite unexciting little things, when approached from the right angle and properly lighted, frequently result in the most expressive pictures. Of course, there is practically nothing that can't be photographed today, in one way or another, from the curvature of the earth and a closeup of the craters of the moon down to a closeup of a germ, but unless a subject contains photographic possibilities, *unless it is "photogenic,"* it will never make an artistically satisfactory photograph. This is a fact that not even the most brilliant "technique" can change.

> Two factors thus emerge as requisites of success in the field of creative photography: First, the subject must be photogenic. Second, its re-creation in a photograph must be based upon technical knowledge, guided and supported by artistic inspiration.

TYPICALLY PHOTOGRAPHIC PROPERTIES

The peculiar vision of the camera, so different from that of the eye, not only compels the photographer to consider these peculiarities from the beginning, while planning his picture, but also offers him the means of discovering and exploring forms of vision hitherto unknown to the unaided eye, creating new and frequently exciting effects. Some of these "effects" may seem to be axiomatic, especially to the beginner, the reason being that one simply cannot help employing them in one form or another when making a photograph. But just this apparent obviousness of typically photographic properties like color transformation into shades of gray, reversal of tone values into the negative form, the change from three-dimensionality into two-dimensionality, etc.—this "obviousness" is what keeps people from giving any further thought to qualities which to the uninitiated appear unalterably rigid and matter-of-fact, thus by-passing opportunities for improving one's pictures. In this respect, a camera can be compared with a typewriter: with practice almost anybody can use a typewriter, can type out a message, an essay, or even a novel that looks neat and clean to the eye, thanks to the technical perfection of the instrument. Upon the value, truth, artistic quality, etc., of what is typed, however, this purely external neatness has no influence whatsoever.

Applied to photography this means: if technique is not coupled with deep understanding of the aesthetic requirements of the subject to be depicted, the resulting photograph, no matter how clean and neat, will be as empty as the brainless head of an otherwise very pretty manikin, and as dead. (Somebody once aptly called pictures of this type "so what? photographs.") In my opinion, anybody using an instrument so full of potentialities as a camera has a certain obligation to use it to best advantage, and this he can do only if his skill is bolstered by knowledge of the "obvious" but intricate and manifold photographic properties discussed on the following pages. Study of the apparently "obvious" (witness Newton's falling apple) pays dividends in photography as elsewhere and gives the student an often decisive advantage over his not-so-curious competitors. . . .

The ability to transform colors into gray tone values should by no means be considered a "weakness" of the photographic process. On the contrary, this apparently "obvious" photographic quality, if properly used, reveals itself as the perfect solution to the old problem of translating an object into an abstract and artistic form of its own while still maintaining its principal characteristics. "Properly used" in this connection means translation of color values into gray tone values not "literally," but "freely," emphasizing the latent graphic possibilities of the object to be depicted. This may necessitate conscious exaggeration of contrasts instead of "true" color translation into grays, or simplification of gray scale and limitation of tone values to a few strong, well-defined steps of black, gray, and white. Thus, powerful and typically "graphic" black-and-white composition with emphasis on line, outline, and pattern replaces the natural colorfulness of an object, creating new and exciting effects out of the natural ones we were compelled to relinquish. Conscious self-limitation, instead of compulsion, enables us to show real mastery of craft. Simplification becomes intensification and concentration, provided the requirements for its employment and the technical means for its execution are understood: a selection of, and frequently a limitation to, simple and well-articulated forms, and an apt choice of emulsion, filter, and gradation of paper.

The ability to transform positive tone values into negative tone values is, strictly speaking, nothing but an extension of the power of translating colors into shades of gray, presenting an exciting means of achieving fargoing abstraction. Negatives, or rather "negative-positives," because they are really negative prints on paper, lend themselves especially well to dramatization of constructional features and reveal and emphasize internal relations between different elements of composition to a higher degree than any "positive" photograph. In this respect they compare favorably with the "photo-graphic" techniques of solarization and bas-relief (see pages 402-409). In many instances, where superlative clarity in the shadows (always the least-defined parts of a picture) is more important than an "emotionally true" rendering of tone values, negative prints will give better results than ordinary positives. A principle similar to this is put to practical use in the common blueprint, showing light lines on darker background, resulting in greater clarity than dark lines on white would give (too much white causes eye fatigue, resulting in halation that detracts from the fine, dark tracings). Incidentally, negative prints should be of special interest to the commercial artist, since their novelty would attract more attention than an ordinary positive photograph. In combination with their powers of clarification this should make negatives the ideal means for advertising technical products whose uninteresting, everyday appearance requires presentation in especially eye-catching form.

Infrared-sensitized negative material opens a perfectly new field of vision, revealing things never before seen by the human eye. With the help of infrared emulsions we can penetrate atmospheric haze and fog, and human skin as well as the leathery skin of insects (chitin), and photograph what's behind them. One of the most exciting photographs ever taken shows the curvature of the earth, a phenomenon known and proven for centuries, but forever destined to be invisible to the naked eye, hidden beyond impenetrable layers of atmospheric haze. Medical-research photographs reveal the spreading of cancer and venereal diseases below the skin, invisible to the unaided eye. In other instances, infrared-sensitized film has exposed forgeries that otherwise might have escaped detection (forged signatures, erasures, alterations, and additions, forgeries on paintings, camouflaged military installations, etc.). And even instantaneous photographs can now be taken in complete and apparently impenetrable darkness, by flashing the picture on infrared film with the help of "black-out bulbs." For the creative photographer, the haze-penetrating quality of infrared material, and also its peculiar intensification of certain colors and contrasts (green leaves are rendered snow-white, blue water and blue sky turn black), are predominantly important. Telephotographs taken over miles and miles of haze-shrouded distance now will still show contrast and perfect definition, and cloudy skies can be rendered much more dramatic than with the help of any other photographic trick. Granted careful choice of subject matter, infrared-sensitized emulsions are capable of artistic effects of the highest expressiveness; they offer a standing invitation to the researcher looking for hitherto unknown effects.

Telephotography with lenses of longer than "standard" focal length opens another door to intensified visual experience. Objects, scenes which hitherto were "unphotogenic" because of insuperable distance from the camera, can now be turned into some of the most exciting pictures. Things, which previous to the employment of the telephoto lens were hardly noticed, now acquire intense meaning: vision and interest in the surrounding world are widened. But many near-by subjects, too (portraits!), gain from the use of the telephoto lens, which renders their intrinsic proportions more correctly than a lens of standard focal length. The reason: the longer the focal length of a lens, the bigger will be the resulting image; applied to portraiture, for instance, this means that a subject can be posed at greater than "standard" distance, with resulting decrease in distortion according to the laws of perspective.

Closeups and photomicrographs introduce us to the fascinating world of extreme nearness, a world whose pictorial potentialities are almost untouched. Where the eye leaves off, the camera carries on and advances. Enlargements up to five times natural size, and more, can be made directly on the negative, the degree of enlargement being mostly a question of available bellows extension. (If using a lens of unsymmetrical construction, the front of the lens must always face the larger of the two images, in order to give the sharpest possible definition; for closeup work where the groundglass image is more than natural size this means that such a lens has to be reversed in the camera. This does not apply to special closeup lenses, as for instance the Zeiss Micro-Tessar, and neither does it apply to lenses of symmetrical design.) Enlarging such an already "over life-size" negative 10 to 15 times more is hardly a problem, especially if finegrain emulsions and developers are used, and the resulting picture showing the formerly insignificant object 25 to 100 times life size can have all the impact and surprise value of an artistic bombshell. Tiny and humble objects of nature—blossoms, seeds, feathers, the antennae of insects, shells, crystals, etc.—often astonish through their ornamental beauty and the technical ingenuity of their construction. A treasure hoard of loveliness and perfection awaits only the extension of your bellows.

Rendering of texture by photographic means, based on the extraordinary sharpness and correction of modern anastigmats, in conjunction with finegrain emulsions and low-skimming side light, permits the cameraman to equal the marvelous achievements of the copper and steel engravers of the nineteenth century. With this difference, however, that where these old masters spent weeks and months of laborious work, the camera does it in a fraction of a second, and a finished print can be ready within less than an hour. Here again, we are confronted with a typical case of "obviousness": what percentage of photographers give a second thought to this typically photographic property of texture rendering and precise definition? How many consciously capitalize on this singular quality by careful crosslighting, and how many disregard it and senselessly "soften" their pictures, either by means of soft-focus devices, or by printing in Bromoil and similar "arty" techniques . . . .

Instantaneous readiness for action. In the wink of an eye, without lengthy preparations, a modern camera is ready for action. A gentle pressure on the release button, and the object, scene, event, or whatever has been registered with documentary exactitude. What possibilities! And what responsibility! Compare this ease with the laborious work of the draftsman using pencil and paper, who may barely have been able to finish one hasty sketch while the photographer, with no more time, covered the same event from every imaginable angle with a descriptive series of unquestionably authentic pictures. Think of the landscape painter who tried in vain to lose a train of benevolent onlookers until at last he felt compelled to pack up, while in the meantime, a photographer with his speedy and inconspicuous minicamera, had taken a series of snapshots, unnoticed and unmolested. BUT, never forget, that the easier the technical part of the picture-taking process has been made for you by an ingenious photo industry, the greater becomes the danger of wasting this precious perfection on unworthy subjects; hence that common accumulation of yards and yards of exposed film that never even warrant printing. By studying the object before you press the button, by making sure that it fits the requirements for a successful picture, by working in accordance with a carefully prepared plan instead of relying on luck and chance, by making every single shot count, you will prove yourself a match for your camera.

Resolving fast movements into single phases is something the eye cannot do; the camera does the trick and does it easily—if necessary by producing ten thousand pictures per second! Once again, photography provides the means for widening the field of vision, for the creation of hitherto unknown visual sensations. Everyday shutters with speeds up to only 1/250 second are capable of stopping surprisingly fast action, especially when used with proper understanding of the laws of motion. Incomparably higher speeds can be achieved, and incomparably faster actions can be "frozen," by means of modern speedlights which nowadays can be bought and used even by photographers with rather limited means. Pictures taken with this kind of light—the stroboscopic multiple exposure of a golfer swinging a club, rifle bullets in flight showing their bow and stern waves of compressed air, the splash of a drop of milk—are among the classics of photography. Edgerton and Mili have pioneered the technique of high-speed photography, invented and designed the equipment, and generally paved the way so that photographers like you and me may use it. Now it is up to us, too, to put those wonderful discoveries to constructive and purposeful use.

The light-accumulation power of photographic emulsions permits, through correspondingly long exposures, adding quantities of light so faint as to be imperceptible to the eye and to keep on adding until their combined power is strong enough to make an impression on film. Stars, billions of miles away, much too small to be visible even through the most powerful telescopes, have thus been photographed successfully, made visible and charted. And night pictures, as well as objects hidden in deepest shadow, can be rendered in amazing detail if only exposed long enough; in fact, in much more detail than even a cat could have perceived at the time of exposure.

The selectivity of the photographic process is another case of "obviousness" which generally escapes investigation. Granted the obvious truth that a photograph is automatically "limited" (by the four edges of the paper it is printed on), this limitation is nevertheless an advantage over the eye, which is incapable of selecting one single segment of the whole range of vision and transmitting this cut-out to the brain, in the form of an independent picture. This advantage of the camera should be used consciously. Instead of indiscriminately slicing off a piece of the surrounding world, the creative photographer should, through proper "cropping," deliberately determine the logical boundaries of his photograph. Often the final touch of clever cropping will compress and concentrate the photographed object until its appearance is more striking in a picture than in reality.

This selectivity of the photographic process applies to all three dimensions in space. Up and down, right and left, it can be controlled through choice of lens, viewpoint and final cropping; with regard to depth, both toward and away from the camera, focusing and diaphragm provide the means for control, deciding position and extension of the "depth of field," the zone in a picture that is rendered sharp.

The recording power is one of the most obvious characteristics of the photographic process, and one which the photographer can hardly help putting to use when taking a picture—unless, of course, one deliberately intends to create a false impression by using the camera to "lie" in a negative sense. How a photographer makes use of this power of documentation, and what kind of subject he chooses to document, is a crucial factor in determining his ability as a creative artist, proving presence or lack of taste and artistic responsibility. Unfortunately, all too many photographers prove by their work a regrettable lack of self-discipline, of taste and discrimination. They flood magazines, "salons," and their own albums and walls with "documents" that were never worth documenting.

More thought and knowledge, discrimination and self-discipline *before* the shutter is released would help prevent so much wasted money, time, and material, and indirectly help photography to gain proper recognition as the artistic means of expression it really is.

Unlimited multiplication of photographs is chiefly of practical interest; the artist is less concerned with limitless multiplication of his work. Photographs, however, always are *originals*, and thus *ipso facto, documents*, and this is the only instance where originals can *easily* be multiplied in limitless numbers. This fact is of importance for educational, scientific, commercial, juridical, etc., purposes. And one more thing: a photographic print invariably shows more detail and brilliance than even the best engraving that could be made from it. And while an engraving invariably deteriorates with the number of prints made from it, a negative is not affected in any way by the number of copies produced, whether it be ten or ten million.

No contrasts—no image—no picture

Differentiation begins—first indication of an image

Well defined contrast—a technically perfect picture

CHAPTER 9

CONTRASTS AND HOW TO CONTROL THEM

EVERY single photograph ever made owes its very existence to contrasts—the contrasts between black and white and intermediate shades of gray. Without such contrasts, there would be no differentiation, no image, no form; even the simplest silhouette or line is nothing but a manifestation of contrasts—a juxtaposition of something light against something darker.

Mastery of contrasts is the first step towards creative camera control.

Methods of control. The photographer has four chances to increase or decrease the contrasts in a photograph during the process of picturemaking:

1. *Before the exposure:* by choice of negative material (see pages 70, 209), color filter (page 223), and lighting (page 302).
2. *During the exposure:* by shortening or prolonging the exposure (pages 122, 211).
3. *While processing the negative:* by varying time of development and type of the developer (see pages 135-139, 211).
4. *While making the print:* by selecting a paper of proper gradation (page 214).

Each one of these factors can be used either alone or in conjunction with one or more of the others. And if at one point or another you overshoot the mark, then you can always use the next step to correct the mistake since all these controls can be made to work both ways: toward an increase, or toward a decrease, of contrast.

Psychology of contrasts. In the majority of cases, contrast control will be used to produce prints of "normal" contrasts in spite of adversities resulting from abnormally contrasty or contrastless negatives, or from mistakes made while selecting the type of film, exposing it, or developing the negative. In certain instances, however, the creative photographer will want to disobey this rule and either increase or decrease the natural contrasts of his subjects consciously in order to achieve certain artistic or psychological effects.

It is interesting to notice in this connection how well photographic and psychological terms cover the same thing: how, for instance, a "soft" mood suggests gentleness, unchallenging mildness, expressed perfectly in a "soft" print; how "hardness" of character, power, and strength are incompatible with "softness" in psychology as well as in photography and would have to be symbolized by strong contrasts between black and white, by "hardness," in a photograph intended to convey such an impression. We talk of "dramatization" in psychology as well as in photography, and mean in both cases "exaggeration." In order to dramatize something in a photograph we have to exaggerate its character to represent a contrastful subject even more contrastfully than it presented itself to the eye, and a contrastless object even softer.

There are hardly any rules to rely on when it comes to subtleties like these; artistic intuition, backed by feeling for psychological undercurrents, will have to be your guide, and the final print will prove whether you were right or wrong.

Terminology of contrasts. Negative and paper contrasts. A "soft" negative shows contrasts that are below "normal," while a "soft" paper permits producing prints with lower contrasts than the negatives they were made from.

A "normal" negative shows contrasts that are easy to print on "normal" or "medium" paper, a paper which does not change the contrasts of a negative while converting it into a positive print.

A "hard" negative shows greater than "normal" contrasts, while a "hard" paper permits producing prints with greater contrasts than the negatives they were made from.

Exposure and development. A "flat" print has hardly any contrasts at all. Everything is more or less "gray-on-gray," usually the result of underdevelopment or overexposure of the negative in conjunction with a printing paper of too soft gradation.

Flat.

Soft.

Normal.

Hard.

Chalky.

A "muddy," streaky, or mottled image tone is usually the result of overexposure of the printing paper coupled with too short development in an effort to save the print from going too dark.

"Normal" of course means normal; a print with contrasts and tones that are pleasing to the eye, strong without being hard, well modulated without being soft.

A "hard" or contrasty print lacks differentiation in its lightest and darkest parts, which consist mostly of pure whites and pure blacks. Intermediate shades of gray are generally missing, usually as a result of overdevelopment of the negative, use of a printing paper of too hard gradation, or both.

A "chalky" print consists overwhelmingly of blacks and whites and is almost completely lacking in intermediate shades of gray, the result of printing a hard negative on hard paper.

CONTRAST CONTROL PRIOR TO EXPOSURE

Negative material for different contrasts. Ordinarily a photographer will choose a particular film because of its speed, its color sensitivity, or its fine grain, but not because of the way in which it renders contrasts. Instead, he will modify and control contrasts by means of exposure, development, and choice of printing paper, which together will give him all the leeway in either direction that he could possibly need—under *ordinary* circumstances.

However, there are always occasions where a photographer either wants to go to extremes with regard to contrasts or where a series of pictures has to be taken under unusual conditions. Then it is simpler to use a special type of film which can be processed "normally" than to use an ordinary all-around film and afterwards upset the whole routine in order to change that film's characteristic contrast rendition.

Two such instances are telephotography, where contrasts must usually be stepped up considerably, and copying black-and-white printed matter, where the utmost contrast is desirable.

Generally speaking, the higher the speed of a film is, the "softer" will be its gradation, and thus the contrasts it renders; and the slower the speed of a film, the "harder" its gradation. Most finegrain films have a gradation that is already somewhere on the "hard" side of normal and needs watching when it comes to exposure and development unless a hard effect is specifically desired. The "softest" films on the market are the super-fast pan films; the "hardest" films belong to the category known as "process films," made especially for the purpose of copying printed matter and drawings, and manufactured by Ansco, Eastman and others.

According to their gradation from very soft to very hard, here is a typical series of Kodak films: Tri-X Pan, Super XX Pan, Plus X, Panatomic X, Contrast Process Film.

Picture at left was taken on a film of very soft gradation; that at right on a film of comparatively hard gradation. Both negatives were printed on "normal" paper for objective comparison of contrasts rendered by these two extreme types of negative material.

Notice, however, that under normal conditions, i.e., when photographing objects of normal contrast range, results identical with the above could have been produced by using only one type of film and printing the negatives on paper of either soft or hard gradation, respectively. Notice how rendering at left gives maximum "detail" and "documentary clarity;" how that at right is more dramatic, graphic with blacks and whites emphasizing masses, light and shadow.

CONTRAST CONTROL THROUGH DEVELOPMENT WITH CONTROLLED EXPOSURE

We saw on page 129 how important the *time* of development is in determining the range of contrasts (the "gamma") in a negative. Anybody who ever watched the development of an orthochromatic film by the red glow of the safelight will recall how a fully exposed (!) negative, after a few moments in the developer, starts to turn grayish almost at once over its entire surface, and how gradually the "highlights" build up in density and contrast, while the "shadows" stay more or less thin and gray. If we interrupted development at such an early stage, we would get a negative with extremely low contrasts, but full of detail in highlights as well as in shadows, provided it had been given a very generous exposure.

On the other hand, if we carried on development far beyond the regular and prescribed time, the relatively briefly exposed shadows would stay more or less as they were, while the plentifully exposed highlights would increase in density until at last they were patches of solid black. Such an overdeveloped negative would show extremely strong contrasts, a fact which under ordinary circumstances would make it impossible to get a decent print from it.

Under extraordinary circumstances, however, either one of these two deviations from the customary rule may give us just what we need. Whenever the natural contrasts in a subject are far below normal and have to be increased for some reason or other, as for instance in the case of many telephotographs over miles of hazy distance, a deliberate shortening of the exposure time by up to 50 per cent, in conjunction with a prolongation of the time of development by up to 100 per cent, will usually result in the desired increase in contrasts.

And whenever the natural contrasts are far above normal, as for instance when taking photographs of desert ranch houses in brilliant sunlight, with entrances and porches in blackest shadow, prolongation of exposure time by about 100 per cent, in conjunction with a reduction of the time of development by 50 per cent, will usually give negatives that can still be printed in the normal manner without loss of detail in either highlights or shadows.

An increase in time of development should always be accompanied by a reduction of the time of exposure, and vice versa, in order to get negatives with fairly normal all-over densities. Overexposure plus overdevelopment would result in extremely black and dense negatives of practically *normal contrasts*, a fact that may come in handy when we have overexposed a negative by mistake and want to develop it to normal contrasts; underexposure plus underdevelopment always means loss of the negative.

1—Short exposure, long development, great contrasts.

2—Normal exposure, normal development, normal contrasts.

Print from negative no. 1 on normal paper. Notice the strong "graphic" black-and-white contrasts.

Print from negative no. 2 on normal paper. Notice well balanced definition in highlights and shadows.

This series of ten pictures demonstrates the very great degree to which contrasts can be controlled in a photograph.

Ordinarily, of course, only one of these six steps would be used. Putting one single picture through all of them was done here merely for theoretical reasons—to show what can be done—and disregarding the fact that in this particular case only the print from negative No. 2 would be usable.

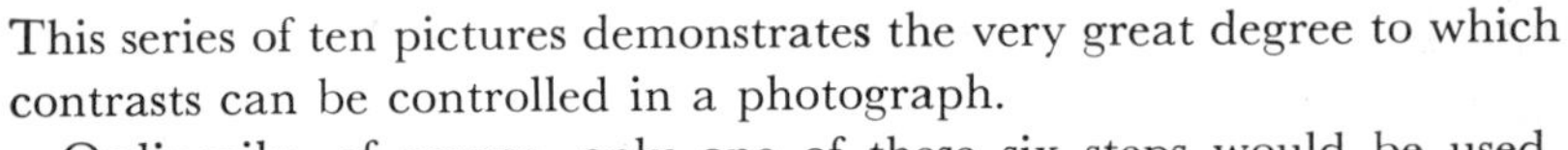

In other instances, however, quite a different treatment might be indicated—a soft one, for instance, if maximum shadow detail is desirable, or a hard one if the picture has to have strong graphic qualities, expressing a mood in terms of masses, light, and shadow.

Contrasts increased as far as possible toward hardness. (Negative no. 1 printed on paper of extra hard gradation.)

3—Long exposure, short development, low contrasts.

4—Very long exposure, very short development, very low contrasts.

Print from negative no. 3 on normal paper. Notice decrease in contrast, useful for rendering over-contrasty subjects.

Print from negative no. 4 on normal paper. Notice perfection of shadow definition even within the deepest crevices.

Contrasts decreased as far as possible toward softness. (Negative no. 4 printed on paper of extra soft gradation).

Combination of all the contrast-controls mentioned in this chapter will naturally permit the most extensive changes in contrast, ranging from practically no contrast at all to purest black and white.

The two lowest pictures, showing the same object taken under identical conditions, give some indication of the control a resourceful photographer has over his medium.

CONTRAST CONTROL THROUGH PAPER OF PROPER GRADATION

The easiest way to control and change contrasts comes with the final step in making a photograph: printing. By selecting a printing paper of proper gradation, from very soft through normal to extra-hard, radical corrections in the negative contrasts can be made with no danger to the negative (as there is to a certain degree in the case of some of the previously mentioned methods). Here, if the first decision proves wrong, a new print on paper of different gradation is readily made, and no harm is done.

However, there is a drawback: prints made on either very soft or very hard paper never show the same richness and brilliance of tone as prints made on paper of normal or just a little harder gradation. So in order to get the best possible results, it is to your interest to produce negatives in which contrasts are already as close to specifications as possible. Then later you won't have to make any more changes but can transfer them practically as they are into the final print on a paper of *normal gradation.*

Soft papers always have a tendency to look flat in areas where contrasts are low, as will be found in practically every negative, even in those with generally strong contrasts. A negative which is very brightly lighted in some spots and whose shadows are thin and deep, for instance, will invariably show very great contrast between its lightest and its darkest parts, but within these lightest and darkest areas themselves, contrasts will probably be very low, and printed on a paper of soft gradation these particular areas would look flat and devoid of definition. And in spite of the fact that a very soft paper probably will still do the trick and give at least a trace of detail in highlights as well as in shadows, a skillfully contrast-controlled negative could probably have been printed on a much harder paper and would have made a much more satisfactory print.

Hard papers always have a tendency to make a print look "spotty" and broken-up, because it is their nature to suppress the more delicate shades of gray. The harder the gradation is, the more they do this. Besides, the harder the paper, the more it brings out the grain of the film. This fact can make a good-sized enlargement on hard paper look as if it were printed on coarse sandpaper.

Soft paper—
mist and fog. . . .

Two prints made from one and the same negative on papers of different gradation, demonstrating how given negative contrasts can be altered during printing or enlarging, and with them the whole mood and character of the photograph. . . .

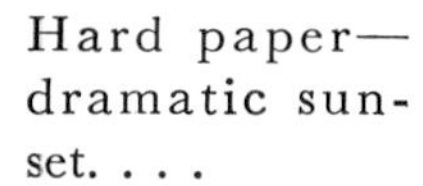

Hard paper—
dramatic sunset. . . .

"Straight prints" made from the same negative as the picture opposite. *Left:* The softer paper brings out all the details of the photograph, in highlights as well as in shadows. But contrasts are too low, and the general impression is one of monotonous flatness. *Right:* The harder paper makes the picture brisk and snappy, but overstrong contrasts kill the detail in the lightest and the darkest parts of the print, leaving an impression of disappointing emptiness. Now compare this with the version on the opposite page.

LOCAL CONTRAST CONTROL THROUGH DODGING

Every experienced photographer knows that there is hardly ever a negative that will make what he calls a "straight print." This would of course be the ideal negative, a negative of such perfection with regard to contrast that all of its parts would have to be exposed for exactly the same length of time in printing.

Usually, the best we can do is to produce negatives of contrasts so well balanced that highlights as well as shadows need *more or less* the same exposure time in order to make a perfect print, but where there will always be some areas that need special attention: a shadow that is just a little bit too thin and would print just a little too dark, *unless* we held the light back during part of the time of exposure of the print; or a highlight that is just a bit too dense and would print too chalky, *unless* we gave it a little extra time while exposing the print. Such local corrections in exposure time are called *dodging*.

Of course, in most cases selection of a printing paper of softer gradation would probably eliminate the need for dodging, but instead we would have the sad results forecast on page 214 in the warning on "soft paper": a regrettable loss of contrast in

"Dodged" final print made from the same negative as the picture on the opposite page, printed on paper of the same gradation as that used to print the right half of the opposite photograph. The darkest parts have been held back during print exposure, and the brightest parts have been "burned in," with the result that this "dodged" print combines the wealth of detail shown in the "soft half" of the opposite picture with the impressive contrasts of the "hard half."

highlights and shadows. To avoid this, to get more contrasts in highlights and shadows, a harder paper will have to be used, and contrast ranges of the negative for which such paper would be too hard will have to be equalized *locally* by dodging.

Dodging of the highlights in a negative is called "burning in," dodging of the shadows is called "holding back." We burn in highlights that otherwise would print too light by shading the rest of the print during part of the exposure with our hands or a piece of cardboard, thus exposing only the reluctant highlights through a crack between the fingers or a hole cut out of the cardboard. And we "hold back" a shadow that otherwise would print too dark by shielding it from the light for part of the exposure time with a piece of cardboard stuck on a wire and held in the path of the enlarger light. In both cases it is an all-important rule that the dodging device (hands or cardboard) must *always be kept slightly in motion* in order to avoid a halo around the dodged parts of the print.

Dodging is the most individualistic of all the different contrast controls and will add that final touch of artistic perfection to your prints.

CHAPTER 10

COLOR AND HOW TO CONTROL IT

SO FAR we have seen how the range of contrasts *as a whole* can be controlled in a photograph to almost any desired degree—how on the one hand it can be stretched to include the extremes of black and white, and how on the other hand it can be narrowed to a few shades of mellow gray-on-gray. But this is only part of the story.

For it is not only possible to influence contrasts as a whole but, to a certain degree, to change them *individually* as well. We can either emphasize certain objects or tone them down. We can make them at will either lighter than they actually were, or darker—and without appreciably affecting the contrasts of the rest of the photograph. The only catch is that the object we wish to lighten or darken, to play up or down, must have a color different in hue from the color of its immediate surroundings.

The desirability of such local contrast control is obvious. That it is actually possible at all is due to the fact that in black-and-white photography, colors are translated into shades of gray, and that during this process of translation a certain color can be singled out and, with the help of *color filters*, can be converted into a gray shade that is either lighter or darker than that particular color actually appeared to the eye. In order fully to understand this phenomenon, and this is necessary if we want to make fullest use of it, we have to take a shallow plunge into the physics of color.

THE PHYSICS OF COLOR

Color begins and ends with light; without light—in darkness—there is no color. So to understand the nature of color, we must learn about the nature of light. Physicists tell us that "light" is a certain form of electromagnetic energy, something like radio waves or X rays, but of a different "wavelength" (see sketch on opposite page). "Light" is a member of that big family of "waves" that starts with the technical alternating currents with wavelengths of several thousand kilometers; that includes radio waves, heat radiation, infrared and ultraviolet waves, and X rays; and that ends—as far as we know today—with the gamma radiation of radium and "cosmic rays" with wavelengths so short that they have to be measured in fractions of the millionth part of a millimeter.

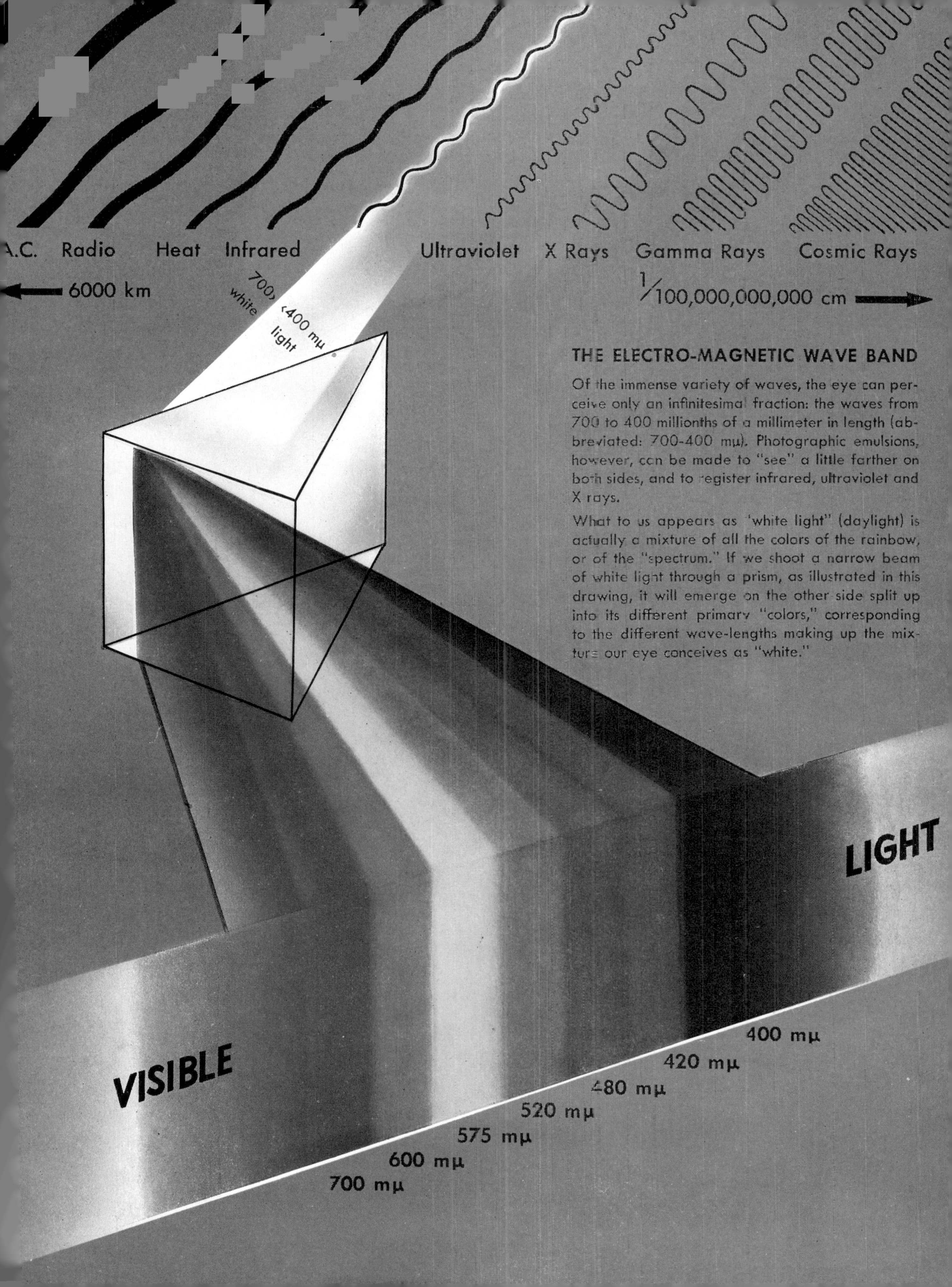

THE ELECTRO-MAGNETIC WAVE BAND

Of the immense variety of waves, the eye can perceive only an infinitesimal fraction: the waves from 700 to 400 millionths of a millimeter in length (abbreviated: 700-400 mμ). Photographic emulsions, however, can be made to "see" a little farther on both sides, and to register infrared, ultraviolet and X rays.

What to us appears as "white light" (daylight) is actually a mixture of all the colors of the rainbow, or of the "spectrum." If we shoot a narrow beam of white light through a prism, as illustrated in this drawing, it will emerge on the other side split up into its different primary "colors," corresponding to the different wave-lengths making up the mixture our eye conceives as "white."

If we shoot a beam of "white daylight" through a prism of perfectly colorless glass, it will emerge all broken up into the colors of the "spectrum," thus demonstrating that what we perceive as "white" light actually is a blend of many different colors. And since these same spectral colors are directly responsible for all the colors of all the things in the world, we may as well say that light and color are one and the same, *that color is light.*

Radiation of wavelengths from 700 to 400 mμ (abbreviation for "millimicron," which means millionth of millimeter) strikes the earth, and our eyes, sensitive receivers for electromagnetic energy of this particular waveband, intercept these radiations and convey them to the brain where they register and produce the sense-impression of "daylight." White daylight illuminates our surroundings and makes things "visible," gets partly reflected and partly absorbed by them, and thus produces "color." For color is not an "absolute" property of things—like shape, or hardness, or weight—but is "relative," depending on an object's ability to reflect and absorb light of wavelengths between 700 and 400 mμ, and on the wavelength of the light that strikes it. If, for instance, an object reflects light waves of 600 to 650 mμ while absorbing waves of all other lengths, we will perceive the reflected waves through our eyes, but not the absorbed parts of the spectrum. Transferred to the brain this radiation from 600 to 650 mμ produces the sense impression of "pure red." If the reflected wavelength were between 500 and 550 mμ, we would see "pure green" if all other wavelengths had been absorbed. Most colors, however, are not "pure" colors because they are produced not by one narrow band of waves alone, but by a mixture of waves of different lengths. The green of plants, for instance, is not only the reflection of "green"-producing waves but contains quite a lot of yellow and even red, resulting from the reflection of waves of approximately 575 and 650 mμ. And so on. An object that appears to the eye as "white" is white because it reflects *all* the "visible" radiation from 700 to 400 mμ; and an object that we perceive as "black" looks black because it doesn't reflect any "visible" radiation at all, but absorbs "light" completely.

Familiar objects show their familiar colors only in white daylight. If we should illuminate a living room, for instance, with *red* light, all the colors would appear changed with the exception of those that were red before. Objects that always appeared red will not change their color because they would still be excited by "red" radiation. But since red light doesn't contain radiation of wavelengths which produce the sense reaction of, for instance, green or blue, objects of these colors will now appear *black* when illuminated by "red light." And white objects, which were white because they reflected the whole range of visible radiation will look *red* under red light because now there is no other radiation for them to reflect.

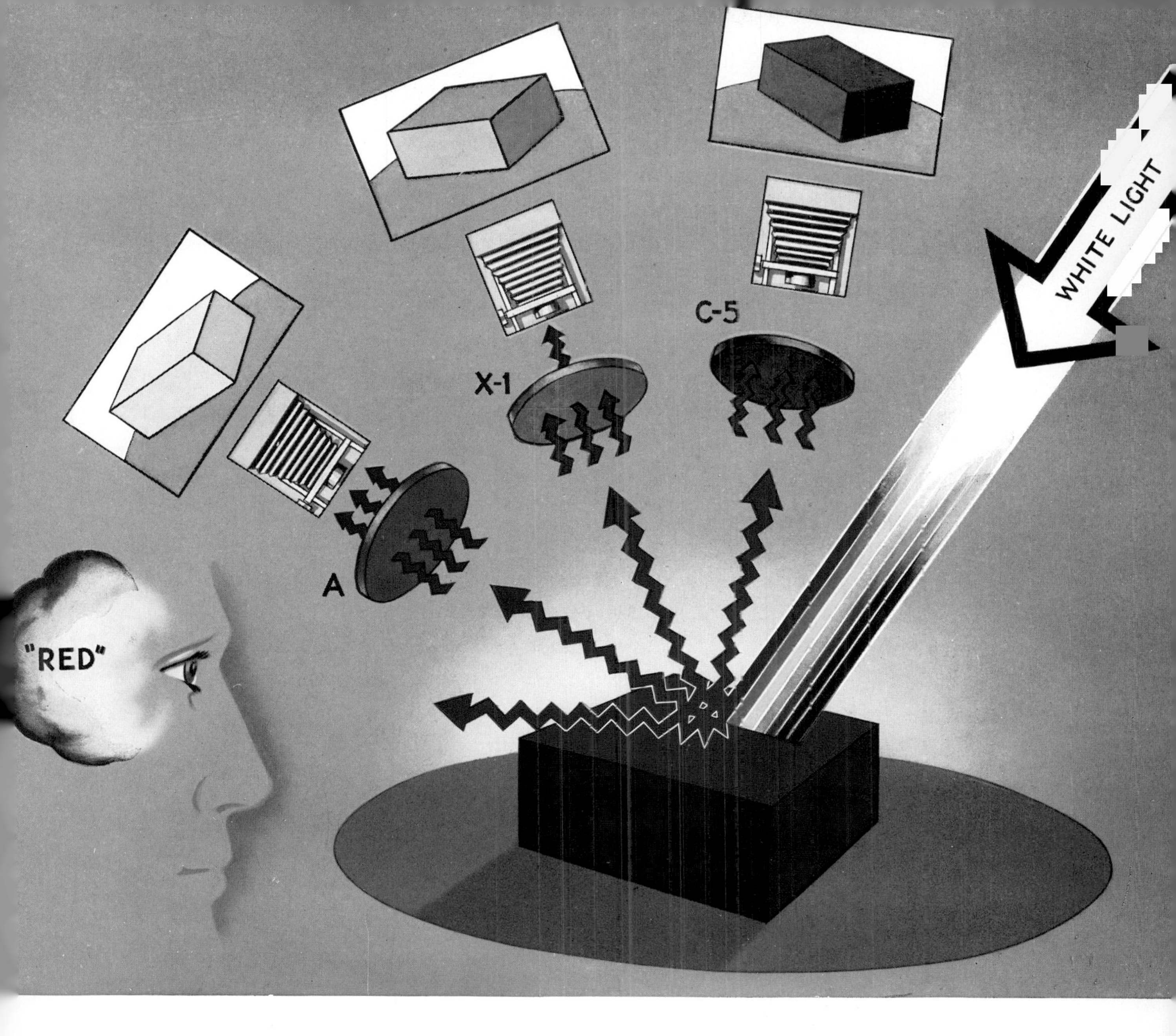

White daylight strikes a red object. This object appears "red," because its surface absorbs all visible radiation with the exception of the red-producing and some of the yellow-producing waves, which it *reflects* so that they can be received by the eye, transmitted to the brain and there produce the sense impression "red."

The sketch further illustrates the action of color filters when taking a photograph. The red filter transmits all of the red, and thus renders red in a photograph as light as it renders white itself (only the fraction of white light that consists of "red" waves can pass a red filter—while the rest is absorbed by the red filter). The yellow-green filter transmits the small number of yellow-producing waves reflected by the red object (remember what we said on the opposite page about "pure" colors!) but cuts off the red-producing radiation, thus admitting only a relatively small amount of light to the film, resulting in a medium gray rendering of the object. The blue filter cuts off red and yellow completely since it transmits only blue light which isn't reflected by the yellowish-red object at all. Thus it doesn't transmit any light reflected from the red object, resulting in a black rendering in the final picture.

We can produce the same effect by looking at the world in white daylight through a piece of red cellophane. Everything will look either lighter and darker red, or black, depending on the different objects' power to reflect "red" radiation from 600 to 700 mμ, which alone can penetrate the piece of red cellophane, and alone reach the eye. The resulting red appearance of everything familiar would be the same as before, but the means of achieving it would be different. In the former case it resulted from illuminating objects exclusively by *red light.* in the latter the actual illumination was unchanged, but instead only the "*red*" waves were permitted to reach the eye, by cutting off all radiation which would produce yellow, green, blue, and purple with the help of a *filter:* the piece of red cellophane. This is actually the way the camera "sees" objects when a picture is taken through a color filter in order to improve, to emphasize, or to reduce an object's contrasts. By working with light from only part of the spectrum, by subtracting and neutralizing certain parts of the waveband, *we darken certain colors, so that other colors may appear lighter by comparison.* Thus, we can never directly render a color "lighter" in a photograph, but by making the other colors that surround this color appear darker, by shutting off that part of the spectrum that made them "light," we can *indirectly* make practically any color in the world appear lighter than any other color. This is done simply by taking the picture through a filter of the same color as the color we want to render light.

To make a certain object appear "lighter," the filter must be of the same color as the object. And to make a certain object appear "darker," the color of the filter must be "complementary" to that of the object. Such "complementary" color pairs are: red and blue-green, orange and blue, yellow and purple-blue, green-yellow and purple, green and red-purple.

COLOR CONTROL THROUGH NEGATIVE MATERIAL

The theory of color control in black-and-white photography outlined above presumes that camera and film react to color values much as do eye and brain. This, however, is not always true. Actually, some emulsions are to a greater or lesser degree "color-blind," while others are even more sensitive to some colors than the eye, thus automatically rendering such colors too light unless retarded by use of the right type of correction filter.

Recalling the examination of the color sensitivity of films in general on pages 68-69, we will remember that there are three basically different types of emulsions:

1. *Blue-sensitive* films that are oversensitive to blue, which they render much too light, while "blind" to all other colors, which accordingly appear black in the print.
2. *Orthochromatic* films that are sensitive to blue, green, and yellow only, but blind to red, which is translated into black in the finished photograph.
3. *Panchromatic* films that are almost equally sensitive to blue, green, yellow, and red, and thus translate *all colors* into gray tones of more or less the same value as recorded by the eye.

It should be obvious that only the last type of film, *pan film which is equally sensitive to all colors*, can be expected to give satisfactory results when it comes to color control, since an emulsion that is "blind" to certain colors of the spectrum cannot possibly give a complete translation of all the colors that surround us. Some shades will always be missing, resulting in involuntary tone falsification and making complete tone control impossible. Obviously, a film that is insensitive to red can never be exposed through a red filter (which, incidentally, is the filter that gives us the most dramatic effects), since such a filter would only transmit light of a color for which such an emulsion is "blind." Films of types *1* and *2* should be used only for special reasons—blue-sensitive films for the black-and-white copy work for which they were especially designed, orthochromatic films for the amateur who is developing a film himself for the first time and wants to watch the process by the red glow of the darkroom safelight.

COLOR CONTROL THROUGH COLOR FILTERS

The purpose of a filter is to prevent light of a certain color (wavelength) from making an impression on the emulsion of the film. Whenever a particular color would photograph too light because the film is oversensitive to that particular color, or whenever we want a color to appear darker in the photograph than it appeared to the eye, a filter of a "complementary" ("opposite") color should be used to darken that color or even make it appear black in the final photograph (see page 226). On the other hand, if we want a particular color to appear lighter in the final print than it ordinarily would, a filter of the same color as this particular color will (indirectly) help to achieve the goal by darkening the rendering of all other colors in the picture and thus making the chosen color stand out lighter by comparison. Since the variety of colors is almost unlimited, and each color theoretically demands two special filters, one to make it appear lighter, one to make it appear darker, the number of available filters is naturally very great (the Eastman Kodak Company alone lists over 100 different Wratten filters). The great majority of these filters, however, is designed for specific scientific and experimental purposes, and the average photographer will seldom need more than three or four filters of different colors.

Color filters are generally designed for one of two different, specific purposes:

COMPARISON of color sensitivity of the three basic types of film emulsions. All pictures taken under identical light conditions, printed on the same grade of paper for fair comparison of color rendition and contrast range.

PANCHROMATIC film translates all colors into closely corresponding shades of gray. In this case, color translation should be controlled by means of filter (see page 198, *bottom*) in order to improve tone separation. Pan film is the ideal raw material for the creative photographer.

ORTHOCHROMATIC film is oversensitive to blue which it renders too light, and is completely insensitive to red, which it renders as black in the final picture. Unsatisfactory rendition of these two important color limits use of ortho material considerably.

BLUE-SENSITIZED film is *blind for all colors but blue*, for which color this film is oversensitive, rendering it as white in the final picture, while all other colors will appear more or less as black. From the creative point of view, blue-sensitized film is obsolete and completely valueless.

1. *Correction filters* alter the response of a given photographic emulsion so that it will record all colors in gray tones that approximately correspond in brightness to the brightness of the original colors as perceived by the eye. For being "sensitive" to *all colors* doesn't necessarily mean that such a film will translate these colors into gray tones of the correct, corresponding *brightness;* as a matter of fact, even the most highly perfected panchromatic emulsions are generally oversensitive to ultraviolet, blue-violet, and sometimes red, and wherever an absolutely correct rendering of color with regard to brightness is necessary ("monochromatic" tone rendering), such an oversensitivity has to be compensated for with the help of the right type of correction filter, which for Kodak films can be chosen from the following table:

Filters for Monochromatic Color Rendering		Wratten Filter	Filter Factor
Film Type (See Table Page 69)	Illumination		
Type B	Sunlight	K-2	2 x
	Tungsten	X-1	3 x
Type C	Sunlight	X-1	4 x
	Tungsten	X-2	4 x

2. *Contrast filters* are used for consciously distorting color values while translating them into gray tone values in order to achieve tone separation between different colors of equal brightness which otherwise would photograph as two nearly or completely identical tones of gray. Red apples among green leaves, for instance, may photograph without a filter as two tones of almost identical gray. Separation between apples and leaves is lost to a great extent, and the picture looks flat and insipid. Use of a contrast filter would prevent this. Photographed through a red filter, which transmits the red of the apples and holds back the green of the leaves, the apples would stand out light against a dark background of leaves. Photographed through a green filter, just the opposite would happen: now the green of the leaves would be transmitted and the red of the apples retarded, resulting in a picture showing dark apples against light foliage.

For selection of the correct type of filter for color separation consult the following table of Kodak Wratten filters for separation of colors of equal brightness:

Color of Object	Filter That Will Make Color Lighter	Filter That Will Make Color Darker
Red	F, A, G	C-5, B
Orange	G, A	C-5
Yellow	G, A	C-5
Green	B, G, X-1, X-2	C-5, A
Blue-green	C-5, B	F, A
Blue	C-5	F, A, G, B
Purple	C-5	B

Total control of one color, here: blue

Blue is the color of a clear and sunny sky, and in the majority of outdoor photographs, sky is one of the most important picture elements. The sky makes a natural background for most outdoor photographs, for mountains and buildings as well as for people and portraits, flowers and trees.

In order to make objects stand out contrastfully against the blue sky, or to capture the fleeting beauty of clouds in our pictures, we have to control the gray-tone rendering of the sky itself, to translate this blue into any shade of gray including white and black. The photographs to the right prove that this can be done. *How* is shown in the following table:

Sky Tone Control

Negative Material	Filter	Tone of Blue Sky
Panchromatic	C-5	White
	None	Lighter than correct
	K-2	Practically correct
	G	Slightly darker than correct
	A	Very dark gray
	F	Almost black
	A + Polarizing filter	Black

Whenever you use the blue sky for a background, remember:

The sky is usually darkest near the zenith but is frequently almost white near the horizon. Shoot portraits of blondes against the sky's darkest part in order to make the blond hair stand out.

The sky is always darker opposite the sun than near the sun.

Rendering of an overcast sky is affected very little by any filter, even if the overcast appears to be very thin.

Slight underexposure always increases, and overexposure always decreases, the effect of filters. Badly overexposed, filtered negatives show hardly any difference from correctly exposed, unfiltered ones.

Blue filter.

No filter.

Yellow filter.

Red filter.

Red filter and polarizer.

The adjoining photographs show what complete control over contrasts and colors is yours for the asking.

Two colors of approximately equal brightness (as illustrated in the Kodachrome reproduction below) can not only be separated in any imaginable way but can individually and independently be translated into any desired gray shade, including white and black. Here we find every possible combination from white-on-white to black-on-black, with all the intermediate combinations of gray.

As a matter of fact, so great is the range of color control that the third picture of this series (*top, right*) and the seventh picture (*bottom, left*) almost look like positive and negative, while both, of course, are genuine positives, as proven by the shadows which in the case of a negative would be lighter than the adjoining tones of gray.

The more complementary (see page 222) two colors are, the easier can they be separated, and the more closely related they are, the more difficult it is to separate them. Still, there is no case where two different colors cannot be separated to fullest satisfaction if the combined possibilities offered by selection of negative material, filter, exposure, development, gradation of paper, etc., are skillfully used together.

Pan film and X2 filter, printed light on hard paper. Both blue and red appear as white.

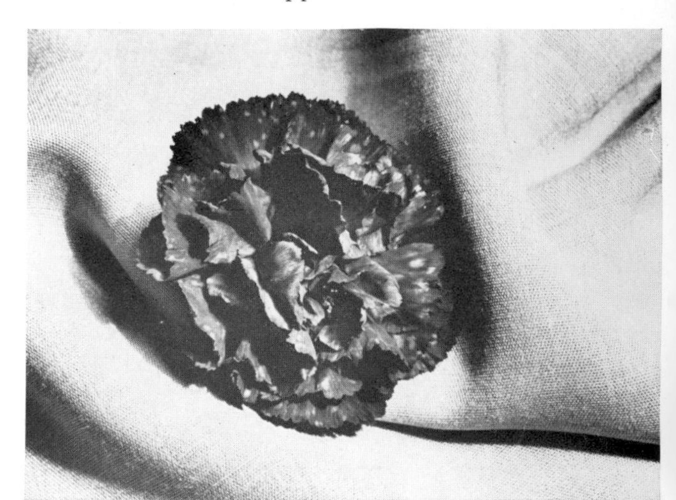

Pan film and C-5 filter, printed on normal paper. Blue appears white, red appears gray.

Reproduction from Kodachrome transparency shows natural colors of carnation and background.

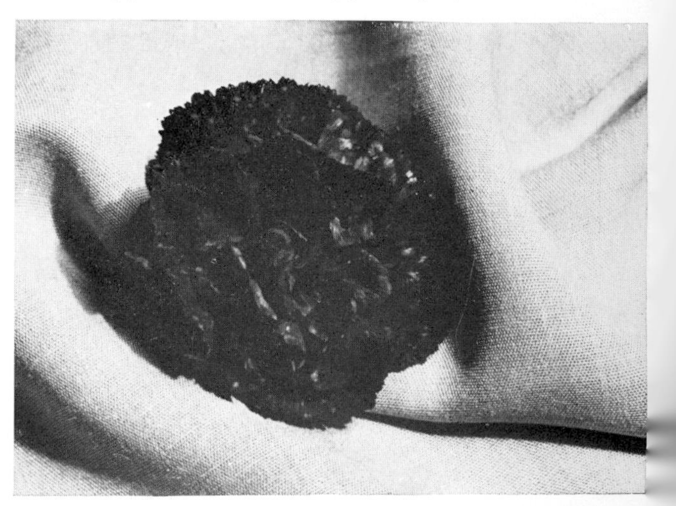

Pan film and C-5 filter, printed on hard paper. Blue appears white, red appears black.

BACKGROUND GRAY ↓

BACKGROUND BLACK ↓

FLOWER WHITE ←

Pan film and *A* filter, printed on normal paper.
Blue appears gray, red appears white.

Pan film and *F* filter, printed on normal paper.
Blue appears black, red appears white.

FLOWER GRAY ←

Pan film and X-2 filter, printed on normal paper.
Monochromatically "correct" rendering.

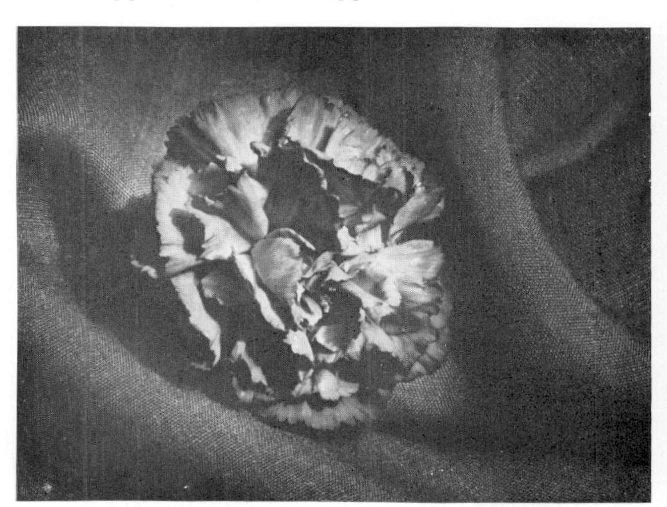

Pan film and *A* filter, printed dark on soft paper.
Blue appears black, red appears gray.

FLOWER BLACK ←

Pan film and C-5 filter, printed dark on soft paper.
Blue appears gray, red appears black.

Pan film and X2 filter, printed dark on soft paper.
Both blue and red appear as black.

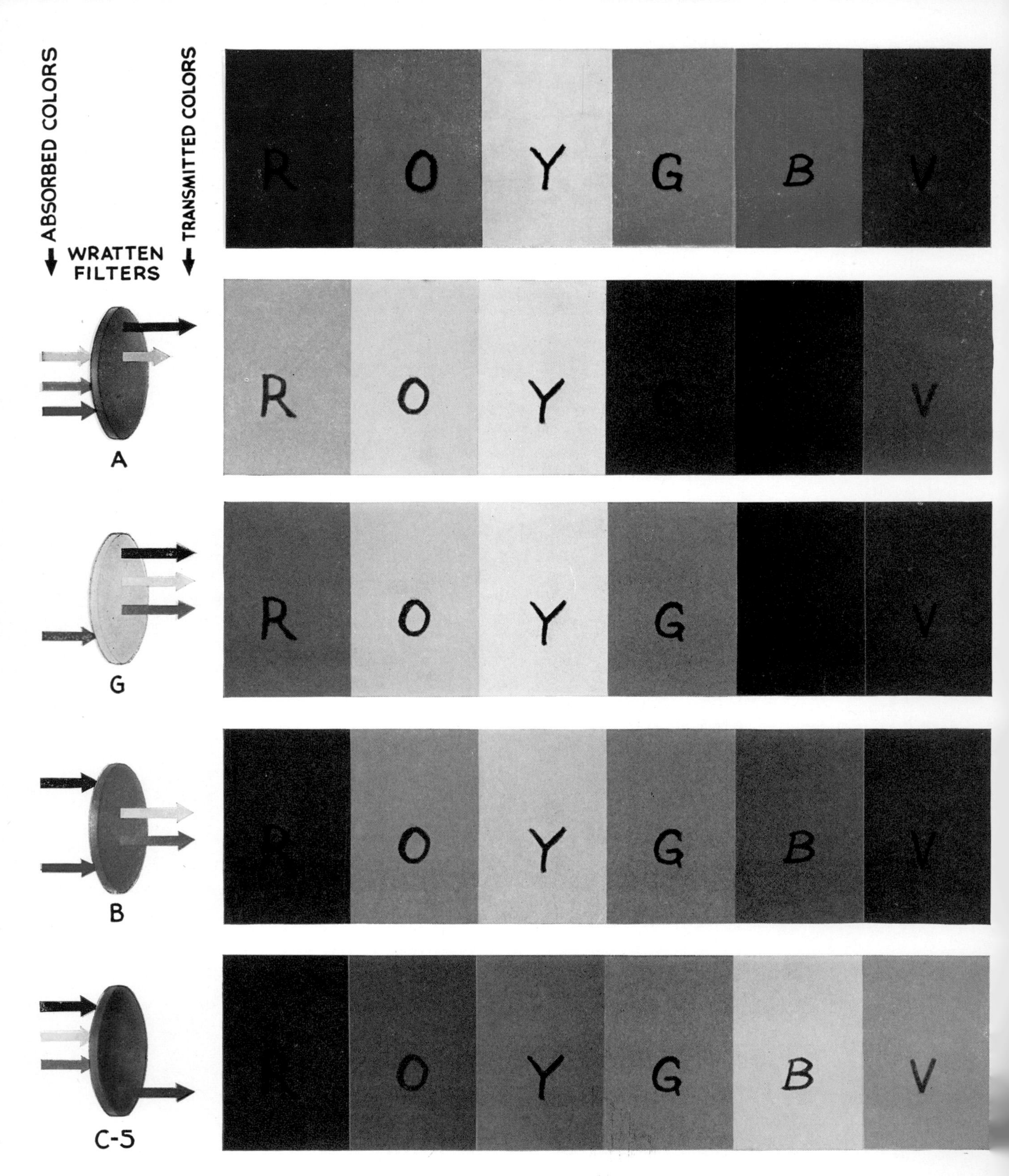

Demonstration of the influence of the four basic color filters on the translation of different colors into shades of gray. The four gray scales are photographs of the color chart at the top, all made on the same type of panchromatic film and printed on the same grade of paper for fair comparison of contrast rendition.

A valuable *visual help* for determining the right type of contrast filter is the Kodak "Contrast Viewing Kodaguide," a card containing red, yellow, green, and blue gelatine viewing filters, identical with the Wratten A, G, B, and C-5 filters, together with filter factors and information pertaining to their use. Looking at colored objects through these filters demonstrates clearly and convincingly the enormous changes in contrasts that can be achieved by using the right kind of filter.

The filter factors

Since the function of a filter is to absorb part of the white light (light of a specific color), this naturally means that with a filter less light is available for making the exposure. The result is *underexposure*, which we must compensate for by *increasing the exposure*. This can be done in two different ways:

By shutter adjustment. Take an exposure-meter reading and multiply the time of exposure by the "filter factor" (see the following tables); if, for instance, the time of exposure without the filter was 1/100 second, and the filter factor is 2, we multiply 1/100 × 2 and get 2/100 = 1/50 second as the new correct exposure time for use with a filter with the factor 2.

By diaphragm adjustment. If we don't want to slow down our time of exposure—perhaps because a slower exposure would result in blurred action, or would necessitate a tripod—we can compensate for the loss of light caused by the filter by increasing the diameter of the diaphragm. If, according to meter reading, we would have to expose 1/100 second at *f* 6.3, and the filter factor is 2, an increase in diaphragm opening from 6.3 to 4.5 would accomplish exactly the same increase in exposure as would prolongation of exposure time from 1/100 to 1/50 second, since diaphragm numbers are chosen so that every step either upward or downward will decrease by ½, or increase by 2, the amount of light that can reach the film (see page 115 for more detailed information).

The measure of the amount by which exposure has to be increased if a certain filter is used is the "filter factor." If this factor is two, for instance, exposure will have to be doubled; if it is five, exposure will have to be five times as long with the filter as without it. Filter factors depend upon color and density of the filter, the color sensitivity of the negative material with which they are to be used, and upon the color of the light source that illuminates the object to be photographed. This means that all filters must have different "factors" when used in connection with different types of film or under different light conditions. To simplify determination of these factors, some film manufacturers have classified their films into groups of similar color sensitivity, thus assigning filter factors to an entire group rather than to individual films. Tables for Ansco and Kodak films are reprinted in condensed form on the following page. Naturally, not all filters can be used in connection with every film. If an emulsion is insensitive to red, for instance, a red filter would shut off all the light that can make an impression on such a film. The result, of course, would be no image at all.

ANSCO FILMS

(Classified according to color sensitivity)

Group I (Non-Color Sensitized)	Group II (Orthochromatic)	Group III (Panchromatic)
Process Commercial	Plenachrome Supersensitive Plenachrome Triple S Ortho Commercial Ortho	Superpan Press Superpan Portrait Isopan Ultra-Speed Pan Supreme Triple S. Pan

FILTER FACTORS FOR ANSCO FILMS

Filter	Color Sensitivity Classification Group			
	II		III	
	Sunlight	Tungsten	Sunlight	Tungsten
Wratten				
K1	2	1.5	1.5	1.5
K2	3	2	2	1.5
G	6	3	3	2
X1	4	3	4	3
X2	6	4	6	4
A	..	..	11	6
B	8	4	8	6
C5	4	4	4	6

KODAK FILMS

(Classified according to color sensitivity)

Group I	Group II	Group III
Verichrome Commercial Ortho Super Ortho Press Ortho-X	Plus-X } 35mm and Super XX } Bantam Plus-X rolls and packs Super XX rolls and packs Super XX sheet film Super Panchro Press B Panatomic-X sheet film	Tri-X Pan

WRATTEN FILTER FACTORS; KODAK FILMS; SUNLIGHT

(Parentheses indicate tungsten light)

Filter	Group I	Group II	Group III
K1	2 (1.5)	1.5 (1.5)	1.5 (1.5)
K1½	2 (1.5)	1.5 (1.5)	1.5 (1.5)
K2	2.5 (2)	2 (1.5)	2 (1.5)
K3	2.5 (2)	2 (1.5)	2 (1.5)
G	5 (3)	3 (2)	2.5 (2)
X1	– (–)	3 (2)	4 (3)
X2	– (–)	– (–)	– (4)
B	8 (5)	8 (8)	8 (6)
A	– (–)	8 (4)	4 (2)
F	– (–)	16 (8)	8 (4)
C5	3 (4)	5 (10)	5 (10)

CONTROL OF REFLECTION AND GLARE

Many of my readers will be familiar with the action of Polaroid sunglasses; they will remember how insufferably bright the reflections of the low afternoon sun can be on a highway, and how looking through Polaroid glasses will eliminate this glare almost completely and will make the macadam appear black once more. This effect is due to the "polarization" of light.

We have to imagine that a beam of ordinary light (regardless of color) vibrates in every direction at right angles to its axis; we could compare it to a tightly stretched string that can freely vibrate "sideways" in every direction. Now let's imagine that we pass such a tightly stretched string through a narrow slit in a piece of cardboard. Obviously, the effect would be that it could not vibrate freely any more in all directions, because now its vibrations would be limited to one plane only—the plane of the slit. In other words, it could vibrate "sideways" in only *one* direction. If we replace the string with a ray of light, and the slitted piece of cardboard with a "polarizing filter" (for instance, Polaroid sunglasses), we change "ordinary" light into "polarized" light, which, as we now can deduce ourselves, means "light that vibrates in *one* plane only." Glare reflected from the highway vibrates mostly in a plane parallel to the road surface, as if the road were a horizontal "slit."

Now let's go one step further and use not just one, but two identical pieces of slitted cardboard and stretch our string through them. As long as both slits are parallel with each other, the ability of our piece of string to vibrate within the plane of the slits is not limited; but as soon as we start rotating one of the slitted cardboards relative to the other, the sideways amplitude of the vibrations of our string is reduced until it reaches zero the moment the two slits cross each other at an angle of 90 degrees. No vibration at all is possible in this position; the pulsation of the string is stopped dead. We can do exactly the same to a ray of light: using *two* polarizing filters, and rotating them slowly relative to each other, we observe clearly how the transmitted light decreases in brightness and how it reaches zero—or blackness—after we have turned one filter 90 degrees from the starting point of greatest brightness. This is how Polaroid sunglasses block reflected glare. Their "slits" are set vertical, 90 degrees from the horizontal road surface.

The unaided eye cannot detect any difference between "ordinary" and "polarized" light, but looking through Polaroid sunglasses will reveal its presence in many unsuspected places. All light *reflected from any nonmetallic surface*, for instance, is more or less strongly *polarized*. Polarization is strongest at an angle of reflection of approximately 35 degrees and is zero at angles of zero and 90 degrees. Blue sky

Straight photograph; reflections obscure magazine page and make it partly unrecognizable. Compare shadows with those in picture on opposite page, proving identical lighting of both.

light at an angle of 90 degrees from the sun, too, is polarized to a great extent. This part of the blue sky seen through Polaroid glasses will look appreciably darker. Hold the Polaroid glasses before the eye and rotate them to determine at what point the strongest effect is achieved.

In photography, we use polarizing filters mainly for two purposes: to control or eliminate all kinds of undesirable reflections, as, for instance, in shop windows, on water, polished wood (furniture), waxed floors, etc., and to darken the sky without affecting the color rendering of all the other objects in the picture. Since both reflected light and sky light at 90 degrees from the sun are already polarized (in other words, since for all practical purposes such light rays have already passed through one imaginary polarizing filter), putting a polarizing filter on the lens

Photograph taken under same conditions as one on facing page, but with polarizing filter on lens. Notice complete elimination of glare and reflections.

and turning it to the right position (which has to be determined by observing the image on the groundglass) will reduce the brightness of such polarized light by almost any desired degree until a maximum of nearly complete extinction is reached, thus helping to eliminate disturbing reflections and to cut down the brightness of the sky. Unpolarized light, of course, *cannot* be controlled in brightness by a polarizing filter, which merely polarizes it. In a studio, however, such a polarizing filter can be used in front of the lights. The subject is then illuminated with polarized light, and a second polarizing filter in front of the lens can then be used for elimination of undesired reflections. Such large-size polarizing filters for use on studio lights are being marketed by the Eastman Kodak Company and by Pioneer Scientific Corporation.

Left: Pan film, no filter. *Center:* Pan film, neutral polarizing filter. *Right:* Pan film, yellow polarizing filter

Neutral polarizing filters are the only practical means of darkening skies in color photography. They are the all-purpose polarizing filters, for reflection control and dark sky effects in both black and white and color. For black-and-white photography, the Polaroid yellow-light-polarizing filter does the work of both a standard yellow filter and a standard polarizing filter.

Since polarizing filters and color filters work on entirely different principles which do not interfere with each other, they can be used together. This makes it possible to control color translation simultaneously with the control of reflections, and very often the one will aid the other. Thus elimination of glare will often bring out the colors which were underneath obscured by such reflections, while the color filter will translate them into gray shades of desired brightness.

The yellow-polarizer permits both color correction and control of reflections in a single unit. The combination of yellow color and polarization darkens the sky even where standard yellow filters are not fully effective. During the midday hours, for example, it darkens the band of polarized sky light extending around the horizon, where the blue of the sky usually is so pale that ordinary yellow filters have little effect.

Since polarizing filters absorb part of the light, a longer exposure is required, as with any ordinary color filter. Exposure-increase factors for polarizing filters are listed in the following table:

TYPE OF FILTER	FACTOR (IDENTICAL FOR DAYLIGHT AND TUNGSTEN)		PURPOSE
	Ortho	Pan	
Kodak Pola-Screen	2.5	2.5	For camera lenses ¾" to 2½" in diameter
Polaroid Neutral Filter	2.5	2.5	For all lens sizes
Polaroid Studio Light Filter	With polarizing filter over camera lens: 8-100		12" diameter, for use in front of studio lights
Polaroid Yellow Filter	—	6*	For black-and-white only

*Tungsten factors are about 15 per cent less.

To determine the increase in exposure for any combination of color filters and polarizing filters, multiply the factor of one with the factor of the other; if, for instance, the filter factor is 4 and the polarizing filter factor 2½, the factor of the combination would be $4 \times 2\frac{1}{2} = 10$.

As everywhere else in photography, however, the fact that we can do certain seemingly incredible things doesn't mean that we have to do them all the time. . . . Often we will find that indiscriminate removal of glare and reflections will harm the effect of our pictures by obliterating the very thing that made them charming, interesting, and alive. . . .

Use the polarizing filter with discretion and with an appraising experimental eye. Look through the filter at the scene; turn it like a wheel until you see the effect you want—which will often be something less than the total effect obtainable; then place the filter over the lens in the same position, so the lens will record what your eye has approved.

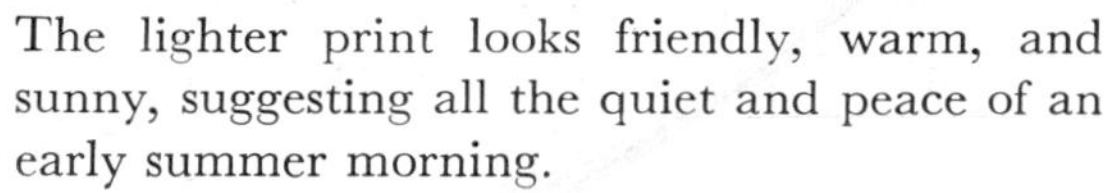

The lighter print looks friendly, warm, and sunny, suggesting all the quiet and peace of an early summer morning.

The same negative, only darker printed, shows the threatening mood of an approaching thunder storm.

LIGHTER OR DARKER

The last control in photography, and the last decision to make after everything else has been decided (selection of negative material and filter, viewpoint and perspective, light and lighting, exposure and development, gradation of paper, proportions and size of print, etc.) is how light or dark to make the print. Here again, different considerations may lead to different results. The documentary approach usually demands a clear and "documentary" rendering, and tone values closely resembling those of factual reality, while the freer, more creative approach once more lends an opportunity to influence the picture according to the photographer's conception of the artistically most effective treatment of the subject.

As said so many times before, fixed rules can be given only for the technical execution of the problem: if we want the print generally light, we have to give the paper a shorter exposure while enlarging than if we desire a darker print. Apart from that, only suggestions can be given. A light print looks generally gayer, more friendly, warmer, but weaker too, than a darker print, which always makes a more serious, heavy, strong, dramatic, and powerful impression. How much a lighter or darker treatment can actually change the character of a photograph is clearly illustrated by the pair of pictures above and on the opposite page, where the effect changes from that of a sunny summer morning to that of an approaching thunderstorm, and from the effect of early dusk to that of darkness at night.

The lighter print suggests early dusk, showing an amazing amount of detail.
The darker print (from the same negative!) gives the impression of midnight.

CHAPTER 11

CONTROLLING SPACE AND PERSPECTIVE

PHOTOGRAPHY as a means of graphic expression is based upon symbols. Light is symbolized by white, color by gray tone, movement by blurs, and space and three-dimensionality by "perspective." But while it is easy to understand white, gray tone, or blurredness, a working knowledge of "perspective" is not so easy to come by.

Perspective is not an "absolute" quality, as, for instance, white or a certain shade of gray, but is "relative," ever changing, elusive, depending on a hundred different coincidences. A phenomenon that would vanish should we try to isolate it by itself, it is nevertheless apparent in almost any photograph. It is the creator of an illusion, the illusion of space and depth in the flat plane of a picture. It provides us with the means for translating terms of space into terms of planes, and its manifestation is "distortion"—distortion of shapes, sharpness, and color shades. Controlling perspective means controlling distortion.

There are three basically different types of perspective by means of which a photographer can create the illusion of roundness and depth. Each one can be controlled to a very great degree, can be used whenever necessary, to exaggerate or minimize the impression of space and distance in accordance with the demands of artistic conceptions. The first type can be used alone, but the other two will generally be used simultaneously with the first. Combined use of all three often will give the most powerful effect.

1. *Linear Perspective.* The apparent convergence of parallel lines toward the distance is the most common and thus the best-known manifestation of perspective (Sketch 1 on opposite page). If lines that we know to be parallel in reality appear to converge in a photograph, we know from reason and experience that the object they represent was not perpendicular to our axis of vision, but inclined at an angle. And from the angle formed by the apparently converging lines we estimate just how much the object was inclined—or in ordinary language, we determine its depth. Similar conclusions can be drawn from the phenomenon of apparent decreasing size with increasing distance from the observer, which actually is only a different manifestation of "linear perspective" (see Sketch 2). The smaller, for instance, a human figure appears in a photograph, the farther away from the

camera we know it to be and vice versa. Hence, by controlling the angle of apparent convergence of actually parallel lines, and the apparent size of objects in a photograph—by deliberately increasing or decreasing them—we can control the rendering of depth in our pictures, making space appear at will deep or shallow, and distances long or short. A special form of space rendering, indication of size through comparison with an object of known dimensions, is only an application of this latter form of perspective (Sketch 3). A picture of a statue against the sky, for instance, doesn't contain any information as to its size. A hand—an object of known dimensions—holding the same statue, however, will immediately give us an exact indication of its actual size—by comparing the one with the other.

2. *Atmosphere.* Simultaneously with the apparent change in object size resulting from a change of distance, changes in tone values frequently occur which can very well be used to symbolize depth in a picture (Sketch 4). The farther an object is from the observer, the lighter it usually appears, and vice versa. Such distortions of tone values are due to atmospheric haze, dust, and smoke, and can be controlled, exaggerated, or minimized by use of the right type of filter.

3. *Limitation of depth of field.* Concentration of sharpness within one plane, objects beyond this plane and in front of it being deliberately made unsharp, will result in a decidedly three-dimensional impression. It will be the stronger, the greater difference there is between sharp and unsharp (Sketch 5). Extension of the sharply defined zone in depth can be regulated to practically any desired degree with the help of the diaphragm.

1. Converging parallels.

2. Diminishing size.

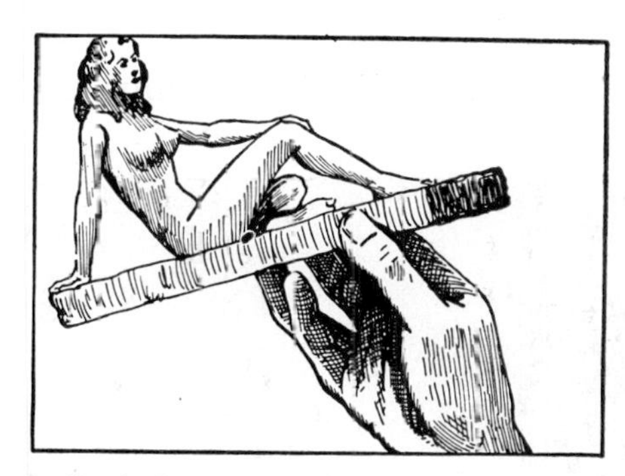

3. Scale by comparison.

4. Atmosphere.

5. Limited depth of field.

THE VIEWPOINT

Deciding on the "best place" from which to shoot a certain picture is one of the most difficult tasks in photography, and one of the most nerve-racking—it is so uncompromisingly final! For it is this decision that principally determines the rendering of space in our picture—the manifestations of perspective are inseparably connected with the point of view.

From any given point of view anywhere in the world, perspective will always be the same, to any eye, to any lens of any focal length. Naturally, a wide-angle lens will photograph a larger area than a telephoto lens, but if we enlarge, out of the negative taken with the wide-angle lens, the section that corresponds to the picture taken by the telephoto lens and bring it up to the telephoto picture's size, then we would find that the "perspective" in these two photographs is identical down to the last and most minute detail. Every angle formed by converging lines, every foreshortening, every apparent decrease in size of any object in the picture, would be exactly the same for both the telephoto shot and the wide-angle blowup, provided both were taken from the identical point of view (see illustrations below).

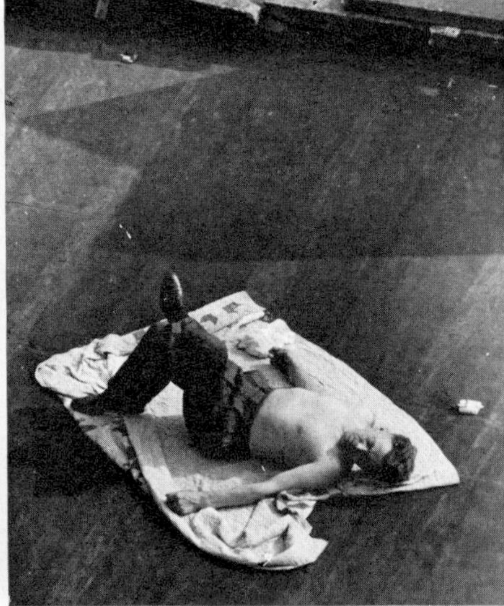

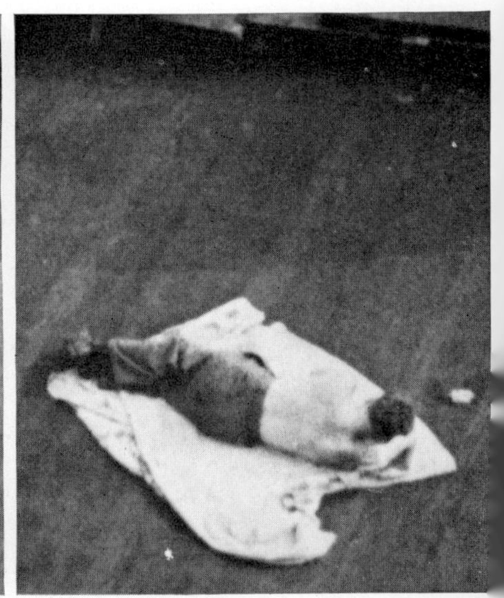

Left: Picture taken with wide-angle lens; rectangle in center corresponds to area shown in picture taken with telephoto lens (*center*). *Right:* Blowup of section of wide-angle shot (as indicated by rectangle, left) to size of telephoto picture (center), illustrating identical manifestations of perspective. The only difference between this and the telephoto picture is in sharpness and graininess resulting from different degree of magnification of the negatives.

Before we finally settle on a definite point of view from which to take a certain photograph we have to find the answers to several questions. The first and most important one is: *Why do we want to take this photograph?* Is it because we want a picture of a certain *object* or because we want to depict a certain *mood?* Should we approach the job from a documentary angle, or from an artistic point of view? Do we want illustration or creation? Remember, the viewpoint settles the question of perspective, and perspective *always* means "distortion" (I will amplify this later see page 260); but we can make our choice from quite a number of different types of distortion, and which one we choose should be decided by the nature of the problem and the purpose of the picture. If it is "documentary," a "conventional" form of perspective is probably the best, because it would most easily be understood by the greatest number of people (under such circumstances, for instance, vertical lines should be kept parallel, and violent angle shots resulting in exaggerated perspective should be avoided). But if the reason for taking the photograph is more abstract, if instead of an object, we want to depict a mood (as for instance: rush hour in the city, sundown, power, soaring height, etc.), then we have much greater freedom in our choice of viewpoint and perspective. Instead of documentation, we have to strive for *dramatization*, which means *exaggeration;* we don't have to be so careful not to distort the shape of familiar objects beyond recognition but can instead choose our own forms of expression, can tilt the camera in any way we think will help to realize our ideas: upward, downward, sideways, changing verticals and horizontals into diagonals, implying speed, action, drama—transforming static perspective into dynamic perspective.

Naturally, our modern way of life has had profound influence on the development of photographic ways of expression. For instance, 50 years ago the average height of a city building was around 50 feet, and people could see the roof of such a building simply by looking more or less straight at it, which of course made vertical lines appear vertical and parallel. Today, many of our city buildings are ten times as high or taller, and anybody wishing to see their top has to do a considerable amount of rubbernecking, tantamount to an object lesson in "perspective." The verticals no longer appear parallel, but *seem to converge.* And the same will happen when looking down from the dizzy height of an observation platform a thousand feet above the canyon of the city streets. Again, lines that we know to be vertical and parallel will appear to converge in depth.

Fifty years ago, people (even artists and photographers, with a very few exceptions) simply didn't connect "perspective" with "vertical lines," because such a phenomenon was outside their ordinary visual experience, and they just didn't bother to imagine it. So for them it simply didn't exist. But today we cannot ignore these forms of space rendering—the *bird's-eye view* and the *worm's-eye view.* They come natural to us and to our light, maneuverable minicameras. We meet them

Which perspective is "right"? *Left:* "Conventional" perspective, where verticals are parallel, and *stay* parallel. *Right:* The "rubbernecker's" version of perspective, which according to the laws of projection, is neither more nor less "correct" than the other one; it is only different.

all around us, every time we look out of the windows of our tall apartment towers, every time we want to see the sky while walking along the bottom of a city street.

We have accepted them, gotten used to them, and now we have to learn how to use them to best advantage in our photographs. It is all a matter of the right "point of view"—not only literally, but figuratively, too. For not too long ago there was a time when bird's-eye views and worm's-eye views were *de rigeur—everything* had to be photographed at an angle, and the cornier the angle, the prouder the photographer.

Naturally, people eventually got fed up with seeing everything cockeyed and distorted, and a reaction set in: *all* angle shots were more or less outlawed as being in bad taste. This, of course, was going from one extreme to the other, and today we seem to have found a happy medium. Most photographers have come to realize that an angle shot, upward or downward, is perfectly all right, *provided there is a reason for it!* Whenever we want to emphasize tallness and give an impression of soaring height, or to illustrate the giddy dizziness that gets us when looking down from a skyscraper, or to convey the creeping claustrophobia we experience when walking through Wall Street—the strongest way of translating these reactions

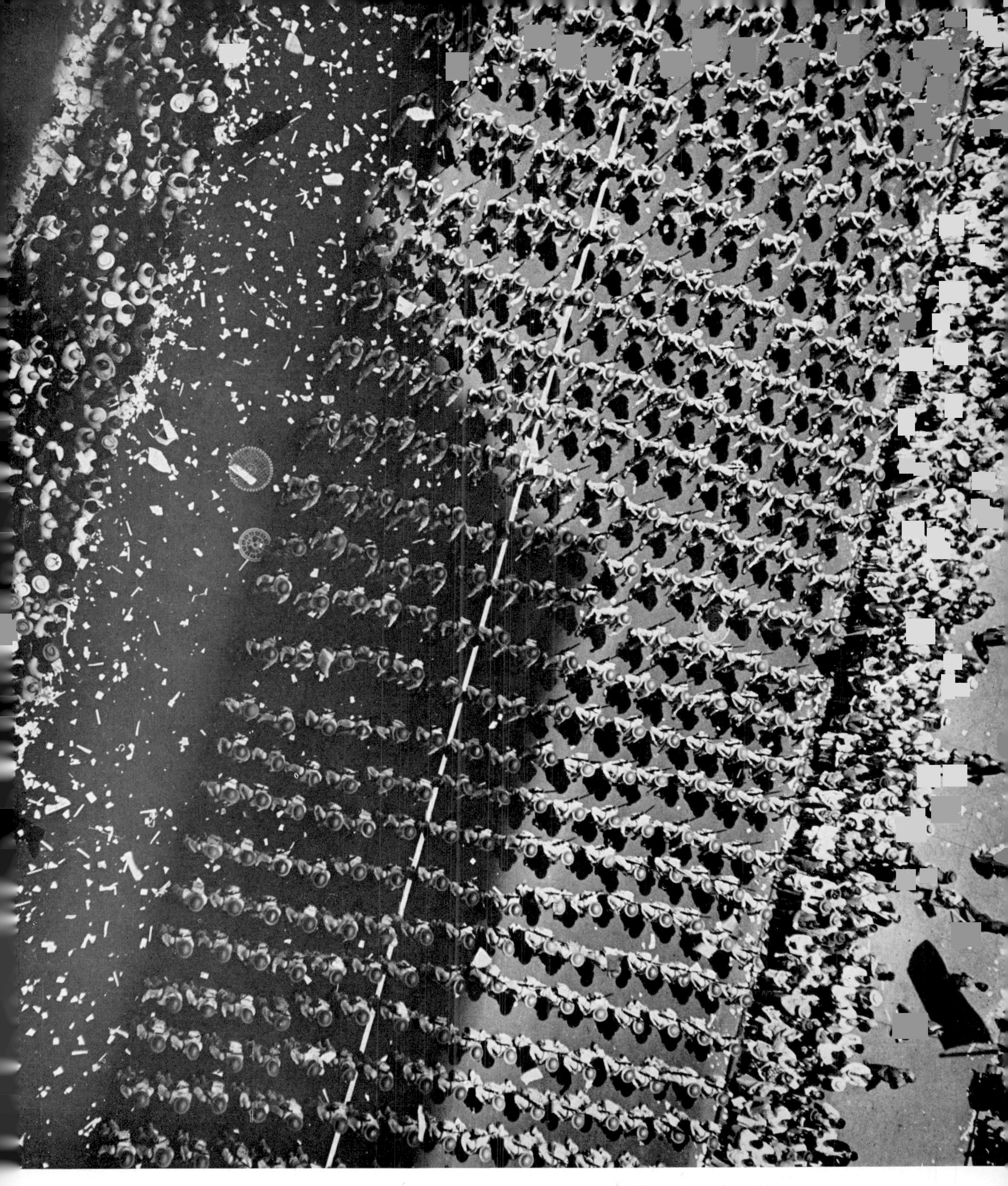

Victory parade on Fifth Avenue, New York City. . . . Camera reproduces sensation of being suspended in mid-air, illustrating that feeling of dizziness that grips us when looking down from a great height, or when hearing news of a great victory. . . .

Courtesy *Fortune* Magazine

Limited framing of a long shot: including part of the ship from which shot was taken gives the picture scale, emphasizing depth by providing the eye with a means of comparing the difference in apparent size between the two ships into photographs will always be by means of converging verticals and dynamic diagonals. However, if there is neither height, nor depth, nor narrowness, not even in a figurative sense (for instance: a person can very well inspire a feeling of greatness and justify an angle shot), then, of course, there is no reason why we should shoot at an angle. And the photographer who can't resist the temptation to be "different" will get nothing but a ridiculous picture. . . . Let's always remember this when we consider our point of view!

Theoretically, there are as many different viewpoints as there are places to put a camera. So we have to adopt certain principles which will help us to reduce this overabundance to a limited number of likely possibilities, from which it should then be easy to make a final selection. Having arrived at a decision as to the type of approach—which normally will be either documentary-illustrative, or artistic-creative—we now have to ask ourselves questions like these: what are *the characteristics* of the subject? What is typical, what do I want to emphasize? On which quality should I concentrate above all? And where will I find the best point of view for depicting these most important elements of my subject?

To illustrate with some concrete examples: let's imagine we have to do a picture story on the making and the uses of glass. This makes *glass* our subject proper, and we should emphasize it in all our pictures. This sounds obvious until we recall pictures on glassmaking that we have seen in magazines and roto sections which showed the workmen, the factory, the background, the confusion of machinery, in short everything but the glass, which thanks to its smallness and transparency was practically lost, and hardly discernible at all. So our first decision should be: pick viewpoints *close* to the object—the *glass*. Concentrate on the essential, eliminate the distracting, less important detail. And not before these all-important closeups are in the bag should we start to round out the picture story with a few carefully selected, situation-explaining over-all shots, and pictures showing the men and machines that make the glass. The next consideration should be: what is the most outstanding property of glass, what should we emphasize especially? Again, the answer seems obvious: "transparency." But how many photographers draw the logical conclusions the first time they are confronted with the problem of photographing glass? How many say to themselves: glass is perfectly transparent, practically "invisible." But a picture of a transparent object that makes it *too* invisible won't get me anywhere—the object won't show at all. So I'll have to make it visible, yet give the illusion of transparency. The only way to do this is by way of reflections. Conclusion: I have to select a point of view for my camera from which I can catch the right kind of highlight on the glass—reflections from furnaces, overhead lamps, and windows, back light—and I have to watch out for the right type of dark and neutral background so that these highlights can stand out contrastfully, unaffected by a mess of superfluous detail. . . . Again, the point of view is all-important, can make or break the picture.

Here is a different example of the vital role location of the viewpoint plays for success or failure in a photograph: we have to take a view from a high vantage point, and a feeling of space and distance is essential (see picture on opposite page). How can we get it? Again, we may choose among many possibilities. Experience shows that the typical snap-happy amateur will simply stick his camera out the window or go as close to the balustrade as possible, and try to slice off as large a piece of America as possible on his film. The experienced photographer will do it just the opposite way. By stepping *back* a little, and consciously *limiting* his sector of view, he will *include part of the nearest foreground* in his picture. He will *frame* his view, and thus by introducing the element of closeness into a picture taken to illustrate "distance" he will create that tension between "near" and "far" that more effectively than anything else conveys the impression of boundless depth. Here, safe and solid foreground; there, horizon hidden in shimmering haze; in between, vastness and space. The eye, before it takes off on its flight into the void, can rest a moment on solid ground, the stepping stone provided by the foreground, can gauge the distance it has to travel before it will reach the horizon, by *comparing* the one with the other.

Selecting the viewpoint so as to include a piece of nearest foreground provides a photograph with *scale*. Simultaneously, it will improve composition by welding the various picture elements together within the boundaries of a *frame*, even if this frame is not always completely closed all around. Framing a photograph will always concentrate interest where it belongs: on the subject. At the same time, it will make it alive with contrast and tension: tension in depth between near and far; tension in tone between dark and light (for such a frame is nearly always naturally dark, more or less a silhouette); tension in definition between fuzzy and sharp (being very close to the camera usually renders such a frame slightly out of focus, which is all to the good since it suggests "closeness." Things very close to the eye always appear unsharp because of limitations of our vision). All this adds up to one of the most important rules of composition, based upon, and inseparably connected with, the selection of the point of view:

> Framing a subject by including parts of the nearest foreground is one of the surest ways to improve depth and composition of almost any photograph, no matter whether it is a long shot or a closeup.

View from Woolworth Building, downtown New York, over Hudson River and New Jersey. Incorporation of nearest foreground matter increases depth of photograph by creating contrast between near and far, concentrates picture elements through "framing," and provides the photograph with scale.

Simultaneous with change in the rendering of space, change of the point of view will result in a change of lighting and its effect on the subject in terms of light and shadow. Often there will be doubt as to which is the more important, perspective or lighting, for not always will the light appear at its best from the point of view that gives us the best perspective. Here again, as so often in photography, a compromise will frequently have to be made, and the artistically successful solution of such a problem will uncompromisingly testify to the creative ability of the photographer.

When working with artificial light, of course, the lighting can usually be arranged to best advantage without sacrifice of good perspective; if working with sunlight, either outdoors or indoors, waiting for the sun to go around will often solve the problem, even if it should involve hours of tiresome waiting or coming back another day. As though we don't know it already, this will acquaint us with one of the most fundamental assets of the successful photographer:

PATIENCE !

Perspective and viewing-point

"Perspective" is determined by the point of view and the focal length of the lens. Regarded as a geometrical projection of space into the plane of a photograph, perspective in a picture is always "right," in spite of the fact that wide-angle shots very often look exaggerated, rendering distances apparently too great and space too deep, while the opposite seems to be true of telephoto shots. This, however, is only an optical illusion, resulting from viewing such a picture from the wrong distance. Any photograph, regardless of the type of lens it was taken with, will look "right" the moment we look at it from a distance which makes the angle of *viewing* identical with the angle of *view* of the lens that made the picture. Thus, if we shoot a negative 5 inches wide with a lens of a focal length of 3½ inches (which would represent a typical wide-angle shot), and if we enlarge this negative to a size of 8x10 inches (in other words, if we enlarge it twice), perspective in such a print would look "right" the moment we view it from twice the distance of the focal length of the lens, or from a distance of 7 inches. Our normal viewing distance, however, is approximately 14 inches, or 4 times the focal length of the lens that took this particular picture. So in order to make perspective look right from the "normal" viewing distance in such a case, we would have to enlarge the negative 4 times, to a size of 16x20 inches. This, of course, would make the print too wide to be contemplated at one glance, and we would be obliged to "scan" in order to see the whole print. But this would be only natural with a "wide-angle" shot, since it includes a wider than "normal" angle of view. Seen under these conditions, however, perspective would appear perfectly "normal" once more. Again, rendering of space becomes a question of the right kind of point of view, for the same principle applies, of course, to telephoto pictures. The photographs on the opposite page will illustrate the influence of the point of view on perspective in a typical wide-angle shot.

Viewing identical pictures of different sizes from the same distance will make their perspective look different. If it is a wide-angle shot, the smaller of the two prints, and if it is a telephoto shot, the larger of the two prints, will look "exaggerated" with regard to rendering of space. This phenomenon and how it can be corrected, is explained on the opposite page.

LINEAR PERSPECTIVE

"Perspective" is one of the most controversial subjects in photography, and the one about which opinion is more divided among photographers than about any other photographic topic. Listening to critics pass judgment upon one and the same photograph, remarks as apparently contradictory as "wide-angle lenses always distort" and "all modern lenses give mathematically correct perspective rendering" will frequently be heard, and the strange fact is that both parties can be right and wrong at the same time, depending on the rule according to which they judge perspective: emotion governed by feeling, or factual optical laws. But the even stranger truth is that, at the same time, all our modern, highly corrected lenses without exception violate the laws of *scientific* perspective in the most outrageous way, recording straight lines straight while actually they ought to be rendered curved (as we shall soon see). And they do this not because they are imperfect, but because they are made that way, so that they can satisfy our present conception of space rendering with two-dimensional means.

This confusion is hardly surprising in view of the fact that for several thousand years artists, trained observers and students of perspective have tried to discover the laws that rule the rendering of space illusions in plane—and so far have more or less failed.

The ancient Egyptians, for instance, when drawing the side view of a row of people, usually made the person farthest from the observer as high as the nearest one, using foreshortening without diminishing size, favoring a perspective (or rather: a lack of perspective) similar to that observed in extreme telephoto shots. They may have reasoned that since the height of people is generally more or less the same, regardless of how close or far away they stand, why shouldn't they be depicted alike? On the other hand, outstanding persons—a king, a queen, a great conqueror—usually were rendered much larger than the common crowd, dominating such people not only figuratively, but literally, too, even if they were farthest back in the picture. The Egyptians were class conscious in an extraordinarily high degree, so no wonder these traits were reflected strongly in their paintings and sculptures, which were their principal means of self-expression. To them, social differences in caste were more important than apparent differences in height resulting from the accident of momentary distance from the artist, and they had sufficient courage of their convictions to express this belief in their art. To them, our modern perspective would probably have looked as clumsy and improper as their drawings look to us today. But let's not feel too superior, because

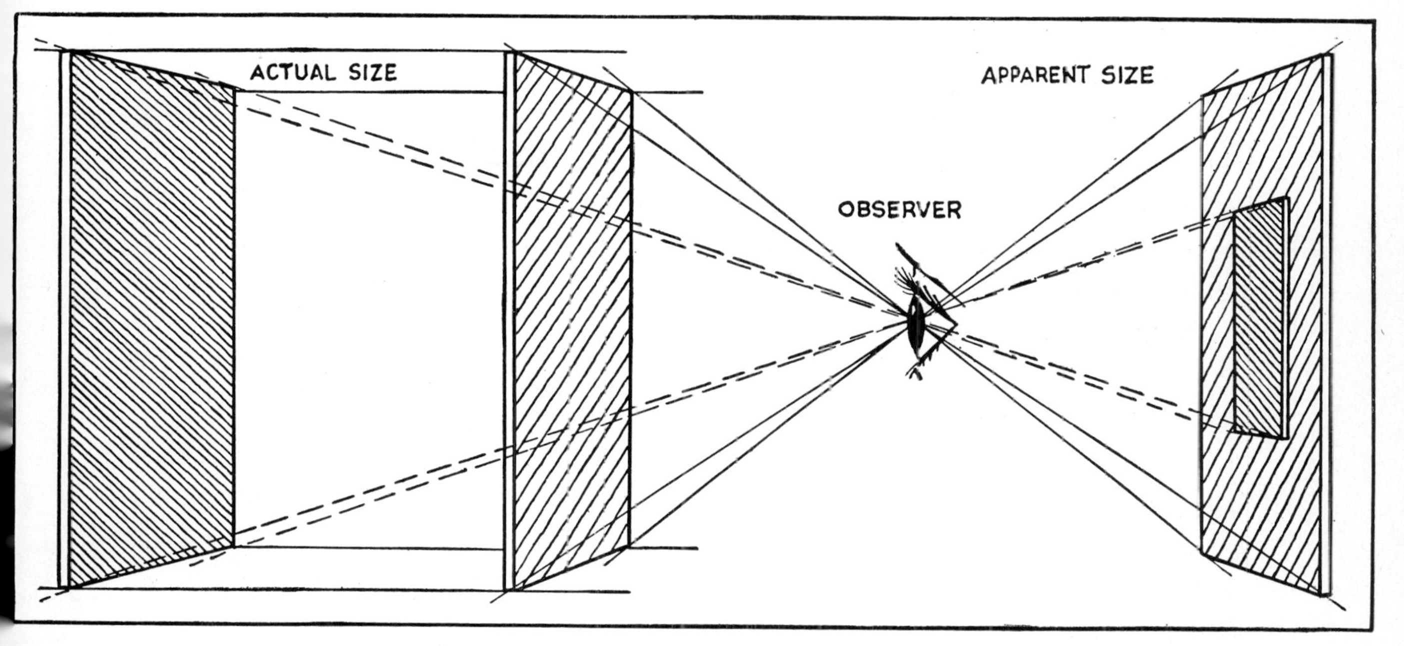

Linear perspective is projection of three-dimensional shapes onto a two-dimensional plane. Although the two objects shown in this sketch are of equal size, they nevertheless appear different in size to the observing eye because of their difference in distance and the different angle from which they are seen. Hence, the distant object will appear smaller than the nearer object, and knowing them to be actually equal in size, we can estimate the interval between them from their difference in apparent size.

to people a thousand years hence, our rectilinear perspective may well appear as outmoded as the Egyptian lack of perspective appears to us today. . . . We'll soon see that there is good reason for such a prediction. . . .

During the Renaissance, artists went to the other extreme. By using an "exaggerated" perspective, by consciously overemphasizing the apparent decrease in size resulting from increase in distance from the beholder, they arrived at space impressions not unlike those encountered in typical wide-angle shots, achieving effects that many of us today would call "distorted" if we saw them in a photograph. Doubtless this was the best way to create the illusion of boundless space within the limited confines of an interior or the constricted ceiling of a cupola. But as a graphic form of space rendering, this super-perspective actually was neither more nor less "true" than the Egyptian lack of perspective.

In a photograph, we can imitate the Egyptian form of perspective as easily as the Renaissance form, and all other forms in between these two extremes as well, by taking our pictures either with a lens of relatively long or relatively short focal length, or with a lens of more or less standard focal length. But before we start discussing when to use what type, and before we can learn how to use any of them intelligently, we have to study the nature of perspective itself.

A typical example of "horizontal" perspective (i.e., perspective manifested in the horizontal plane only). To eliminate all traces of "vertical" perspective (converging of vertical lines), the camera was held perfectly level while taking the photograph. Besides, the plane of the film was perfectly parallel with the front of the building at the left side of the picture.

Principles and rules

Linear perspective is the graphic application of the fact that objects appear to decrease in size with increasing distance from the beholder. If we go out into the country and see a man standing in a field, to his right a horse which appears about as tall as he does, and to his left a two-story farmhouse which doesn't quite reach up to his shoulder, we know at once that the horse is standing close to the man, but that the house is far behind him. If it really were right next to the man (as it appears to be), it would appear about five times his height. On the other hand, if this two-story farmhouse appeared not five times, but let's say ten times as high as the man, then we would know right away that actually it must be much closer to us than the man.

Evaluation of the preceding photograph with regard to perspective. The more important horizontal and vertical lines, determining the perspective of the picture, are overlaid and emphasized in ink.

Thus, by comparing the apparent sizes of objects, and by knowing from observation and experience how high certain things appear when seen from certain distances, we orient ourselves in space and gauge the intervals that separate us from the objects of our surroundings.

Now let's apply this theoretical knowledge to the practical case of a photograph. Let's examine the above pictures of a street and see what we can learn from them with regard to the nature of perspective:

Studying the diagrammatic photograph, we will observe how four distinguishing features determine its perspective:

1. All lines and angles within a plane parallel to the plane of the film (left side of photo) remain undistorted. Here, parallels are still parallel, horizontals are still horizontal, and verticals are still vertical. Angles appear in their true shapes.

2. All true verticals remain vertical, regardless of their position within the picture.

Photograph taken from the same point as the pictures on the two preceding pages. But the camera was tilted upward, so that the film was no longer parallel to true verticals. As a result, verticals converge toward a common vanishing point.

3. All lines receding from the camera appear to converge toward vanishing points. If they are true parallels, they converge toward a common vanishing point (as, for instance, the base and roof lines of the buildings on both sides of the street). If they are true horizontals, their vanishing points always lie on the true horizon.

4. All straight lines are reproduced straight.

These four facts represent the acknowledged, conventional, academic rules for linear perspective. They apply to photography only as long as the film within the camera remains perfectly parallel to true verticals. The moment we tilt the camera so that the film is no longer parallel to true verticals, we introduce the new element of "vertical perspective" into the picture, i.e., true verticals will behave like "receding lines" and converge toward a common vanishing point. Such a photograph is reproduced above.

Disturbing the parallelism between film and true verticals immediately washes out rule No. 2. This is only natural since rule No. 2 is nothing but an artificial rule, with no foundation in fact. Actually rule No. 1 takes care of *all* lines, regardless of their direction and position, and as long as the verticals conform to this rule, i.e., as long as they are parallel to the plane of the film, they will be reproduced vertically; otherwise—not. In this respect, photography has taught us a valuable lesson. It has made us conscious of the fact that perspective exists not only in the horizontal plane, but in the vertical or any other plane as well. "Horizontal" and "vertical" are merely human conceptions, designating certain positions relative to our own solid earth; they have no meaning in abstract space, where all positions are of equal value. Thus it is only logical that the law of "perspective" should be the same for all lines regardless of relative position. Horizontals, verticals, diagonals and all lines in between follow one common law—according to which they must appear converging the moment they recede from the camera. If we don't like this converging of verticals (which often makes buildings look as if they were about to collapse), we know now how to avoid it: by keeping the film truly vertical. However, wherever we want to emphasize and dramatize height, there is no better means than conscious use of "vertical perspective," as the picture on page 264 will show. . . .

According to the universal laws of linear perspective, all lines receding from the camera have to converge toward vanishing points. This sounds simple until we ask ourselves: what kind of lines do *not* recede from the camera? The usual answer is: lines parallel to the plane of the film, like the horizontals and verticals on the left side of the demonstration photograph on pages 254 and 255, which consequently were reproduced in their true positions and did not converge. So far, so good. But now let's imagine that we stand with the camera on one side of the street and look straight across the pavement toward the other side. We put the camera on a tripod and carefully adjust it until the plane of the film is aligned perfectly parallel to the fronts of the houses on the other side of the street; then we take a picture. Obviously, under these conditions we will get a photograph where horizontals are reproduced horizontally, and verticals vertically, a picture as free from perspective (which, remember, is distortion!) as an architect's "elevation." Now, let's imagine we exchange our regular lens for a super wide-angle lens (as, for instance, the 160° lens of a Robin Hill camera) which can include all of the other side of the street, toward the right and toward the left as far as we can see—perhaps a quarter of a mile in either direction. We take another picture. Obviously, the horizontals and verticals should still be rendered parallel on the film, but will they? Can you imagine the fronts of houses a quarter of a mile away to the right or left reproduced as high as the front of the house directly opposite your camera? In other words, can you imagine that the horizontals will still be rendered horizontal and parallel throughout the length of your picture? I can't, and I don't suppose you can either. . . .

Apparently, somewhere something is wrong with our reasoning, and reconsideration of our line of thought shows us where we made our mistake: there are no such things as lines that do *not* recede from the camera, because mathematically speaking, any line is automatically a "receding line" because it runs away from the optical axis of the lens in one direction or another, even if in so doing it should happen to run parallel with the plane of the film! The only possible "line" that actually does not recede from the camera is not a line at all, but a point—the point of intersection between the optical axis and a perspectivic line. But if all lines in a picture are *ipso facto* "receding lines," then they should all converge toward vanishing points, if "perspective" is to be mathematically correct.

That lines running parallel to the plane of the film don't conform to this demand is due only to the "rectilinear correction" of modern lenses, which counteract such tendencies because according to our present conception of perspective they make a photograph appear "untrue." But mathematically speaking, it is this "corrected" type of "rectilinear" perspective that is "untrue."

This statement is easily proven: just take a ruler, hold it straight up and down at arm's length, and measure the apparent height of the windows of the building directly across the street from you. Obviously, the top and bottom edges of such a row of windows form horizontal parallels, and they are situated in a plane that is parallel to your plane of observation, which is the plane of your window (assuming the front of your building is parallel to the front of the building across the street). Under these conditions, parallels should appear parallel according to the rules of conventional perspective, but your check-up with the ruler will show you that the apparent height of the window directly opposite you is a little bit greater than the height of the window next to it, while window No. 3 appears still smaller, window No. 4 smaller than window No. 3, and so on. And you would get the same result if you were to measure the apparent width of the vertical column of windows exactly opposite your window: again, the window that is on the same level as you are would appear wider than the windows above and below it, despite the fact that actually they are all equal in width.

Now let's imagine you go one step further and put your findings down in the form of a graph. Draw crosslines on a piece of paper, transfer onto them the positions of the center of each of the windows within one horizontal and one vertical row from your axis of vision and mark down the apparent height and width of each measured window according to a uniform scale. Finally, connect all points of equal denomination with a line (tops connected with tops, bottoms with bottoms in the

Picture taken with the 180-degree Robin Hill camera, which was constructed especially for the purpose of taking meteorological photographs of the whole sky with one single shot. It marks the beginning of the practical evaluation of this newly "discovered" spherical perspective.

horizontal row, right sides with right sides, and left sides with left sides in the vertical column), and you will find: your connecting lines will (*a*) converge and (*b*) will be, *not* straight, but *curved*!

Such an experiment will give you a true picture of the only mathematically correct perspective, which is not "rectilinear," but "spherical," where *all* lines converge and straight lines become curves. The reason that it doesn't appear "true" to us is that our eyes and brains deceive us: the eye, when contemplating a large object, "scans" it and takes it in bit by bit, overlooking the minute deviations from true parallelism inherent in every such small sector; and the brain, because of its knowledge of actual parallelism automatically compensates for the apparent convergence of truly parallel lines, unless such convergence is too obvious to be ignored. . . .

Parallelism, as we see it, is nothing but an optical illusion . . . and the reason for my initial doubts as to the durability of current conceptions of perspective will be more obvious now. . . .

Step by step, we shall now proceed to construct a linear perspective mathematically as correct as is possible with present photographic means.

To facilitate comparison, all pictures were taken from the same point of view.

A regular "rectilinear" photograph taken with a wide-angle lens with an angle of view of 120 degrees (Goertz Hypergon, the most extreme wide-angle lens that is corrected for rectilinear perspective). Since the film was parallel with the plane of the object, this rendering is free from "distortion"—horizontals are reproduced as horizontal, verticals as vertical, parallels as parallel. None of the lines converge, and the picture appears "true" according to the conventional rules of perspective.

A composite picture, made from two photographs taken at a 30-degree angle toward the left and the right, respectively, with a lens of standard focal length with an angle of view of 45 degrees for each of the two halves. Verticals are still vertical, since they were parallel to the plane of the film, but horizontals converge toward two vanishing points because the plane of the film was inclined toward them. The angle at the junction of the two picture-halves is artificial, objectionable, and actually nonexistent.

A picture composed of three photographs eliminates the angle in the center of the picture but introduces two new ones, not quite as abrupt, but still definitely untrue. The convergence of receding lines (here: the horizontals) as demanded by a theoretically correct perspective appears more gradually than in the previous picture; a definite pattern begins to emerge.

Composing the picture out of many sections, "scanning" it piece by piece as the eye would scan it—produces even smoother convergence of the receding horizontals, makes the angles where different sections of straight lines join even flatter and less obtuse. Instead of looking straight and angled, the horizontals begin to appear curved, confirming the finding of our experiment with the ruler as recommended on page 258.

Photograph taken with a panoramic camera, in which the lens describes a short arc while it takes the picture. The horizontals are evenly curved, converging toward their vanishing points in the distance. This photograph corresponds to the impression we get when turning the head from left to right while contemplating an object of wide horizontal extension. The rendering is no longer rectilinear, but "cylindrical." Verticals are still vertical and straight.

The "spherical" perspective of the uncorrected meniscus lens. All lines are curved, the more so the farther they are from the imaginary point where the prolonged optical axis would penetrate the object of the rendering. Theoretically, this is the only mathematically correct type of "linear" perspective. Perhaps in the faraway future it will replace contemporary "rectilinear" perspective, which may then appear as old-fashioned as ancient Egyptian perspective seems to us today. . . .

The foregoing considerations and conclusions apply to perspective in the vertical as well as in the horizontal or any other plane. The practical form they would take when applied to objects of predominantly vertical extension is shown in these two photographs. *Left:* Camera tilted upwards, verticals are still straight but converge. *Right:* Photo taken with a panoramic camera, lens swinging vertically up and do n; verticals curve toward a common vanishing point.

Rockefeller Center, New York. Conscious employment of "converging verticals" as a means of expressing "distance toward height," creating a feeling similar to that experienced by the man in the street below.

Controls for linear perspective

Perspective is distortion, the degree of which is determined (*a*) by the point of view, (*b*) by the position (inclination) of the film with regard to the optical axis of the lens. The lens itself has nothing to do with "distortion," and if used from the same point of view, *all* types of lenses, short-focus and long-focus alike, will give exactly the same kind of perspective distortion. As long as the center of the lens, the optical axis, and the plane of the film are in the same relative position, pictures taken with *any* camera, 35 mm miniature or 8x10 view camera, will render perspective identically. If blown up to the necessary size, the minicamera shot will register perfectly with the photograph taken with the 8x10. Naturally, the angle of view of one camera may differ from the angle of view of another, depending on the type of lens being used (remember page 242), but as long as the above conditions are fulfilled the perspective of their pictures will be the same.

With this in mind, we deduce that control of perspectivic distortion can be effected in two different ways, which can be used either separately or together:

1. By changing the point of view;
2. By changing the position of the film with regard to the optical axis.

Control Through Changes of the Point of View

Most readers will know what is bound to happen if we take a portrait with the camera too close to the face of the model: the nose will seem too large, the ears too small, and the features will look "distorted." Usually, we connect this type of warped perspective with wide-angle shots, which actually is wrong, for it can happen with any kind of a lens, even a telephoto lens, *if*—and this is the point—the distance between camera and object is relatively too short. We have here a typical case of selecting the wrong point of view. For all we have to do in order to avoid such a contorted perspective is to keep a long enough distance between object and camera. As long as we remember this, we may even take a portrait with a wide-angle lens and still get a natural perspective.

The first rule for natural-appearing perspective is: watch the distance between camera and subject. Don't go too close!

Distortion resulting from too short a distance between camera and subject. *Left:* Face raised, chin appears too massive, forehead too low. *Right:* Face lowered, chin appears too weak, forehead bulges too much. If distance between subject and camera is relatively short, even slight changes in position will often lead to gross "exaggerations of perspective."

The bad reputation of wide-angle lenses is really not quite deserved because most of the time it is the fault of the photographer if he gets that typical "wide-angle distortion." Because of their wider angle of view, wide-angle lenses naturally render objects in smaller scale than "standard" lenses, and in his effort to compensate for this loss in image-size the inexperienced photographer often selects a viewpoint that is too close to some prominent object. It then of course looks "distorted" and out of proportion to the rest of the picture. With wide-angle lenses, it is always the foreground that bears watching, while the background usually comes out all right by itself. When working with wide-angle lenses, objects with great extension in depth normally should be kept out of the foreground as

→

The business end of a 16-inch coastal defense rifle, undergoing inspection at the Watervliet Arsena Albany, N. Y. Only a wide-angle lens, used in violation of all rules for wide-angle photograph could have made this picture. Point of view was extremely close to an object with exceptionall great extension in depth. While it is good policy for the beginner to stick to the rules, many of tl most striking photographs owe their existence to the bold violation of these same rules by photog raphers with enough experience to turn disadvantage into advantage. . . .

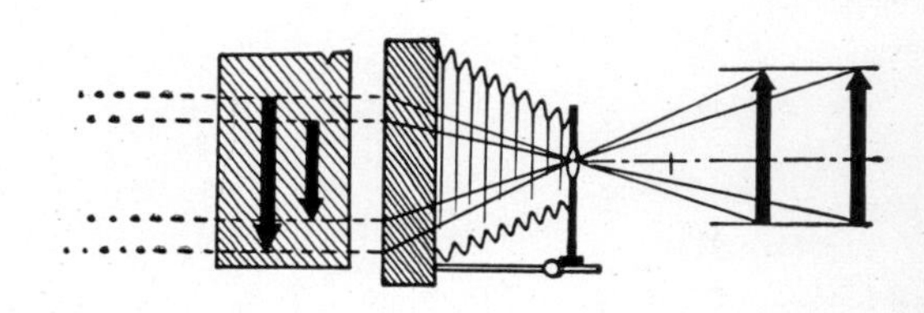

Point of view close to object (short-focus lens): depth appears exaggerated, proportions between objects in picture seem distorted, things in foreground look too big, things in background look too small. Notice difference in size of images of arrows on groundglass.

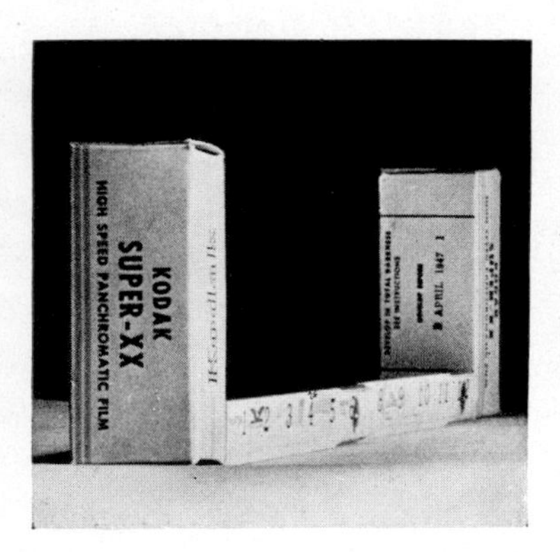

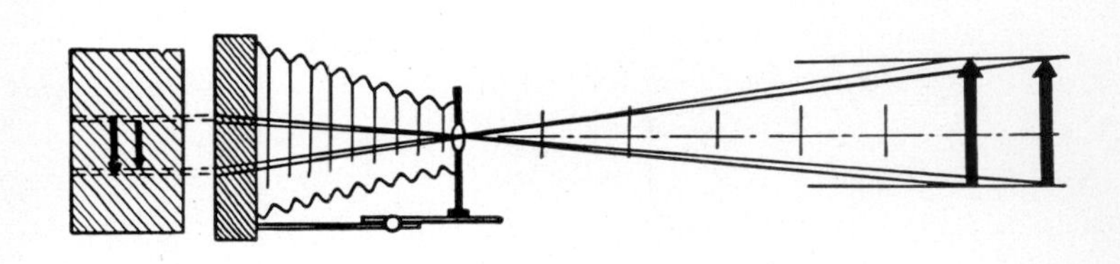

Point of view far away from object (long-focus lens): depth appears shallow, proportions between objects in picture are well preserved, distortion is avoided. Notice difference in size of images of arrows on groundglass.

much as possible; but occasionally it is just this "distortion" of objects close to the lens that gives a photograph its special "something," as witness the picture on the preceding page. . . .

The more we reduce the distance from camera to object and the more pronounced becomes the difference in scale between foreground and background, the greater the illusion of depth will appear and the more "exaggerated"-looking a perspective will we get. On the other hand, the farther away the point of view is from the object, the better will the natural proportions of this object be preserved in the image, but the depth of such an image will appear less extensive and its scale will become increasingly smaller. The relationship between the different factors that determine the character of perspective is demonstrated in graphic form in the illustrations above. As a rule, unless that typical "wide-angle effect" is desired, it is advisable to put the requirements of good perspective first, to stay far enough away from the object, and to compensate for the loss in size of image by

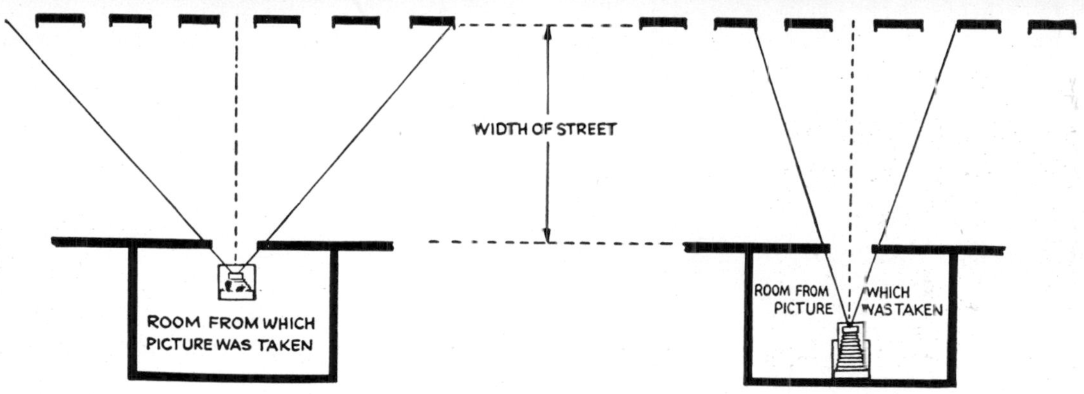

Through proper selection of point of view and focal length of lens, space can be made to appear large or small at will, in accordance with the intentions of the photographer. *Left:* Picture taken with wide-angle lens, camera close to window. *Right:* Picture taken with telephoto lens, camera far back in room. The apparent distance between the window in foreground and the house across the street, actually the same in both instances, varies from large to very small.

afterward enlarging only the center section of the negative. The slight loss in definition, a price that has to be paid for every enlargement, is usually preferable to bad perspective. Of course, a telephoto or long-focus lens eliminates even this small disadvantage; its use permits the photographer to get a negative-filling image from a viewpoint far enough from the object to be safe from undesirable distortion. In this respect, a telephoto lens is especially valuable in portraiture, infinitely superior to all so-called "portrait slip-on lenses" which shorten the focal length of the lens they are being used on, actually converting it into a wide-angle lens, and for this reason making it as unsuitable as possible for the taking of portraits.

Possession of lenses with different focal lengths enables a photographer to choose his viewpoints solely with regard to perspective, freeing him from worry about image size and scale. If he wants to emphasize things in the foreground, he can now make them dominant with the help of a wide-angle lens, exaggerating and dramatizing them to any desired degree. If his motif proper lies more or less in the background, he can still make it large and impressive on film, thanks to his tele-

Brownstone fronts, Harlem, New York—*Left:* Wide-angle shot. *Right:* Telephoto shot. Employment of lenses of different focal length enables the photographer to emphasize different features of one and the same object: *left,* the length of the row of houses; *right,* the narrowness of the individual buildings.

photo lens. Wherever he wants to preserve an object's natural proportions to the greatest possible extent, a telephoto lens will help him to do so. On the other hand, if he feels that exaggeration is indicated to express some typical feature more strikingly in a photograph—height, length, bulkiness, the vastness of the sea, the immensity of the sky, etc.—nothing but a wide-angle lens will give satisfaction. In this respect, a wide-angle is even more useful than a telephoto. While in an emergency enlarging of a section of the negative can substitute for a telephoto lens—at least to a certain degree—there is no surrogate for a wide-angle lens. Typical examples of pictures that could *only* have been taken with either a wide-angle or a telephoto lens, respectively, are the photographs on pages 267 and 271.

View of 42nd Street, Manhattan, from across the Hudson River, from Weehawken, New Jersey. A pic of this type can be taken only with an extreme telephoto lens, since a section of a negative taken wi lens of standard focal length would have to be enlarged more than 20 times before it would match photograph; the loss in definition connected with such a procedure would of course be prohibitive, page 378-379.

Notice how well the typical "tele-perspective" preserves the natural proportions of the buildings, towers more than two miles away from the camera still dominate the picture, and how the lower struct in the foreground still appear low and subdued in spite of their closeness to the point of view.

HOTEL DIXIE
DIXIE BAR & LOUNGE
HOTEL HOLLAND
SWIMMING POOL
ROOF LOUNGE
DEWEY
NEW YORK CENTRAL SYSTEM
N. Y. O. & W. RY.

Control Through Changes in Film Position

According to the first rule of rectilinear perspective, "all lines within a plane parallel to the plane of the film remain undistorted" (see page 255). Hence, whenever we want distortion-free reproduction of some object, all we have to do is to take care that the plane of the film is parallel to such lines of the object as we want to render in their natural, undistorted positions. For instance, if the vertical lines of a building have to be reproduced in a photograph as vertical and parallel (instead of converging toward the top of the picture), the film inside the camera has to be kept perfectly vertical; and if in the oblique view of an automobile the wheels have to appear as circular disks instead of as foreshortened, oval shapes, the film inside the camera has to be kept parallel to the plane of the wheels, i.e., parallel to the side of the car. I deliberately use the expression "film inside the camera," because the actual position of the camera itself is of no importance in this respect; it is *only* the position of the film that matters.

Most of the time, the relative positions of camera and object will be predetermined by reasons such as immovability of the object, angle of view, light and shadow, scale, general appearance of perspective as determined by distance between camera and object, degree of foreshortening, etc. In such cases, the point of view should be selected in accordance with these demands. After all other adjustments have been made, the plane of the film should be swung parallel to the lines that have to be reproduced undistorted, by means of the "swingback" of the camera (if it has one). Degree or absence of distortion will have to be checked on the groundglass. Usually, readjustment of focus will be found necessary. Stopping down the lens will give the desired degree of sharpness in depth.

The step-by-step procedure of adjusting a camera for the undistorted reproduction of verticals is illustrated in the series of pictures on the opposite page. In the case of the undistorted automobile wheels, the horizontal back swing of the camera would have to be used in similar fashion. In more difficult cases, where distortion-free rendering in two planes is desirable, as, for instance, the undistorted reproduction of a package of merchandise for an advertisement, both horizontal and vertical swings can be used simultaneously. Frequently, a corresponding change in the position of the lens—a vertical shift up- or downward, a lateral slide, a slight turn in the right direction—will materially aid the achievement of the necessary all-over sharpness of the picture. Groundglass observation of the image will immediately tell if such adjustments have been made in the right direction.

Many cameras have neither swing backs nor adjustment facilities for the lens. In that case, distortion can be corrected later while enlarging the negative; see in-

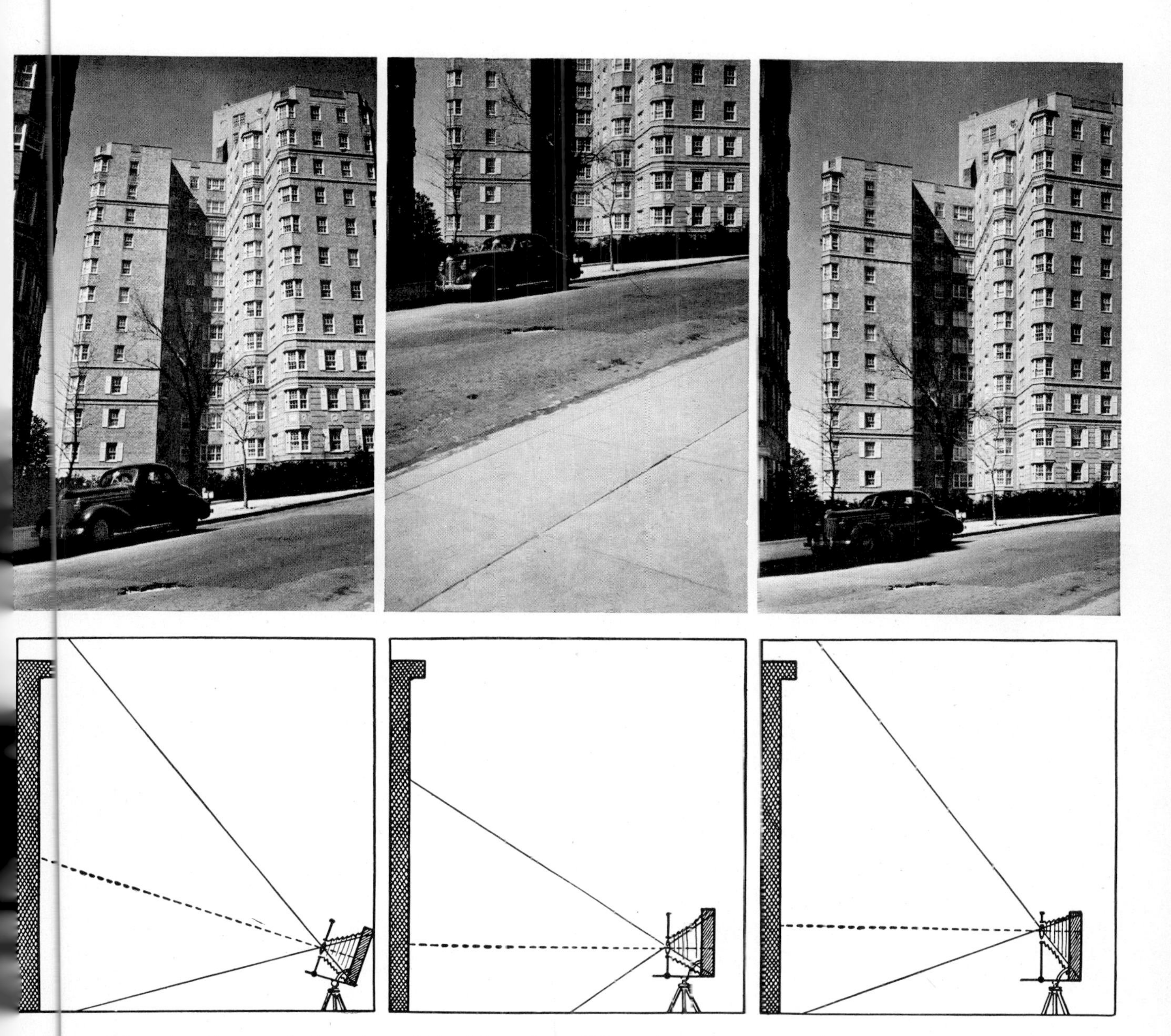

Distortion-free rendering of a tall building. *Left:* Tilting camera and film to include top of tall building results in converging of verticals toward the top of the picture. *Center:* Keeping camera and film level renders verticals parallel, but cuts off top of building. *Right:* Keeping film parallel to verticals prevents distortion; raising the lens changes direction of angle of view so top of building is included in the picture. If covering power of the lens in extreme raised position is too small to illuminate image evenly, a slight backward tilt of the lens will improve the situation, but sharpness will suffer unless diaphragm is stopped down considerably. Such tilting of the lens does not affect the perspective of the picture.

structions on page 163. There is no visible difference between an enlargement made from a distortion-free negative and a print made from a negative in which distortion had to be corrected with the enlarger. In extreme cases, best results

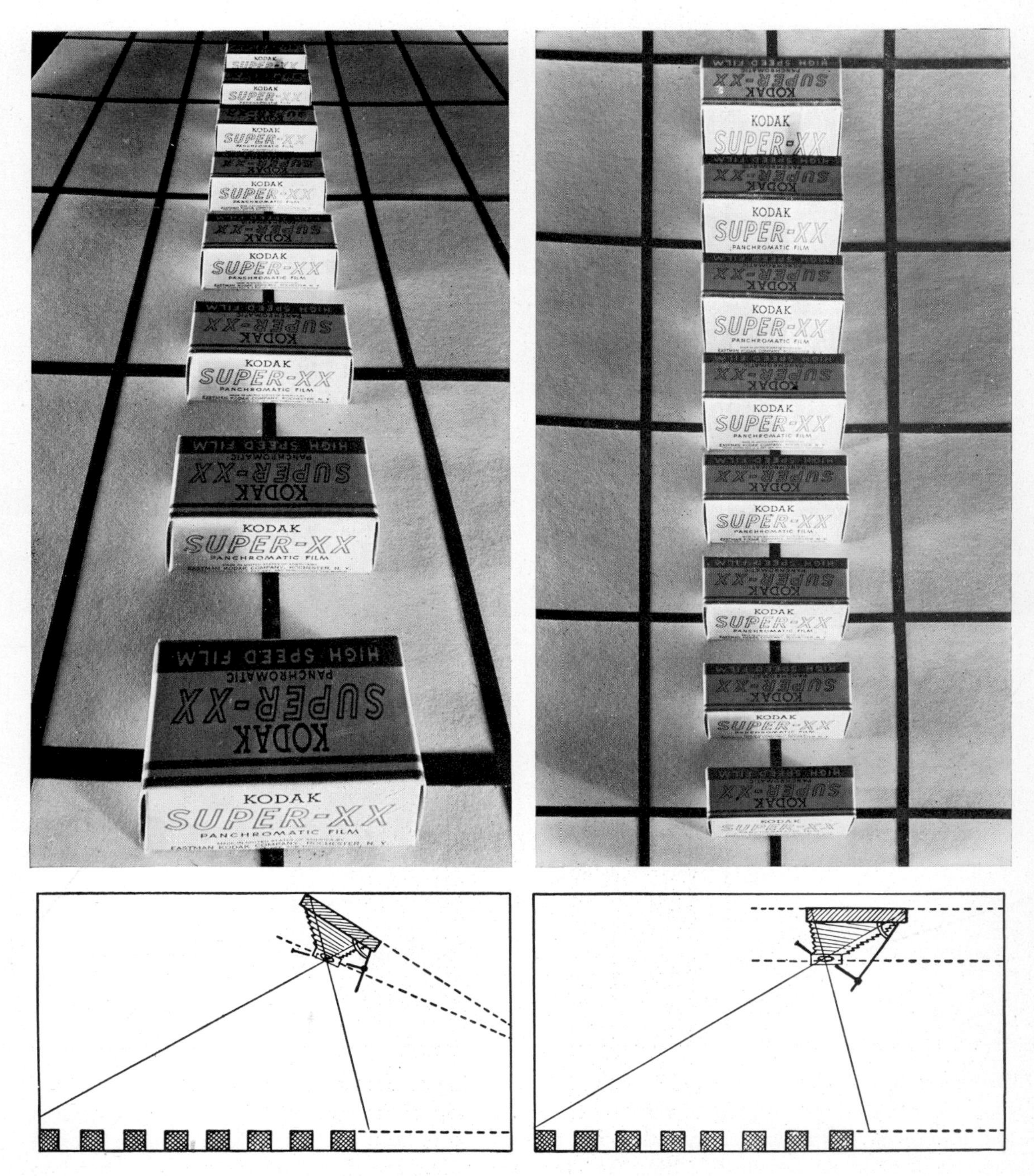

Comparison of two extreme types of perspective, both taken from the same point of view. The sketches illustrate how the tremendous difference in rendering was achieved simply by making use of the swings provided for camera back and lens. Naturally, all steps in between these two extremes can be achieved as easily merely by changing the positions of the swings.

will be obtained if part of the distortion is corrected while taking the picture, and the remainder while enlarging the negative. This will be necessary especially if the covering power of the lens is relatively limited.

Two views of New York City, taken with the same camera and lens from the identical point of view. In both cases, certain corrections have been made with regard to perspective: *Above*, the plane of the film has been aligned with the verticals of the buildings, and the lens has been lowered, resulting in a rather conventional, but not uninteresting pattern shot. *Below*, the natural tendency of receding lines to converge has been artificially increased by swinging the plane of the film in the opposite direction to that in the picture above, amplifying the convergence of verticals instead of correcting it. An example of turning an apparent disadvantage into an advantage, further distorting an already distorted motif and thus creating a startling and attractive "sunburst effect" which makes this rather unorthodox picture far more interesting than the conventional view above.

SPACE ILLUSION THROUGH SCALE

Many of the world's most stirring subjects make notoriously disappointing photographs. Standing on high dunes overlooking the boundless sea is one of the most profound sensations anybody can experience—but a picture taken from that point of view usually doesn't look like much. . . . A view of the Grand Canyon takes one's breath away—but I'm still waiting for the photograph of this gigantic landscape that will give me more than a fleeting impression of pretty-pretty dime-store art. . . . The cathedral of Chartres is one of the greatest works of architecture ever conceived by man—but in a picture it usually looks like a toy and fails to move one. . . .

All these examples are characterized by huge dimension, expanse, greatness—literally as well as figuratively. Actually, they are so tremendous that it is difficult for a human being to grasp how overwhelmingly big they really are. And then a little photographer comes along and snaps a picture with his little camera and after he sees what he got on his little piece of film he has the nerve to be disappointed at the result, because he was conceited enough to think that he could catch the spirit of this hugeness in his little 8x10 print.

Apparently there are obstacles that even the best photographer cannot overcome without compromise. "Greatness" is one of them. Nothing that is really and truly "great" can be expected to retain its greatness when reduced to a size of 8x10 inches. Greatness must always be expansive in order to be effective, and it is small consolation that "greatness," like all qualities is "relative": the cathedral of Chartres is big, but not when compared to the Grand Canyon—which again is dwarfed by the sea. . . . The same applies to photography: a 4x5 contact is small, an 8x10 print is "normal," an 11x14 looks big until you see too many and get used to them. Only sizes way above the "normal" will really and truly look "big": 3x4 feet, 5x7 feet, murals. . . . Only when plastered over an entire wall does the Grand Canyon begin to look really "great" in a picture—unless. . . .

. . . Unless we tackle the problem from the other end. After all, there is a limit to blowing up photographs to giant sizes, even more so when it comes to reproducing them in magazines and books. But "greatness" is a relative quality which exists only in contrast to something "small." In other words it depends on *scale*, on a measure by means of which we can express its size in units, so-and-so-many-times as big as such and such. Hence, by introducing such a scale into the picture we can still get across the idea of greatness in a photograph of relatively small dimensions—by comparing something great to something small. And the smaller the unit we use for measurement, the "greater the greatness" will appear.

The human figure as an indicator of scale in a photograph: Despite his smallness, this lonely runner is the most important element in the picture, making sea and sky look big by contrast. Just for fun, cover the figure with your finger and see how all dimensions seem to shrink, and how the photograph becomes empty and dull. . . .

Now let's imagine a photograph of the sea, containing everything we love: the boundless space, the snowy beach, white-capped waves, and a glorious sky. We walked far along the dunes to escape the noisy crowds, to find the solitude that alone gives rest and peace; we found it; we took a photograph to keep this mood forever, and now we are contemplating the result. It is—to put it mildly—disappointing: emptiness instead of solitude, no indication of greatness, the vastness of sea and sky looks dull. In short, the picture is a dud. The reason: *it has no scale!* Nothing is there to indicate the size of the landscape, nothing to tell us whether the beach is 50 feet long and the waves are big, or 500 feet long and the waves are small. Admittedly, the spacing of the oncoming breakers toward the horizon results in a certain impression of depth, but since we have no means of measuring the actual extent of this space, this, too, is of little use. Space without scale doesn't impress us very much.

On the other hand, let's have a look at the photograph on the previous page. At once the sea appears broad and deep, the sky boundless, and we experience something of the lure of endless space that incited us to take the picture. This is it. This space is not wishy-washy, but definitely huge. This photograph has scale. And still, the only difference between this and the first imaginary picture is a tiny little figure running along the beach: a human being, an object of known dimensions! And tiny as it is, this little figure is the most important thing in the whole picture, the unit that gives it scale, the object that by contrast to its own smallness makes the sea and the sky and the whole of space look big!

Usually it is easy to achieve some illusion of space in a photograph. But this alone is not enough if this space is undefined with regard to size: how big, how high, how long, how wide, how deep? This can develop into a serious problem—especially when taking photographs of open landscapes—and the usual solution is to "get some human interest into the picture." This is perfectly correct, even if the reason for the resulting improvement of the picture isn't always clear to the photographer himself. For actually it isn't the interest in the figures as human beings that exerts the good influence on the appearance of the photograph, but their usefulness as units of a definite scale. Comparison of the sizes of the objects in the picture—trees, buildings, rocks, mountains, etc.—with the apparent size of these figures—objects of familiar dimensions—becomes the means for measuring the actual size of all those other objects, their distance from the camera, and the dimensions of the space included in the picture.

Many different objects of well-known and uniform dimensions can be used to give a photograph "scale." Best of all, of course, is the human figure; man is vain and loves to see all things in relationship to himself . . . and not for nothing does he measure distances in "feet." For closeups, a hand usually makes a good scale, while inclusion of part of a finger or two provides a more interesting and organic scale for many super closeups than the conventional matchbox, or the more scientific ruler. However, the character of the hand must be in accordance with the content of the picture. Long, carefully manicured fingernails on the hands of a girl machine operator will make a photograph look ridiculous.

Wherever the human figure or part of it would appear out of place or is undesirable for some other reason, other objects of familiar and uniform size can be used instead. Here are a few suggestions: cows or horses in a pasture; cars on a highway or one car on a country road; telephone poles; boats and ships of all

Artificial jewels for bearings in precision instruments made by Bulova. Since closeups of individual bearings didn't look interesting enough even when strongly magnified, this was the form selected for presenting the finished product: a glass vial containing 2,500 jewels, held between the fingers to indicate scale. In order to make the jewels appear as small as possible, a large man's hand was chosen instead of the smaller hand of a woman.

S. S. *Kungsholm* off Coney Island, sailing for Europe. Scale as sole creator of space illusion: a practically "perspectiveless" photograph—no converging lines, no limited depth of field, no atmospheric haze—but the smallness of the big liner on the horizon convincingly suggests depth and distance and boundless space.

kinds, because their differences in shape automatically indicate their sizes (see picture on opposite page). Buildings with standard-sized windows, since windows are one of the best nonorganic units for scale. And so forth.

By changing the real or apparent size of the measuring unit we can control the scale and space impressions of our photographs. Whenever something has to look big, the measuring unit has to be small, and vice versa. If, for instance, in the picture on page 277 the figure had appeared twice as large, which could have been achieved easily by placing it closer to the camera, the whole proportions of the photograph would have been changed, and the sea and the sky would have looked only half as big as they do now. In case the measuring unit must be too close to the object to reduce the unit's apparent size by increasing its distance from the camera (since this would change the apparent size of the object, too), selection of a relatively small indicator of scale will help to make such an object look larger; instead of an average-sized figure, for instance, we would have to use a smaller one. Or if in a closeup we want to get the opposite effect and make the object appear even smaller than it actually is, having a big hand with thick and heavy fingers hold it (instead of a hand of normal size or smaller) will help to do so. Especially in industrial and advertising photographs, the indication of an object's size is often highly important, and using the wrong-sized scale can actually spoil such a picture.

While scaleless photographs of large subjects invariably look disappointing, just the opposite is true of closeups of very small objects. Lack of scale makes them appear much larger than they actually are, resulting in pictures that often look surprisingly interesting, fantastic, and stimulating to the imagination. Subjects especially fitted for "scaleless" photographs are small objects of nature—flowers, insects, shells, crystals, etc.—which enlarged to several times their natural size make exceptionally striking pictures. They provide a challenge to any photographer who combines imagination with a sense of the beautiful and the bizarre.

SPACE ILLUSION THROUGH CONTROL OF DEPTH OF FIELD

Every time we look at some particular object, the lens of the eye automatically adjusts until it gets this object "in focus," with the result that we see the object "sharp." If we let our gaze wander toward some other object farther away, lightning-fast readjustment of the eye will immediately take place because, as a result of the relatively large aperture of the human eye, we can never see objects in different planes really "sharp" simultaneously. Hence, if two objects are "apparently' side by side in a photograph, but one is sharp and the other is unsharp, our subconscious mind tells us that this side-by-side effect is only an optical illusion (otherwise we would be able to see both of them sharp at the same time), and that actually one of the objects must be closer than the other one. For this reason, the simultaneous presence of sharp and unsharp elements in a picture evokes depth associations, and from its degree of unsharpness we conclude that an object is in front of, or behind, another one which is rendered "sharp."

Contrast between sharp and unsharp creates the impression of "depth" in any picture.

From a purist's point of view, photographs that are perfectly sharp in depth could thus be rejected as "unnatural," since they represent a form of vision different from that of the eye. Of course, nobody would seriously think of doing this. On the contrary, one of the greatest assets of photography is the ability of the camera to widen the range of visual experience by presenting familiar objects in new and exciting forms. But actually there is at least a grain of truth in such a radical opinion. For whenever we get really absorbed in a certain object, our eyes concentrate on this object alone, singling it out from its surroundings and literally isolating it, by presenting it to the mind in the form of a sharply defined image, making all other things around it unimportant by reducing them to different stages of blurredness. Judged with this in mind, a photograph in which sharpness is concentrated exclusively on the subject proper has an advantage over other pictures which treat the essential and the unimportant alike. Contrasts between sharp and unsharp permit accentuating the most important parts in a photograph.

This selective action of the eye can be imitated in photography, at least to a certain degree. By focusing carefully on the subject proper, and by using a relatively large diaphragm opening, sharpness in depth can be confined to a certain plane in a picture, or to a certain zone of predetermined depth, with objects behind or in front of it appearing increasingly blurred the farther away they are from this sharply rendered zone. Such conscious limitation of sharpness in depth can improve a photograph in two ways: first, by increasing its illusion of depth; second, by concentrating the interest on its most important elements.

Limitation of depth of field always tends to stress the "mood" of a picture and to create an "atmosphere" through obliteration of "facts"—the details that are drowned in blurredness. If all the objects in a picture were of equal importance,

Comparison of photographs showing different extension of sharpness in depth. *Left:* Focused on a point about one-third between foreground and street, lens stopped down to *f*22. Uniform all-over sharpness results in documentary clarity of detail, but destroys impression of depth. Equal treatment of foreground and background makes them equally important, divides interest between them, and leads to confusion. *Right:* Focused on figure in foreground, diaphragm wide open at *f*3.5. Limitation of sharpness to foreground concentrates interest on the figure, making it the motif proper of the picture; unsharp rendering of street stresses its unimportance. Clear differentiation between near and far results in pronounced feeling of depth.

limitation of depth of field would mean the loss of some important elements and should be avoided. But any time we wish to emphasize a single object in a photograph, any time we want to play up a mood, conscious limitation of sharpness in depth is an effective way to do so. It stirs imagination into action by giving it something to work on—the re-creation of the facts hidden in blurredness, the reconstruction of the background of the subject, literally as well as figuratively, the savoring of the atmosphere of the picture. . . .

> Limitation of depth of field often makes a photograph more interesting by leaving a little to the imagination.

The extent to which sharpness in depth can and should be limited depends on the type of picture desired and the kind of subject to be depicted. If *the photograph is primarily documentary*, limitation of sharpness in depth should be used only sparsely because it would obscure the facts, which are here important. *In industrial photography* limited sharpness is one of the most valuable means of bringing order into pictorial chaos; by concentrating interest it often provides the only means of getting a clear and understandable picture, of separating the objects to be photographed from a messy-looking background, of concentrating the interest on the subject proper, of subduing distracting detail behind it—and still achieving an impression of space where other manifestations of perspective are lacking. Besides, limited depth of field helps to re-create the mood that is so typical of most industrial settings—that mixture of smoke and heat, of noise and vibration—impressions which cannot be photographed directly but have to be interpreted in symbolic form by the photographer, so that the beholder of the picture can later reconstruct them in his imagination. . . . *In portraiture*, controlled limitation of sharpness in depth is often the only way of creating a three-dimensional impression, thanks to the usual lack of other means such as converging lines, scale, atmospheric haze (we'll hear about this later), etc. Besides, confining sharpness to a face alone draws attention to it immediately, and underlines its importance as the proper subject of the picture; no photograph looks as confusing as a portrait that blends the head into the background, thanks to an equally sharp treatment of both. . . . *In outdoor* photography, the illusion of space can often be improved considerably through "framing" a long shot by including part of the nearest foreground in the picture (see pages 248-249). Emphasizing the difference in distance through difference in treatment—faraway things sharp and close things out of focus—will make this impression of depth even stronger.

Situation and extension of the sharply defined zone depends on its distance from the camera, the plane of focus, the diaphragm stop, and the focal length of the lens. Since stopping down a lens makes sharpness in depth increase twice as fast beyond the plane of focus as toward the camera, focusing should be done on a plane one-third within the zone we want to render sharply. Its depth will be more limited the closer this plane is to the camera, the larger the diaphragm stop is, and the longer the focal length of the lens. And vice versa. A checkup on the groundglass is always better than relying on the depth-of-field scale on certain lenses or on tables, which should be employed only in case the camera is not equipped with a groundglass. For more exhaustive information, see pages 107 to 115.

When photographing an object of very great extension in depth, the problem is not one of limiting the zone of sharpness but of making it deep enough to cover

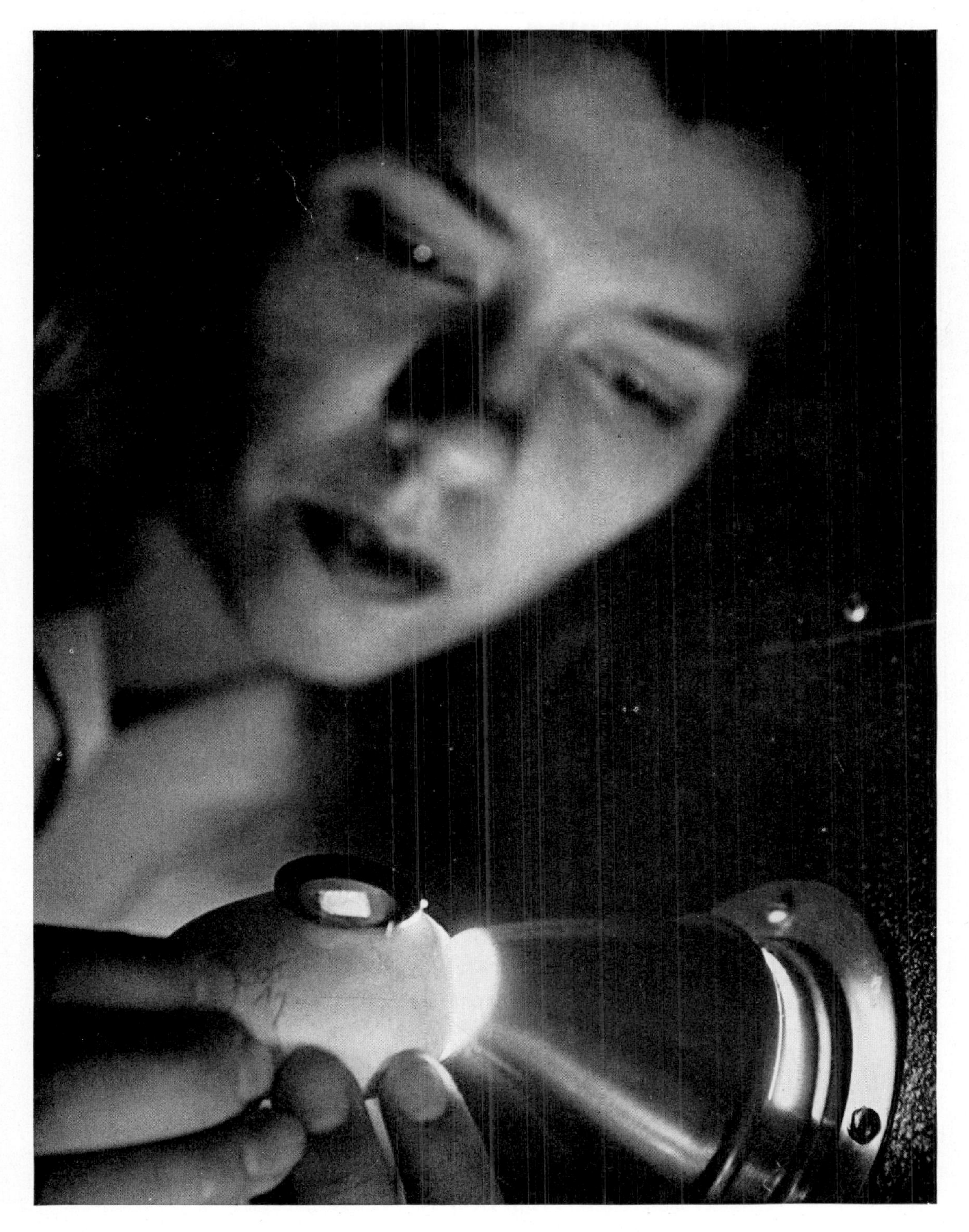

Cancer research—candling of a chicken egg with implanted cancer tissue. Limiting sharpness to the egg makes it the subject proper of the picture and concentrates the interest of the beholder where it belongs. The intense face in the background, deliberately rendered blurred, suggests the anonymous laboratory assistant doing research work all over the world.

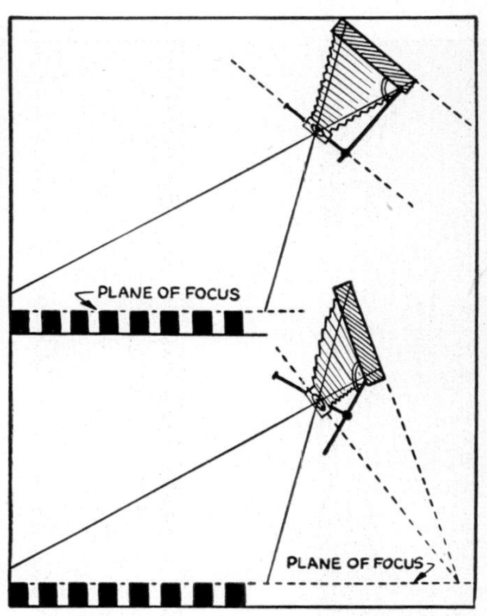

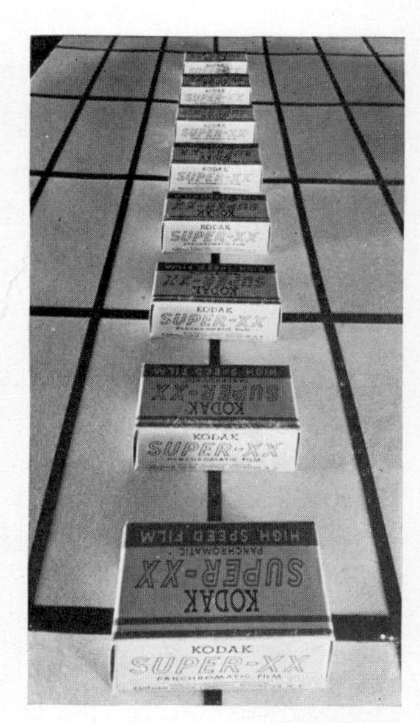

Swings for greatest extension of sharpness in depth. *Left* and *top:* Picture taken in ordinary way, film parallel with lens, diaphragm stopped down to *f* 4.5. *Right* and *bottom:* Plane of film swung backward until imaginary lines drawn through the planes of object, lens, and film converge in common point. In this position, sharpness in depth is distributed evenly over the whole picture (with the same stop, *f* 4.5, as before).

the entire object. If even the smallest diaphragm stop doesn't give enough sharpness in depth, or if for the sake of a shorter exposure the lens cannot be stopped down far enough, the following method will usually give results, *provided* the whole of the object lies more or less within *one plane*: by means of the camera swings, arrange the relative positions of object plane, lens, and film according to the illustration above, and watch the result on the groundglass. The object will be more or less in focus in its entire extension—the more so the less of it protrudes from the plane of focus—even with the diaphragm wide open! Such parts of the object as protrude from the plane of focus proper will have to be brought back into focus by stopping down the diaphragm, the same as in any ordinary photograph. But instead of having to cover the entire depth of the object, such stopping down has only to cover the smaller difference between the plane of focus and the protruding parts of the object, with the result that we can get away with a much larger stop than otherwise (see page 106). Pictures like that on the opposite page could never have been made without the help of a swing-back camera.

Propeller hubs on conveyor, Curtiss-Wright plant, Clifton, New Jersey. Every object is somehow important in this industrial-documentary picture. Hence, despite its very great depth, it had to be rendered sharp from beginning to end. Use of the swing back made it possible to get the necessary depth of field even at *f* 12.5, while without its help not even the smallest available stop would have given the desired coverage in depth. Besides, unreasonable prolongation of exposure time would have made it impossible for the workmen to "hold it" during the time exposure.

SPACE ILLUSION THROUGH ATMOSPHERIC HAZE, LIGHT, AND SHADOW

All forms of space rendering with two-dimensional means are founded on the common fact that objects change in appearance with increasing distance from the beholder. Most of these changes are constant under all conditions, as, for instance, apparent decrease in size, or converging of parallel lines, or contrast between sharp and unsharp. Thus the same combination of object-position, distance, and point of view will always cause the same degree of "perspective distortion," regardless of whether it happens to be in New York or Tuscaloosa or on the moon. . . . But there is one special type of perspective distortion that is never twice the same, that changes with the position of the sun and the clarity of the air, that is very much in evidence one day and the next day hardly noticeable and that, instead of affecting an object's shape, distorts its colors and contrasts and suppresses its finer detail. It is *aerial perspective*. . . . The earth's atmosphere is never a perfectly transparent medium, is saturated to a greater or lesser degree with minute droplets of water, with particles of dust and soot. Each of these reflects, deflects, and scatters light, reducing the transparency of the air and causing things to appear lighter and less contrastful the thicker the layer of intervening air is. This effect can best be observed on a hazy day in the mountains, when range after range appears lighter and lighter until near the horizon, mountains and sky almost blend together in white. For this reason, distortion of the familiar color of an object toward white generally suggests distance, and in a photograph, contrasts between light and dark create the illusion of space.

Aerial perspective gives the photographer an opportunity to produce a feeling of depth even when other means of perspective are lacking, as occasionally in landscapes. More often it is useful in suggesting "mood" and "atmosphere," in separating different planes in depth through different shades of lightness, and for suppression of unwanted detail for sake of a more powerful form of presentation with accent on contrasts and masses. As the name suggests, aerial perspective depends largely on atmospheric conditions. But it is not limited to long shots. Actually, on very hazy or foggy days, long shots are all but impossible, and aerial perspective invades the field of the medium-long shot and the closeup. Occasionally it can be effective even in interior shots, as the picture on page 290 demonstrates.

When viewing the mountain ranges mentioned previously, the eye uses the different shades of increasing lightness as stepping stones which guide it toward the depth. Thus, in a photograph, the longer the scale of stepping stones, i.e., the longer the gradation of the photograph and the greater the contrast between dark foreground and light background, the more convincing will be the illusion of space, and vice versa. Consequently, control of aerial perspective depends upon control of the gradation of the photograph.

Distance and haze are bluish. Increasing the haze effect will increase the depth illusion, which according to the table on page 226 necessitates the use of a C-5 (blue) filter. On the other hand, to bring things nearer, either literally by using the magnifying telephoto lens, or figuratively by rendering them as sharp and detailed as possible, the veiling effect of haze and atmosphere has to be decreased to a greater or lesser degree or cut out entirely. This can be achieved through use of the proper filter from light yellow through orange to dark red, which will increasingly cut down on atmospheric haze until finally it is practically eliminated.

The most complete elimination of even the last traces of haze effect under difficult conditions can be accomplished through the use of infrared-sensitized film under the proper filter if certain radical changes in color values are permissible—green foliage, for instance, will appear white in the photograph, and blue water will be rendered black.

Pan film under blue filter: haze effect exaggerated, strongest contrasts between dark foreground and light background result in strongest feeling of depth.

Pan film, no filter: haze effect as it appeared to the eye, medium contrasts between near and far objects produce a "natural" appearing impression of space.

Pan film under red filter: haze effect completely eliminated, uniform tone and clearness of foreground and background makes picture appear "flat."

MESTA

Members' penthouse, Museum of Modern Art, New York City. Light as creator of space impressions: converging shadows make up for lack of actual converging lines, creating a feeling of depth that couldn't be surpassed by any other means. Contrasts between the shadow-darkened foreground and the haze-filled lightness of the city beyond the windows further strengthens this space illusion.

Creation of a feeling of depth and space is not confined to actual physical means. Since all our space impressions are nothing but "illusions," "illusionary means" will often give even better results, as do the shadows in the picture above, or the light shafts on the opposite page. In both cases, the powerful converging lines that are first of all responsible for the "perspective" are "illusionary" lines that actually didn't exist. Their source is back light, about which we will hear more in the following chapter on lighting. Pictorially, it is the most beautiful of all types of light, and that which more than any other type of light can play an effective, positive, and important role in the creation of three-dimensional effects in a photograph.

> Back light is probably the surest of all the different means of perspective to insure an illusion of space in any type of picture.

osit page: Strip mill, United States Steel Corporation, Pittsburgh. In dust-filled or smoky interiors, ial perspective is the most effective of all the different means for the creation of the illusion of space. fts of sunlight amplify with a touch of linear perspective the already pronounced feeling of depth. mospheric effects" contribute more than anything else to give this picture its particular "atmosre" of heat and smoke and work.

CHAPTER 12

LIGHT AND LIGHTING

LIGHT is to the photographer what paint and crayons are to the artist. In perfect darkness even the best photographer is helpless. On the other hand, through clever use of light a good photographer can do almost incredible things. He can make dark objects appear light (by strongly illuminating them) and light objects appear dark (by keeping them in the shadow). He can create or destroy the illusion of space. Without help of light—and of shadow, which after all is nothing but "negative light"—he could never translate the beauty of the female form into the flatness of a photograph—but if he is clumsy, he can just as easily flatten the curves of a veritable Venus in a flood of uncontrolled light. . . . A good photographer plays with gradations of light as a violinist plays on the strings of his instrument, creating any mood he may desire, high key for youth and joy and happiness, somber tones for seriousness, darkness for tragedy and sorrow. . . . He builds up contrasts to symbolize strength and uses flatness to indicate monotony. . . . He accentuates with brightness, suppresses with shadow, dramatizes with contrasting light and dark.

Not until he masters light and lighting can a photographer expect to create according to a predetermined plan or to express emotions in his pictures.

There are two basic types of illumination—"natural" (sunlight) and artificial (incandescent or flash). Their principal difference lies in the number of light sources ordinarily employed: one for "natural" lighting, several for "artificial" lighting. Of course, "natural lighting" can be imitated in the studio, too, by using a single powerful spotlight as the main source of illumination, together with several well-diffused weaker floods to "fill in the shadows," carefully controlled so that these auxiliary lights won't cast any "secondary shadows." On the other hand, heavy shadows in sunlit, outdoor portraits, for instance, can be "filled in," either with flash or with sunlight thrown back from a reflector (aluminized board). . . . But this type of outdoor picture usually has an unmistakably "artificial" flavor, resulting not so much from the lights themselves as from the complex shadows they cast—especially noticeable and ugly if they happen to crisscross.

The following series of demonstration pictures (pages 293 to 299) was photographed by Philippe Halsman.

Examples of basically correct lighting. *Left:* Sunlight-type lighting, one set of shadows only. *Right:* Artificially lighted portrait employing several sources of light. Notice, however, the presence of not more than *one set of shadows*, and—naturally—absence of cross-shadows. . . .

Exceptions like these, however, do not affect the intrinsic validity of the two basic rules for pictorially effective lighting:

> Any illumination will look "natural" (like sunlight) if it appears to come from a single source of light and casts a single set of shadows.
>
> The number of lights employed for "artificial" illumination has little to do with the quality of the lighting. It is the way in which such lights are used that matters, and how their shadows fall. *Any* illumination casting shadows within shadows is automatically bad lighting.

DANGERS AND MISTAKES

Most mistakes in lighting are caused by the use of too much light and too many lights. Beginners are especially likely to make the mistake of trying to kill an un-

Shadow within shadow—caused by a faultily placed and insufficiently diffused fill-in light.

Double shadows—caused by equally strong lights placed at equal distances from the face.

desirable shadow by filling in with another light, which only casts a new set of shadows, which they attempt to obliterate with a third light, which again casts . . . and so on . . . instead of changing the position of the light that produces the offending shadow. But recognizing a mistake is already half the cure, and even if he doesn't know as yet how to build up a good illumination, knowing what *not* to do will materially aid a beginner, who will do well to memorize the third basic rule for pictorially effective lighting:

> Too much light and too many lights will ruin any lighting!

On this and the following pages are illustrated some of the more disastrous mistakes that can occur in portrait lighting. A few minutes study of the ugly effects that faultily placed lights can have on a portrait should be considered time well spent if it helps to avoid similar accidents in the future. Mistakes of this kind are usually fatal picture diseases, as impossible to cure after they happen as they are easy to prevent. . . .

Main light was placed too low, producing a theatrical and unnatural effect. If subject is close to background, hovering shadow resembles a sinister ghost.

Nose shadow looks like a mustache—caused by a main light placed too directly overhead. A nose shadow that crosses or touches the lips will always look ugly.

"Blind spots" in a face are the cavities of the eyes, the corners between nose and mouth, the neck beneath the chin. Make sure they are sufficiently "filled in."

Insufficiently screened accent light struck the lens, causing flare that ruined the picture. Use a cardboard screen. Lensshades are too short for this purpose

1. The main light—its purpose is to bring out form and texture of the object and to determine the mood of the picture.

The main light

LIGHTING FOR FORM

Step by step we shall now proceed to light a portrait with the help of four lights, each of which has a different function. After posing the model comfortably and naturally in front of a neutral background, we darken the room illumination until there is just enough light left to see what we are doing, but not enough to make it difficult to judge the effect of the portable lights upon the subject.

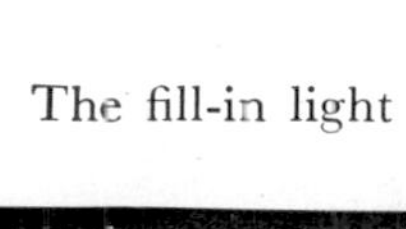

The fill-in light

2. Main light and fill-in light. The purpose of the fill-in light is to lighten up the black shadows left by the main light so that they will show traces of detail in the finished print.

A lighting scheme should always be built up step by step, beginning with the most important light. No further light should be added until the previous light has definitely been placed to the satisfaction of the photographer.

The first step. We place the "main light" (picture on opposite page), which should preferably be a large spotlight (but a flood will do). The purpose of the

The accent light

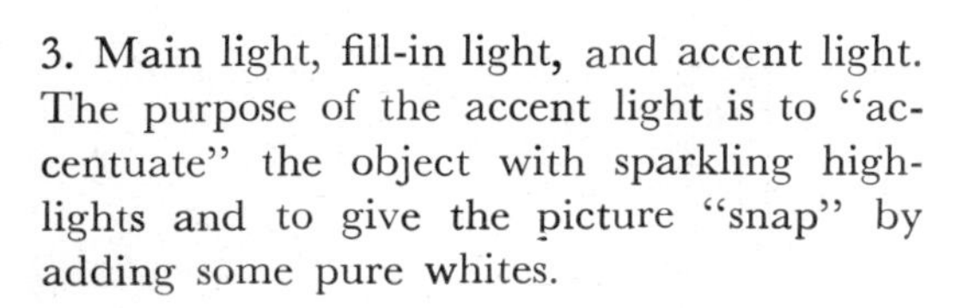

3. Main light, fill-in light, and accent light. The purpose of the accent light is to "accentuate" the object with sparkling highlights and to give the picture "snap" by adding some pure whites.

main light is to bring out the form and texture of the subject, and by roughly fixing the proportions between light and shadow to determine the mood of the picture. If the main light throws more light on the subject than it casts shadow over it, the general impression of the photograph will naturally be more gay or bright or youthful, etc., than if the shadows dominate over the lights—creating a more mysterious, glamorous, or serious mood. As so often in photography, equality between two opposite elements should be avoided as boring. Either one-third light and two-thirds shadow, or vice versa, will usually result in a pleasing effect. If a photog-

4. Main light, fill-in, accent light, and background-separation light, the purpose of which is to separate object from background and to lend a feeling of roundness and three-dimensionality to the picture.

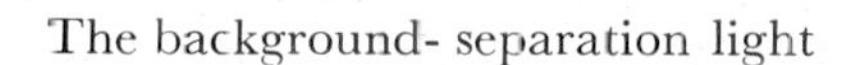

The background- separation light

rapher knows how to handle lights, disregarding this guide rule and increasing the proportions between light and shadow can lead to even more interesting and unusual pictures. . . . With this in mind, we place the main light approximately 45 degrees to one side and 45 degrees above the subject. Again, this is only a guide rule to start with and may later be disregarded, but it will help the beginner to place the main light so that it can fulfill its other important task: to illuminate the object so it becomes recognizable in every respect. How much or how little we actually see by the rays of this first light doesn't really matter so long as what we see makes sense and doesn't consist of just a number of unrelated, incomprehensible spots of light. Remember, this first light plays a decisive role in determining the appearance of the future picture, not only with regard to mood but to composition as well. It fixes the relative position of illuminated and shadow-hidden areas and thus determines composition with regard to light and dark. Make sure that the pattern thus created is satisfying in shape and proportions even from a purely abstract point of view, and could stand up as a self-contained, "abstract" picture even if left exactly as it is. . . .

The second step. We place the "fill-in" light. Its purpose is to lighten ever so slightly the too-black shadow areas left by the main light—just enough to make them light enough to show a trace of detail in the final photograph. Remember, the contrast range of the photographic emulsion is relatively limited (when compared to the eye), and the task of the fill-in light is to balance the illumination so that highlights and shadows will photograph equally well and thus look "natural." However, shadows should never be lightened beyond a certain point (which depends on the contrast range of the film, and the method of its development), since too much fill-in light will result in a flat and washed-out picture. Generally speaking, the fill-in light should not change the appearance or character of the main-light illumination; it is nothing but a technical necessity.

With the fill-in light we introduce the danger of cross-shadows (remember page 293). To avoid this, the fill-in should always be a well-diffused floodlight (there can be two or even more fill-ins as long as they are diffused enough not to cast any "secondary" shadows within shadows cast by the main light). The larger its reflector and the better diffused the light itself, the less danger of secondary shadows, which can be lessened even further by placing the fill-in as close to the camera as possible (best of all: right on top of it), because then all possible shadows will fall behind the parts of the subject that cast them and thus will be hidden from the lens.

The third step. We place the "accent light." So far, we have carefully avoided extremes of light or dark, areas that would photograph either too white or too black to show detail in the final photograph. If we want snap and contrast in the picture, however, we have to employ the full scale of gradation from pure white to pure black, and the accent light makes this possible. By adding a few "highlights," pure white accents, in strategic positions we make sure that the gradation of the print will include at least a few spots of snowy white.

The accent light should be a spotlight that can be focused on just the parts of the subject we wish to accentuate. It is most commonly placed somewhat behind the subject where it cannot cast secondary shadows, but it should be shielded to prevent it from shining into the lens of the camera and causing halation and flares on the film (see example on page 295, *bottom right*). Since the parts it strikes will be overexposed (purposely; otherwise they wouldn't print white), and thus be empty of detail, accent light should be used only sparingly, just to highlight the outline of a face or a shoulder, and to put a halo-like glow around the hair. . . .

Accentuating highlights are the final touches that give pictures life and sparkle and make prints colorful and rich. They are the seasoning that flavors the picture, and if we overdo them, the effect is comparable to that of too much pepper in the soup.

The fourth step. We place the "background-separation light." The model should be well lighted by now, but one extremely important thing is still missing: the illusion of three-dimensionality. On the shadow side, there doesn't seem to be any "air" between figure and background—they blend into each other too much to permit an impression of space. . . . This is where the separation light enters the picture. By throwing some carefully controlled light on the background we lighten it on the shadow side of the figure, while still keeping it dark on the figure's highlighted side, so that *now both* the shaded and the highlighted contours of the model stand out clearly *separated from the background.*

The background-separation light can be either a spot or a floodlight; what matters is not so much the quality of its light (with regard to crispness of shadow), as its correct intensity and position, both of which have to be adjusted carefully by placing it at the proper distance from the background it has to illuminate.

Conclusions. The method described on these pages produces a standard illumination that can be used to light any conceivable object, a girl as well as a grasshopper . . . a dahlia as well as a drill press. . . . It is always reliable and can be varied in innumerable different ways merely by changing intensity or spread of one or several of the four basic lights. Decreasing the intensity of the main light, for instance, while increasing the brightness of the background-separation light and using a slightly weaker and well-dispersed accent light for back illumination (to light the object more or less from its back side, producing a halo effect all around it) will produce highly dramatic lighting, especially useful for symbolizing action in industrial photographs. Another variation— decreasing the intensity of the fill-in until shadows photograph practically black, while increasing the spread of the accent light and balancing proportions between light and shadow until darkness fills most of the picture—is part of the secret of the famous Hollywood "glamor lighting," guaranteed to produce the most seductive effects.

As so often in photography, the number of different possibilities is in direct proportion to the imagination and creative ability of the photographer. . . .

Glass wool emerging from furnace at Owens-Corning fiber-glass production line. Illumination for texture with two flashbulbs: the mainlight, behind the stream of glass wool, just skims the surface of the white wad of spun glass to bring out its texture. The fill-in, a smaller flashbulb on an extension far to the right, lightens the shadows just enough to show a trace of detail. Exposed at 1/250 second to stop the motion of the stream of glass, which would have caused blurredness that would have destroyed the texture.

LIGHTING FOR TEXTURE

Realism in photography depends to a great extent on the amount and precision of detail recorded in a picture (in contrast to mood, which is best expressed by simplification through use of masses, and light and shadow which swallow the detail, leaving it to the imagination to reconstruct it in a more abstract way). Detail, as we understand it here, sometimes consists of small independent forms, but more often it is "form within form" or *texture.*

When taking a portrait, for instance, the most important task, along with posing and composing, is to arrange the lights so the forms of head and face will be brought out in a natural manner. We learned how to do this in the preceding section by studying the effect of light on a living model. Actually, however, a dummy would have served the purpose just as well, since in a photograph the only difference between the head of a well-made manikin and the head of a living person is the difference in appearance of the textures of plaster and skin. The converse of this realization is that color and shape of an object may change, but its texture remains the same. Human skin, for instance, can be white or brown or black, can be flat or sharply curved, but its texture is always the same. Texture gives a surface its character, and since most photographs are concerned with surfaces of different objects, we may safely state that texture lends additional character to almost any picture. Actually, texture is often the only means by which we can tell the nature of an object in a photograph; a white mass, for instance, may be either snow or sand or plaster or glass wool or cotton or flour or sugar or salt, and whichever it is can be told only if its texture is rendered clearly enough to make recognition possible. Even apparently textureless objects such as clouds have some kind of texture, and when appearing unsharp and "textureless" in a picture will immediately lose their character and may as well be suspended masses of cotton or white blobs painted on a canvas backdrop.

Texture in photography depends on sharpness; an unsharp picture obviously cannot show any texture. But sharpness alone is rarely enough to bring out texture, unless texture has been made "visible" first through proper lighting. Texture, when examined under a magnifier, is nothing but a repetition of minute forms as, for instance, hairs, pores, wrinkles, crystals, grains, etc. It consequently obeys the same rules for lighting that we discussed in the previous section on lighting for form, i.e., flat and shadowless light suppresses texture, while shadow-throwing side light and back light brings it out in the form of contrast between highlighted elevations and shadow-filled depressions. Naturally, if the differences in height between the texture-creating elevations and depressions of a surface are relatively large, moderate side light striking the object at an angle of about 30 degrees already creates enough differentiation between light and shadow within the surface to bring out texture (coarse textures, like fur, bark, gravel, etc.). But if the texture is very finegrained, as, for instance, human skin, paper, sand, etc., such shadows are much too short to be visible in a photograph, and have to be made longer by readjusting the source of light until its beam just skims across the surface of the object, at an angle of perhaps five degrees or less.

A spotlight or the sun provides the best illumination to bring out texture, since their light is "hard" enough to make even the very smallest forms throw crisp and clean shadows (grains of sand, fibers of paper, fine fabrics, etc.). Light from a flood is too soft for texture rendering but can be made "hard" enough to substitute for a spot in an emergency by taking off the reflector and using only the naked bulb, which in this case, of course, must be shielded so its light cannot strike the lens.

Shadowless lighting kills texture.

THE PRINCIPLE OF

Low-skimming, shadow-creating light brings out texture. This picture was taken with a single flood. Texture is apparent, but looks mushy because of pronounced diffusion of light.

The concentrated light of a low-skimming spot makes texture appear crisp and clean. Exaggeration of contrasts dramatizes the object pictorially, but is contrary to "true" appearance of the bread.

TEXTURE LIGHTING

Same setup as above, but shadows filled in slightly with a flood. Texture appears similar to picture at left, only crisper and cleaner. This is the best lighting for a "documentary" picture.

Sea dollar—low-skimming illumination brings out texture, filling valleys with shadow, hitting elevations with light.

Iron filings (magnetic attraction)—practically shadowless illumination presents magnetic pattern in clearest possible form.

EXAMPLES OF

Steel—characterization of material and texture (hardness and smoothness) through precise definition and multiple-reflections.

Snow—low-skimming backlight brings out the granulated surface texture. The car—an object of known dimensions—provides the picture with scale.

Cold rolled steel—side light emphasizes thinness of layers; reflection inside coil demonstrates its smoothness and shiny texture.

Raw glass—reflections from back light indicate smooth but slightly rippled surface; dark horizontals are rollers beneath glass.

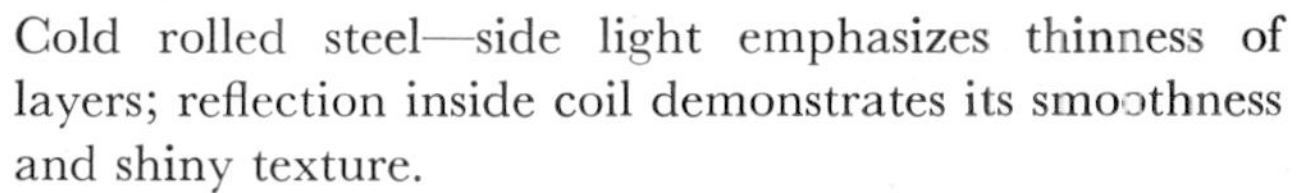

TEXTURE LIGHTING

Fabrics—low-angled side light makes texture clearly visible, while a fill-in flood illuminates shadows otherwise too dark.

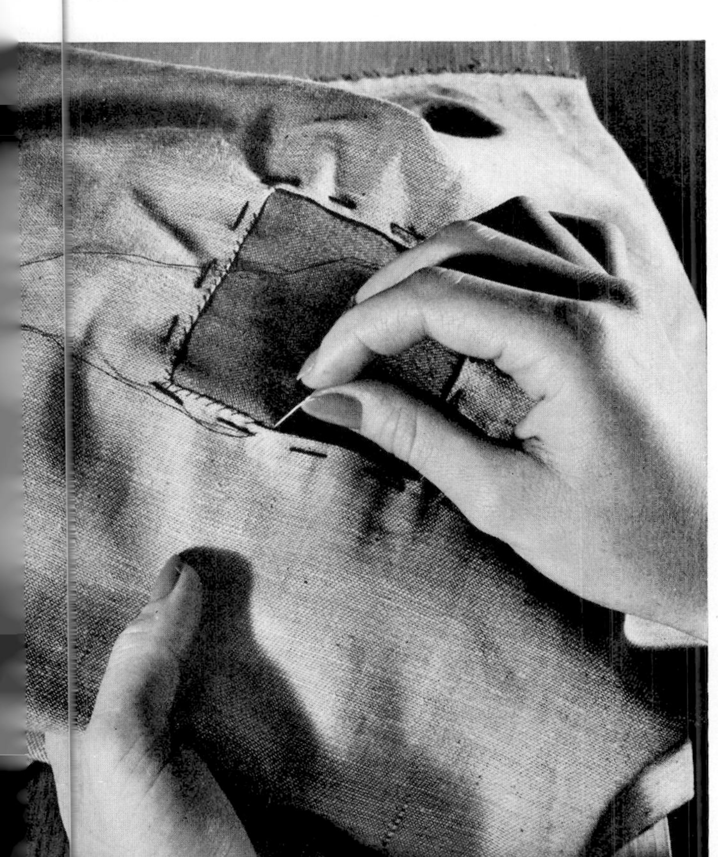

Water—sparkling back light animates rippled surface which otherwise could scarcely be distinguished from (for instance) a meadow.

LIGHTING FOR MOOD

Creative photographers are not exclusively concerned with realism. Ever so often, either of their own volition or because called upon by a magazine editor to illustrate a certain story, they go out to photograph the unphotographable and come back with pictures of the invisible.

What they are trying to do, and, if they are good, succeed in doing, is to capture a certain mood and to suggest in symbolic form and with (naturally!) visible means, thoughts and ideas and feelings that cannot directly be put on film and paper. They do so by photographing objects that are already suggestive in themselves, either because there is a story connected with them or because they naturally lead one's imagination in the direction called for by the theme they have to interpret. And in order to get away from realism and start the beholder on the track of the story, the good photographer further increases such objects' suggestive powers by lighting them in a way likely to stir the imagination of the person who looks at them.

Imagination can work only if it has something to work on. A "realistic" photograph, a picture that is perfectly sharp all over, showing every little bit of detail, is "self-explaining" and can be understood at a glance; such a photograph seldom contains food for the imagination. But if a photograph shows only glimpses of things and veils the rest in darkness—if a picture hints but doesn't explain—then the beholder has to figure out the puzzle for himself, his mind and imagination have to work, and if led in the right direction through subject choice and mode of lighting, will usually get into the mood the photographer intended when he started out on his task of photographing the "invisible."

Lighting a photograph for "mood" is just the opposite from lighting it for "realism." Instead of clarifying everything with light, of painstakingly separating the various elements of the picture and avoiding vague masses of light and shadow, most "moods" can best be created by a sense of mystery. Consequently, light and darkness, masses, shadows, and occasionally even unsharpness, have to be employed to create a feeling of suspense, of eeriness and unreality, accentuated by only occasional glimpses of clarity—just enough to steer the thoughts of the beholder in the right direction. Naturally, before he can illustrate, or rather "interpret," a certain mood, the photographer must himself experience the feeling he wants to depict—fear, loneliness, danger, exuberance, reverence, or whatever it may be. And only if he is capable of doing so can his pictures look "genuine." Otherwise, they will merely succeed in being "arty."

Light—the sun—suggests reality, clarity, joy, and happiness. The opposite of

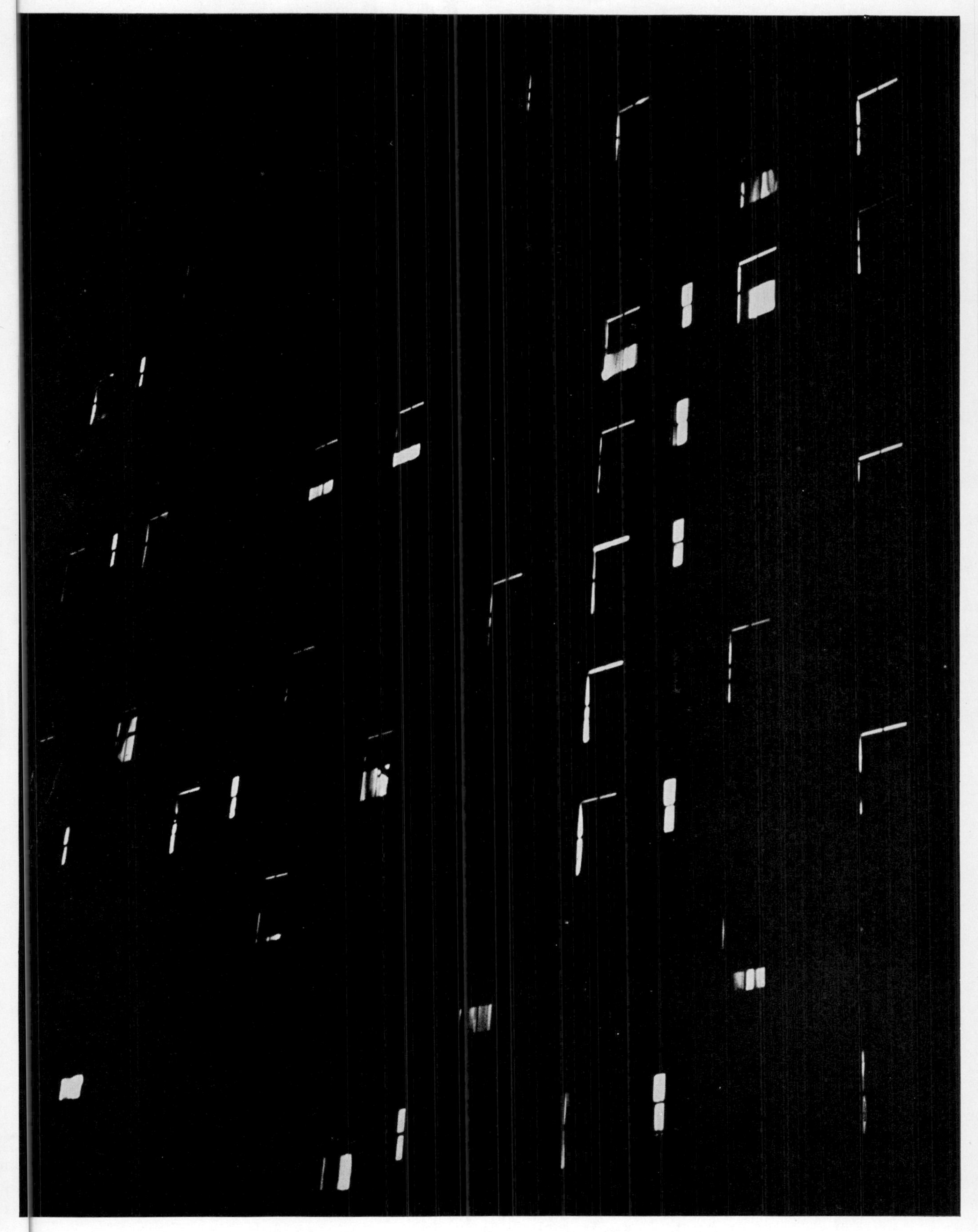

Dim-out 1943. Symbolization of the feeling of tenseness and suspense through darkness. Repetition of identical forms—the L-shaped cracks of light leaking from behind the black-out curtains—suggests masses of people hiding behind darkness, united in fear. . . .

Photograph by Margaret Bourke-White, courtesy *Life* Magazine.

Ruins of a German town—symbolic of war, destruction, and despair. Shadow used as form (see page 315), to reconstruct the ghostlike shadow of a once beautiful and happy little town.

light, its negative form, is shadow and darkness, suggesting unreality, mystery, seriousness, and fear, elements that are closely associated with "mood"—as we know it in photography. So, if he wants to emphasize a feeling rather than the subject he is depicting, the photographer should try to "say it with shadows" instead of light. An excellent example is the photograph above, which suggests war's terrible desolation by means of the *shadows* of burned-out buildings. Notice, the naked walls of the ruins themselves are barely discernible—reality is treated negligently in this picture—but the resulting feeling of utter misery is masterfully brought out through the medium of ghostlike shadows, creating with this "city of shadows" a mood of horror and destruction that nobody will easily forget.

→

Photograph by Philippe Halsma

"Mood" in portraiture. Dramatizing a sensitive face with light and shadow (the photographe Weegee, photographed by Philippe-Halsman). Notice how carefully detail is restricted . . . wir finder of the camera, police card, and cigar are merely indicated . . . darkness here symbolize night, the time when Weegee the photo-reporter is on the prowl . . .

APR.
PRESS
THE BEARER

Pennsylvania Station, New York City, during the dim-out, 1943. *Left:* Undodged, "straight" print, a documentary picture without much feeling. *Right:* Picture made from same negative as left, but corners of print "burned in." Additional darkness creates a somber, war-conscious effect, reflecting the thoughts of people saying good-by under the flag. . . .

In contrast to this symbolization of ravage, feel the warmth and coziness radiating from the picture on the opposite page. Again, the objects depicted here are only media for the creation of a mood, and the treatment confirms in every respect the principles outlined on page 308. But this time, the theme of the photographer was *light.* A lantern is the focal point of the picture, and the deep surrounding shadows serve only to make its brightness appear more radiant in contrast to their own darkness. Again, objects are indicated only sparsely, their nature chosen with intent to lead the thoughts of the beholder towards warmth, security, and peace. . . .

Shadow can be darkness, and shadow can be form; examples for both were given in the two preceding pictures. As darkness, shadow serves admirably to hold a composition together—to "frame" the motif proper (see pages 248-249)—and to make white and light stand out more brilliantly in contrast to its own blackness. This emotional quality of darkness can be emphasized even further when enlarging a "moody" negative by "burning in" the corners of the print, i.e., by giving them additional exposure to make them darker than they would have printed if left alone, thus creating a framelike effect (see the two pictures above). Many a negative that would look comparatively uninteresting if printed "straight" will acquire a surprisingly "dramatic" quality as a result of this "trick."

Photograph by Fritz Goro, courtesy *Life* Magazine

Symbolic of homelike security—shadow used as darkness. The focal point of the picture is light, its radiance made even brighter by contrasting it with the darkness of its surrounding, creating a feeling of warmth and coziness. The nature of the objects, selected by the photographer to symbolize the mood he wanted to create, suggests quiet and peace.

Photograph by Walter Sanders, courtesy *Life* Magazine.

House of Morgan, at half-mast. Sleet falling in Wall Street on the day of J. P. Morgan's death conveniently symbolized the drab misery of mourning. Photographically, notice deliberate use of monotonous gray tones (the "mono-tone"!), reduced contrasts to indicate a depressing mood.

As form, shadows can make a picture more interesting through the grotesqueness of their shapes. In this respect, an object and its shadow are reminiscent of Dr. Jekyll and Mr. Hyde: here conventional reality, there fantastically distorted dream. Frequently, a photographer can create his own opportunity when striving for "mood" by placing his lights low so that they will cast strange shadows on walls and ceiling. Especially in portraiture, illumination from below can produce the weirdest and most dreamlike expressions. Light from below is rare in nature, and thus automatically seems "unreal"; lighting faces from beneath will make them look like the faces of witches sitting around a brewing cauldron.

Occasionally, carefully restrained unsharpness, which should never go too far, can be used to blur reality in a photograph and to induce a feeling of mood (see picture on page 285), provided there is a reason for softness. Some legitimate reasons: an attempt to symbolize "heat" (remember the vibrations of hot air over a car radiator?), or fog (which seems to blur the shapes of things), or night (when objects cannot be seen as clearly as in daylight; see picture on page 360), or brilliant light (which blinds the eye to a certain degree—and the lens, too), or whenever a photographer wants to create a dreamlike effect in a picture.

However, in my opinion, such unsharpness should be treated with the same respect as a good poison, which can have a beneficial effect if taken knowingly in minute quantities, but if taken at the wrong time or in too great a dose, will prove fatal.

BACK LIGHT

Years ago, the first rule for successful picture-taking was that the source of light had to be behind the camera (remember?). Technical reasons made this more or less a necessity, but today, in the age of anti-halo emulsions and coated lenses, rather the opposite is true, and one of the surest ways to improve almost any illumination is to add a touch of back light (the accent light on page 300 is a certain form of back light).

By "back light" we mean any kind of light that is directed more or less against the camera, lighting the subject wholly or partly from the rear (as seen from the camera). If properly placed, its good influence on a photograph is threefold: it separates objects in depth by outlining them with a halolike "silver lining"; it improves the illusion of space by throwing perspective-creating shadows toward the camera (see picture on page 291); and it facilitates the rendering of surface texture.

Back light is one of the most photogenic forms of illumination, since it almost automatically creates strong, dramatic contrasts between white and black, highlights and shadows (see picture on page 249). It can serve equally well to reveal

delicate detail, or to simplify composition with masses of shadow and veils of light (see picture on page 290). Back light animates almost any motif, makes water glistening and alive (picture page 280), weaves halos around the hair of beautiful women, and even glamorizes others not so beautiful. . . . Back light permits placing accents where they will do the most good and helps to hide undesirable features in shadow. It makes clouds more luminous, wet streets more sparkling, shiny objects brighter, and the very air and space itself visible with radiant shafts of light breaking through the clouds at sunset. . . .

Any conceivable source of light can be used for back-light illumination: outdoors, the sun, or street lights at night; indoors, spots of floods or flashbulbs. The only danger a photographer faces when using back light is flares or undesired halation on the film. If working with a coated lens and anti-halo film, of course, even shots directly into the light are possible today. Otherwise, only groundglass observation can tell whether flares are present, since different lenses react differently, even when used under otherwise identical conditions. Ordinary lens shades are usually much too short to prevent back light from striking the lens; better, watch whether the lens itself is lighted by back light, and, if so, shade it with the help of a screen between light and lens, the hand, a hat, etc., but not enough to cut off part of the image.

Backlighting can be used either as auxiliary illumination for better rendering of texture and for background separation, or by itself. Examples showing back light as the only source of illumination are the photographs on page 321 and on the opposite page, proving with an outdoor and an indoor shot, respectively, that under certain conditions shooting smack into the light is the best way of getting an outstanding picture. Notice, however, that in both cases the actual source of light was hidden from the camera. In the indoor shot, the groundglass background acted as a diffuser that softened the light sufficiently to avoid the danger of flares on the film, while in the outdoor shot, the rising sun was hidden behind the largest cactus.

Under different conditions, however, or when using a coated lens (see page 176), the source of back light can itself be included to improve a photograph even further. Such occasions will arise outdoors about sunrise and sundown, when the disk of the sun, dimmed by haze or misty clouds, can become the very focal point of a picture. Or indoors or at night, when a back-light-giving desklamp, store front, street light, movie entrance, etc., provides a background of light against which an object can be outlined in relief-like silhouette, showing only a minimum of shadow detail brought out by a carefully restrained fill-in (outdoors at night: fill in with a highly diffused flashbulb at the camera, combine with short time exposures).

← Laboratory glassware. All illumination comes from behind a piece of groundglass, which serves as a background for the glass vessels. An example of pure back light illumination without auxiliary lights or fill-ins, which would only cast disturbing reflections on the glassware.

Simplification through light and shadow.

Silhouette, graphic black and white.

TYPICAL MANIFESTATIONS

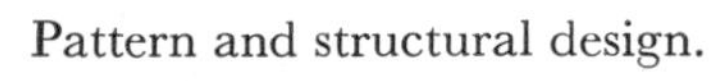

Pattern and structural design.

Long shadows toward camera.

Monumentality and impact through darkness.

Luminous clouds.

OF BACKLIGHTING

Glitter and sparkle animates water.

Reflections enliven wet streets at night.

DIRECT LIGHT

We all know that modern negative material is pretty nearly perfect (Eastman, Ansco, etc., won't let us forget that), but, paradoxically, in certain instances and for certain purposes it is already overperfected to such a degree that it can no longer do the things that it did very well not so many years ago.

I am referring here to the rendering of direct light in photography. Today, if shooting backlighted subjects (especially with a coated lens) and the source or sources of light are part of the picture (as, for instance, street lights at night), such light sources will often lose their character as "light" and look just plain "white"—small and perfectly defined pinpricks or disks of ordinary white. Such a difference between "light" and "white" may seem small, but it is significant: "light" is always luminous, radiant, often blinding, something warm and alive, while "white" is nothing but a flat and "colorless" color, or the lightest shade of gray, something that lives on borrowed light and would be black if this source of borrowed light were shut off.

If "light" thus photographed on modern negative material is reproduced in a magazine or book as a half-tone engraving, matters become even worse, for now such "light" doesn't even appear as "white," but as a muddy gray containing up to 40 per cent of black. No wonder that little of the radiance and brightness of direct light is left in pictures. . . .

Years ago, in the days of the first still imperfect anti-halo plates and films, things were different. Then the difference between light and white was apparent even in a photograph, for if something was white it was white, but if it was light it appeared luminous and radiant even in the picture, surrounded by a beautiful and symbolic halo of light resulting from diffusion within the emulsion. Examples of such halos are shown in the pictures on page 324. They are reminiscent of the halos that artists of all times have loved to draw around their renderings of light, in order to symbolize its radiant character. Photographers once had them for the asking, but purists considered them "faults" since they couldn't actually see them around their sources of light, and an obliging and progressive-minded industry soon eliminated these "flaws" by perfecting the anti-halo backing of present negative material.

The creative photographer was the loser and had to look for new means for symbolizing the radiance of direct light in his pictures. Since I have always been par-

→

Sunrise over Tucson, Arizona. Back light from the sun behind the largest cactus creates the illusion of space, converging lines of shadow delicately traced through early morning mist provide perspective, gradual increase in lightness from the silhouetted saguaros in the foreground to the hazy mountains in the distance leads the eye toward the faraway horizon.

Circular halo (glass plate).

Out-of-focus image.

MEANS FOR SYMBOLIZING

Halation on film.

Time exposure of moving lights.

Four-pointed stars (single screen).

Eight-pointed stars (double screen).

THE RADIANCE OF LIGHT

Eight-pointed clusters (double screen).

Diaphragm star pattern.

Symbolizing direct light by means of halos resulting from light reflection from the base of the emulsion (glass plates). Pictures taken in 1932. Manufacturing of these particular plates has since been discontinued, but there may still be plates on the market that will give similar results.

ticularly interested in the rendering of direct light in a photograph and its pictorial symbolization, I started considerable experimenting as soon as I found myself cut off from my source of raw material when manufacturers discontinued making the plates that made those beautiful halos. I tried different types of plates and film, found some that gave acceptable results in certain limited cases, but none that gave me as beautiful and suggestive an effect as the old-fashioned glass plates. I used soft-focus lenses and softening devices and heartily disliked the way they made the whole picture mushy, despite their good influence on certain forms of direct light (such lenses are excellent for sunlighted water and backlighted blondes). Finally, just when I was about to give up, I happened to look at the headlights of an approaching car through ordinary window screen (I was sitting on a screened porch), and noticed how this screen transformed those lights into four-pointed stars. That gave me an idea, and I began to experiment with wire cloth (brass wire) of different gauge, cutting it to fit into filter-holders, placing it in front of my lens and taking pictures of different types of light. The results were rather encouraging: a single screen transformed any bright source of light into a four-pointed star, while a double screen, made of two pieces of metal cloth, one rotated 45 degrees counter to the other, produced eight-pointed stars.

Chatham Square Elevated station, New York City. *Left:* A straight photograph, taken with an ordinary lens without filter or screen on ordinary film. *Right:* Picture taken with the same lens on the same type of film as *left*, but with a double screen in front of the lens. Notice the remarkable mprovement in the character of the lights, which all at once appear radiant.

The wire mesh of single screens used for this purpose should be medium-fine, since too fine a screen results in all-over blurredness. For double screens, however, the mesh can be rather coarse, as otherwise too little light reaches the film and the result is general unsharpness. For both types of screen, exposure times should be increased about one-third above normal to compensate for the inevitable loss of light. Shorter exposure will produce only very small stars and may result in underexposure of the picture, while with prolonged exposure the stars will keep on growing and finally may reach across the entire film, crossing each other and generally messing up the picture. Weak lights, as, for instance, lighted windows at night, are practically unaffected. If wire cloth of the right gauge is used for making the screens, the sharpness of the picture will not suffer noticeably, even if definition naturally is not quite as good as without a screen. However, since this method will be used almost exclusively for night photographs, where masses of darkness and light accents are more important than definition and fine detail, such a slight decrease in sharpness is rarely objectionable. The picture on the following page will give an idea of the kind of light effect that wire screens can produce.

Occasionally, it is possible to get pictures of street lights at night in star form

Night impression of a city. With almost super-realistic intensity, the eight-pointed lights blaze out of the night, while underneath the never-ending stream of traffic flows like a ribbon of light. . . . Can you imagine how much would have been left of this impression if this picture had been taken without the double screen, and with an instantaneous exposure (which would have been possible at $f/1.5$), instead of the time exposure recording the headlights of all the passing cars?

The Statue of Liberty at dusk. Picture taken during the wartime dim-out, 1943. The starlike pattern surrounding the few lights, produced by light reflected from the leaves of the diaphragm, indicates in pictorial form the glitter and sparkle of radiant light. The smallness of the star shapes conveys the idea of small and dimmed-down lights, reflecting the somber spirit of the dim-out.

without using any kind of screen. In such cases, the star pattern is produced by light reflected from the leaves of the diaphragm, and the stars are always small and many-pointed, the number of points corresponding to the number of leaves in the diaphragm. This phenomenon is typical only of certain lenses, while others are practically free from it. Stars of this type appear only if the lens is stopped down considerably; they are difficult to control and will always remain comparatively small. Whenever they occur, they will add welcome sparkle to the photograph, but they are too unpredictable to be of any real value. The picture of the Statue of Liberty at dusk is reproduced here as a typical example.

Photograph by George Karger from *Pix*

Picture taken with a Rodenstock *Imagon* lens. Beautiful and symbolic rendering of sparkling light. The starlike eff of glitter and radiance is due to the special correction of the lens in conjunction with interchangeable, sievelike d phragms with holes of different diameters arranged in concentric circles, permitting adjustment of the degree of ha tion in accordance with different types of light.

Waterfront street. Symbolizing light through unsharpness. Throwing the images of the street lights out of focus expands tiny white dots into big luminous circles, producing a feeling of the radiance of direct light. In a picture of this kind, where detail neither exists not matters, a slight degree of blurredness in the background only adds to the eeriness of the mood (see page 308).

All star-shaped light symbols have a certain aggressive quality, thanks to the sharpness of their points. They convey very well the idea of brilliant electric light, the glitter of city streets at night, but they are less suitable for creating a softer mood. Here the old-fashioned glass plates and their circular halos would be ideal, their soft, round shapes suggesting the mildness of gaslight, of Chinese lanterns, of big white globes radiating softly diffused light. Ever since these plates disappeared from the market I have tried to get a similar effect by other means, but so far without much success. The closest resemblance I ever got was by deliberately throwing a picture out of focus, which, of course, can be done only in a few isolated instances without ruining the entire photograph (see picture above). The idea came to me because of my nearsightedness. Looking at any kind of lights without my glasses transforms them into big radiant disks, while everything else appears unsharp and unreal, like a picture out of a dream. This dreamlike quality, unnatural though it may be, is by no means unpleasant, and more often than not, strangely fascinating. An out-of-focus photograph contains a good deal of this unrealistic effect, and occasionally it will be found that such an impression is just what is needed to depict the mood we want to convey (see page 315). This is especially true of photographs at night, when things appear magically transformed, when trees become gremlin-like figures leading a strange life of their own, and buildings loom like modern monsters with glowing eyes. . . .

The more a photograph is thrown out of focus, the larger will become the disks made by the light, but the more blurred will, of course, be the rest of the picture, too. The right degree of unsharpness is a compromise that gives enough of the disk effect without making the rest of the picture unrecognizable. A checkup on the groundglass is indispensable for satisfactory results.

The best way to symbolize direct light in motion (headlights of moving cars, flying sparks, fireworks, etc.) is by means of time exposure. We will hear about this later; see page 360. Below, and on the opposite page, are reproduced two typical examples, illustrating the suggestive power of such time exposures of moving lights.

Left: Saw cutting steel rails. Only a time exposure (here: two seconds) can record the graceful arcs of the flying sparks and give an indication of the beauty of the manufacturing process as it appears to the sustained vision of the eye.

Right: Night at the Fair. A four-second time exposure symbolizes with circles of blurred light the whirl of Ferris wheel and merry-go-round. Motion revealed in graphic form, each light recording on film the part of the path it traveled during the time the shutter of the camera was open.

FLASH

Many of our best photographers are prejudiced against flash illumination, claiming that flashbulbs produce a harsh and flat light not suitable for high-quality photography. Time and again I have seen commercial photographers of national reputation tackling assignments with batteries of big floods and spots, trying to do things that could have been done at least as well, perhaps better, and certainly easier, with flash. Generally speaking, flash is neither better nor worse than spots and floods. It is merely a different type of light that must be used differently. But the man who knows how to handle flash can often get pictures far superior to those obtainable with incandescent light, over which flash has three invaluable advantages (about the disadvantages, see page 52): 1. A flashbulb the size of a child's fist packs more punch and intensity than a 5,000-watt spot, permitting the use of smaller stops (greater depth of field) and higher shutter speeds down to hundredths of seconds (motion can be stopped, action can be taken unposed). 2. Flashbulbs can be fired with battery current, or house current of low amperage, eliminating the embarrassing nuisance of blown fuses or the necessity for temporary powerlines. 3. Flash equipment large enough for simultaneous use of a dozen or more lights can be accommodated in one large suitcase if clamp reflectors that stack tightly into each other are used; compare this with the space a dozen or more large floods and spots would take with their heavy and cumbersome stands.

Naturally, quality photographs can only occasionally be produced with only a single bulb, which in such a case would have to be on an extension and *not* at the camera. As a rule, however, it isn't quite as simple as that, and today the normal minimum for closeups is two bulbs (the main light on an extension and the fill-in at the camera), while long shots can require any number of bulbs from three on up to ten, fifteen, and more. But the ease and the simplicity with which this number can be handled, transported, set up, and fired is almost unbelievable when compared to the job it would be to work with an identical number of incandescent lights. And, if done according to the rules of good lighting, the result will in no way be inferior to those obtainable with incandescent lights—more often than not superior, for the reasons stated above.

Like any other type of artificial light, flash can never fully replace natural or local illumination. Everything we have learned so far about light and lighting still holds good for flash, too—especially what we heard about the advantages of making use of natural or local illumination, with portable lights playing only the auxiliary role of boosters and fill-ins. This means that a photographer has to restrain himself frequently, to fight the temptation to take the "easy way out" by relying completely on flash. In order to preserve typical local illumination, for instance, a combination time-and-flash exposure ("open flash") is often necessary, the time-exposure permitting the relatively dim local light to register on the film, while the flash is merely used to lighten heavy shadows, to accentuate points of interest, and to separate different objects from each other and from the background. Naturally, if cases where this is imperative are not recognized by the photographer and dealt with accordingly, the result can be nothing but a harshly lighted picture with neither feeling nor atmosphere (figuratively as well as literally)—another one of those typical "flash shots" that have discredited the whole method of flash photography. Remember whenever you see such a picture that the photographer alone is to blame, and not the process of flash photography as such. . . .

Some photographers experience difficulties when calculating the exposure times and diaphragm stops for flash pictures. To help determine these data, manufacturers of flashbulbs have computed special exposure tables for different combinations of shutter speeds, film speeds, and types of flashbulbs, assigning each such combination a so-called "guide number." When using these very handy tables, all a photographer has to do is to *find the guide number* for the combination of shutter speed, film speed, and flashbulb type he intends to use, and *to divide it by the distance in feet from flashbulb to subject. The resulting figure is the correct diaphragm stop number. Notice, however, that this stop number is correct only if direct front light is used* and needs adjustment for any other type of light. For side light, for instance, a stop one step larger has to be used, while back light demands a stop two steps larger than necessary for front light according to the table—provided that only one bulb is being used. If two or more flashbulbs are used simultaneously, *only* the one used for the main light determines the exposure, while the fill-ins and back-light bulbs have to be disregarded when making the exposure calculations. If several bulbs are used together as the source of main light, all directed side by side toward the same subject, either the time of exposure should be divided by the number of these bulbs, or the diaphragm should be stopped down one step for each two bulbs. If in an over-all shot a number of flash bulbs of the same type are strung out in order to cover a large area evenly, each one being approximately the same distance from a section of the subject, this average distance should be used to determine the proper diaphragm stop for a shot made with *all* of the bulbs.

These few rules are all there is to flashbulb exposure. Following them will almost automatically lead to perfectly exposed negatives, regardless of the type of lighting or the number of bulbs being used.

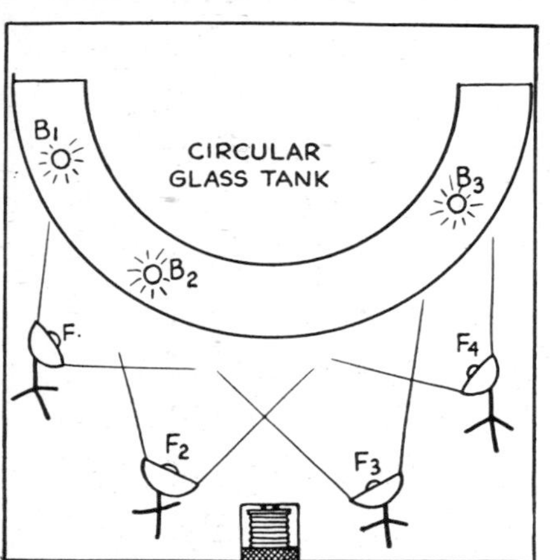

Above: Blowing blueprint cylinders at the Corning glass works, Corning, N. Y.

Diagram of illumination at left: *B-1, B-2, B-3* are three Press 40 flashbulbs for main and back light, used "naked" without reflectors for even light distribution all around, bulbs hidden behind men and objects to prevent direct light from reaching the lens. *F-1, F-2, F-3, F-4* are four fill-in lights, No. 22 flashbulbs in reflectors, spaced for even illumination of the whole setting.

All seven bulbs synchronized to camera shutter and flashed simultaneously with 115-volt house current and Abbey multiple flash at *f* 11 and 1/50 second.

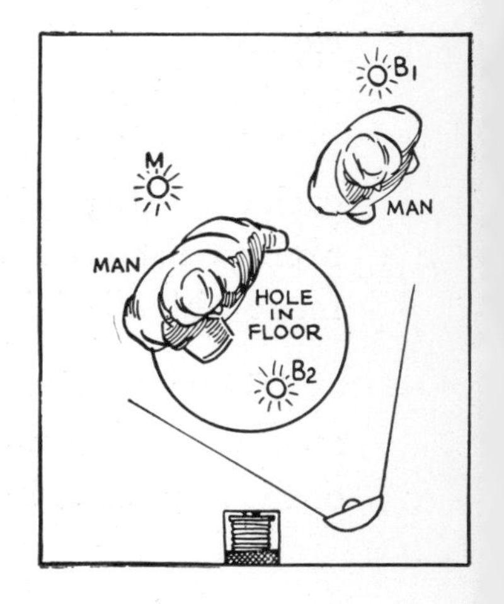

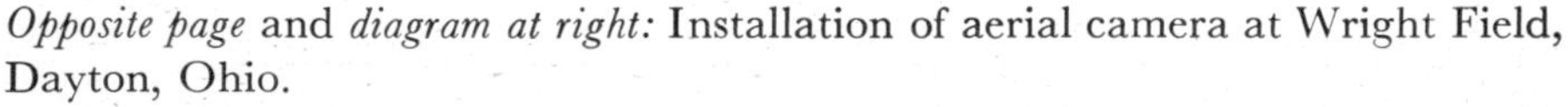

Opposite page and *diagram at right:* Installation of aerial camera at Wright Field, Dayton, Ohio.

Illumination with four flashbulbs. *M* is the main light, a No. 22 flashbulb used as side and back light. *B-1* and *B-2* are two Press 40 bulbs used as back light without any reflectors, *B-1* hidden behind a man and *B-2* inserted into camera hole in plane floor to light up hole and front of aerial camera. A Press 40 fill-in was used at the camera, held high up on an extension to avoid shadows behind men on background. All four bulbs synchronized to camera and flashed with four-cell battery, exposure 1/250 second at *f*16.

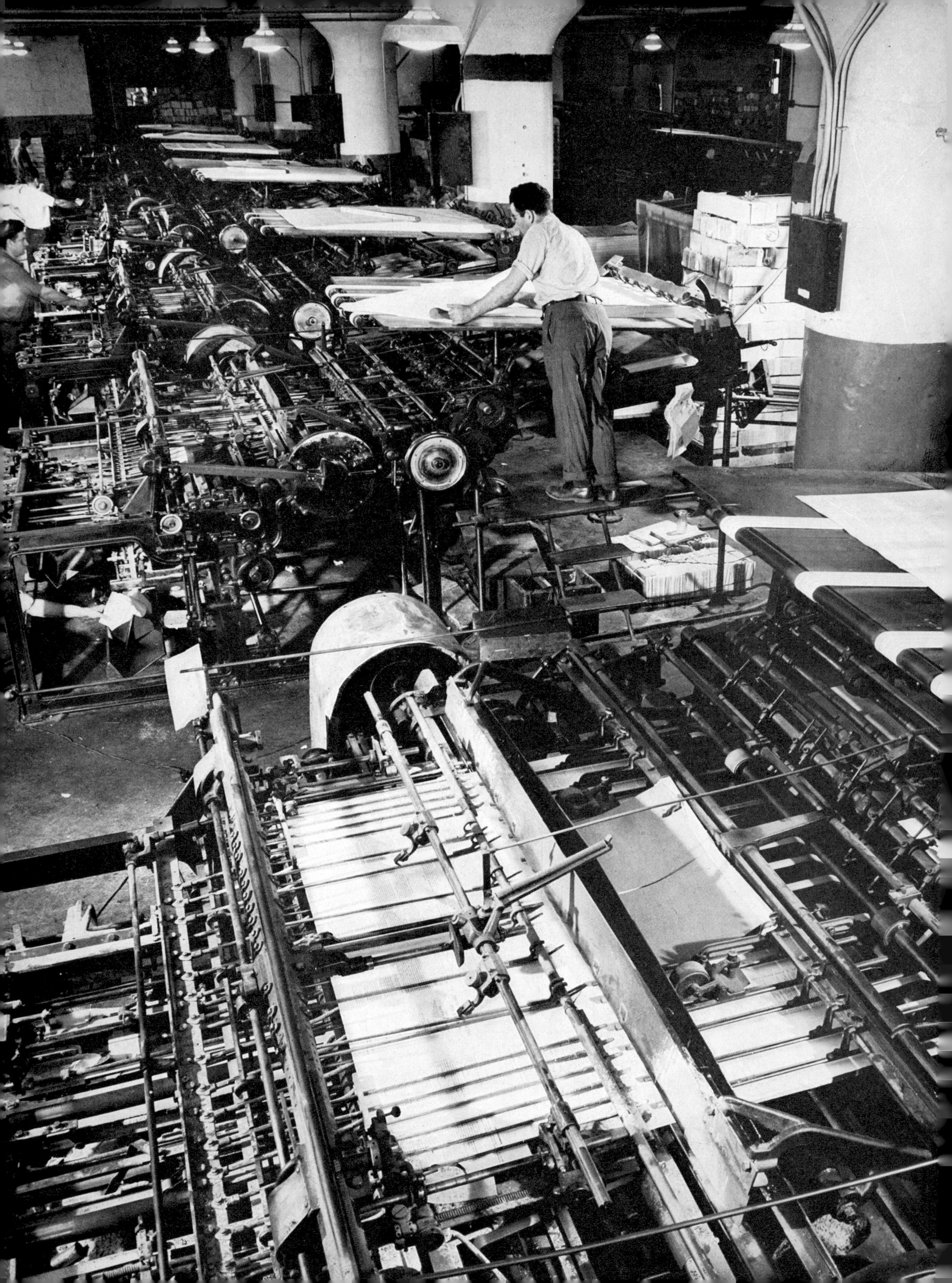

Above: Final checkup at the Curtis propeller plant, Clifton, New Jersey.

Combination time and flash exposure (see illumination diagram at right): daylight through the skylight provides the main illumination together with *M* a No. 22 flashbulb. *F* is the fill-in, another No. 22 flash twice as far away from the object as *M* and thus much weaker in effect.

Picture taken late in the afternoon, with daylight already rather weak. Shot at *f* 22, open flash plus five seconds time exposure.

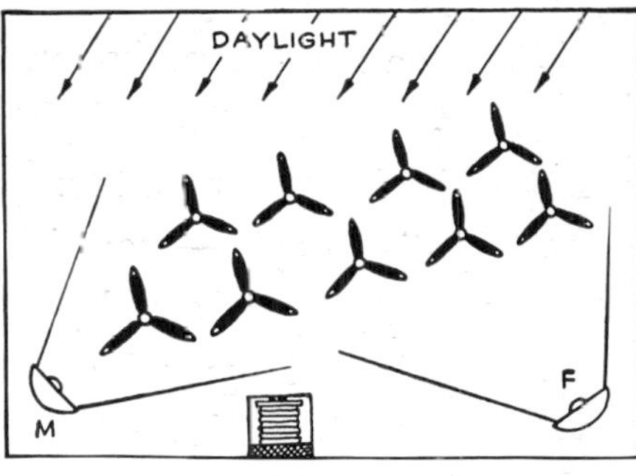

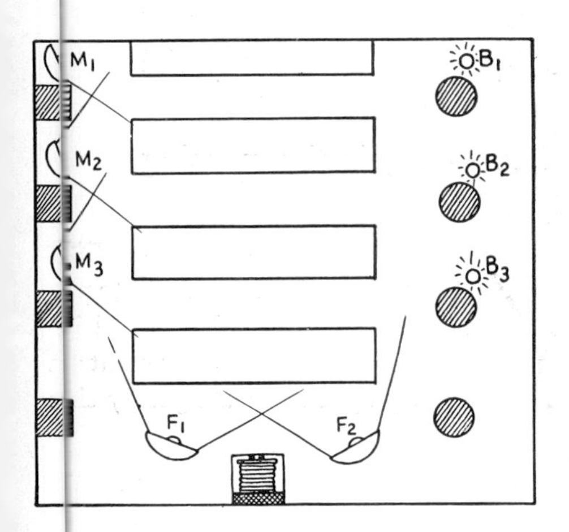

Opposite page and *diagram at left:* Folding machines at H. Wolff, book manufacturers, New York. A typical example of multiple-flash picture where each bulb is assigned to illuminate only a small section.

M-1, M-2, M-3 are three No. 22 flashbulbs acting as main lights, placed inside the window-casings to boost the weak daylight. *B-1, B-2, B-3* are three Press 50 flashbulbs used without reflectors as back light hidden behind pillars from the lens. *F-1, F-2* are two fill-ins, No. 22 flashbulbs in reflectors, placed on both sides of the camera.

Picture taken with "open flash" (i.e., the shutter was set on "time" and opened, the flashes were fired with a switch instead of being synchronized to a high shutter speed, and the lens was closed again), at *f* 22.

DAYLIGHT

Practically everything we have heard so far about good and bad lighting applies to daylight, too—especially the sections on back light and lighting for texture and mood. But while previously we had as many individual lights to work with as the occasion warranted, we now have to solve all our lighting problems with the help of only a single source of light—the sun. This handicap, of course, makes certain forms of lighting impossible, and will generally tax not only the ingenuity and resourcefulness of the photographer to a much higher degree than artificial light, but even more so his *patience*, since now he cannot shift his lights around at will, but is obliged to wait patiently until the sun has reached a favorable position. We have here a typical case where Mohammed must go to the Mountain, since this Mountain certainly won't come to Mohammed, the photographer. . . .

While taking mediocre outdoor shots is the easiest of all forms of photography, nothing is more difficult than making really first-class outdoor pictures. You can check this for yourself by trying to remember how many of all the outdoor photographs that you have seen made a lasting impression on you—compared with the percentage of other types of pictures.

The reason: outdoor photographs *seem* so easy. . . . If only the sun is shining high and bright, the whole world, full of light and color, smiles gay invitation to the cameraman. Too late he realizes that actually there was *too much light* (and too little shadow), and that color doesn't count for much in black-and-white photography if translated carelessly into contrastless shades of gray.

Two words must be learned if one is to avoid such pitfalls and disappointments in outdoor photography: "discrimination" and "self-restraint." *Before* you release the shutter make sure that your subject is "photogenic," that it shows the right balance between light and shadow (especially shadow), and that it isn't only meaningless color that tempts you to take a shot. . . . And if you are convinced that after all—maybe— conditions *aren't* quite right for a successful picture, then *leave it alone!* Satisfy your soul by taking in the beauty of the scenery with your eyes, and preserve it in all its grandeur in your memory—but don't degrade it by taking a meaningless snapshot which through its very insignificance eventually will only destroy the colorful image you hold in memory.

As a rule, the best times for outdoor pictures are the hours early in the morning

→

Moonrise over Manhattan. Patience is one of the first conditions for successful outdoor photography. Many times had I seen the moon rise over Manhattan, but it took me seven years and innumerable unsuccessful attempts before I finally succeeded in capturing this spectacular sight on film. This picture was taken with a telephoto lens of 40 inches focal length from the Jersey side across the Hudson River.

and late in the afternoon, when the low sun casts long pictorial shadows that bring out forms and textures equally well (see picture page 321). Around noon, the sun is usually too high, and light becomes flat and expressionless (occasionally, of course, this may be just what a photographer needs to create a certain mood).

> On outdoor assignments, early morning and late afternoon should be the time for work, while noon should be the time for rest—or travel.

Unfortunately, however, just the opposite of the above is usually the case: a photographer goes out in the morning, arrives at the scene of shooting at noon, takes his pictures when light is at its worst and tries to get back in time for dinner. This may be another reason for the predominance of meaningless outdoor pictures. . . .

Control over daylight is naturally more limited than over artificial light, a good part of it being confined to the negative qualities of selection and limitation. Instead of moving the source of light we have to move the subject into the right position for best illumination, which is simple with regard to persons or easily movable objects, but can require an awful lot of patience if it is a building or a landscape and the photographer has to wait for the earth itself to move around far enough to bring the object into proper position with regard to the sun. Frequently, being half an hour too late necessitates a full day's wait before illumination is right again—provided it doesn't rain the next day. . . .

Much more than in indoor photography, filters play an important part in providing the necessary contrasts through controlled color separation—contrasts which indoors would have been created with the help of auxiliary lights. But in spite of all these difficulties, a surprisingly great amount of control can be exercised over daylight by the man who knows how, and even the appearance of everyday objects can be changed to a great degree—from flat to contrasty, from light to dark, from gay to somber, etc.

When worried about daylight that doesn't seem right, be patient and remember that things are bound to change sooner or later (I know your time is limited, but trying to save time by rushing the shooting in spite of adverse conditions actually means wasting time, since bad pictures are of no more value than no pictures at all). Watch how daylight changes with the time of the day, with the seasons, and with atmospheric conditions. Notice how sometimes on windy and cloudy days the sun breaks through the overcast and lights up parts of the landscape like a giant spotlight; watch these patches of light racing across the countryside and shoot when they reach the point you want to emphasize. If the light seems flat in one direction, turn

Utah State Prison, Salt Lake City. A combination backlighted sun and indoor flash exposure. Notice how back light from the sun just skims along the prison wall and brings out its stone texture, while the source of light itself, the sun, is hidden behind the awning to prevent it from striking the lens and causing flares on the film. A single flashbulb on an extension to the right illuminates the interior of the guardhouse just enough to reveal detail, but not so much as to give an unnatural appearance of artificial light. The whole secret of such a combination, sun and flash exposure, is proper balance of light, with the sun playing the role of main light and the flash the role of the carefully restrained fill-in.

around—it may be different. Remember, in daylight, too, back light is always the most pictorial illumination, lending sparkle to water and beach grass alike when shooting pictures at the seashore, glamorizing people as well as landscapes, and providing dramatic contrasts even where other means of dramatizing fail. . . .

Learn how to evaluate color in terms of black and white, so you will be able to use filters intelligently for the creation of contrasts through color separation when translating colors into shades of gray. Always keep an eye out for clouds, they can enliven even the dullest photograph. Use filters to make them stand out contrastfully against the blue of the sky (see page 227). If shooting people, watch your background; try to keep it clean. There is no better background for outdoor pictures of people or for portraits than the sky. Hold your camera close to the ground and shoot upward at an angle; outline your figures against the sky. Avoid daylight flash for filling in shadow—all advertisements to the contrary. It is bad technique and bad taste. Rather, learn how to make use of sunlight or skylight reflected from bright objects—a whitewashed wall, a pastel dress, or the clean sand at the beach. Use this reflected light to lighten shadows in faces or figures which otherwise would photograph too dark. If no such natural reflectors are handy, make your own: a piece of white board or cloth, a shirt. Get somebody else to hold it while you take the picture, or prop it up with sticks, or fasten it to some object with safety pins. . . . A little ingenuity will get you out of almost any difficulty. . . . Never forget, the difference between a good and a bad photographer is a difference in approach (to the picture), in selection (of subject), in creation (of a theme), and in presentation (of the final composition). . . . And *not* in their equipment.

SUMMING UP—Twenty-five pointers on good lighting

Whenever possible, make use of natural light or local illumination.

When using artificial light, build up illumination step by step; never add a new light before the previous one is placed to your satisfaction.

Flat front light and single flash at the camera are the worst of all types of illumination; try to avoid them under any circumstances.

Side light brings out texture, which is often the only clue to the identity of an object.

Sunlight and spotlights are better for rendering texture than are floods.

Back light separates objects in depth and is pictorially the most dramatic and exciting form of light.

The back light is the most important of all your lights. Even if several flashbulbs fail to fire, you may still have a picture if your back light went off.

Watch out for "blind spots" in faces when lighting portraits. You'll find them in the corners of the eyes, the angles between nose and mouth, and underneath the jaw. Use fill-ins to make them light enough to show detail.

In portraiture, the nose casts the most important shadow. Never let it touch or cross the lips.

Shadows from different sources of light should never cross each other openly. Shadows within shadows signify the beginner or the blunderer.

Always place your fill-in lights high, so that their shadows will fall low. Few things are uglier than meaningless shadows from low-placed fill-ins messing up an otherwise clean background.

Balance your lighting. Keep your fill-in rather too weak than too strong. And don't forget your back light.

A fill-in that is too strong has the same effect as single flash at the camera.

Always keep your fill-in well diffused in order to avoid the danger of shadows within shadows.

Concentrate your light toward the depth and keep your foreground darker.

A dark foreground has the effect of a frame on your picture. It leads the eye toward the center of the photograph where interest belongs.

Light foreground combined with dark background gives an artificial night effect, typical of single flash at the camera. People in the foreground look like plaster dummies, faces in the background appear black. Don't let this happen to you.

If you like your photographs snappy and sparkling, make sure that you have pure white and pure black somewhere in your picture.

Don't be afraid of jet-black detail-less shadows, as long as such shadows are expressive in form and placed right with regard to composition.

Light attracts the eye more than darkness. Use light to accent your pictures, to guide the eye to points of interest within the photograph.

Be careful when placing spots of brightness close to the edge of a picture. They may lead the eye out of your photograph.

Differentiate between white and light. If you have to photograph a source of direct light, indicate its nature with a symbolic treatment, which will make it look different from a mere spot of white.

Light is the strongest creator of moods. Make use of its potentialities.

A light all-over treatment suggests happiness, joy and youth, sunshine, warmth and friendliness. A dark all-over treatment indicates seriousness and sorrow, night, loneliness and fear, strength and power, problems, drama. . . .

Dramatize with light and shadow, create expressive contrasts between white and black, simplify and symbolize. . . .

CHAPTER 13

MOTION

IN CONTRAST to "moving pictures," every single photograph, even the most violent action shot, is a "still." Nothing that happens in time and space—a change, a motion—can be photographed instantaneously without stripping it of its most outstanding quality: movement, the element of time. . . . No ordinary action shot can "reproduce" an action, because it reduces change and movement—the basis of all action—to a standstill, freezing it into immobility. . . . In photographing action, more than anywhere else in still photography, we must rely on "symbols" and on "translation" if we are to capture the essence of that action in a "still."

When taking a photograph we open the shutter for a certain time so that the light can get through the lens at the film and leave an impression on the emulsion. This is the moment when "time" can influence the rendering of the picture—*if* we give it "enough time"—and I mean this literally! Ordinarily, the faster the action, the higher shutter speed the photographer must use in order to "stop" this action, to "freeze" it into sharply defined immobility. These photographic terms "stopping" and "freezing" are significant. Most photographers don't even want a picture of the real action—they want a needle-sharp photograph, and the sharper it is, the more stiffly frozen, the prouder they are of themselves and their "fast" cameras and lenses. But the spirit of the action, its direction, speed, character, is lost. . . . They won't give it "time enough" to leave its imprint—the blurredness that provides the first indication of action—the streaky unsharpness the eye associates with speed—on the film.

How many times have you seen, in a railroad ticket office or on a wall calendar, a blowup of a crack train, photographed "at full speed," but needle-sharp with detail. How the picture was actually taken is irrelevant, but didn't the train *look* as though it were standing still?

When did you ever see a streamliner roar past with this supernatural sharpness? Rather, didn't it appear to you as a blast of staccato flashes merging into one blurred streak, thundering ahead in a shock-wave of air over trembling ground, gone as abruptly as it came?

In contrast to this tame train "speeding along at 80 miles per hour," have a look at one of Robert Capa's immortal invasion photographs, taken on D-Day on the beaches of Normandy (*opposite*): your first impression is blur and unsharpness, flatness, low contrast . . . from the viewpoint of the photo-perfectionist, this

Photograph by Robert Capa, courtesy *Life* Magazine

D-Day, 1944. Storming the beaches of Normandy.

picture is a flop. . . . But seen as human documents, these same, apparently technically "bad" photographs pack the most terrific emotional wallop I have ever seen crammed into "stills" in my life—and I must have seen tens of thousands of photographs, among them very many of the world's best. . . . Just that same blurredness and flatness that makes them "technically bad" is what gives them their emotional punch: it makes you almost physically *feel* the concussion of heavy guns, the trembling before the barrage, gives you a taste of salty spray, the clammy feeling of being soaked to the skin, the numbness of ice-cold hands still holding on to automatic rifles, puts you right amidst these men struggling through swirling water and whining bullets on to the beaches, to blood and death and victory. . . .

If these pictures were "technically perfect," contrastful, nice and clean and sharp, they would look as pretty-pretty and as false as a Hollywood set—and leave you emotionally as cold. . . . It is the reality of *action*, masterfully expressed in terms of photography, that shocks you to the core.

Naturally, I am not advocating that from now on, every action, every object in motion should be photographed blurred. As always, a photographer has to use common sense and discretion in deciding whether to use one medium of expression or another. What I want to get across here is simply the idea that it isn't the degree of sharpness that makes an action shot good or bad, as the majority of photographers (and picture editors, too) seem to believe, but the impression it makes on the beholder. If his first thought is, "Golly, how beautifully sharp!"—the picture probably is not too good. But if the contents of the photograph affect him somehow emotionally or intellectually before he notices its technical execution, the picture has served its purpose. This fact alone should be enough to classify it as a *good* photograph, regardless of whether it is blurred or sharp.

The decision between sharp or blurred action rendition depends on a number of different factors. Most important is speed: the faster a movement actually is, the more blurred it appears to the eye, and the more reason for a blurred rendering. Even in real life we gauge the speed of moving objects frequently by their degree of apparent blurredness, and the more unsharp they appear, the greater we know their speed to be. In this respect it doesn't matter *where* the blurredness occurs—in the object itself or in the background. Often we follow a moving object with our eyes, keeping it centered within our field of vision (as, for instance, horses on a race track). In such a case, however, the background behind the moving object will look blurred, and its degree of blurredness will be the indicator from which to gauge the moving object's speed. Without such contrast between sharpness and blurredness, speed is very difficult to judge. Following a low-flying plane in a cloudless sky with the eyes, the plane will always appear sharp and its speed not very impressive, because we have no means of measuring it against a background at rest. But if we were inside this same plane and looked at the earth, watching the ground race past some part of the plane in streaky blurredness (this part of the plane being at rest relative to us), this same "speed" would now appear terrific.

Thus, by controlling the degree of blurredness in our pictures, by playing it up or playing it down, we can control the feeling of movement, speeding action up, slowing action down, or making it appear as we felt it. Speed is relative too, and motion that appears fast to one photographer may seem slow to another who is used to much higher speeds.

Next to its speed, the character of an object in motion should decide its treatment in an action shot. In this respect, we have to differentiate between two types of objects: those that always look the same, in motion or at rest; and those that change their appearance the moment they begin to move. In the first category belong all inanimate objects, like cars, locomotives, trains, plains, ships, etc. (While themselves remaining the same, they may nevertheless produce direct effects indicating motion: the wake of a ship, smoke trailing a locomotive.) In the second class belong all living beings, people and animals alike. From the way they hold their legs and arms and wings as well as from their general appearance in outline, we can tell at once if they are in motion or at rest. Objects belonging to this second class can usually be photographed either sharp or blurred, depending on the speed of action, and seldom will there be any doubt as to whether they were moving or standing still. When we see the picture of a bathing beauty diving head-first through the air, needle-sharp against a cloudless sky, we never for a moment believe that she is standing still in mid-air, but from the way she is dressed and from the position of her body we rightly deduce that she has just jumped from a springboard and is enroute to the water, even if neither the one nor the other is shown in the picture.

Of course, we can always add a touch of blurredness to such an otherwise sharp picture, selecting a shutter speed that will make only the object's fastest moving parts appear slightly blurred—a hand, a foot, a hoof, a wing—not so much to indicate motion that is already evident, but rather to stress the feeling of *speed*, to indicate the *rate* of such motion. There are always certain situations which obviously cannot occur at rest—a horse over a hurdle, a football player standing on his head in the middle of a game, etc. In such cases a photographer can go right ahead without worrying much about how to symbolize motion in a "still"—the photograph will look animated because of the very nature of its subject.

Quite the opposite is true with regard to pictures of inanimate objects. With very few exceptions—as, for instance, an airplane in flight—we cannot tell from a sharp photograph of such an object if it was in motion or at rest when the picture was taken, and even less do we sense its speed. In such cases, motion and speed have to be symbolized through controlled blurredness, either of the object itself, or of its background, or have to be otherwise indicated by means of dynamic composition. Combination of both will usually produce the most convincing feeling of speed.

MOVEMENT THROUGH COMPOSITION

Unlike most beginners, who carefully center their subjects in their pictures, more experienced photographers exert equally great care to avoid such symmetry, knowing that it tends to make a picture dull and tensionless. With regard to action pictures, symmetry means balance, balance suggests rests, and rest is the opposite of motion and action. Consequently, the first thing to avoid when composing an action shot is having the action take place in the dead center of the picture.

6200

The same reasoning holds true with regard to lines. Horizontals and verticals are "static" symbols, representing equilibrium and suggesting order, symmetry, and rest. Composing an object in motion perfectly horizontally is the surest way of counteracting and destroying any feeling of speed we may have been able to inject through use of controlled blurredness. On the other hand, deviation from these lines of rest immediately implies action. Tilting an object in a picture seems to throw it out of balance, makes it slip, sets it in motion . . . A good example is the picture on this and the opposite page, showing a locomotive at full speed. Since this was a technical demonstration photograph, where detail is of greatest importance, blurredness as a medium for suggesting speed could not be used, and the shot was taken at 1/500 second. A "regular" print, with the engine in a "natural" horizontal-vertical position, gave not the slightest impression of motion, let alone of "speed." Tilting the locomotive ever so slightly, however, immediately produced a very definite illusion of high-speed motion . . .

Turbine locomotive of the Pennsylvania Railroad crossing the Susquehanna near Harrisburg, Pa.

Explanation of this print and that on the opposite page is in the text above. Both prints made from the same negative, the only difference being in cropping.

Ninth Avenue Elevated, New York, 1940. Straight and bold, the tracks bisect the photograph from corner to corner, following the diagonal, the line of action, the longest straight line in any picture, transferring some of their dynamic power to the elevated train speeding down the center track.

Tilting an object in a photograph transforms its verticals and horizontals into diagonals, or near-diagonals, with similar effect. Diagonals are the longest possible straight lines in any picture, the longest possible distance an object could travel through a photograph, and thus they imply action and speed. Artists have long known about this peculiar capacity of diagonals to suggest movement and action, and whenever a painter wants to dramatize, for instance, a fighter plane, he depicts it either climbing or diving or peeling off—showing it in a diagonal position, but never in level flights, which would suggest tensionless stability and would be the correct way to portray a commercial airliner. . . .

Photographers can make use of these facts in several ways: by tilting the image of an object in motion (see picture on page 348); by composing the photograph so that the action takes place somewhere along one of the diagonals of the picture, but of course not in its center; or by combining the advantages of both possibilities. The picture below and the one on the opposite page illustrate some of the possibilities of diagonal composition.

Symbolizing speed through composition. Diagonals—lines of action—make this picture: the wake of the Chris-Craft racer cutting its foamy path from corner to corner, the overleaning figures of the girls trying to keep their equilibrium through the curve, the crazy tilt of the horizon suggesting the banking of the boat—all add up to give a strong impression of speed.

Photograph by Charles Steinheimer, courtesy *Life* Magazine

Fast motion is here proven by the very nature of the object—an airplane in flight cannot possibly stand still. . . . In such a case, sharp rendering is indicated, as it will improve interest by showing detail of the object in action too fast to be seen and understood by the eye.

"FREEZING" MOVEMENT AND ACTION

Whenever the presence of movement and action is obvious in a photograph either because of the nature of the object (a plane in the air) or the character of the situation, sharpness of rendering will not only not be detrimental to an impression of motion and speed, but can actually promote interest by giving the beholder an opportunity to study details of the action which in reality were too fast to be observed by the eye. A horse taking a hurdle, for instance, is so obviously in motion that no further proof in the form of blurredness, etc., is needed. On the other hand, the tense expression in the rider's face and the taut muscles of the horse, too, are unmistakable corollaries of action, and may be of even greater interest than mere speed. So, we either have to compromise, or to choose one or the other: either blurredness symbolizing speed, or sharpness recording some other equally convincing expression of action. Another opportunity for the photographer to prove that he is more than just a shutter-clicker. . . .

Technically, motion can be "stopped" in a photograph in three different ways, all based on the same principle: the faster the movement, the shorter the exposure.

1. Normally, we "stop" movement by using a "fast" enough shutter speed. In this case, the shutter stays open during exposure for a time so short that the image of the moving object has too little time to move an appreciable distance across the film while the lens is open.
   Shutter-speeds for "freezing" the motion of objects traveling at different speeds are listed in the table below.
2. If the shutter of a camera isn't equipped with speeds high enough to stop fast motion, the apparent speed of the moving object can be reduced by using the camera like a gun: get the image of the moving object in your viewfinder and keep it there by following the object with the whole camera. Trip the shutter while in motion.
   This method of reducing relative speeds can advantageously be used even when shooting at the higher shutter speeds (see above). It will result in pictures with a definite feeling of action by rendering the moving object sharp and the background behind it blurred. This is the only instance where a camera should *not* be held still while making an exposure.
3. Instead of timing an exposure with the help of a shutter, it can be timed with the help of "speedlights" that illuminate the moving object only for an extremely short moment. Such lights have to be used in a relatively dark place, too dark to illuminate the moving object enough to let it make an impression on the emulsion during the whole exposure of about 1/100 second. For it is not the shutter that times the exposure, but the flash of the speedlight which lasts from 1/500 to 1/10,000 second and has to be synchronized to the shutter. Such a flash is short enough to give a tack-sharp picture of a bullet leaving the muzzle of a gun.

The following table shows minimum exposure times for stopping movement and action.

Subject	Distance: Object-Camera	Direction of Motion	Focal Length of Lens					
			2 in.	3 in.	4 in.	5 in.	6 in.	10 in.
Pedestrians walking, or children playing, or slow-moving animals	25 ft.	↔ ↖ ↗ ↕	1/60 1/40 1/25	1/75 1/50 1/30	1/100 1/75 1/40	1/125 1/85 1/50	1/150 1/100 1/60	1/250 1/150 1/80
Horses galloping, bicycles racing, or automobiles moving 30 mph	50 ft.	↔ ↖ ↗ ↕	1/180 1/120 1/60	1/275 1/180 1/90	1/360 1/240 1/120	1/450 1/300 1/150	1/550 1/360 1/180	1/900 1/600 1/300
Horses trotting, bicycles coasting, or children racing	25 ft.	↔ ↖ ↗ ↕	1/200 1/120 1/75	1/300 1/180 1/100	1/400 1/240 1/126	1/500 1/360 1/160	1/600 1/450 1/200	1/1000 1/750 1/330
Automobiles, trains, etc., at 40-60 mph	100 ft.							
Fast athletic events	25 ft.	↔ ↖ ↗ ↕	1/300 1/200 1/100	1/425 1/300 1/150	1/550 1/400 1/200	1/700 1/500 1/250	1/850 1/600 1/300	1/1400 1/1000 1/480

All shutter speeds are in fractions of seconds and are short enough to insure adequate sharpness (the condensed table on page 102 is intended for inexpensive cameras with simple shutters and less critical demands with regard to sharpness). If a camera doesn't have the exact shutter speed recommended here, the one that is closest to it should be used. When indicated distances are doubled, exposure times may be twice as long; when distances are halved, shutter speeds have to be twice as fast.

To outline her path across the ice and through the air, *Life* photographer Gjon Mili fastened battery-fed flashlight bulbs to the skates of Carol Lynne, then photographed her with a combination time and speedlight exposure. On a stage too dimly illuminated to register on the film, the skater traced her figures in front of the camera while the shutter was open, the film registering nothing but the moving flashlights. . . . Then, at the height of a leap, Mili flashed his speedlights, getting the image of the jumping skater, waited another moment for the continuation of the movement as demonstrated by the flashlight paths and closed the shutter of his camera.

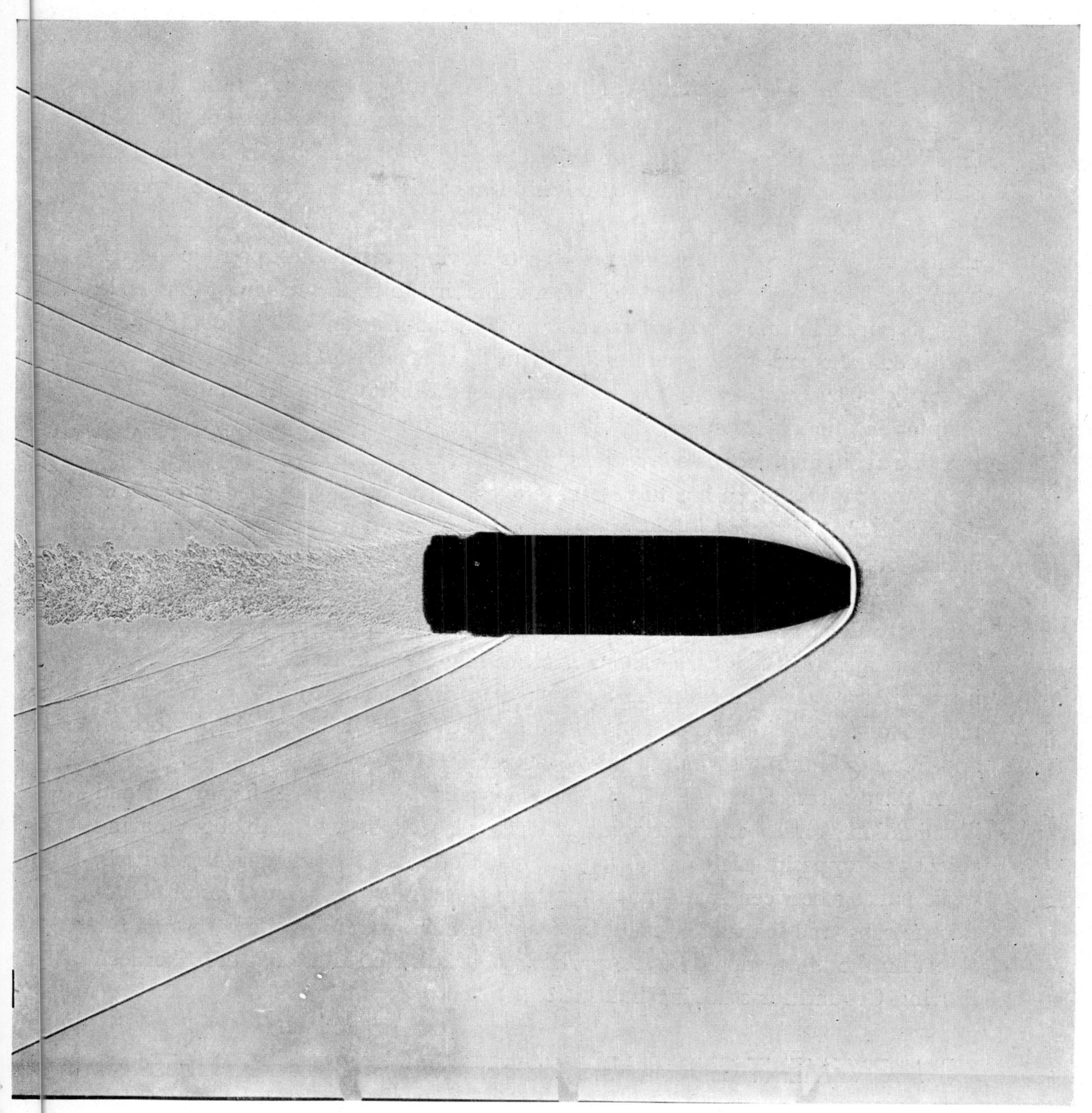

Spark photograph of a bullet in flight, taken at the Aberdeen Proving Ground.

The shortest exposure times regular camera shutters are capable of range from 1/500 to approximately 1/1400 second. This, of course, is fast enough to stop any object at ordinary speed, up to and including racing horses and cars, fast trains, vigorous athletics, etc. Beyond these speeds, however, ordinary shutters fail because of their mechanical nature and the laws of inertia, and shorter exposures have to be timed by some nonmechanical means, the most convenient of which is the "speedlight" referred to above. Instead of admitting light to the film by opening and closing the shutter, exposure is timed by the on-and-off-flash of the light that illuminates the object. The source of this light is a gas-filled tube in which an electrical discharge takes place; its duration depends on the type of the lighting unit and varies between 1/500 and 1/100,000 second. This, of course, is fast enough to give sharp pictures even of objects moving at the fastest possible speeds, from the lightning-fast wingbeat of a hummingbird to bullets leaving the muzzle of a gun or splinters ripped from armor plate at the moment of impact of a shell.

Speed lights are easily synchronized with the camera shutter, which is usually set for 1/100 or 1/250 second, during which time the light will flash, simultaneously illuminating the object, "freezing" its motion, and timing the exposure of the picture. To avoid all traces of blurredness, the general illumination of the place where the photograph is taken has to be dim enough not to register on the film during the 1/100 or 1/250 second the shutter is open. A checkup with the exposure meter under consideration of shutter speed and diaphragm stop will make sure of this.

A variation of the speedlight is the stroboscopic light, which emits a series of extremely short flashes at predetermined intervals. Photographs taken with stroboscopic light look like time exposures of moving objects, in which blurredness is interrupted at short intervals and chopped up into a sequence of needle-sharp pictures of the moving object taken along the path it traveled, resolving its motion and freezing it into a series of step-by-step single phases.

A third form of high-speed photography uses electric sparks for timing and illumination. A number of such spark-units are placed along the path of the moving object and opposite each unit is a photographic plate. The moving object itself, while passing between spark-unit and photo plate, releases, via a series of photoelectric cells, one spark after another, each of which makes a shadowgraph of the object on the plate opposite it. A spark range of this kind is used at the Aberdeen Proving Ground for studying ballistics.

MOVEMENT THROUGH CONTROLLED BLURREDNESS

One of the first photographers to recognize the speed-suggesting quality of controlled blurredness was Dr. Arnold Fanck, a German photographer who in the early thirties published a picture book on skiing. Fanck had the courage to take the illustrations for his book not with the customary focal-plane shutter at 1/1,000 second, but with an ordinary movie camera at 1/30 second. From each strip of pictures showing a certain phase of skiing he selected the most typical frames and blew them up to page or half-page size. Thanks to relatively long exposure times,

Symbolization of motion through controlled blurredness. By deliberately taking his ballet photographs at a comparatively slow shutter speed, Alexander Brodovitch attains an incomparably stronger feeling of movement than any perfectly sharp rendering could ever give.

motion was not "stopped" but appeared slightly blurred—the more so, the faster his subjects had moved. This gave a surprisingly strong feeling of action, making motion look real and alive. You could almost see those figures moving, gliding down the slopes, turning, jumping, flying through the air. Blurredness symbolized action so effectively that you practically became a skier in looking at the picture.

Instead of "freezing" motion, of showing only an infinitesimal instant from the flow of a movement, controlled blurredness enables a photographer to show within a single picture a whole sequence of such infinitesimally short phases simultaneously, enough to permit the beholder to reconstruct at least the direction of the movement. Instead of taking 33 single phases of an action in 33 single pictures at 1/1,000 second each—with no feeling of movement in any one of them—the

Forging of a heavy crankshaft at the Wyman & Gordon plant, Chicago. Flash exposure, synchronized at 1/50 second instead of the customary 1/250, short enough to stop the relatively slow motion of the workmen, but long enough to insure enough blurredness of the down-beating hammer to create a feeling of action. An example of the "happy compromise" recommended on page 347. Only the fastest-moving element in the picture appears blurred.

photographer now takes only one single picture at 1/30 second, combining the features of those 33 single phases into a short one-picture sequence. Thus, through introduction of the element of *time*, he retains a feeling of speed and direction of the actual motion, expressed in the photographically symbolic form of "blurredness."

The degree of such voluntary blurredness depends on several factors. In general, the faster an object actually moves, the more blurred can it appear in a photograph and still retain its character. Whenever we want motion to appear faster than it really was, we can accomplish it through increasingly blurred rendering; on the other hand, if a detailed rendering of a moving object is more important than its actual speed, the degree of blurredness will have to be restrained. Often a happy compromise is the best solution: by shooting at an intermediate speed, the greater part of the picture can be rendered sharp, and only the moving object's fastest-moving elements will appear blurred, as, for example, the feet of a sprinter, the fists of a boxer, or the wing-tips of a bird in flight.

Selection of a shutter speed which will give the right degree of blurredness needs some experience. The table of minimum exposures on page 353 can serve as a guide for the beginner if he prolongs the times recommended there two or three times (instead of 1/200 second, for instance, use 1/100 or 1/70 second). This will give a medium degree of blurredness, which in special cases can be increased or decreased. Wherever possible, however, it is advisable to take several different shots of the same moving object at different shutter speeds to make sure that one of them will give just the right feeling of speed. This is not amateurish waste of film, but sound practice, and customary even with the most experienced photographers. After all, what is the cost of a few frames of film when compared to the cost and effort involved in retaking a certain picture provided that a retake is possible at all?

Because of its resemblance to the very common fault of plain accidental unsharpness, controlled blurredness is a medium that isn't easy to use properly. It should never degenerate into sloppiness, and should usually be contrasted by perfect sharpness in some part of the picture, since it is just this contrast between sharp and blurred that creates the illusion of speed, similar to the space impression resulting from the contrast between sharp and unsharp we learned about in the discussion of perspective (page 282). Controlled blurredness should give that certain final touch that sets objects in motion, comparable in this respect to the indication of "slip stream" which commercial artists love to airbrush to wing tips and tails of airplanes and on radiator caps and wheel hubs of cars, in a creditable if fanciful effort to symbolize speed. Blurredness should indicate that an object is in motion, but not make a mess out of a picture. . . .

Vision of a city at night—a symphony in light and motion. Each passing car records its presence with a double line of light drawn by its headlights. Movement and action, noise, street lights and advertising signs—the whole orderly chaos of a big city at night is here symbolized in photographic form by carefully controlled blurredness. This is the impression a strange city makes on you by night when you first glimpse it in short staccato flashes through the window of a swiftly moving taxi.

MOVEMENT THROUGH TIME EXPOSURE

The maximum degree of action-suggesting blurredness is limited by the speed and nature of the moving object. If we were to expose a darkly dressed pedestrian too long, his image would appear in ghostlike transparency in the picture, with the lighter parts of the background shining through the figure, and his character as a pedestrian would be lost. And if we were to take a time exposure of Manhattan at night across the water, ferries passing through the field of vision during the exposure wouldn't register on the film at all—and would cause no blurredness either—but every single light on board would burn a fine horizontal white line across the picture, indicating the path it traveled while the shutter was open.

These two examples can teach us several interesting things: First, the more we increase the exposure time, the more the character of the moving object becomes diluted and distorted (the pedestrian who appeared transparent), until it finally

Occasionally, even a subject photographically as time-worn as the Statue of Liberty in New Yo
harbor can be transformed into a new and fascinating picture with the help of a time exposu
Instead of using the lens wide open and shooting at a minute or two, a 20-minute time exposu
was made with the diaphragm stopped down far enough to prevent the sky from registering t
light, in order to give the stars time enough to trace their paths in the sky, forming a symbo
background for the Statue.

gets completely lost (the dotlike lights of the ferry that became a line). Second, with increasing exposure time, a dark object moving in front of a light background becomes increasingly transparent and will finally disappear entirely. Incidentally, this is the reason why a darkly dressed person can walk in front of a camera during a time exposure without leaving a trace of his presence on the film; this is almost unavoidable when taking time exposures on a street at night and shouldn't worry the photographer as long as such a passer-by is dark and keeps on moving. Third, light objects moving across a darker background (the ferry lights) will register on this background, leaving a graph of the path they traveled during the exposure. Incidentally, this is the reason why at night the headlights of cars in motion appear in time exposures as long white lines running across the picture.

Of these three lessons, the first one contains a warning (don't expose too long!), the second one useful knowledge (don't worry about people crossing in front of your lens at night), while the third points the way to a new and fascinating type of picture, based on time exposures of moving lights: instead of shooting the picture at a shutter speed fast enough to stop the motion of the source of light—and being satisfied with a mere pinprick of white—we deliberately increase the time of exposure until we get the path of the moving light on the film, a diagram of its motion, a graph registering time itself. . . .

Once more photography presents us with something new, something the eye can never experience unaided: pictures of patterns drawn by light—graphic records of action and changes in time. . . .

There are quite a number of occasions when an increase in exposure time automatically increases the interest in a picture involving lights in motion. In industrial photography, flashing the shot of a welder or a grinder at the customary 1/250 second invariably kills the most attractive part of the picture, the flying sparks . . . while shooting it at a second or two will register all the forceful beauty of these bursts, the rich and graceful arcs, the drama of fire and action. City streets at night look positively empty in a picture without the diagrammatic lines of traffic traced by the headlights of passing cars. At a carnival, nothing can symbolize the noise and excitement, the ceaseless rotation of merry-go-round and Ferris wheel, as suggestively as a time exposure of whirling lights. . . . Fireworks in a photograph can be more beautiful and fascinating than they actually were, if with the help of a time exposure, a number of skimpy single bursts of rockets are added up into one well-filled picture, displaying the collected excitement of many minutes at a glance. . . . And with the help of a time exposure, occasionally even a subject as time-worn as the Statue of Liberty can be transformed into a new and fascinating picture, as witness the photograph on the preceding page.

Keystone-Underwood

A typical example of "focal-plane shutter distortion," the vertical elongation of the front wheels strikingly conveys the feeling of forward motion and speed.

MOVEMENT THROUGH FOCAL-PLANE SHUTTER DISTORTION

In contrast to between-the-lens shutters, which admit light to all parts of the film simultaneously, focal-plane shutters expose the emulsion successively either from top to bottom or sideways from left to right (or from right to left), through a wider or narrower slit (according to exposure time) in a curtain rolling down right in front of the film (near the "focal-plane," hence the name) like the lid of a roll-top desk. Naturally, even at very fast exposures the passage of the slit across the film takes a certain amount of time, and if objects traveling at very high speeds are being photographed, they will be in different positions at the beginning and at the end of the exposure. Consequently, there will be a certain amount of lateral distortion if the exposure of an object moving across the camera is made with a focal-plane shutter traveling downward. And since the top of the film is exposed before the bottom, and since the lens-projected image of an object appears upside-down on the film, the lower part of a horizontally moving object will be exposed earlier than its upper part, which in the meantime will have moved a little bit further, with the result that in the finished picture such an object will appear to lean over forwards in the direction it is going.

This typical "focal-plane shutter distortion" has rather limited practical value, since it occurs only if very fast action is photographed with shutters traveling vertically (shutters working sideways cannot have this effect for obvious reasons—unless the action is vertical), and I wouldn't mention it here at all except that:

Most photographers condemn this form of distortion simply because it is "untrue," which admittedly it is: the front wheel of the car on the preceding page was certainly round, not oval as shown in this picture. On the other hand, isn't it just this oval distortion, typical of focal-plane shutter exposure, that gives this photograph its singularly suggestive impression of speed? Doesn't this picture seem to contain the very essence of auto racing, the frenzied recklessness of the drivers, the mad dash to the finish line?

Seen from the viewpoint of the artist, focal-plane shutter distortion puts into a picture everything that symbolizes speed in graphic form: a certain touch of blurredness, direct evidence of time expressed in the time-lag between the lower and the upper parts of the moving object, and composition along diagonal lines with their implicit action. Wherever it can be used, it gives a better illusion of breathtaking speed than any other form of symbolizing action; it is pictorially suggestive and direct to the point. Commercial artists have long since recognized these possibilities, and often when they want to express speed and power in a poster or an ad, they depict a locomotive, an ocean liner, a racing car, etc., forward-bent as if reaching out for the goal. Little does it matter if they discovered this effect by themselves, or if they got the idea from focal-plane shutter distorted photographs; what matters here is that photographers who can have this effect simply for the asking, usually don't appreciate it "because it isn't true. . . ." And this isn't the only instance, either, where convention-bound photographers (and this means the majority) condemn some of their strongest means of expression because "they don't seem to be true." "Converging verticals"—expression of distance in height, "wide-angle distortion"—expression of extreme closeness, "halation"—expression of the radiance of bright light, are other typically "photographic" forms of expression which many photographers deny themselves, and even laboriously try to avoid and to counteract "because the eye doesn't see things that way. . . ." Little do they realize that in order to get a "true"-appearing picture, a photographer, thanks to the abstract nature of his medium, often has to use forms of expression that "actually" are "untrue."

MOTION AND ACTION THROUGH PICTURE SEQUENCES

There are differences between speed and speed: it is one thing to watch the Limited thunder past—120 feet per second!—while waiting at a railroad crossing, and another thing to stand at the end of a pier and see a fishing smack approaching under sail, sluggishly heaving with the swell, coming closer, rounding the break-water, jibbing, and entering the harbor at five feet a second. Two examples of motion, but what a difference in speed!

Obviously, it is quite impossible to symbolize the motions of the train and the boat by identical means. The impressions they make are far too different: there, a shock-wave of air, a flash, a blur, and everything is over; here: slow and peaceful motion giving the eye plenty of time to notice detail—oblique view approaching, side view while passing, stern view while disappearing. There it is again, the element of *time*, the factor we always have to consider when talking about speed as well as when trying to translate the feeling of speed into a picture. In the case of the train, we hadn't "time" enough to see much more than a blur. In the case of the fishing boat, we had plenty of "time" to see *and photograph* several different views.

Whenever a motion is too slow to give an impression of blur, it has to be symbolized by some other means: tilting or diagonal composition or if it is very slow, by a sequence of pictures showing different phases of its progress. In the case of the fishing vessel, such a series could be as follows:

Picture 1. The approaching boat seen from an oblique angle, still rather distant, therefore small in size. Don't enlarge the boat too much and make it appear too near! Symbolize the distance it still has to travel by placing its image rather close to the side of the picture it came from.

Picture 2. The boat is already nearer and thus much larger, almost negative filling, and seen more from the side, its image close to the center of the photograph.

Picture 3. The boat is passing our pier, as close to us as it can get. This closeness has to be expressed in the size of the image of the boat, which should fill the full frame of the film and may even be larger, so that parts of it have to be cropped off. Here, we want a real "portrait" of the vessel, rich in tone and full of detail; every block and tackle, every sail and stay rendered crisp and clear.

Picture 4. Stern view of the slowly disappearing boat, already much smaller and silhouetted, image placed close to the edge of the picture for which the boat is bound.

Analyzing such a series of pictures point for point will teach us several interesting things. There is, for instance, the difference in object size: the farther away we want the ship to appear, the smaller must we render its image, which may occasionally necessitate the use of a wide-angle lens in order to get enough sky and water around the boat (for instance, if we have to photograph a big liner instead of a small fishing vessel, and are crowded for space). Of course, it would be a simple matter either to use a telephoto lens, or to enlarge the small image of the approaching ship afterwards—but this would destroy the feeling of "approach," expressed in the smallness of the image of the ship and the distance it still has to travel before it gets to us. . . . On the other hand, the moment we have to symbolize "closeness," the moment the ship is opposite our pier, we have to make the vessel appear big and "near," and the larger and the more negative-filling the boat, the closer will it appear (a telephoto lens may come in handy here). Extreme closeness could be symbolized by showing only the center part of the ship, cropping off its ends and the top of the mast. Thus, by consciously stretching the difference in image size, we make the motion of the ship—its course—appear more "real." And we can go even further in this respect by treating the approaching and the arrived boat differently: there a simplified, "hazy" silhouette, a sharply outlined mass of gray (blue filter)—here a precisely rendered, clean-cut portrait of the boat, vividly detailed (yellow filter).

Next point to consider is the position of the boat within the picture. By placing it properly, we can further emphasize the sequence of approaching, passing, and leaving, already manifested by varying the angle of view and image size. When the ship is far away, it still must travel quite a distance before it reaches us, and this distance should be made visible in the picture, by placing the image of the approaching boat close to the edge of the picture it came from. On the other hand, a boat that has left us has already put some distance between itself and us, and this distance again should be indicated pictorially by placing the image of the ship comparatively close to the edge of the picture for which it is headed—the closer, the more pronounced the feeling of "leaving" we want.

Questions like these should first be faced in theory so that you will become familiar with them and have some idea of what to do when the time comes to face them in the field. Photographing objects in motion usually doesn't leave much time for theorizing, and the better we are prepared, the more we can concentrate on those problems that can only be solved on location. . . .

The number of single pictures necessary to describe a motion or action in a photo-series varies with the speed and nature of the subject. The slower a motion (within reason!), and the more complex an action, the greater the number of steps that have to be shown in order to compile an intelligent report, and vice versa. In the simple case of our passing boat, where motion was uniform and only three different views were possible, four pictures were enough for a complete pictorial description of the event. In complicated cases, however, the number of different steps can easily go up to ten, twenty, and even more, which makes this type of photography especially suited to the fast-shooting, economical miniature camera, and if the action is too fast for it, the "Magic-Eye" camera.

Since it is seldom possible to decide in advance how many different steps to shoot, it is always advisable to be prepared for at least three or four times the number of pictures one originally expected. Especially where fast and complicated actions have to be depicted it will happen time and again that the photographer seemingly cannot afford to miss a shot, takes it and realizes the next moment that the situation has changed for the better and necessitates another shot, more interesting than the last one and still so much like it that only one of the two could possibly be used later, making the first shot practically valueless. The same thing may happen three times within the next two minutes, but unless the photographer wants to take the risk of missing an important step in the development of the action, he cannot act differently and has to consider this waste of film the price to be paid for completeness of his story. It is an especially common fault to miss the beginning and the end of a series—the beginning because it didn't look interesting enough to shoot, and the photographer realized too late how important it is to show a situation before the action proper starts; and the end because he ran out of film.

Thus, four important rules emerge for taking picture series:

1. Take plenty of film with you—and I mean *plenty!*
2. Start shooting early enough so you don't miss the logical beginning!
3. Take 50 pictures too many rather than miss that one important shot without which the whole series may be valueless!
4. When feasible, preserve the same angle of view throughout the series.

When speaking of motion and action we shouldn't think only of the obvious motion of a passing ship, or the obvious action of a brawl. Actually, other more subtle forms of motion and action are much more frequent themes for picture series, such as the changing expressions of a woman trying on a hat, the "stationary" motion of a piece of pottery growing on the wheel, or the "quiet" action of the thrower who forms it. Here, the principles as discussed above are of course still valid, but besides, something new and equally important has to enter the picture: planning and directing on the part of the photographer.

CHAPTER 14

PLANNING AND DIRECTING THE PICTURE STORY

A PICTURE story should be taken according to a preconceived plan to insure continuity and to economize on time, material, and effort. If a photographer *happens* upon a picture story accidentally, fast thinking must substitute for a shooting script, with which he should be equipped for other than spontaneous stories. Before he goes out on a definite assignment the photographer should make himself thoroughly familiar in advance with his story's possibilities. He should select his equipment and make up his film supply accordingly, and have a picture-by-picture shooting script in his possession. Even if he doesn't follow such a script literally, which hardly ever is possible—and not always advisable anyway—it is still the best insurance for an orderly continuity and a guarantee that no important shot will be missed.

In composing such a shooting script four major points need special attention:

1. The number of different pictures depends on the complexity of the theme and the amount of space (number of pages) the story may take up when published. Space is a matter of editorial judgment. The following figures are therefore the result of my inspection and study of material—both mine and others—after publication. To fill six pages in a magazine, editors need an average of 30 pictures from which to select the 6 to 15 photographs finally used. This usually means that about 40 different shots have to be taken, out of which 30 ought to be good enough to be submitted to the editors. Figuring on an average of two different angles or different exposures on each shot this means that the photographer should have film enough to take 80 single pictures, out of which at least six should, ideally, be good and important enough for possible full-page use.

2. Every picture story should have one "lead picture," a photograph containing the essence of the whole series in one single shot. It is used in full-page or near full-page size to begin the story and to introduce its theme. Pictorially, it should be unusual and interesting enough to attract immediate attention, an "eye-catcher" which makes the reader curious to see more of the story. Trick lighting, dramatic composition, unusual perspective, or interesting framing help to achieve this effect. A picture story of the size mentioned above should have at least four shots with lead-picture possibilities.

3. The beginning, middle, and end of a picture story should be clearly and logically defined. In the case of a manufacturing story, for example, the first and last photograph should show the raw material and the finished product. The forms in which these first and last steps are presented depend on the length of the story and its theme: In a magazine story on steel, for instance, the first picture could show the ingot coming out of the soaking-pit and the last one a finished coil of sheet metal. A book on steel, however, probably would begin with mining the ore and end with the use of steel in bridges, ships, or locomotives.

4. To hold the interest aroused by the lead picture, variety in contents and size of the remaining photographs is most important. An average story should be composed of three types of pictures: over-all shots which give the general setting of the story, orientating the reader and assisting him in understanding the pictures which follow. "Long shots" of this type frequently and advantageously are taken from elevated vantage points: roofs, scaffolds, ladders, or airplanes. The next type of pictures are "medium-long shots," to which the majority of photographs in a story belong. They show people, groups, interiors, action. Finally, there is the explanatory group of "closeups," pictures taken at very close ranges showing faces, hands doing things, small objects of importance such as the working parts of machinery. Pictorially, closeups can be more interesting than any other kind of pictures. They give the photographer an opportunity to prove his imagination, to do tricks with lighting, viewpoint, and perspective, in short, to use the camera as a means of widening the field of visual experience.

While shooting pictures on location, the photographer should keep an eye open for one more thing if he is working for a magazine: photographs with cover possibilities. The main quality editors look for in a cover picture is "poster effect," which means that such a photograph should be so simple and clear in content and rendering that it can be seen and understood from a distance. To achieve this effect, three conditions should be observed: 1. The subject should be simple and clean-cut in outline, not too burdened with fine detail, and should be rendered large enough to fill most of the frame. 2. The background should be quiet and neutral in design and tone. 3. The space where the name of the magazine is to be inserted should be kept clear from important picture elements. Other points that further improve a photograph's chance to make a cover are: selection of *one* large space-filling motif instead of a group of smaller ones; the closeup of a head, for instance, usually has a better poster effect than a full figure. A sitting figure is usually better than a standing one, which because of its narrowness doesn't provide a full enough composition. The subject of a cover depends on the magazine and is related to its contents. For picture magazines, almost any subject theoretically can "make" the cover: faces of people, groups of from two to twenty persons, animals, machines, buildings, airplanes, landscapes.

There are in general three types of picture stories: First, there are those stories a photographer happens upon accidentally and in the execution of which he must depend upon theoretical knowledge and experience gained from earlier occasions. Second, there are those stories concerning which he knows in advance what to expect. In such cases he cannot take an active part in the story's development, he has to work fast and, if he misses something, knows that he has missed it for good. Third, there is the "ideal" story for which everything is staged especially for his benefit, where he knows not only from the beginning exactly what to expect, but can arrange and change things to suit his own ideas and can retake difficult shots until he is sure he gets them right. Under these last conditions, success depends in equally high degree on his ability as a photographer and on his capacity for working with people.

When assigned to photograph a story in the third group I usually follow a fixed routine, the result of many years of practical experience. I begin with a study of the shooting script, which afterward I discuss with the editor to get his personal point of view with respect to the story, to find out where he wants the emphasis and what he wishes to avoid. If I don't agree with him on certain points I suggest changes, mostly motivated by technical reasons. I always find these discussions advantageous for both editor and photographer as they prevent misunderstandings and disappointments. The editor, with "the story behind the story" in his mind, sometimes doesn't think clearly enough in terms of pictures and isn't sufficiently familiar with the possibilities and limitations of photographic technique to realize that pictures he suggests will not be interesting pictorially, important though they may be in making a story's points. If a photographer slavishly follows a shooting script the result may be disappointing to both editor and photographer. The script I always consider as simply suggestive and do not hesitate to put it aside when I learn upon inspection of the actual story situation that its points had not been fully anticipated. Rarely can they be.

When I have been briefed by the editor and have studied the script, I select my equipment for the particular job and make ready my supply of film and (if necessary) flashbulbs. I like to work with as little technical ballast as possible. I take the vast majority of all my pictures with the same camera and only two lenses (see page 10). I find that in this way I can concentrate much better on the task of picturemaking than if I waste time and thought on the selection of highly specialized tools each time before I take a shot. The result is that I always travel very light, usually with two small suitcases.

Once on location, the first thing I do is to contact the man (there is one in every story situation!) who will help me arrange things. With him I discuss the whole story in advance. I explain to him what I want, and he usually makes suggestions based on his better knowledge of the subject in hand. The good will of this contact man, who usually knows everybody we must photograph and work with, is as important as the ability of the photographer himself, and every effort should be made to obtain his confidence and cooperation.

I don't even unpack my equipment before I have become thoroughly acquainted with the place of my activities to be and have talked to most of the people who are to become the actors in the picture story. When on a big industrial assignment, for instance, I often spend all of the first day orientating myself. I let my guide show me the plant, I talk to foremen of departments where later I will take photographs and make notes on picture possibilities. I am thoroughly convinced that this practice has saved many precious hours or even days of futile camera work.

The essence of a good picture story is action, and every effort should be made by the photographer to get action or an impression of it in each picture. Action, however, more often than not would look chaotic if photographed "as is." It has to be arranged and directed before it makes a good picture. As a matter of fact, the majority of first-class action shots are not "snapped" during the original action at all, but are carefully posed re-enactments, dramatically lighted and taken from an interesting angle that frequently is not obtainable during the "real thing." Before taking an action shot, I usually watch the "actors" until I understand what they are doing, at the same time moving around them and investigating picture possibilities from every angle. After I have made up my mind how to shoot the picture, with proper consideration of background and lighting conditions, I talk to my subjects, explain what I want them to do and tell them the idea of the story. Here again, a few minutes spent on friendly talk may not only save precious time later, but will insure the quality of the picture itself, for otherwise it might turn out to be stiff and valueless.

Frequently people who are to be photographed are shy and self-conscious before the camera. They lose their spontaneity and become awkward. If he uses the psychologically right approach, a clever photographer can overcome the most serious case of self-consciousness. This he can do by keeping up a running conversation, which consists not of talking about himself but of asking leading questions designed to get his subjects to talk and, in talking, to forget the threatening camera. When faced with such a situation, the photographer should have some of the psychological wisdom of a good dentist: the more he fusses with his instruments, the more seriously he takes them and himself, the more nervous the patient becomes.

On the other hand, if the photographer handles his camera and equipment with ease and confidence, apparently paying attention only to the subject he wants to put at ease, he usually will reach his goal. I remember especially a famous scientist and inventor who was willing to pose but simply couldn't help "freezing" the moment a photographer got down to business. Before I went to Washington to try once more where so many others had failed I read up on the scientific problems he was working on at the time. From the moment I met him I did not even mention photography, but made him instead talk about his own work. At his laboratory my assistant helped me change flashbulbs (I used two lights on extension). I told my subject I had to test my lights first and asked him not to pay any attention to occasional flashes. Then we settled down, he with a contraption he was working on first in his lap and later in his hands. He proceeded to explain its features and became more and more oblivious of everything around him. I listened and asked more questions while adjusting my camera until he got used to it and had forgotten all about pictures. From then on it was easy, and I got shot after shot without his even noticing the flashes. The resulting series of pictures was one of the most animated and natural I ever made.

An assistant is a most valuable asset. Usually a magazine doesn't provide a helper, but so far I have never failed to secure somebody to assist me in carrying lights, plugging in cables, and changing flashbulbs on extensions. A local helper is often more useful because he knows the people to be photographed. If no helper is available the local contact man usually can furnish one without difficulty. If I am working in an industrial plant, the public relations department is cooperative in this respect. Many times the plant photographer himself offers me his assistance, especially valuable because he knows every person in the place and gives me invaluable hints, pointing out interesting spots and warning of possible pitfalls, both pictorial and real. There are photographers who object to letting other photographers see them work and do not like to give away their little secrets. Personally I regret this attitude. Much preferred in my opinion is mutual exchange of ideas and methods. To imitate successfully somebody else's style is impossible anyway. In my own case, chance contacts with plant photographers have developed into genuine and lasting friendships.

When photographing people and their actions, a photographer should remember that those people know as much about what they are doing as he knows about photography. Any really good photographer will respect skill and knowledge in others. If, for pictorial reasons, changes in a setup become necessary and people have to be made to do things in a different and more pictureable way, he should not persuade anybody to do something that is incorrect from a workmanlike point of view. I always listen to—and frequently act upon—my subjects' suggestions as to how they should "perform" before the camera. More often than not such suggestions are most helpful. Following them has saved me several pictures that otherwise would have illustrated certain actions wrongly because to me—the layman—they looked more pictorial that way.

Most picture stories are concerned with people. Sometimes these people—our "actors"— are predetermined, but often they have to be selected by the photographer, who, in such a case, besides his other duties assumes the role of a casting director. This requires taste and a working knowledge of the particular duties of models. A photographer will find that the most valuable quality of any model is thorough familiarity with the action she or he has to perform before the camera. Beauty, glamor, fame are not half so important. A fashion model, for example, above all has to know how to wear clothes. Pretty face nor lush figure nor golden hair ever made a convincing picture unless supported by poise and personality. And the photograph of a girl machine operator with beautifully manicured fingernails holding the controls the wrong way is a deplorable sight. In my opinion, familiarity with the job on the part of the model takes at least half the professional worry off a photographer's mind.

It frequently happens that a photographer would like to switch persons on a job. He may have to photograph a certain operation which usually is performed by one and the same man, but, for pictorial reasons, may want to use a different person—somebody taller or smaller or younger or older. This sounds quite simple but actually requires much tact and discretion and should usually not be done by simply asking the original operator to step aside and the other person to take his place. More often than not, such direct proceedings end by offending the first operator who feels that he isn't good enough, while the intended new operator probably refuses to take orders from an "outsider." In such a case, only diplomacy and cooperation of the foreman or boss of the two workmen can effect the switch painlessly, and sometimes white lies have to be used as an excuse for the switch in order not to hurt anybody's feelings.

Once on a job, the good photographer is all eyes. He must see not only the close up things but—and this is all too often overlooked—the distant background. Busily occupied arranging persons or objects within his immediate vision, the photographer sometimes forgets to notice the chaotic confusion in the darkness farther away. Afterward, of course, he is flabbergasted when he sees how the penetrating light of his flashbulbs has brought out the whole deplorable background mess in brilliant clarity. If messy background cannot be cleaned up for a picture a different camera angle might help to keep it out of a photograph. Proper screening of lights often enables the photographer to hide it in a merciful veil of darkness.

In many industrial operations the law and plant or union regulations demand the use of safety devices. Because of carelessness or laziness on the part of some workers such devices—screens, helmets, goggles, or gloves—are not always used. It is up to the photographer to insist on their use when taking pictures. If he forgets to do so the company can refuse to release his photographs for publication.

Light conditions on location frequently are difficult. Wherever possible I find it advisable to use the natural light for main illumination (see pages 55-56), as it gives a place its "typical" character, which would be lessened or lost if drowned in the brutal light of flashbulbs. Here are picture-story scenes where added light can cause grievous effects in detracting from their authenticity: very large interiors such as steel mills, cathedrals, auditoriums; plants where every machine or workbench is illuminated by its individual lamp (restaurants and night clubs belong in this category, too). In these places all-over gloom punctuated by numerous small sources of light is typical, and the equalizing light of flashbulbs hopelessly destroys the atmosphere. In those cases, even relatively long time exposures with all the risks involved are preferable to the disillusioning flatness of flashlighted pictures, and, if properly prepared, are usually much easier to take. Sometimes, as in certain closeups or small interiors, it is possible to replace the ordinary incandescent bulb of a desk or other lamp with a flashbulb synchronized to the camera. Then, of course, a photograph can be flashed and the motif will still retain much of its natural atmosphere. The good photographer always keeps an eye open for such opportunities. If he is resourceful and imaginative he will more often find a way to preserve the character of a setting by using the right type of illumination than his less observant or not so gifted fellow-photographer.

Nobody will ever become a great photographer without this feeling for mood and atmosphere, which revolts at the very thought of killing the subtle light of an organically illuminated place with the brutal glare of flashbulbs. Nobody will ever make great pictures without a genuine understanding of subtleties which makes a photographer feel instinctively the difference that tallness or smallness of a person in a photograph can make for scale or proportions of a picture. . . . I frankly believe that a great photographer cannot be made but has to be born, and his main qualifications have to be a burning curiosity about people, places, and things, and a genuine feeling and love for the objects or subjects he wants to photograph. Without this feeling he can be a good illustrator, and with the help of a first-class photo-technique even a brilliant one. But what people will mostly admire in his pictures will be their clever way of execution, the sparkle, and the cleanliness—emotionally they will be empty and they will be soon forgotten.

CHAPTER 15

COMPOSITION

REALITY is as boundless as three-dimensional space. We contact reality mainly through our eyes, elevating objects to temporary importance by focusing on them, but never for long. Soon we move on and concentrate on something new that meanwhile has captured our attention. We move, and everything seems different: objects change their positions relative to each other, perspective and foreshortening appear in new and different forms. Importance shifts with interest from one thing to another, but always temporarily. Values are ever-changing, reality is always relative. . . .

All this stops suddenly and completely the moment we capture part of this reality on film and paper. At once everything becomes final, limited, and frozen. Taking a picture at once establishes a definite and unchangeable order, creating a self-contained world of its own. Objects are cast into a definite form of perspective; size and proportions of things become fixed on paper. And no matter how much we turn and twist a photograph, whatever the angle or distance from which we look at it, nothing will ever again change the composition of this picture, its perspective, its distribution of light and dark, its pattern of lines and forms. What once was relative has now become absolute, reality has been transformed into art. Or if not art, at least into something artificial.

NECESSITY FOR COMPOSITION

Every photograph is final. A painter can always make last-minute alterations if he is dissatisfied with his work, can change it even after he has finished, can paint over, or start the same work anew. But a photographer can do nothing of the kind. Once he has trimmed his picture, he holds the final result in his hands, and if he isn't satisfied there is nothing he can do but throw it away. Because of this finality inherent in any finished picture, a photographer should learn from the start to pay to "insignificant" things the same attention he knows he has to pay to "important" ones when executing a picture. For usually it is just one of these "insignificant" things that he has overlooked because he didn't think it was important which later ruins his picture. A famous example is the case of the glamor portrait that had everything—light just right, the pose natural and interesting, technical execution perfect, and the only disturbing element a potted flower in the background which in the finished portrait seemed to sprout right out of the model's head.

We have here a typical example of faulty composition resulting from carelessness. Moving the camera a few steps to one side or another would probably have saved the picture, since the photographer doubtless knew what a disastrous effect a flower sprouting out of his model's head would have on the appearance of the portrait. But the trouble was that he didn't notice the presence of this potted flower while there was still time to do something about it, and this negligence cost him an otherwise successful picture. In a different case, a photograph was cropped too short, cutting off part of the composition which provided the base for the motif proper. But nothing could be done about it because there was nothing else on the film. A fraction of an inch more on the negative would have saved that picture. Still another time . . . a bright patch of uncontrolled light detracted from the center of interest . . . a horizon was too high, creating a false impression of space . . . a line running into a corner of the picture seemed to split the photograph . . . faulty balance between light and shadow created a lopsided effect . . . and so on. Compared with "technical" mistakes like bad exposure or use of paper of the wrong gradation, such "faults of composition" may seem of small importance, but in the end they have an equally disastrous effect. They thoroughly spoil the appearance of a picture.

This just goes to show again what we have seen already: even the most perfect "technique" cannot guarantee the success of a picture unless it is used according to the rules of composition.

THE PURPOSE OF COMPOSITION

Composition means more than merely arranging objects in the form of an *S*-curve or an *L*-shape, or having the horizon divide a picture five by eight . . . which, it would seem, is about all a photographer can hope for according to the average textbook.

"Composing" means "arranging" and the purpose of "composition" is to arrange the various elements of a photograph in such a way that it becomes a self-contained independent unit, to create order, to balance the distribution of light and dark in graphic equilibrium, to arrange lines and forms into harmonic patterns, to direct and concentrate interest where interest belongs, and to create organic boundaries which hold the picture together like an unobtrusive natural frame.

PLACING THE SUBJECT WITHIN THE NEGATIVE

Most photographs are relatively small, and common sense alone should tell us not to waste any of their precious space on the rendering of superfluous or meaningless things. Consequently, one of the main rules of composition demands that the whole picture should be filled with interest, each one of the picture elements should have a meaning, and everything that doesn't belong should be cut off and left out of the picture. This has to be kept in mind even when planning a photograph, before the actual shooting begins. Conditions beyond our control, for instance, often prevent us from getting close enough to the subject proper to make it fill the full size of the negative if shooting with a standard lens. Under such circumstances, we have three possibilities: one is to take the picture with the standard lens and leave it as it is; this means that the subject proper will be surrounded by a lot of detracting and, for our purpose, meaningless detail, resulting in a diluted, wishy-washy impression. The composition of such a picture as a whole would be definitely bad. However, the basis of this composition, as far as the subject is concerned, may be sound, and a blowup of the section of the negative containing the subject proper may solve the problem. Then the subject proper would fill the entire picture (enlargement), and the superfluous parts of the negative would be cut off. This is possibility number two.

Doubtless the second picture is a tremendous improvement over picture number one, but under certain conditions it still has one big disadvantage: if the subject proper was very small on the negative, a high degree of magnification is necessary to enlarge it to a representative size, and this we know results in a proportionally great loss of sharpness and definition, and lowered picture quality. In such a case, possibility number three provides the anwer: instead of enlarging the subject proper afterward on paper, we enlarge it directly on the film by shooting the picture with a telephoto lens. This would be the ideal solution to the problem, regardless of whether the actual case was a candid shot of people whom the photographer didn't dare to approach more closely for fear of being observed, or a skyline picture that had to be taken from a very great distance. The three pictures across the following pages illustrate this problem, demonstrating at the same time the difference in quality between an enlargement made on paper and one made directly on the film with a telephoto lens.

Unless it is known right from the start exactly how a picture is going to be used, cropping the subject on the film has to be done cautiously. If such a picture is intended for editorial use in a magazine, for instance, demands of the layout have to be taken into consideration. Quite often, composition can be arranged

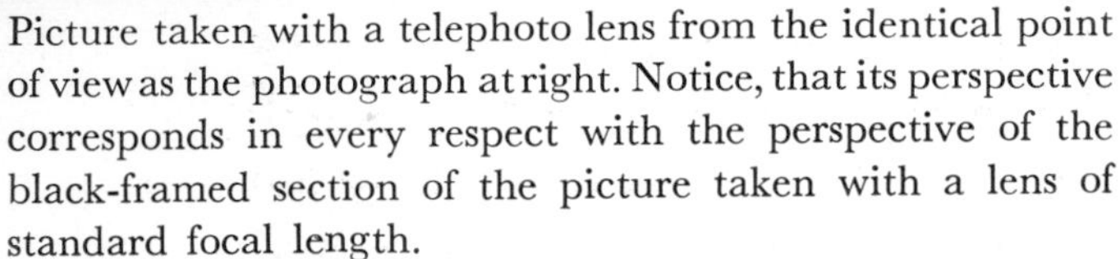

Picture taken with a telephoto lens from the identical point of view as the photograph at right. Notice, that its perspective corresponds in every respect with the perspective of the black-framed section of the picture taken with a lens of standard focal length.

Picture taken with a lens of standard focal length from the identical point of view as the telephotograph at left. Compared to the telephoto shot, the only difference is one of scale, resulting from the greater angle of view of the standard lens. The "perspective" of both pictures is identical.

for both a horizontal and a vertical picture. Only one or the other will later fit into the layout, but the experienced photographer plays safe by taking important pictures both ways, once vertically and once horizontally. If, for reasons of composition, a picture can be taken only horizontally or only vertically, enough space should still be left on the film around the subject proper so that minor corrections in the proportions of the final picture can be made by the layout man. Naturally, the size of the film must be considered here, too, and such leeway for alterations will be smaller for a 35 mm negative than for a 4x5 film.

In this connection I want to draw attention to the special problem of the square negative. Among *Life* photographers, for instance, the most popular camera is the Rolleiflex which takes a square negative and has a large square groundglass for focusing. It would be only natural to assume that making a decision between horizontal and vertical composition would be especially easy with a Rolleiflex

Enlargement of the black-framed section of the picture taken with the lens of standard focal length to the size of the telephoto shot. Notice that the perspective of both is the same in every respect, the only difference being one of sharpness.

because its square groundglass in effect shows both the horizontal and the vertical versions at once. The fact is, however, that after using the Rolleiflex for a while most of *Life's* photographers more or less stopped composing their pictures on the horizontal or vertical. Instead, they subconsciously arranged their subjects to fit the square, to the consternation of the editors who couldn't make effective use of these squares in their layouts. Naturally, after the photographer's attention was drawn to the undesirability of pictures with square proportions, things became better again. But the interesting fact remains that even experienced photographers subconsciously compose their pictures to fit the proportions of their negative material, while actually the opposite should be the case. *The subject should be the factor that determines the proportions of the composition*, and the proportions of the film should be regarded as merely accidental. Even the fact that demands of the layout occasionally make it necessary to arrange objects to fit into a picture of pre-determined proportions cannot change the principal validity of this rule. This should always be kept in mind—and especially when using a camera that takes square pictures.

CONCENTRATING ON A SINGLE SUBJECT

When contemplating our surroundings, we focus our eyes on only a single object at a time. For instance, if following a conversation between two people, we usually look at the person who does the talking, and when this person stops and the other answers, our attention quite automatically shifts to this other person, since we cannot concentrate on two different subjects at once. The same applies to photography: *A photograph should never have more than a single theme.* If it contained two or more subjects of equal importance, interest would have to be divided be-

Photographs by Nina Leen, *Pix*

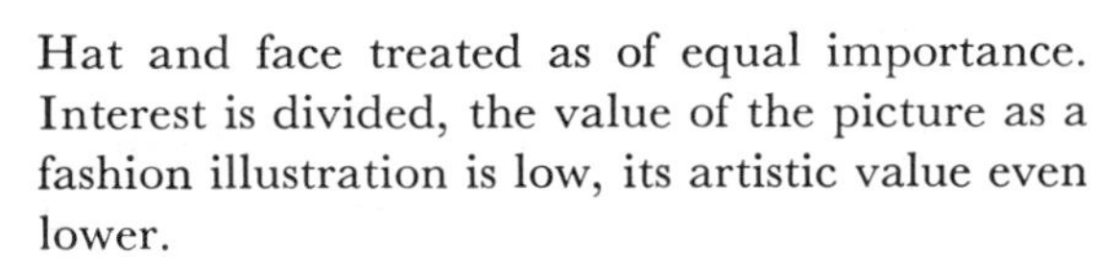

Hat and face treated as of equal importance. Interest is divided, the value of the picture as a fashion illustration is low, its artistic value even lower.

Casting a shadow over the face of the girl forces attention on the hat, the subject "proper" of this fashion picture. Artistically, a much better photograph is the result.

tween the two, and the result would be a weakened impression of the picture. Whenever a photographer finds two interesting subjects very close together, he should resist the temptation to take them on one and the same piece of film. Instead, he should split them and treat them as two separate pictures. This sounds so obvious that I am almost ashamed to write it down here. But it is a well-known fact that the "multiple motif" is one of the most common faults of composition. Beginners, especially, seem to be the happier, the more different things they can crowd onto one piece of film, almost as if they felt that this way they would get more for their money. . . . Consequently, whenever a photograph seems overloaded and overcrowded, whenever you feel that something is wrong, especially with a long shot, without your being able to put your finger on the cause of such a bad impression, check on multiple motif!

Occasionally, even experienced photographers who ought to know better, make the same mistake. This happens especially often in fashion photography, where the conflict between emphasizing the dress or hat, etc., on one hand, and a pretty but distracting face on the other hand, constantly produces good examples illustrating the danger inherent in every two-subject picture. Attention is divided equally between the fashion and the face, the picture is neither fish nor fowl, and loses its potential power. Of course, the idea is to use the pretty face as an "eye-catcher" to attract attention to, for instance, a hat (see picture, *opposite, left*). But a photographer—at least a photographer with artistic aspirations—cannot compose his pictures according to the rules of advertising and high-pressure salesmanship without forfeiting his artistic claims. And besides, the underlying idea is wrong, at least with regard to fashion photographs. For the woman who might buy that hat is certainly not interested in the face of the model who displays it in the picture; while a man, who might be attracted by the face, would hardly be interested in the hat. Of course, some people strive to please everybody, even if the price is a cheap-looking picture.

Now let's analyze the other photograph (*opposite, right*). Here, a shadow is thrown like a veil over the face of the model, drawing attention away from her subdued features and directing it toward the hat where it belongs. Obviously, in a fashion photograph, the fashion must be the motif proper—the center of interest—and not the person who happens to display it. But there is more to it than just an artistic principle. Sound psychology is behind it. As long as the face of the model is clearly shown, a discriminating customer may reason: "That hat looks good on that girl, but unfortunately she is not my type, so I doubt if I could wear it myself—better look for something else." And then she sees the other picture where the features of the model are unrecognizable in shadow, and she can easily identify herself with the wearer of the hat—on which her undivided attention is now concentrated—and if she likes the hat, she is much more likely to buy it.

Naturally, if Lady XYZ happens to wear that hat in a fashion photograph instead of little Miss Nameless, conditions will be just the opposite. Then Lady XYZ becomes the motif proper, which should now be treated with all the reverence due a fine portrait, while the hat becomes more or less accidental. Besides—it really hardly matters in such a case how the hat is treated photographically—women will buy it anyway.

Whenever two strong themes are as closely related as person and fashion in a fashion photograph, they obviously cannot be split and made into two separate pictures. In such a case, one of the two has to be played up, and the other played down, as explained in the example above. How this is going to be done must be planned carefully *before* the picture is taken, since afterward very little can be done to repair any damage. Possibly the "secondary motif" can be printed-in to make it less conspicuous, or part of it may be cropped off. . . . But the result can be only a compromise, and believe me, it will always look it. In other cases, however, where two or more equally strong subjects are rendered side by side in one picture, something can often be saved by enlarging only sections of the negative containing a single motif each. Treated in this manner, one overcrowded, hopeless-looking negative occasionally will yield several surprisingly good pictures.

The danger of multiple subjects is always most acute in long shots that take in a multitude of objects. The shorter the distance between camera and subject, the less acute becomes the danger of interest being divided between two or among several equally important objects. Least dangerous in this respect are typical closeups, where there is hardly ever a chance of getting two subjects at once. This partly explains the fact that closeups as a rule are more photogenic than long shots: they generally have only *one center of interest*, and the motif proper covers proportionally more of the picture than the motif proper in long shots, resulting in higher "concentration of interest per square inch."

CONDENSING AND CONCENTRATING THE INTEREST

Having decided *what* to take—what to regard as the proper subject of the picture—the next step is to decide *how* to handle the subject so it will attract maximum attention. Attention is always proportional to interest: the more interesting a photograph looks, the more attention it will command. Consequently, the next question a photographer should ask himself is, "How can I make my picture as interesting as possible?"

Since I have already discussed in great detail different ways of making pictures interesting through lighting, framing, selection of proper perspective, etc., I will confine myself here to composition. In this respect, we can learn a great deal by analyzing the reason why closeups have special attraction. What actually is it that makes almost any closeup interesting? Or rather: what is it that makes almost any object interesting as soon as we show it in the form of a closeup?

I have previously mentioned the "higher rate of interest per square inch" as one of the reasons for the special attraction of closeups. But there is considerably more to it. There is a psychological reason, too: closeups bring objects closer to the beholder, and closeness creates an atmosphere of intimacy which is difficult to resist. By bringing objects closer to the beholder we oblige him—we practically force him—to take a *personal interest* in them. If a girl snuggles very close to a man he can be pretty certain that she wants to be kissed. . . . Consequently, one of the surest ways of making objects interesting in a picture is to show them from as close a distance as is consistent with their size. This, of course, is actually only a different

Photographs by Phillippe Halsman

Left: Impression of formality and distance—this is the way a stranger sees a person. . . . *Right: Impression of intimacy* and closeness—this is the way a husband sees his wife, a child his mother, a lover his beloved. . . . Which one of the two pictures commands more attention?

way of expressing the first rule for good composition which demanded that all of the picture be filled with interest.

Naturally, the photographer has to use common sense and discrimination when trying to approach his subject as closely as possible. A landscape, for instance, doesn't have to be reduced to a closeup of a few sticks and stones in order to become effective. On the other hand, confining the presentation of this landscape to an interesting group of rocks or a few expressive trees will often make a more attractive photograph than a sweeping view of the entire countryside.

In the final analysis, it all boils down to one very simple rule: the whole secret of the successful isolation of the "motif proper" is successful separation of the "typical" from the "superfluous." Always ask yourself: *what* is really typical of this subject, what are its most characteristic features? Approach this question impartially, honestly, and sincerely, disregarding everything you may have seen or heard that could influence you. And don't be surprised if you arrive at the conclusion that the "typical" of, for instance, a landscape is not something concrete—like rock formations—but an abstract quality like loneliness, or fertility, or bound-

Two versions printed from the same negative. *Left:* "Documentary" version showing the whole building. *Right:* "Pictorial" version, cutting off the top of the building to emphasize its height.

less expanse. . . . If such is the case, try to get this feeling into your picture, symbolizing this mood in graphic form according to the principles discussed in the chapter on light and lighting; see page 308.

On the other hand, if you do find the "typical" to consist of weird rock formations, or clusters of tall trees, or patches of spring flowers, then you will discover that presenting these features in concentrated closeups, will usually re-create the character and atmosphere of the landscape more effectively than a long shot, which would naturally show these typical features on a much smaller scale, surrounded and "diluted" by any amount of conventional scenery (clear sky, level ground). In this respect, a picture showing gigantic rock formations from perhaps a hundred yards is as much a "closeup" as a photograph of a patch of spring flowers from three feet.

Once more the purpose of the photograph becomes important. Let's imagine, for instance, that we want to take the picture of a skyscraper. We could do this for two reasons: either we want a documentary photograph of the building for the record's sake, or we want to express the feeling we experienced when standing in front of this building and looking up at it. In the first instance, we need a "straight" picture of the skyscraper, showing it as clearly as possible. We would try to make it fill most of the negative in order to get it big, and make it look as tall as feasible without losing any part of it in the picture. In the second instance, however, completeness of the rendering is not important as long as the rendering expresses that feeling of *height*. Height, however, is something abstract, a relative creation of the imagination. Compared with the buildings that surround it our skyscraper may seem high, but compared to Mount Wilson it would look small. In our first "documentary" picture (*opposite, left*) the height of the tower had to be treated as a concrete quality—so-and-so-many stories tall—necessitating a complete picture of the building. In the second case, however, "absolute height" is not only unimportant, but actually detrimental to the purpose of the rendering, which is to create as strong as possible a feeling of tallness—since absolute height is a fact and kills rather than stimulates imagination. To do this, we have to give the imagination something to work on, to create a problem, and the best way to achieve this is by cutting off the very top of the building in the photograph (see *opposite, right*). Then, instead of *knowing* that our skyscraper is, for instance, 60 stories tall (we could count them all in the first picture), we now can count only 58, but obviously this cannot be the full height of the building. Immediately, imagination becomes interested and takes over, visualizes story upon story in never ending tiers . . . the "true" impression of a skyscraper.

Cutting off part of the motif proper and treating it as a "super closeup" is one of the most effective means of composition for arousing interest. It can be used to improve the rendering of any kind of object, regardless of actual size—flowers and portraits as well as buildings and scenery—as long as completeness is unimportant. Actually, it is nothing but the logical consequence of the first rule of composition demanding interest throughout the picture, followed through to its very end. This principle is nothing new. Sculptors of all times have made use of it. Every sculptured torso demonstrates it: instead of showing the complete "motif"—the human form with head and arms and legs—the artist condenses his conception into the main mass of the body—the torso—thus achieving an artistically stronger effect. Just imagine the Venus de Milo complete with arms (even if absence of these arms may be due to an earlier accident)—and you will *realize why part of an object often makes a stronger impression than its whole.*

STATIC OR DYNAMIC COMPOSITION

We have already seen (page 366) what an important influence the relative position of the subject proper has on the feeling of actual motion imparted by the picture. There the subject was a little boat, and we symbolized approach and departure by placing the image closer to one side of the photograph or the other.

Actually, similar consideration should be given every photograph, regardless of whether it shows objects in actual motion or not, for "emotional" motion, too, can be expressed in this way. For instance, let's reconsider the picture of a skyscraper on page 384, *left*. Quite obviously, this building is not in motion. On the other hand, its extension is more pronounced in the vertical than in the horizontal plane, which gives it definite direction: up and down. Such a direction has a two-way character, going up as much as down. We might compare it to a road connecting two towns, *A* and *B*, which leads from *A* to *B* as much as it leads from *B* to *A*. In other words, such a road expresses no motion (which can occur in only one direction), neither "actual" nor "emotional." It is "static"—as static as the up-and-down direction of the skyscraper in the left-hand picture on page 384. We can express this in graphic form as shown in the illustrations below.

This tower rests squarely on solid ground in perfect equilibrium, and both tower and photographic composition are "static."

Now let's turn to the right-hand picture on page 384. The purpose of this picture was to illustrate the emotional quality of height. Height, however, is definitely a one-way conception and can be compared to a one-way road which leads from *A* to *B*, but *not* from *B* to *A*. Emotionally, as well as from the viewpoint of composition, such one-way direction represents motion—a "latent" motion which in the skyscraper example is directed upward. We symbolized this latent motion by cutting off the top of the building, so the picture included the beginning of the motion (the base of the tower) but not its end, leaving it to the imagination to continue the upward flight ad libitum. Thus, we disturbed the static equilibrium of the composition by introducing a state of dynamic tension, which could be expressed diagrammatically as follows:

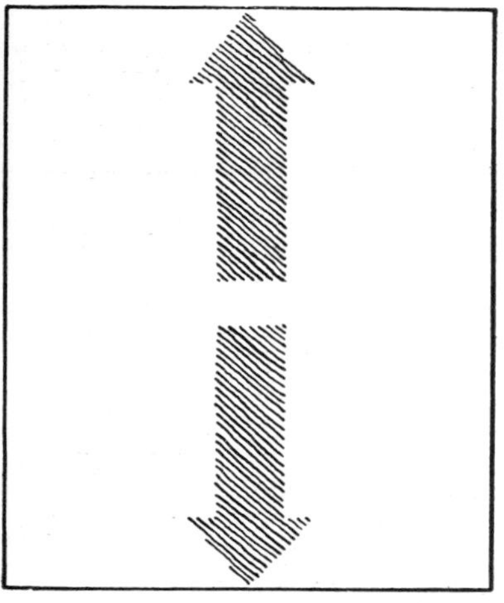

In this form the tower appears somehow projected, reaching up into the sky. It still has connection with the ground at its foot; it is still a basically "static" composition. But the upwards sweep of latent motion is already indicated, the foundation for a "dynamic" composition is already laid. To emphasize this upward movement even more we can make use of "vertical perspective," symbolizing "distance in height" by means of converging verticals:

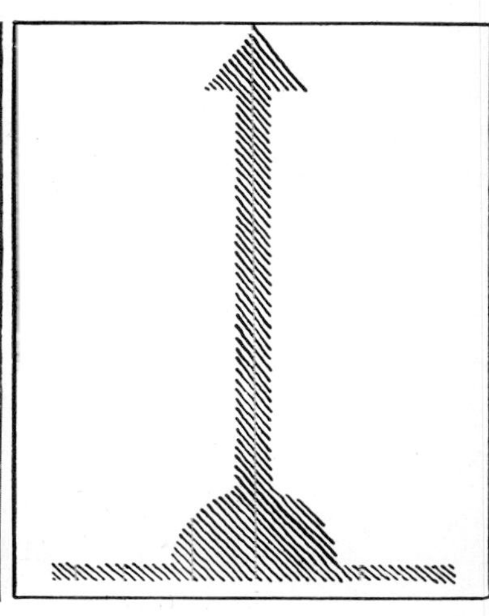

The impression of height is now even more pronounced, and we begin to feel that dizziness that always grips us when standing at the foot of a skyscraper looking up. To liberate the upward movement and to indicate this upward surge in symbolic form we have to complete the change from "static" to "dynamic" composition by changing the position of the tower from vertical to diagonal. This way, we transform verticals into diagonals —introducing dynamic symbols of motion:

Now, upward movement is completely unrestricted; nothing holds the soaring power of the building back. Our eyes sweep upward, higher and higher, following the lines of motion, the diagonals, toward the clouds and the sky. . . .

The composition is now one hundred per cent "dynamic."

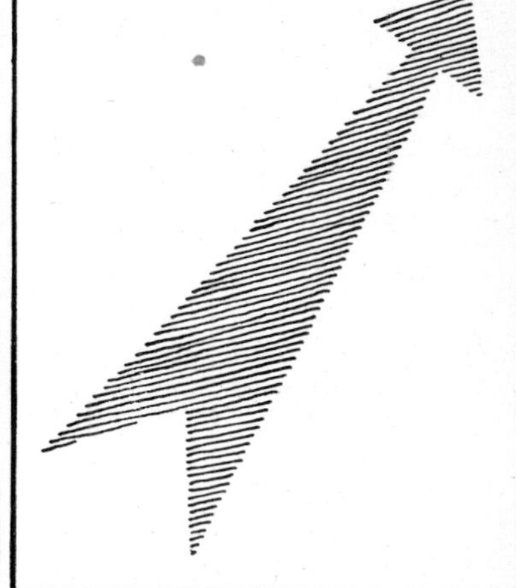

Step by step this little series demonstrates three increasingly effective means of transforming a static composition into a dynamic one: 1. The "*super closeup*" which cuts off parts of the subject proper and makes it appear close and intimate, challenging the imagination to reconstruct the missing parts. 2. *Perspective which through converging parallels* transforms static two-way direction into dynamic one-way motion, regardless of whether such motion is "real" or only "latent." 3. *Change of position of the subject itself* within the frame of the picture, transforming verticals into diagonals, symbolic of action.

Analysis of the relative value of each of these three steps will show that the last was the most effective, mainly because of the dynamic power of its diagonals. We discussed this motion-suggesting effect of diagonals in the chapter on motion (page 347), but here is one additional point:

A rectangle can be crossed with one straight line in three different ways:

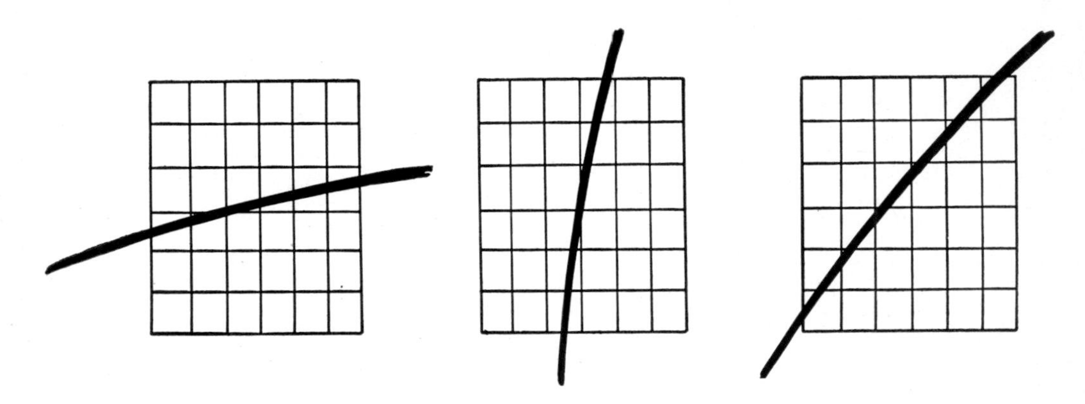

Which of these lines is the most effective? That at the left, which crosses only the verticals? Or the one in the center, which crosses only the horizontals? Or the one at the right—the *diagonal*—which equally effectively crosses *both* verticals and horizontals, sweeping the entire rectangle?

Translated into terms of composition these three alternatives appear as follows:

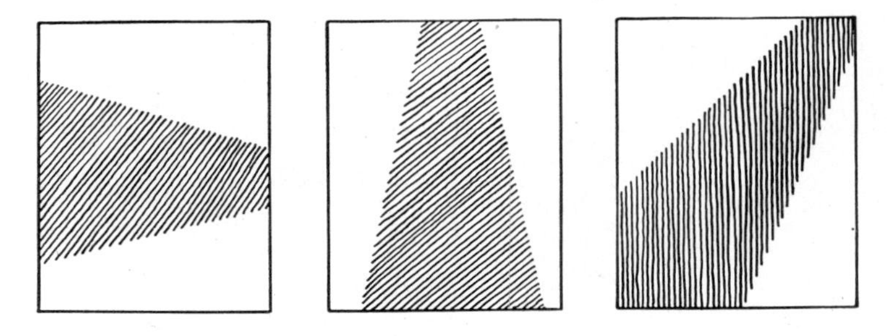

Again, which one of these three diagrams gives the strongest suggestion of motion, of sweep and surging power? Is there any need for further proof?

Dynamic composition is preferable to static when a suggestion of actual motion or strong emotion is desirable in a picture. The surest way to achieve this is by means of a diagonal composition. This, of course, doesn't mean that actual diagonals must always be present. Frequently, diagonals can be suggested simply by placing the subject proper on one of the diagonals of the photograph (but never in its center; see page 351), and the feeling of motion or emotion will be just as strong. In this respect, compare the psychological effects of the following three diagrams:

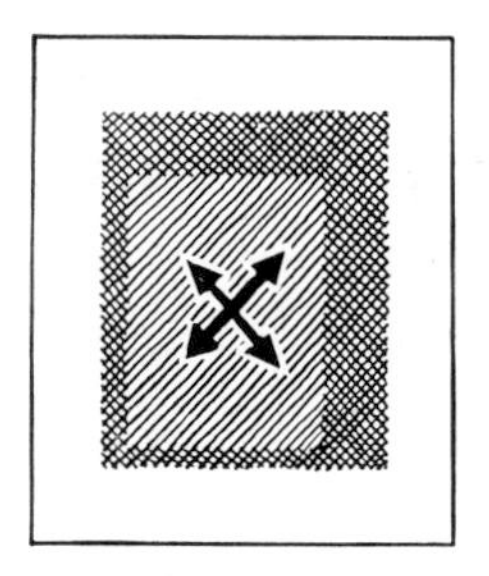 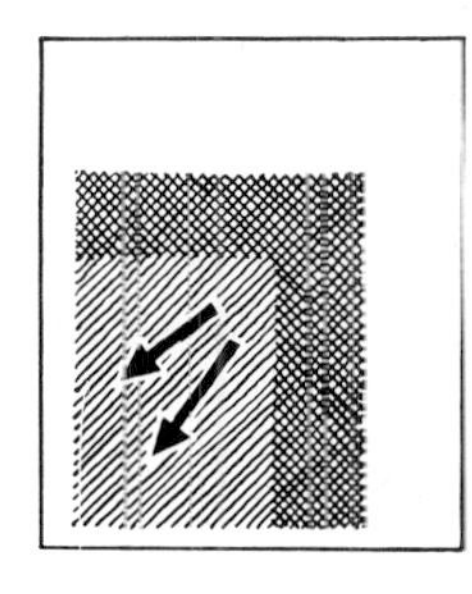 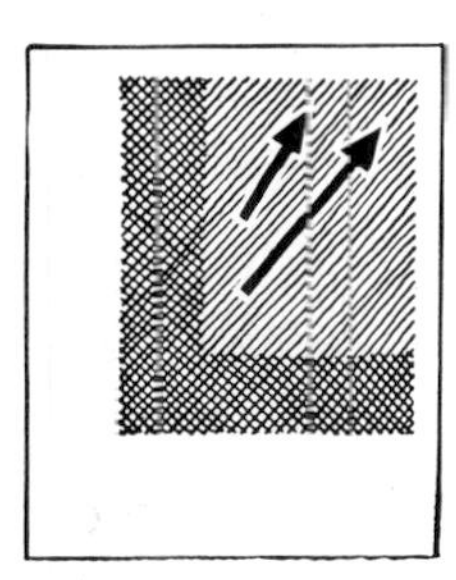

Doesn't it seem as if the object is at rest in the left-hand composition, but in motion in the other two diagrams? Can't you imagine the object moving toward you in the center picture and going away from you in the picture at right? If these three diagrams represented pictures taken horizontally, the object would appear static at left, going down in the center, and going up at right. And if they represented pictures looking downward at an angle, they would suggest movement in the horizontal plane, directed toward the camera in the center and away from it at right . . . further proof of the importance of the placement of the subject within the frame of the picture.

BALANCE OF COMPOSITION

In order to make a pleasant and harmonious impression, the elements of a photograph should be in a state of balance. This applies to the arrangement of lines and forms as well as to the distribution of light and dark. Out of balance, a picture looks lopsided and accidental, a product of chance, a careless snapshot—not the well-planned, intelligently assembled, independent, and self-contained unit every good photograph should be.

Balance in a photograph has nothing to do with symmetry; for this is not a balance of volumes, but of weight. In this respect, important picture elements carry much weight, and less important ones carry correspondingly little weight. Again, this applies to formal as well as to tonal picture elements.

When balancing a composition, the photographer should start with the "center of interest"—the subject proper, the spot where the action takes place. This center of interest is the most important part of the photograph, and consequently carries the greatest "weight." It should become the focal point of the picture, its "center of gravity," around which everything rotates. It has to be put into a prominent place, usually *not* too close to one of the edges of the picture, or directly in the center. which would result in a symmetrical, dull, and tensionless composition. Remember, balance is *not* symmetry.

Apart from this, the center of gravity can be practically anywhere within the limits of the picture, high or low or left or right, depending upon the type of motif and the intentions of the photographer. Remember, however, that its position will give the picture its direction; or rather, that real or latent movement on the part of the subject should be considered when fixing the position of the center of gravity in a picture.

As a rule, placing the center of gravity within the upper half of the picture tends to make a composition more dynamic, while placing the center of gravity within the lower half will make for a more static composition. However, there are quite a number of possible exceptions.

Placing the motif proper in the right position within the limits of the picture is relatively simple wherever action or actual motion are involved. All the photographer has to do is to follow through with his composition, emphasizing the direction which is already clearly indicated in the action or movement that has to be depicted (see chapter on motion, pages 347-351). However, matters are more complicated in cases where movement is "latent" and can be felt only emotionally—as, for instance, in our much-discussed skyscraper, where unusual height produced a feeling of "upward sweep."

This height, however, can produce an exactly opposite feeling—a feeling of tremendous depth—when we look at it from the other end, taking a shot downward from the top of the skyscraper. To symbolize such a feeling the photographer would use practically the same means as in the case of "upward sweep," only the verticals would now converge toward the depth. And "scale" (see page 276) could be introduced; by showing tiny figures of people down on the street below, their smallness exaggerated through use of a wide-angle lens, tension between near and far in vertical direction can be increased even further, making for an even more pronounced sensation of "depth."

A field where "latent" movement is not given sufficient consideration is portraiture, where the direction of the gaze of the subject should determine the position of the head within the frame of the picture. In this respect, closed or sleepy eyes need less space around them than eyes that are wide awake and alert. The profile of a sentry watching for the enemy, for instance, should command as much space in the direction of his gaze as the size of the photograph permits. This means that such a head should be placed with its back at the edge of the picture. Here is one of the exceptions to the rule that the subject should not be placed too close to the edge of the photograph, but extremity of situation demands extremity of means. And again, in the opposite case, a prisoner will look all the more caged the more we cut off his gaze by placing his face as close as possible to the bars. . . .

In this connection, I want to draw attention to the position of the *horizon* in a photograph. Emotionally, the horizon divides a picture into two parts, the lower of which is dedicated to closeness and objects, while the upper is dedicated to distance and space. Even the fact that, more often than not, objects of the close foreground, as, for instance, trees, people, or buildings, etc., will cut across the horizon into the part representing distance and space, doesn't affect the principal validity of this definition. What matters from the point of view of composition, though, is the position of this dividing line of the horizon. If we place it high in a picture, we emphasize foreground, nearness, and objectivity; and if we place it low in a picture, we emphasize distance, space and abstract qualities. (Having the horizon divide the picture into two equal parts usually results in a dull and uninteresting composition, dividing the interest as do photographs with two equally important motifs; see page 379.)

Just for fun, make the following experiment for yourself: take two pictures of the same object, identical in every respect with the one exception that in the first picture the horizon is high and the foreground dominating, while in the second the horizon is low and the sky dominating. Then notice how differently they affect you emotionally. The first one should "bring you down to earth," while the latter should "give you a lift."

The main thing to consider when balancing *the tonal elements* of a picture is the fact that *light* and *white* attract the eye much more than darker shades. Consequently, the center of interest in a photograph can often be made the most "attractive" part of the picture by accentuating it with the brightest white of the whole composition, even if such an accent is very small and the main part of the subject proper is dark. Leaving the center of interest comparatively dark will give the picture a negative quality. Taking the brightest white away from the subject proper will detract the interest from the point where interest belongs.

Proof of the important role white plays in attracting attention can be found in any portrait. In a portrait, the most important element is doubtless the eyes. They are the center of interest which should catch the attention of the beholder more

Flame thrower. Example of concentration of interest achieved through cropping and darker printing. *Left:* Full negative. *Opposite page:* Final picture.

BASIC PRINCIPLES OF COMPOSITION

When using a lens of comparatively short focal length the only way to avoid distortion is to stay far enough away from the subject (*left*).

Afterwards, composition has to be pulled together by enlarging the most important section of the film (*right*).

than any other part of the picture. However, it is a well-known fact that because of the darkness of iris and pupil, even the most beautiful eyes look listless and dead in a picture *unless animated by a "catchlight"*—that tiny dot of brilliant light reflection which more than anything else draws attention to the eye.

Because of its special "attraction," white carries the greatest weight when balancing a composition. If only the whites are placed properly in a picture, the photographer doesn't need to worry much about the rest, because the grays and blacks will usually take care of themselves. For in order to show up white as "white," we have to offset it against other darker tones—dark gray or black—which automatically places such darker shades in their appropriate positions. And the more brilliant we want a white to appear, the darker has to be the tone next to it. White never looks whiter than when it is completely surrounded by black.

As a result, whenever a photographer wants to emphasize "depth" in a picture, he should take care to keep the distance light and "attractive" while the foreground stays dark. Incidentally, this partly accounts for the special depth impression of properly "framed" motifs, which I mentioned in the discussion of perspective on page 248. On the other hand, it explains the "flat" impression of pictures taken with single flash at the camera, the foreground of which is usually overexposed and too light while the background fades into darkness.

CROPPING TO PROPORTIONS

The majority of photographs we take will be either "horizontals" or "verticals," which means that either length is greater than height or height is greater than length. Pictures where length and height are equally large (squares) are rare, and quite correctly, too. For from the viewpoint of composition the square is not a very pleasant form, and pictures so composed usually appear dull, monotonous, and lifeless. . . . Beware of the square.

(This, of course, is by no means a criticism of cameras that take square negatives. On the contrary, such cameras eliminate the often time-consuming change from horizontal to vertical camera position [or vice versa]. The square negative, however, should never influence composition, and merely means that transformation from a square into a rectangle will have to be made later in "cropping" the negative with the help of an enlarger while making the print. But keep in mind what was said about the danger of the square negative on page 378.)

The decision whether a photograph should be composed for a horizontal or vertical picture depends entirely on the *direction of the motif*, which again depends on one or more of three factors:

1. *Actual movement* on the part of the photographed object. The picture of, for instance, a plane traveling in horizontal flight would probably demand a horizontal composition, since the direction of the motion of its subject proper is horizontal. A picture of the same plane in a power dive, however, should be composed vertically; for even if the actual motion of the plane is not strictly vertical but follows the diagonal, the character of such a dive is much more "downward," i.e., "vertical" rather than "sideways" or horizontal.

2. "*Latent*" *movement* inherent in the character of the motif. Remember, for instance, the latent upward or downward movement of our skyscraper on pages 386-389, which was produced by a feeling of "height" or "depth" as a direct result of the tallness of the building—which can be expressed in satisfactory form only in a vertical composition. In other cases, however, latent movement may have a horizontal direction (remember, for instance, the example of the sentry watching for the enemy on page 391), in which case composition should be horizontal.

3. *Physical extension* of the subject proper. In case there is neither actual nor latent movement, objects that are of predominantly horizontal extension should be composed horizontally, and objects of predominantly vertical extension should be composed vertically. Occasionally, however, it can be questionable which is the more dominant direction of the two. An oil derrick, for instance, or even a small group of three or four derricks standing close together, would probably have to be composed for the vertical, since height is more predominant in an oil derrick than width. But things would be different in a photograph of an entire oil field. In that case, repetition of many vertical forms in the horizontal plane would result in a predominantly horizontal motif; these forms now become an oil field instead of a collection of derricks, and would necessitate a horizontal composition, as illustrated in the following:

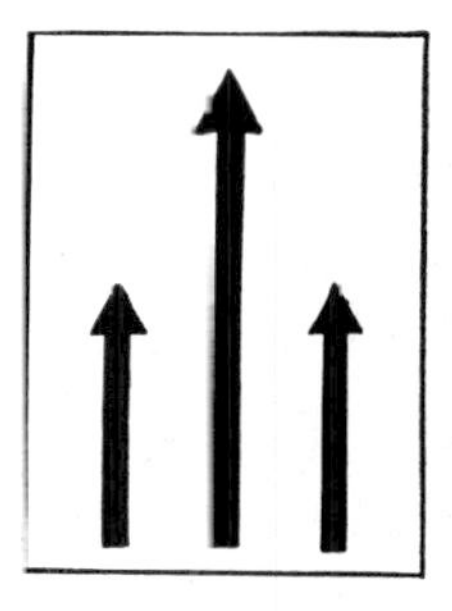

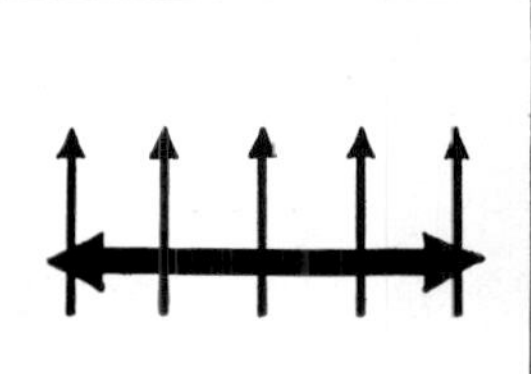

Incidentally, analyzing a photograph in diagrammatic form as demonstrated above is the surest way to settle any question of horizontal versus vertical composition. Actually, all that is needed is a simplified sketch of the main trends of the picture indicating their direction and distribution. Disregard trends of minor importance and concentrate on the motif proper, emphasizing the general direction by means of a heavier arrow.

Such a graphic analysis of the composition of a picture is especially valuable in the final adjustment of the proportions of a photograph. For more often than not, simply deciding between horizontal and vertical is not enough to get the utmost out of a picture, since many times a subject doesn't fit exactly into the stereotyped proportions of four by five. Certain subjects simply demand a narrower or wider rectangle. Otherwise, the subject proper would either have to be cut off, or else its concentration would suffer because of the necessity of filling extra space with superfluous and distracting detail. In this respect, the greatest danger usually lies in the vertical direction, so watch out for unnecessary foreground and sky.

Another reason for carefully tailoring the proportions of a picture to fit the requirements of the motif is the fact that usually the one will help the other. Narrowness, for instance, is the main impression of New York's old Downtown alleys, and cropping the picture of such an alley into an extremely narrow vertical with proportions of perhaps one to four draws attention through its very narrowness to the canyon-like character of the alley. On the other hand, giving such a photograph the standard proportions of four by five would necessitate including the nearer buildings of the street, whose horizontal rows of window would detract from the vertical character of the alley.

Finally, giving each picture its "personal" proportions will result in greater variety and make the layout more interesting, as the photograph to the left will prove.

ENLARGING AND FINAL ADJUSTMENTS

Having decided on the proportions of a photograph, the next step is to determine *exactly where to trim* the picture. The easiest way to settle this question is with the help of an enlarger: Project the negative on the easel and keep on adjusting the mask until you finally arrive at a pleasant solution. At this stage, a photographer should be on his own and work according to his personal taste and ability. Experience has shown, however, that observation of a few simple rules will often be beneficial. You will find them listed below.

Tips for the Final Trimming of Pictures

Symmetry in a photograph is generally bad and should be avoided. Don't place your center of interest directly in the center of the picture. Don't let the horizon cut your composition in half.

If the camera has been tilted accidentally when taking a picture, turn the easel so that your main lines will appear vertical and horizontal in the print. A slightly slanted horizon looks especially objectionable unless there is a reason for it (see picture on page 351).

On the other hand, tilting a picture boldly can often transform a dull and static composition into an interesting and dynamic one. Try this when everything else fails. . . .

If you have a negative with multiple motifs (see page 379), try to split it up into two or more separate pictures. Don't be afraid to use a high degree of enlargement to blow up tiny sections as long as your negative is sharp.

Don't hesitate to cut into the subject proper (see page 382). It is one of the surest ways to intensify the concentration of a composition, as many closeups prove. . . . If anything, trimming off too much (in the print) is preferable to leaving a lot of senseless and distracting detail (if you cut off *too* much, a new print is easily made).

Lines running directly into a corner of a picture seem to split the corner. Trim your composition to avoid this. Let such lines run either into the horizontal or into the vertical edge of the photograph at a safe distance from the corner.

Curves should never just touch the edge of a picture. Either keep them safely within your composition, or boldly cut into them.

Small spots of white running along the edge of a picture make a photograph look as if rats had gnawed its border. Cut them off entirely if possible. Otherwise make them dark by burning them in when exposing the print (see page 312).

Beware of the square! Its symmetry makes it a dull and tensionless shape that ought to be avoided (see pages 378 and 394).

The size of the final print should depend on the character of the motif. Many subjects never look well in a photograph unless they are presented *big*, while others are effective as smaller prints. As a rule, subjects that actually were big, and complicated objects rich in fine detail, need a larger scale in order to be effective than smaller and simpler subjects which are frequently unimpressive when enlarged out of proportion. Landscapes, for instance, almost invariably look dull and commonplace unless blown up to impressive dimensions (minimum 11x14 inches), even if they were exciting in actuality. . . . On the other hand, if enlarged to the size of a mural, even a dull and ordinary landscape will become impressive. . . .

If we had to make a general rule, maybe we could put it like this: any subject can be enlarged up to its natural size (if possible!) and will still look good in a picture. Further enlargement, however, will often make it coarse and less effective, with one important exception: closeups of very small objects always gain with size, the larger the better, as long as they are still sharp. . . .

Many photographers make the common mistake of enlarging all their photographs to one standard size. Especially when presenting a picture story to the editors of a magazine, variation in size is important, since it is the simplest way to draw attention to key pictures and highlights of a series. Personally, I try to make up an average picture story as follows: a few selected 11x14 prints for lead pictures (see page 368), for the pictures that are most important for the understanding of the story, and for the pictorially most beautiful pictures. But I am always careful not to have too many prints of this large size in a single story since this would dull their effect. I print the majority of "general" single pictures 8x10, but in case a story contains a picture series showing step-by-step operations (see page 367), I make such pictures only 5x7. Such series have to be seen as a continuity, like frames of a movie film, and making them too large (8x10) makes it difficult to spread them out on a table and look at them all at once.

Finally, *all* prints should be trimmed and spotted carefully before presentation. It is really only a small job, taking very little time, but it makes a tremendous difference in the appearance of a story. Nothing looks more sloppy and "don't give a damnish" than lint spots and raggedy edges.

CHAPTER 16

CONCLUSIONS AND THE "PHOTO-GRAPHIC" TECHNIQUES

PHOTOGRAPHY is the youngest of all the arts and is still in a state of violent evolution. To be successful, the best qualifications a prospective photographer can have are, in my opinion, good taste, ingenuity and imagination. While photo-technique is getting simpler from day to day, easier to learn and easier to practice, the demand for originality and freshness in a photograph is growing daily, too. People have finally begun to realize that good photography is art, that good photographers are artists, and that artists are born and simply cannot be "turned out" by photography schools. . . .

Neither this book, nor any photo school, can ever do more than help a beginner on his way, teach him photo-technique, and develop him into a first-rate craftsman. Beyond this point, all he can ever get from *without* is the stimulation provided by the problems of daily experience. But the way in which he meets these problems and transforms problems into pictures, must always be his own. This is my personal belief and the reason why I talk here so freely about my methods and "secrets" without being afraid of training "competitors." I know too well that at worst all I can train are "imitators."

The creative photographer must be an experimenter, always curious about new things, always looking for new ideas, trying to develop them, to improve them. . . . To a great extent his success as a photographer will depend on this inborn curiosity. . . . Today more than ever I believe that imagination and sense of composition are more important for making good pictures than perfection of technique. Technique can always be acquired, and if mastered once, soon becomes subconscious routine. Technique is always basically the same, in shooting still life as well as action, in portraiture as much as in scientific photography. Uniformity of photo-technique will never result in monotony.

Quite the opposite is true of ideas. Every assignment, every single picture, presents the creative photographer with new problems, problems of approach and composition. Almost every subject he tackles has been photographed before. His problem is to find a new approach to that old subject—and that requires an idea. Here is the test of the true photographer. If his idea is good, he will produce an "original" photograph—even though the subject is old. If it is bad, he will produce only another mediocrity. . . . But even if he succeeds, he knows his success is only temporary. Every new subject requires still another approach, another idea, and so on. . . . Uniformity of ideas soon means failure as a photographer.

It is with this in mind that I want here—almost as an afterthought—to draw attention to the young techniques of "graphic" stylization: solarization, controlled reticulation, the bas-relief technique, and combinations of two or more of these interesting forms of picture presentation. I know they are considered "radical" and "arty" by many, public and photographers alike. But then, ridicule is often the first reception radically new ideas get, ideas that included among others, the airplane, the submarine . . . yes, and the camera.

At the beginning of this book I drew parallels between photography and the art of writing. This comparison still holds good, for photography is at least as complex a form of art as writing. In writing, several forms, each quite different from the other, are commonly used: narrative prose style, the clipped style of the journalist, the even shorter style we use in telegrams, and poetic style. In photography, styles as different as the softness of the Misonne-school pictorialists, and the precision of the Weston-school *f* 64 purists, are practiced peacefully side by side. But as soon as anyone dares to think of "photo-poetry," more often than not he will get the horse-laugh or the Bronx cheer. . . . Personally, I think this is rather thoughtless, since one can never know which way a new idea will develop and how useful it may become in time. Remember the airplane and the submarine. . . . And please take notice of the fact that *Life* has already run several ads that were illustrated with photographs in bas-relief.

The "graphic" techniques can be called "the poetry of photography." They frequently permit farthest-going simplification, condensation, and stylization of motifs without infringing on the typical character of the objects they depict. Actually, just the opposite is the case (and the reason why we use these techniques): they concentrate through elimination. By suppressing superfluous detail and detracting matter more completely than even the most careful form of lighting or composition could accomplish in an "ordinary" photograph, they almost automatically reduce a subject to essentials. To mention but one example: A photographer wants to put all his emphasis on the outline of a form as the most characteristic feature of his subject. All he can do in an "ordinary" photograph is to show this form either black against white or white against black. In both cases, the best he can get is a positive or negative "silhouette"—a plane—but he can never isolate the "outline" of this plane all by itself. . . . This would be a case for one of the "graphic" techniques, and how the result might look is shown in the "bas-relief" photographs on the opposite page and on page 403.

Bas-relief. Reduction of a motif to its basic forms, boldly outlined in "graphic" black and white. Notice how such a stylization intensifies the "typical" of an object by eliminating distracting detail, instead of making it less recognizable. . . . Careful choice of subject matter, as well as proper technical treatment, of course, are all-important for satisfactory results. In this case, both negative and diapositive of the picture were developed to more than ordinary contrasts, and printed on extra-hard paper in order to eliminate every trace of gray and to get this purely black-and-white effect.

Painting and the graphic arts offer a great variety of different techniques to the discriminating artist, who can always find a medium that will express his intentions especially well: oil, gouache or water color, pencil drawing, etching or woodcut are only a few of the best known of these forms. In photography, such choice is much more limited, partly because of the nature of photo-technique, but even more so because photographers as a rule are either too busy or too lazy to experiment, and too conservative to use new forms of expression even if they are presented to them on the proverbial silver platter. . . . The few exceptions, men like Man Ray, Blumenfeld, Herbert Matter, Alan Fontaine, etc., merely confirm this rule. . . .

If nothing else, this alone, I think, should be reason enough to mention the "graphic" techniques in this book, and to give the really discriminating and creative photographer a chance to get acquainted with them.

BAS-RELIEF

Make a contact print of your negative on film or glass plate, develop, fix, wash, and dry it like any ordinary negative. Glass plates are easier to handle than film. The type used for making lantern slides is best and can be processed under a yellow safelight. Take this "diapositive" (after it is dry, of course) and place it on top of your original negative, emulsion sides together, adjust them until they are just slightly off-register, put them sandwiched like this into the enlarger, and print them. The result will be a "bas-relief picture," where the width of the lines corresponds to the degree of off-set between negative and diapositive.

If you want to use bas-relief in the negative form, print your "sandwich" on a lantern slide plate instead of on paper, process this new diapositive and use it as a "negative" for making your negative bas-relief prints. If the lines were black on white before, they will now be white on black, providing you use a hard enough gradation of paper.

The possibility of using either the positive or the negative form is a further advantage of all the graphic techniques, increasing the variety of means a photographer has at his disposition by one hundred per cent. "Graphic" photographs are already so much "abstracted" that it no longer matters if they are presented black on white or white on black, as little as it matters whether a drawing is made with pencil on paper, or with chalk on a blackboard. . . .

For getting best results, graphic pictures should be conceived with special attention to the characteristics of the process. Choice of clean-cut simple forms facilitates stylization. Good contrasts in negative and diapositive are essential for getting "graphic" black-and-white effects. Watch the outlines of shadows, since

Bas-relief. Condensation through simplification, presentation of a theme in its most concentrated form. Only the "leitmotive" is shown, just enough to recognize the "melody" and to stimulate the imagination into reconstruction of the rest. . . .

a graphic treatment will emphasize them and make them much more prominent than they would appear in an ordinary photograph. A figure, for instance, that is well lighted for a "regular" picture may be lighted all wrong for a bas-relief photograph, and uncontrolled shadows may easily upset the whole composition. The only way of telling when a shadow is right and when it is wrong is from experience derived from personal experiments, for in this field a photographer is working as freely as any other creative artist.

Solarization. Skyline of a small city. If bas-relief pictures can be said to have the boldness of "woodcuts," then this solarized form could be compared to an "etching" because of the delicacy of its lines with their graduated shadings.

SOLARIZATION

After a negative has been developed for the prescribed time, turn on the *white* light for a few seconds and expose the negative while it is still in the developer. Turn the white light off and continue development for a few more seconds. The negative will, of course, turn black almost immediately, but not uniformly all over. Beginning with the centers of the thinnest parts, blackness spreads toward the areas that already were black before exposure. Interrupt development just before the negative appears completely black by putting it into a concentrated shortstop bath, then fix, wash, and dry it as usual. If second exposure and development were timed correctly, fine white seams will trace all outlines of the rendering if the finished negative is observed against a strong white light. Printing such a negative will give you a "solarized" photograph.

Since the process of "solarizing" is a rather delicate one and will result in the loss of the negative if timing is not absolutely right, it is advisable to use either a

Solarization. Creation of a vision by photographic means. Don't expect naturalistic values from such a picture; rather look at it as you would at the picture of a dream. . . . Let it stimulate your imagination like a good sonnet. See the fantastic creation, the picture of a girl on a South Sea atoll at night. . . . Of course, you may not be interested in poetry. But, if not, don't criticize, either.

Reticulation. Vacation mood, symbolized by "photo-graphic" means. Fine grains of reticulation suggest the graininess of seashore sand and of sun-heated air vibrating over the dunes. All-over lightness of the picture gives the impression of merciless noontime light.

duplicate negative (made on "direct-positive film") or a "paper negative" (which should be an enlargement in the size of the final print, which would then have to be contact printed from it) in order to avoid the possible destruction of an irreplaceable original. Treatment and result are in both cases the same.

RETICULATION

Reticulation of the emulsion is often produced accidentally if the temperature of the developer or of the rinsing water is too high. Usually, the result is a total loss of the negative since this type of "uncontrolled" reticulation usually happens only in spots. Once in a while, however, such accidental reticulation develops evenly all over the surface of a negative and produces a very interesting effect, comparable in many respects to that achieved through use of special "screens" through which to print a negative. But while the textures of such screens invariably introduce alien and unworkmanlike elements into a photograph, creating a false and ugly effect, the grain of a reticulation will always look "photographic," since, instead of obliterating fine forms and design through superimposition of a mechanical and unrelated pattern, such grain actually accentuates the rendering of a picture by following the outlines of its design organically. At the same time, its coarseness eliminates superfluous detail, thus making reticulation a valuable means for achieving stylization in a picture through uniform treatment of its various elements in a typically photographic manner.

To reticulate a negative evenly over its entire surface, soak a dry film or plate for about 15 minutes in water, until its emulsion is thoroughly softened. Or you can start working on a negative directly after it comes out of the rinsing water. (One thing, however, is important in both cases: the negative should not be hardened too much, since this would prevent reticulation either entirely, or would produce reticulation only in spots.) Reticulate the negative by letting its emulsion swell in warm water of 86 to 96° F. Different emulsions react differently, and best conditions have to be found by making tests. According to type of emulsion, temperature of water, and degree of hardening of the negative emulsion, reticulation sets in after 5 to 25 seconds. If nothing has happened after half a minute, either the water is too cold or the emulsion too much hardened. In the first case, increase the temperature gradually; in the second case, nothing can be done before the negative has been de-hardened. Once it has started, reticulation usually spreads and grows rather fast and has to be watched carefully in order not to miss the moment when the film or plate has to be lifted out of the warm water and put into a cold solution

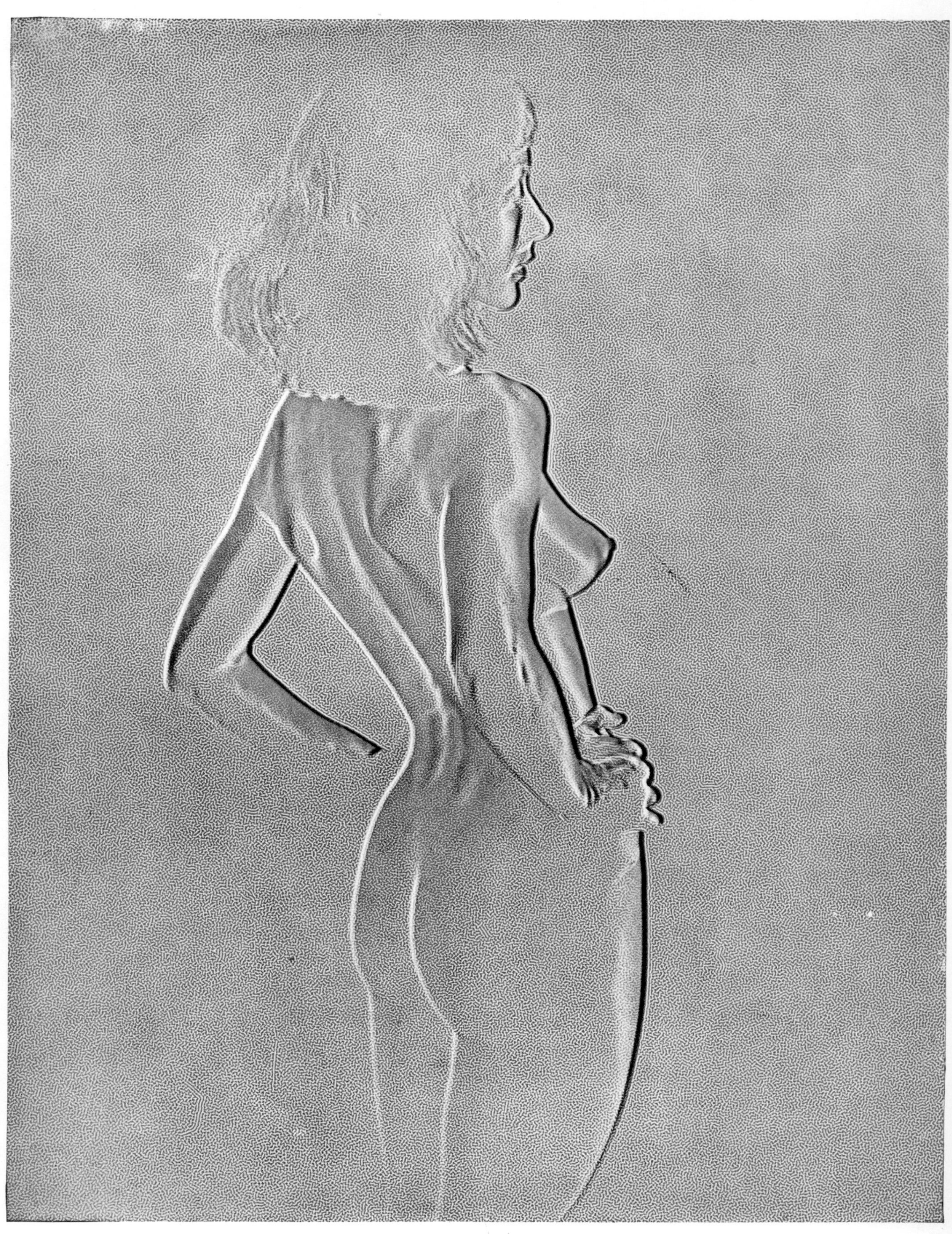

Combination of reticulation and bas-relief. Creation of a unifying all-over pattern through reticulation, emphasizing the motif proper by means of the bas-relief technique. An example of the possibilities resulting from combined use of two different "graphic" techniques.

of hardening hypo, where the emulsion stiffens almost instantaneously. Don't tilt the negative while taking it out of the warm water, since some emulsions become so soft that they flow off their base if given the opportunity. Since reticulation is a rather delicate process, and failure invariably results in the loss of the negative, only duplicate negatives should be reticulated in order not to risk destruction of a valuable original.

COMBINATIONS

In many instances, two, or even all three, of these graphic techniques can be combined in one and the same picture. The photograph at the left, for instance, combined two techniques: a negative was reticulated, then contact printed on film in order to get a reticulated diapositive, and finally both of them were sandwiched together slightly out of register and enlarged according to the bas-relief technique. In other cases, a bas-relief paper print is solarized and—used as a paper negative—a solarized bas-relief picture is contact printed from it. Or a negative could be solarized, contact printed on a glass plate and in this state might be solarized once more, which would give a double-sided solarization effect instead of a one-sided one. And so on. Possibilities here are as unlimited as the imagination and energy of the photographer. . . .

CONCLUSIONS

Photography may be the youngest of all the Arts, but it follows the same timeless rules. The substance of his surroundings provides the raw material for the photographer, which he has to form and to transform into pictures. Discrimination, selection, and limitation should precede the making of any photograph. Condensation, concentration, and stylization are indispensable for making it a work of art. And as tons of ore finally yield a few ounces of gold—a whole landscape may yield a few blossoms crystallized on film in the intensified form of a closeup, surpassing by far in its concentrated composition, its richness of detail, its graphic black-and-white effect, and its symbolic suggestiveness, the vague impression made by the original flowers as the eye swept the scene. If that has been achieved, Nature has been transformed into Art.

Thus century-old laws of artistic creation are found to be as valid as ever for photographers of today, even though the means for their realization have changed. *Imagination* and *feeling for the material* will always remain conditions for any creative activity, *selection* will always be the starting point, *condensation* and *stylization* the main elements of composition. That established, what difference does it make whether the executing tools are the chisel, the brush, or—the camera?